California Politics

A Primer

Renée Van Vechten
University of Redlands

CQ PRESS

A Division of SAGE
Washington, D.C.

CQ Press
2300 N Street, NW, Suite 800
Washington, DC 20037

Phone: 202-729-1900; toll-free, 1-866-4CQ-PRESS (1-866-427-7737)

Web: www.cqpress.com

Cover design: Paula Goldstein
Composition: C&M Digitals (P) Ltd.
Image credits:
AP Images: 36, 41, 43, 48 (Bowen, Chiang, Leonard, Lockyer, O'Connell, Poizner), 53, 60, 66, 73, 87, 104, 108
Brian Fairrington/Cagle Cartoons: 3
Corbis: 9, 44 (Jesse Unruh)
Getty: 2, 5, 17, 25, 44 (Bass, Brown, Villaraigosa), 48 (Brown, Chu, Garamendi, Schwarzenegger), 50, 76, 81, 91, 105
International Mapping Associates: inside front cover, 8, 21, 69, 97
Office of Betty T. Yee, Chairwoman and First District Member: 48
Steve Greenberg: 94
Wikipedia Commons: 10, 48 (Steel)
WILLIS/San Jose Mercury News: 26

♾ The paper used in this publication exceeds the requirements of the American National Standard for Information Sciences—Permanence of Paper for Printed Library Materials, ANSI Z39.48–1992.

Printed and bound in the United States of America

13 12 11 10 09   1 2 3 4 5

Library of Congress Cataloging-in-Publication Data

Van Vechten, Renée
California politics : a primer / Renée Van Vechten
    p. cm.
Includes bibliographical references.
ISBN 978-1-60426-995-6 (alk. paper)
    1. California—Politics and government. I. Title.

JK8716.V36 2010
320.4794—dc22
                           2009032805

Contents

Tables, Figures, Maps, and Boxes   vi

1. Introduction   1

  Principles for Understanding California Politics   3

2. Critical Junctures: California's Political History in Brief   7

  Early California   7

  The Rise of the Southern Pacific Railroad   9

  Progressivism   11

  The Power of Organized Interests   13

  Growth and Industrialization in the Golden State   14

  The Initiative Process Takes Hold   14

  Hyper-Diversity in a Modern State   16

  Recalling a Governor   18

  Conclusion: Political Earthquakes and Evolving Institutions   19

3. Direct Democracy   20

  The Initiative Process   20

    Drafting Stage   24

    Qualification Stage   24

    Campaigning Stage   24

    The Power of the Initiative Process   26

  Referendum   27

  Recall   27

  Conclusion: Frustrating Collective Action   29

4. The State Legislature   31

  Design, Purpose, and Function of the Legislature   31

  California Representatives at Work   32

Policymaking and Lawmaking   36

Annual Budgeting   40

Constituency Service and Outreach   40

Executive Branch Oversight   41

Leaders   42

Conclusion: Of the People, For the People   44

5. **The Executive Branch**   **46**

California's Plural Executive   47

California's Governor   49
 Head of State   49
 Chief Executive   49
 Legislative Powers   50
 Budgeting Power   51
 Chief of Security   51
 Party Leader   51
 Sources of Power   51

The Constitutional Executive Officers   52

Administrators and Regulators   54

Conclusion: Competition for Power   55

6. **The Court System**   **59**

The Three-Tiered Court System   59

On and Off the Court   62

Court Administration   63

Juries   64

Criminal Justice   64

Conclusion: Administering Justice   66

7. **Other Governments**   **68**

Municipal Government   71

Special Districts   75

Regional Governments   77

Federalism   77

Tribal Governments   79

Conclusion: The State's Interlocking Systems   81

8. The California Budget Process 83

California Budgeting 101 84

Political Constraints 84

Mechanics of Budgeting: Revenue 87

Mechanics of Budgeting: Deficits and Expenditures 90

Tax Burden: Too High, Too Low? 92

The Budget Crisis and Beyond 94

Conclusion: Change the Rules? 95

9. Political Parties, Elections, and Campaigns 96

A Weak Party State 96

Party in the California Electorate 98

Party in Government 101

The Party Organizations 103

Elections: Continuity and Change 104

California Campaigns 106

Major Voting Trends 108

Conclusion: A Complex Electorate 110

10. Concluding Thoughts: Political Paradoxes and Governability 112

Appendix A: List of Counties, Including Median Income per County 116

Appendix B: Current Constitutional Officers and Leaders of the Legislature, Including Salaries, July 2009 118

Appendix C: Recent Governors, Senate Presidents pro Tempore, and Speakers of the Assembly 120

Tables, Figures, Maps, and Boxes

Tables

3.1 Selected Landmark Initiatives in California, 1966–2009   22

3.2 Five Most Expensive Ballot Measure Campaigns   25

4.1 Day in the Life of Sen. Denise Ducheny   39

6.1 Diversity of California's Justices and Judges   63

8.1 General Obligation Bonds Passed, 2006–2008   88

9.1 Modern Era California Governors by Party Affiliation   103

9.2 Largest Campaign Contributors to State Campaigns by Industry, 2008   107

Figures

2.1 Timeline of California's Population   12

3.1 Sample Ballot with Initiatives   23

3.2 2003 Governor Recall Measure Question on the Sample Ballot   29

4.1 Profile of California's Population vs. California State Legislature   33

4.2 How a Bill Becomes a Law   37

5.1 California's Executives and Musical Chairs   48

5.2 Organization Chart of California's Executive Branch   56

6.1 California Court System   61

7.1 County Revenues and Expenses, 2006–2007   72

7.2 City Revenues and Expenses, 2006–2007   74

7.3 Tribes Are Recognized Sovereigns   80

8.1 The Annual Budget Process   85

8.2 State Revenue, 2007–2008   89

8.3 State Expenses, 2007–2008   90

8.4 California's Sales Tax in Context   93

9.1 Party Registration in Presidential Election Years, 1924–2008   99

9.2 Registration by Political Party in California   101

9.3 Differing Perceptions about the Role of Government   109

9.4 Ethnic Makeup of California's Likely Voters   110

Maps

2.1 California's Missions   8

3.1 States with the Initiative Process, 2009   21

7.1 California's Fifty-eight Counties   69

9.1 California's East-West Partisan Divide   97

Boxes

1.1 Comparative FAST FACTS on California   4

3.1 Reforming the Initiative Process   28

4.1 FAST FACTS on the California Legislature   32

4.2 Term Limits: Political Earthquake   34

5.1 FAST FACTS on California's Plural Executive   47

6.1 FAST FACTS on California's Criminal Justice System   65

7.1 FAST FACTS on California's Other Governments   70

7.2 The Feds vs. California on Air Quality   78

8.1 The California Teachers Association: Major Player in Education   91

9.1 How to Party in California   100

Introduction

I magine California as one of the ten largest countries in the world. With a gross domestic product of about $1.8 trillion,[1] its economy rivals those of Russia, Spain, and Brazil. Its land mass includes coastal stretches, fertile farmland, deserts, the highest and lowest points in the continental United States, dense urban zones, twenty-one mountain ranges, and ancient redwood forests. Imagine further how approximately 38 million ethnically diverse inhabitants govern themselves: they generally distrust representative institutions and assume that bickering politicians will squander taxpayers' money. Many eligible citizens never vote, and 20 percent of registered voters spurn the two major parties by registering as "Decline to State" voters. Well-funded citizens, interest groups, and corporations routinely use the initiative process to force policy changes that will affect the entire citizenry. Virtually everyone relies on such public goods as roads, emergency services, and schools, yet the state can't pay for all that's demanded of it; it comes up short by billions of dollars, year after year, and voters rebuff tax increases.

Given all of this, California certainly appears "ungovernable." Consider also that a global economy, immigration, climate change, federal mandates, terrorist threats, and a host of other factors place conflicting pressures on those who make policy decisions even as such essential resources as expertise, time, and money are frequently in short supply. Further, some of the state's rules encourage conflict without compromise. If **politics** is a process through which people with differing goals and values try to manage their conflicts by working together to allocate values for society—which implies that government

The California coastline: a metaphor for a state teetering "on the edge."

institutions should enable officials to craft long-term solutions to major problems—
then California's system is in need of serious repair.

It wasn't always so: a newly "modernized" constitution implemented in the late
1960s transformed the legislature into a highly paid, well-staffed institution that
quickly gained a reputation as a policy and political reform leader among the states.
In 1971 the legislature was described as "having all the characteristics that a legislature should have," having "proved itself capable of leading the nation in the development of legislation to deal with some of our most critical problems."[2]

It didn't take long for popular perceptions to change, however. In 1978 the people
revolted against "spendthrift politicians" by passing Proposition 13, a measure that
addressed ballooning property tax rates.[3] In the 1980s, as immigration was blamed
for bigger government and rising costs, Californians passed the first of many initiatives that would attempt to give "guidance to the legislature" about redefining the
state's responsibilities toward immigrants.[4] Legislators were also targeted for acting
"arrogant and unresponsive" and for spending money on themselves while neglect-
ing "schools, transportation, and basic needs."[5] By the time term limitations were
passed in 1990 (a measure limiting the number of terms any state elected official
could serve in a lifetime), it seemed the legislature's reputation could sink no lower.
Many observers regarded California's legislators as simply incapable of governing.

Today, California's issues exist on a massive scale. For example, more than one of every eight U.S. residents lives in California, and one of every four Californians is foreign born. In summer 2009 the estimated budget gap reached the staggering sum of over $26 billion, representing a huge chunk of the state's approximately $95 billion annual budget that would need to be balanced by universally slashing state services. It is little wonder that in May 2009 only 21 percent of adult Californians approved of the job the legislature was doing, while only 34 percent approved of Gov. Arnold Schwarzenegger's performance.[6]

Despite being held in low regard, state legislators work hard year-round to represent hundreds of thousands of people—a job that requires them to balance the needs of their own districts against those of the entire state. That balancing act is but one reason why California politics is complex and often appears irrational, but like the U.S. government's structure the system was designed that way, mostly through deliberate choice and sometimes through the unintended consequences of prior decisions. California's crazy quilt of governing institutions reflects repeated attempts to manage the conflict resulting from millions of people putting demands on a system that creates both winners and losers, not all of whom give up quietly when they lose. As happens at the federal level, state officials tend to respond to the most persistent, organized, and well-funded in society, but unlike the national scene, losers have more opportunities to use state power by employing the tools of direct democracy to bypass state lawmakers altogether.

Principles for Understanding California Politics

It may seem counterintuitive given the depth of its problems, but California politics can be explained and understood logically—although the results of the process are just

BOX 1.1 Comparative FAST FACTS on California

	California	New York	United States
Capital:	Sacramento	Albany	Washington, D.C.
Statehood:	Sept. 9, 1850 (31st state)	July 26, 1788 (11th state)	Declared independence from Great Britain July 4, 1776
Number of U.S. representatives:	55	27	435
Number of counties:	58 (since 1879)	62	50 states
Largest city by population:*	Los Angeles, 4,065,585	New York, 8,363,710	
Total population:*	38,292,687	19,490,297	304,059,724
Foreign-born persons:**	26.2%	21.6%	12.5%
Median household income:**	$59,928	$52,944	$50,233
Persons living below poverty level:**	12.4%	14.6%	12.5%

*California Department of Finance, January 2009 estimates; New York State Data Center, 2008 estimates; U.S. Census Bureau, 2008 estimates.

**U.S. Census Bureau, 2007 estimates.

Ethnic Makeup of California:

Category	California population
White, Non-Hispanic	43.5%
Hispanic	36.1%
Asian	11.7%
Black	6.1%
Other	2.5%

Sources: California Department of Finance, www.dof.ca.gov/research/demographic/reports; and U.S. Census Bureau.

as often frustrating and irresponsible as they are praiseworthy and necessary. In short, the fundamental concepts of choice, political culture, institutions, collective action, rules, and history can be used to understand state politics just as they are used to understand national or even local democratic politics. These concepts are used throughout this book to explain how governing decisions are made on behalf of Californians and to provide a starting point for evaluating how governable California is.

We begin with the premise that **choices** are at the heart of politics. Citizens make explicit political choices when they choose not to participate in an election or when they decide to cast a vote, but they also make implicit political choices when they throw aluminum cans in a recycling bin or send their children to private schools.

Legislators make explicit choices every day, such as when they decide to return certain phone calls but not others or voice support for their colleagues in committees.

In large and diverse societies such as that of California, in which people are motivated by different goals, interests, and values, a successful political system will provide a process for narrowing choices to a manageable number and allow many participants to reconcile their differences as they make choices together. The decisions that emerge from this process express the customs, values, and beliefs about government that a society holds and give that political system a distinct culture—a **political culture** that varies from state to state. One of the features that defines California's political culture is a historical fondness for reform and an aversion to politicians—a theme that will resurface throughout this book.

Political systems also facilitate compromises, trade-offs, or bargains that will lead to acceptable solutions or alternatives. **Institutions** help organize this kind of action. Political institutions are built to manage conflict by defining particular roles and rules for those who participate in them. In short, they bring people together to solve problems on behalf of society. Democratic elections are a good example: there are rules about who can vote or run for office, how the process will be administered, and how disputes resulting from them will be resolved. Through institutions like elections, **collective action** can take place. The same can be said of other

Arnold Schwarzenegger is sworn in as California's thirty-eighth governor on the steps of the state capitol in Sacramento on November 17, 2003.

institutions—such as traffic courts, legislatures, and political parties—for in each people work together to solve their problems and allocate goods for a society.

Rules also matter. **Rules** define who has power and how they may legitimately use it, and rules create incentives for action or inaction. For instance, legislators who do not face term limits may extend their political careers by choosing to run for reelection in perpetuity, but term-limited legislators who want to remain in public service have an incentive to run for other offices when opportunities arise. Rules are also the result of choices made throughout **history**, and over time a body of rules will change and grow in response to cultural shifts, natural disasters, economic trends, and other forces, creating further opportunities and incentives for political action.

Recognizing that both choices and the rules that condition them are made within a given historical context goes a long way toward explaining each state's distinctive political system. A state's political culture also contributes to that distinctiveness. These are the elements that make New York state government so different from the governments of Nevada or California, and they should be kept in mind as we consider how California's governing institutions developed. In essence, a unique set of rules, culture, and history is the key to understanding California politics and helps explain why elected officials have such a difficult time governing the state.

Is California ungovernable? From online blogs to *New York Times* editorials, the consensus is an unqualified "yes." The current arrangement of political institutions makes it nearly impossible to solve the state's pressing problems or plan for the future. This book explores the reasons for this state of affairs and pushes the reader to ask what it will take to restore government's ability to serve the public's interests effectively, comprehensively, and sensibly.

Notes

1. California's gross domestic product in 2008 was $1.846 trillion. Taken from the Bureau of Economic Analysis, U.S. Department of Commerce, www.bea.gov/regional/gsp/action.cfm. This figure is compared to country GDP data compiled by the World Bank, "Gross Domestic Product 2008." Taken from http://siteresources.worldbank.org/DATASTATISTICS/Resources/GDP.

2. John Burns, *The Sometime Governments: A Critical Study of the 50 American Legislatures, by the Citizens Conference on State Legislatures* (New York: Bantam Books, 1971), 8.

3. Howard Jarvis and Paul Gann, "Arguments in Favor of Proposition 13" (Sacramento: California Secretary of State, 1978 Primary Election Ballot Pamphlet). Taken from the University of California–Hastings, http://holmes.uchastings.edu/cgi-bin/starfinder/9679/calprop.txt.

4. S. I. Hayakawa, J. Orozco, and Stanley Diamond, "Arguments in Favor of Proposition 63." (Sacramento: California Secretary of State, 1986 General Election Ballot Pamphlet). Taken from the University of California–Hastings, http://library.uchastings.edu/cgi-bin/starfinder/9720/calprop.txt.

5. Paul Gann, "Argument in Favor of Proposition 24" (Sacramento: California Secretary of State, 1984 General Election Ballot Pamphlet). Taken from the University of California–Hastings, http://library.uchastings.edu/cgi-bin/starfinder/9720/calprop.txt.

6. Public Policy Institute of California, Statewide Survey: "Californians and Their Government, May 2009"; www.scribd.com/doc/9281785/PPIC-Statewide-Survey-Californians-and-Their-Government. Survey included 2,005 adults; 1,515 registered voters; and 1,080 likely voters. Interviews took place April 27–May 4, 2009. Margin of error +/- 2 percent.

OUTLINE

Early California

The Rise of the Southern
Pacific Railroad

Progressivism

The Power of Organized
Interests

Growth and
Industrialization in the
Golden State

The Initiative Process
Takes Hold

Hyper-Diversity in a
Modern State

Recalling a Governor

Conclusion: Political
Earthquakes and Evolving
Institutions

CHAPTER 2

Critical Junctures: California's Political History in Brief

Early California

The contours of California's contemporary political landscape began to take shape in 1542, when Spanish explorer Juan Cabrillo claimed the Native American lands now known as San Diego for a distant monarchy, thereby paving the way for European settlements along the West Coast. Aided by Spanish troops, colonization accompanied the founding of Catholic missions throughout Baja (lower) and then Alta (northern) California. These missions, as well as military presidios (army posts), were constructed along what would become known as El Camino Real, or the King's Highway, a path that roughly followed a line of major tribal establishments. Over the next two hundred years, Native peoples would either be subordinated or decimated by foreign diseases, soldiers, and ways of life, and the huge mission complexes and ranches, or rancheros, that replaced these groups and their settlements would become the focal points for social activity and economic industry in the region.

The western lands containing California became part of Mexico with that country's independence from Spain in 1821, and for more than two decades Mexicans governed the region, constructing presidios and installing military leaders to protect the cities taking shape up and down the coast. Following the Mexican-American War of 1848 that ended with the Treaty of Guadalupe Hidalgo, California became the

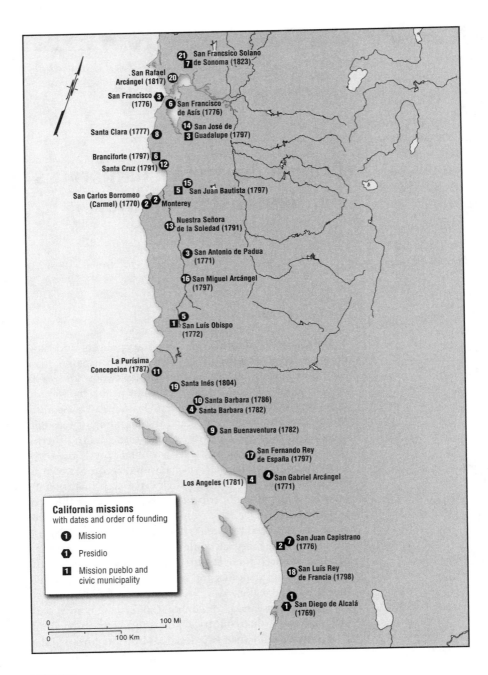

MAP 2.1

California's Missions

new U.S. frontier astride a new international border. The simultaneous discovery of gold near Sacramento provoked an onslaught of settlers in what would be the first of several significant population waves to flood the West Coast during the next 125 years. The rush to the Golden State was on.

The Rise of the Southern Pacific Railroad

Spurning slavery and embracing self-governance, a group of pre–Gold Rush settlers and mayors convened to write a state constitution in 1849; a year later the U.S. Congress granted the territory statehood, and shortly thereafter Sacramento became the state's permanent capital. Although gold already had lured nearly 100,000 adventure-seekers to the state in less than two years, the region remained a mostly untamed and distant outpost, separated from the East Coast by treacherous terrain and thousands of miles of ocean travel. Growing demand for more reliable linkages to the rest of the United States would lead to the building of the transcontinental railroad in 1869, an undertaking that would result in the importation of thousands of Chinese laborers and was enabled by millions of acres of federal land grants to a few railroad companies: 11 million acres in California to the Southern Pacific alone.[1]

Despite persistent racial discrimination, punishing conditions, and a lack of labor and safety protections, Chinese immigrants laid thousands of miles of railroad tracks between the 1880s and 1900s.

THE CURSE OF CALIFORNIA.

The wildly successful enterprise not only opened the West to rapid development but also consolidated railroad power in the Southern Pacific Railroad. Owned by railroad barons Collis Huntington, Mark Hopkins, Leland Stanford, and Charles Crocker—the "Big Four"—through the early 1900s the Southern Pacific extended its reach to virtually all forms of shipping and transport. This had direct impacts on all major economic activity within the state, from wheat prices to land values and from bank lending to the availability of lumber. As famously depicted in Edward Keller's "The Curse of California," which appeared in San Francisco's *The Wasp* on August 19, 1882, the "S.P." dominated every major sector of the state's economy—and politics—like a determined octopus.

Progressivism

The Southern Pacific's hold over California government during the late 1800s cannot be underestimated. One historian describes the situation in this way:

> For at least a generation after the new constitution went into effect [in 1879] the great majority of Californians believed that the influence of the railroad extended from the governor's mansion in Sacramento to the lowest ward heeler in San Francisco, and that the machine determined who should sit in city councils and on boards of supervisors; who should be sent to the House of Representatives and to the Senate in Washington; what laws should be enacted by the legislature, and what decisions should be rendered from the bench.[2]

The Southern Pacific's grip over California industry and politics was finally smashed by muckraking journalists, whose stories were pivotal in the passing of new federal regulations aimed at breaking monopolies; in the prosecution of San Francisco's corrupt political boss, Abe Ruef; and in the rise of a national political movement known as "Progressivism" that quickly took root in California. Gov. Hiram Johnson (1911–1917) personified the idealistic Progressive spirit through his focus on "eliminating every private interest from government" and restoring power to the people.

To that end, Governor Johnson spearheaded a historic reform agenda that addressed a wide range of social, political, and economic issues that were attracting the attention of Progressives in other U.S. states. Not only was his agenda grounded in a fundamental distrust of political parties, which had been hijacked by the Southern Pacific Railroad in California, it was also built on an emerging philosophy that government could be run like a business, with efficiency as the focus. Workers' rights, municipal ownership of utility companies, universal education, environmental conservation, morals laws, and the assurance of fair political representation topped the list of items Johnson tackled with the help of the California legislature after he entered office in 1911.

Changes in electoral laws directly targeted the ties political parties had to both the railroads and potential voters. Although secret voting had become state law as early as 1892, the practice was strengthened and enforced as a means to control elections and ensure fairness. The ability of party bosses to "select and elect" the candidates for political offices was undercut with the establishment of direct primary elections, in which any party member could become a candidate for office and gain the nomination of his fellow party members through a regular party election. The legislature also reclassified local elected offices as "nonpartisan," meaning that the party affiliation of candidates would not appear on the ballot if they were running for positions on city councils, local school boards, or as judges. Efficiency, the Progressives believed, demanded that voters and officials be blind to partisanship, because the conflicts caused by it wasted time and resources that could be channelled elsewhere and the important thing was who was the best person for a position, not his political affiliation.

A more ingenious method of controlling parties was accomplished through cross-filing, a new law that allowed any candidates' name to appear on any party's primary election ballot without the candidate's party affiliation being indicated. In effect, Republicans could seek the Democrats' nomination and vice versa, thereby permitting a candidate's nomination by more than one party. This rule, which remained on the books until 1959, initially helped Progressives but later allowed Republicans to dominate state politics despite state party registration that favored the Democrats after 1934.

Civil service exams were also instituted, which changed the hiring of local and state government employees from a system based on patronage (*who* one knew) to one based on merit (*what* one knew about a position and *how well* one knew it). But perhaps most important of all the reforms instituted by the Progressives was a transformation of the relationship citizens had to California government, in the first place by guaranteeing women the right to vote and in the second place by adopting the tools of direct democracy: the recall, the referendum, and the initiative process (discussed in chapter 3). By vesting the people with the power to make laws directly, even laws that could override those passed by the state legislature and signed into law by the governor, Progressives

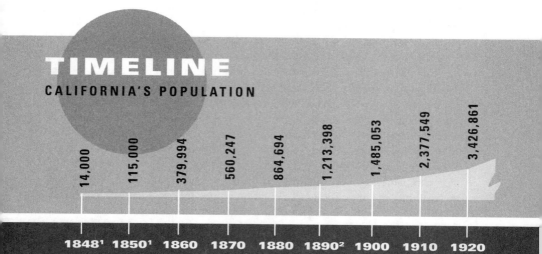

TIMELINE

CALIFORNIA'S POPULATION

14,000	115,000	379,994	560,247	864,694	1,213,398	1,485,053	2,377,549	3,426,861
1848[1]	1850[1]	1860	1870	1880	1890[2]	1900	1910	1920

[1] Source for population estimates 1848–1850: Andrew Rolle, *California: A History* (Wheeling, Ill.: Harlan Davidson, 2003).
[2] Population estimates from 1848–1880 are for non-Native populations. Native populations were not included in the U.S. census prior to 1890.

redistributed political power and essentially redesigned the basic structure of government. No longer would California be a representative democracy; its representatives would now compete with the people and special interests for power through the initiative process. The Progressives had triggered the state's first giant political earthquake.

It should be noted that Progressives' efforts to widen access to political power did not extend to every group in California, and some of the laws they passed were specifically designed to exclude certain people from decision making and restrict their political power. The most egregious examples reflected the white majority's racial hostility toward Chinese-born and other Asian-born residents, which took the form of "Alien Land Laws" that denied land ownership, full property rights, and other civil rights to anyone of Asian descent—laws that would not be removed from the state's books for another half century.

The Power of Organized Interests

Ironically, the Progressives' attacks on political parties and the Southern Pacific created new opportunities for other kinds of special interests to influence state government. Cross-filing produced legislators with minimal party allegiances, and by the 1940s these individuals

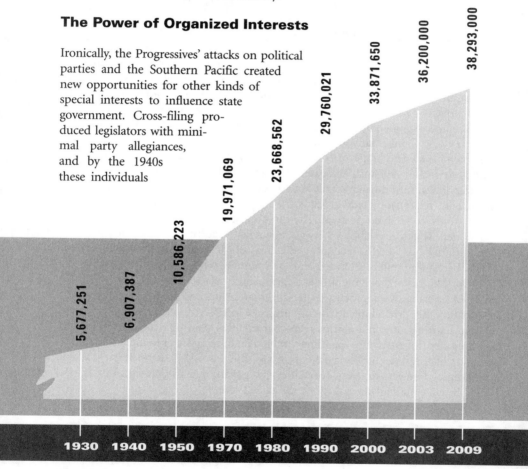

Source for population estimates 1860–2000: U.S. Census Bureau.
Source for population estimate 2009: California Department of Finance, Demographic Research Unit.

had come to depend heavily on lobbyists for information and other "diversions" to supplement their meager $3,000 annual salary. The legendary Artie Samish, head of the liquor and racetrack lobbies from the 1920s to the 1950s, personified the power of "The Third House" (organized interests represented in the lobbying corps) in his ability to control election outcomes and tax rates on industries he represented. "I am the governor of the legislature," he brazenly boasted in the 1940s, "To hell with the governor of California." He would be convicted and jailed for corruption not long after making this statement, but his personal downfall hardly disturbed the cozy relationship between lobbyists and legislators that continued to flourish—and taint—state politics in California.

Growth and Industrialization in the Golden State

Rapid urban and industrial development during the first decades of the twentieth century accompanied the invention of the automobile and the step-up in oil production preceding World War II. Ribbons of roads and highways rearranged cities, and people kept arriving at a spectacular rate. This was particularly true during the Depression years of 1935 to 1940, when hope for a new and better life beckoned approximately 350,000 farmers from the Dust Bowl states to what they believed to be a vast land of golden opportunity. The plight of those destitute "Okies" (the pejorative used by Californians to describe unskilled American migrants), depicted in John Steinbeck's *The Grapes of Wrath*, did not begin to change until war production created new labor demands and eased the pangs of their assimilation.

Industrialization during World War II restored the state's golden image, bringing defense-related jobs, federal funds, manufacturing, construction, and a prosperity that only accelerated postwar. The building sector boomed while orange trees blossomed. To address labor shortages, a federal "Bracero" program created a new agricultural labor force by facilitating the entry of Mexican laborers into the United States, beckoning millions of men and their families whose efforts laid the foundations for California's thriving modern agribusiness sector.

Tract housing developments materialized at an unprecedented rate and so did roads and other critical infrastructure projects. In 1947 the state fanned the spread of "car culture" with an ambitious ten-year highway plan that cost $1 million per working day. Infrastructure spending centered on moving water to the thirsty southern part of the state, building schools, establishing a first-class university system, and keeping freeways flowing—priorities that governors Earl Warren and Edmund "Pat" Brown would advance through the early 1960s.

The Initiative Process Takes Hold

The political landscape was also changing. Cross-filing, which had severely disadvantaged the Democrats for forty years, was effectively eliminated through a 1952 initiative that required candidates' party affiliation to be printed on primary election ballots.

With this important change, Democrats finally realized majority status in 1958 with Pat Brown in the governor's office and leadership in both legislative houses.

Several U.S. Supreme Court cases also necessitated fundamental changes in the way that Californians were represented in both the state and national legislatures. Between 1928 and 1965 the state employed the "Federal Plan," modeling its legislature after the U.S. Congress with an upper house based on geographic areas (counties rather than states) and a lower house based on population. Though many attempts had been made to dismantle the plan because it produced gross overrepresentation of northern and inland rural interests and severe underrepresentation of southern metropolitan residents in the Senate (three-fourths of sitting senators represented low-density rural areas), it remained in place until a federal court struck it down; per the U.S. Supreme Court ruling in *Reynolds v. Sims* (1964), the California system was found to violate the "one person–one vote" principle.[3] After 1965 political influence passed from legislators representing the north to those representing the south and also from rural to urban interests. Moreover, putting legislators in charge of redrawing their own districts reopened the possibility for gerrymanders, the practice of manipulating district boundaries to virtually ensure the reelection of incumbents and the continuation of the majority party in power.

Parties' revival in the legislature during the 1960s was greatly assisted by the Democratic Speaker of the Assembly, "Big Daddy" Jesse Unruh. Well aware of how to control the flow of campaign donations and influence the reelection of loyal partisans, Unruh also helped orchestrate an overhaul of the legislature through Proposition 1A, a measure designed to "Update the State!" via constitutional cleanup in 1966. Prop 1A professionalized the lawmaking body by endowing it with the "three s's": salary, staff, and session length. Lawmakers' pay would double to $16,000 to reflect their full-time status, and ample staff would help them write and analyze bills. The hope was to create a legislative body that could separate itself from the enticements of lobbyists by giving it the necessary resources to compete on more equal footing with the executive branch, and 73.5 percent of California voters welcomed the political shake-up.

Such professionalization helped refresh the legislature's image, but the shine soon faded. It quickly became apparent that these changes still did not adequately equip legislators to deal effectively with all of the major issues facing Californians. And so voters took matters into their own hands, and in 1978 the power of the initiative process would be fully realized in Proposition 13. This citizen-generated anti-tax measure would forever change the rules regarding taxation and state budgeting, effectively altering the balance of power in the state by transferring that authority from cities and counties to state government.

Propelled by anger over the legislature's inability to reconcile skyrocketing property taxes and a multibillion-dollar state budget surplus, voters overwhelmingly approved Prop 13's annual property tax limit to 1 percent of a property's assessed value.[4] Moreover, a two-thirds vote of the legislature would be required to raise any tax, a rule that empowers a minority determined to forestall any tax increases. This has had significant impact on the legislature's ability to pass budgets on time. Finally, Prop 13 sparked the dramatic use of the initiative process that continues today.

The faith in self-governance and mistrust of politicians that spurred Progressives into action and citizens to approve Prop 13 continued to cause political tremors in California politics. The view that citizens were more trustworthy than their representatives only intensified during the 1980s after three legislators were convicted of bribery, reinforcing the perception that Sacramento was full of irresponsible, self-indulgent politicians. Similar political reforms have since targeted *governing institutions* such as the legislature, with the most notable of these being Proposition 140 (discussed in chapter 4), which in 1990 imposed term limits on lawmakers and constitutional officers.

Parties and elections also have been targets: Proposition 198 (approved in 1996) would have allowed all persons to vote in any political party's primary election regardless of party membership, but the measure was in effect only for the 1998 elections. It was later overturned by the U.S. Supreme Court, but a measure on the 2010 ballot revisits the issue (see chapter 9). *Policymaking* has been altered through changes in the rules. Proposition 98, approved in 1988, significantly constrains the legislature by mandating a minimum funding level for K–12 and community colleges, an amount equal to about 40 percent of the state budget each year; and Proposition 39, approved in 2000, affects the voters' ability to approve school bonds by lowering the supermajority requirement to 55 percent (from two-thirds).

Hyper-Diversity in a Modern State

Probably no condition defines politics in California more than its great human diversity, which is as much a source of the state's rich heritage and culture as it is the root of competing and sometimes divisive political pressures. Differences stemming from ethnicity, race, religion, age, sexuality, ideology, economic class, and geography (to name but a few sources) do not *inevitably* breed conflict; however, these differences often are the source intense political conflict. The political realm is where those differences are expressed as divergent goals in the search for group recognition, power, or public goods, and the vital challenge for California's political representatives and institutions is to aggregate, rather than aggravate, differences.

A post–World War II baby boom swelled the state's population even as waves of immigration and migration throughout the mid- to late twentieth century produced minor political tremors. A marked national population shift from the Rust Belt to the Sun Belt boosted California's economy as well as its population over the latter half of the twentieth century. Another wave arrived during the late 1960s to the mid-1970s, following the Vietnam War; and the most recent occurred during the 1980s and 1990s, when the state's economic prosperity encouraged large-scale immigration from Mexico and other Central and Latin American countries.

Immigration, both legal and illegal, as well as natural population growth, has therefore produced a hyper-diverse state in which many groups vie for political legitimacy and attention, for public services and goods, and for power and influence. Same-sex couples demand the right to be wed in the same manner as heterosexual couples; children of immigrants seek to pay for their state college education at resident rates rather than as out-of-state applicants; women seek workplace promotions at the same frequency and pay rates as men. In California, those groups that are well endowed with voting strength, money, political power, or some combination of these have had an easier time using the instruments of state power (usually the initiative process) to achieve their goals, which may or may not represent the public interest. Groups that do not possess these assets may try to make a statement in other ways. For example, racial tensions have occasionally erupted into large-scale riots, as happened in Southeast Los Angeles in 1992 (and in 1965 in what came to be known as the Watts Riots).

Continuing ethnic diversification will dominate California society in the coming years, and the resulting social changes will undoubtedly have important political dimensions and ramifications. California is already a state in which whites are a minority; Latinos are projected to become the absolute majority segment of the state's population by 2050. Will members of this group, currently underrepresented among voters, become fully active participants in California politics? If so, how? Will they do so with or without the help of the state? What kinds of political earthquakes, if any, will the shift produce?

Changing demographic patterns have influenced and continue to drive public policy debates. Among the topics frequently and often passionately discussed are whether to

A foreign culture transplanted or an American culture transformed? Ethnic subgroups in California have established communities of character, as this barrio in East Los Angeles shows.

make English the state's official language (approved by 73.2 percent of voters in 1986), whether to teach children only in English (passed by 60.9 percent of voters in 1998 as Proposition 227), and whether to deny citizenship to children born to undocumented workers. The issue of whether or not to grant driver's licenses to undocumented immigrants is another political hot potato for government officials at the state level.

Settlement patterns also raise questions about cultural assimilation versus cultural preservation. Some subpopulations tend to concentrate into geographic areas identified by a dominant ethnic community, such as "Little Saigons," "China Towns," or barrios. Areas such as these at least partially absorb foreign laborers and refugees, including the approximately 50,000 Vietnamese who arrived after the Vietnam War or the 3 million or so Latinos who joined family members in the United States as part of a 1986 federal amnesty program. The dual trends of "balkanization" (communities separated by race or ethnicity) and "white flight" (the movement of Caucasians out of urban zones and to the inland counties) have become more pronounced during recent decades and have political implications, particularly for voting (see chapter 9).

The sheer volume of basic and special needs created by this hyper-diversity has tended to outstrip government capacity in the areas of public education, legal and correctional services, environmental protection, public welfare, and health services. Constant and growing population needs will continue to animate budget and policy debates, providing plenty of fissures that will test the foundations of state government.

Recalling a Governor

Prior to the budget crisis of 2009, the most significant political earthquake of the new millennium in California hit in 2003 with the "chaotic" and "dizzying" recall of Gov. Gray Davis, a circus-like event that solidified the state's image as a national outlier. Though the petition drive gained momentum slowly at first, it built on growing discontent over rising electricity costs, a weakening economy, and an overdue budget that contained unpopular fixes such as raising the car tax. Davis's unseemly relationship with public employee unions had also raised more than a few eyebrows, and he had come to be perceived as a "pay-to-play" politician who accepted campaign funds from these unions and rewarded them with larded contracts. Few would have guessed that political mayhem could be whipped up by combining a mild-mannered, uncharismatic governor with a dollop of public disgruntlement and a large infusion of campaign cash, but that is exactly what happened.

Early in 2003 the stalled petition drive took on new life after Republican U.S. representative Darrell Issa donated $1.75 million to the cause, enabling professional signature gatherers to finish what volunteers had started. Eventually, 1.6 million signatures were collected, almost twice the amount needed to call a special election. For the first time in the state's history, Californians would be asked if they wanted to keep their sitting governor in office or replace him; and if enough voters wanted to replace him, they would have the opportunity to choose a successor from among what became an extensive list of candidates. Indeed, much of the excitement came to revolve around the hundreds of citizens who lined up to become candidates, including one Arnold Schwarzenegger, who surprised Jay Leno and the audience of *The Tonight Show* by announcing his candidacy during an appearance on the show.

On October 7, 2003, 55.4 percent of voters selected "yes" on the recall question, with 48.7 percent of those same voters choosing Schwarzenegger to replace Davis and 31.6 percent placing their support behind his nearest rival, Democratic lieutenant governor Cruz Bustamante. Though the spectacular election season lasted only seventy-six days (a normal cycle is about twice as long), it nonetheless contained elements of a "normal" campaign: approximately $80 million was spent during the campaign (Schwarzenegger spent $10 million of his own money and accepted almost $12 million in donations); the captivated mainstream media uncovered as much background information on the candidates as was possible in such a short amount of time; and a closely watched, formal televised debate featured the top candidates. Yet the recall election also differed significantly from a regular gubernatorial election: low barriers to entry onto the ballot netted 135 qualified candidates; the media focused intently on the process and California's politics; and the electorate became intensely engaged in the process, with 61.2 percent of registered voters eventually casting votes in the election. In demonstrating that they'd had enough "politics as usual," the voters had used the tools of direct democracy to shake up their government once again.

Conclusion: Political Earthquakes and Evolving Institutions

Political earthquakes throughout California's history have reconfigured relationships between the elected and the governed, between citizens and their governing institutions, and among citizens. Each of these upheavals involved choices about who may use power and how they may do so legitimately. Rules also mattered: in some cases the shake-ups were about changing the rules themselves, whereas in other cases the rules shaped the alternatives available and determined who could choose among them. Finally, history also plays a role in creating opportunities for action or creating conditions that shape alternatives. As this historical review demonstrates, California's past lives in the political institutions, culture, rules, and choices of today.

Notes

1. Andrew Rolle, *California: A History* (Wheeling, Ill.: Harlan-Davidson, 2003), 174.
2. Quote is attributed to Robert G. Cleland in Evelyn Hazen's "Cross-Filing in Primary Elections" (Berkeley: University of California Bureau of Public Administration, 1951), 9.
3. *Silver v. Jordan,* 241 Fed. S. 576 (1965) and *Reynolds v. Sims,* 377 U.S. 533 (1964), following *Baker v. Carr,* 369 U.S. 186 (1962).
4. Proposition 13 limited property tax rates to 1 percent of a property's assessed value in 1975; for properties sold after 1975, the rate would be 1 percent of the property's sale price, and this rate could not increase more than 2 percent per year.

CHAPTER 3

OUTLINE

The Initiative Process
    Drafting Stage
    Qualification Stage
    Campaigning Stage
    The Power of the
    Initiative Process

Referendum

Recall

Conclusion: Frustrating
Collective Action

Direct Democracy

Until 1911 California government reflected the U.S. Founders' belief that representatives working in competing branches (executive and legislative) would check each other with overlapping powers, would filter the passions of their constituents through a deliberative process, would find compromises, and would create good public policy. Progressive reformers removed those checks with the institution of the initiative, referendum, and recall, creating a hybrid government that is part representative, part direct democracy.[1] What we might call the "first branch of California government" is the people's power to govern themselves through the instruments of direct democracy.

The Initiative Process

The *direct initiative* gives Californians the power to propose constitutional amendments and laws that fellow citizens will vote on without the legislature's involvement. Twenty other states also have an initiative process, though each has different requirements for bringing measures to the voters; the *indirect* method allows legislatures to consider citizen-initiated measures first before they are presented to the public for a vote.

Today, Californians use the process more often than residents in any other state: from 1979–2009 voters considered 175 initiatives, compared to 137 in Colorado and 87 in Oregon during the same period.[2] Far more measures were attempted but never qualified for the ballot.

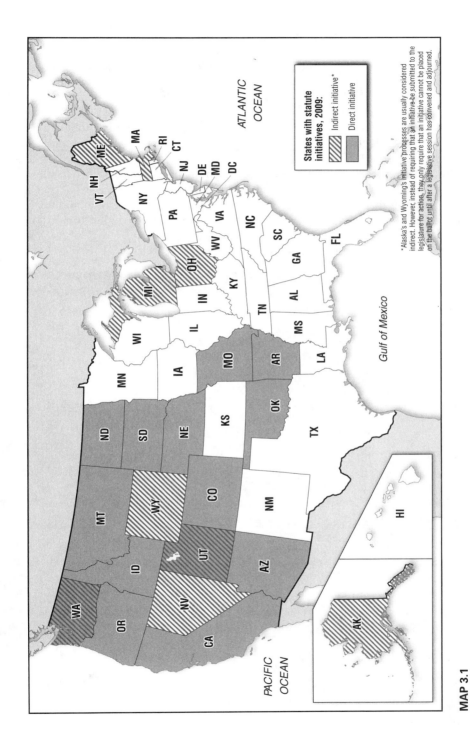

States with statute initiatives, 2009:

▨ Indirect initiative*

▥ Direct initiative

*Alaska's and Wyoming's initiative processes are usually considered indirect. However, instead of requiring that an initiative be submitted to the legislature for action, they only require that an initiative cannot be placed on the ballot until after a legislative session has convened and adjourned.

MAP 3.1

States with the Initiative Process, 2009

Heavier use of initiatives over the past three decades has been marked, and measures cover all manner of subjects. Prevalent are political reforms intended to change the rules for political engagement or control the behavior of elected officials, and it is no coincidence that term limits for statewide officials exist only in states with the initiative process. Taking the redistricting process away from legislators (discussed further in chapter 4) is another example of how Californians have played a vital role in setting the context for political decision making by imposing major institutional changes. Without a doubt, initiatives have fundamentally altered California government and politics (see Table 3.1).

Unfortunately, such piecemeal reforms are forced on government incoherently, resulting in political rules that overlap and encourage stalemate and inflexibility. The bottom line is that both directly and indirectly the initiative process conditions the actions of all California elected officials, who work in fragmented institutions

TABLE 3.1   Selected Landmark Initiatives in California, 1966–2009

Number	Description	Year
Proposition 1A	Constitutional reform, legislative professionalization	1966
Prop 9	Political reform act	1974
Prop 13	Property tax limitation	1978
Prop 8	Victims' bill of rights	1982
Prop 98	Minimum funding levels for education	1988
Prop 140	State officeholder term limits	1990
Prop 184	Three strikes law	1994
Prop 187	Ineligibility of illegal aliens for public services	1994
Prop 198	Open primary elections (overturned by U.S. Supreme Court)	1996
Prop 209	Ending affirmative action in state institutions	1996
Prop 215	Medical use of marijuana	1996
Prop 5	Tribal state gaming compacts, tribal casinos	1998
Prop 227	Elimination of bilingual education	1998
Prop 39	Lowering supermajority vote requirements for school bonds to 55 percent	2000
Prop 48	Court consolidation	2002
Prop 11	Legislative redistricting	2008
Prop 8	Definition of marriage	2009

OFFICIAL BALLOT

SAN DIEGO COUNTY, CALIFORNIA
PRESIDENTIAL GENERAL ELECTION - November 4, 2008

MEASURES SUBMITTED TO THE VOTERS

STATE

PROP 8 ELIMINATES RIGHT OF SAME-SEX COUPLES TO MARRY. INITIATIVE CONSTITUTIONAL AMENDMENT. Changes California Constitution to eliminate the right of same-sex couples to marry. Provides that only marriage between a man and a women is valid or recognized in California. Fiscal Impact: Over next few years, potential revenue loss, mainly sales taxes, totaling in the several tens of millions of dollars, to state and local goverments. In the long run, likely little fiscal impact on state and local governments.

YES ⬭

NO ⬭

PROP 9 CRIMINAL JUSTICE SYSTEM. VICTIMS' RIGHTS. PAROLE INITIATIVE CONSTITUTIONAL AMENDMENT AND STATUTE. Requires notification to victim and opportunity for input during phases of criminal justice process, including bail, pleas, sentencing and parole. Establishes victim safety as consideration for bail or parole. Fiscal Impact: Potential loss of state savings on prison operations and increased county jail costs amounting to hundreds of millions of dollars annually. Potential net savings in the low tens of millions of dollars annually on parole procedures.

YES ⬭

NO ⬭

STATE

PROP 10 ALTERNATIVE FUEL VEHICLES AND RENEWABLE ENERGY BONDS. INITIATIVE STATUTE. Authorizes $5 billion in bonds paid from state's General Fund, to help consumers and others purchase certain vehicles, and to fund research in renewable energy and alternative fuel vehicles. Fiscal Impact: State cost of about $10 billion over 30 years to repay bonds. Increased state and local revenues, potentially totaling several tens of millions of dollars through 2019. Potential state administrative costs up to about $10 million annually.

YES ⬭

NO ⬭

PROP 11 REDISTRICTING. INITIATIVE CONSTITUTIONAL AMENDMENT AND STATUTE. Changes authority for establishing state office boundaries from elected representatives to commission. Establishes multilevel process to select commissioners from registered voter pool. Commission comprised of Democrats, Republicans, and representatives of neither party. Fiscal Impact: Potential increase in state redistricting costs once every ten years due to two entities performing redistricting. Any increase in costs probably would not be significant.

YES ⬭

NO ⬭

FIGURE 3.1
Sample Ballot with Initiatives

that are not necessarily organized to encourage collective action. As a result, representative and direct democracy coexist uneasily.

Citizens can propose laws at the local, county, and state levels in California. Any registered voter may propose a law (an *initiative statute*) or a change to the state constitution (a *constitutional amendment*). However, because the initiative process contains funding and time barriers that most citizens cannot overcome, well-funded interest groups now dominate a system that was intended to *reduce* their influence. Interest groups use the state's initiative process to circumvent regular lawmaking channels because it "is the only way for some groups to get the policy they want."[3] Though the process remains primarily a check against government corruption and unresponsiveness, the Progressives of the late nineteenth and early twentieth centuries would probably be surprised at how the process works today.

Drafting Stage

The first step in bringing an idea to the ballot is **drafting,** or writing, the text of the proposed law. Measures are carefully worded to fit the needs and goals of their sponsors, and it is the authors' responsibility to correct errors that may later provide opponents with a convenient excuse to challenge it in court. The attorney general's office assigns each proposed law a title and summary that captures the measure's purpose, and from that point on the wording of a proposed law cannot be changed. The state will also prepare a fiscal analysis of the proposed law if the attorney general requests one.

Qualification Stage

During the **qualification** stage the initiative's proponents must circulate petitions throughout the state and gather enough valid voter signatures to qualify the measure for the ballot. Signature requirements are based on a percentage of all votes cast for governor during the previous election: from 2007 to 2010 the requirements were 5 percent (433,971 signatures) for an initiative and 8 percent (694,354 signatures) for a constitutional amendment. Proponents have 150 days to circulate and collect signatures on their strictly formatted petitions, and all signatures must be submitted 131 days before the next election. For these reasons, proponents usually hire a consulting firm to help with the legwork. The rule of thumb is to gather twice as many signatures as required, because many will be invalidated later. At an average cost of $1 to $2 per signature, it can easily cost $1 million or more to qualify a measure.

Campaigning Stage

A measure qualifies if the secretary of state verifies that enough registered voters signed the filed petitions. Initiative attempts often fail at this point. For successful proponents, the **campaigning** stage has just begun, and they will usually raise and spend millions of dollars to mobilize or sway voters. A thriving initiative industry has grown up around the need to coordinate fund-raising, television and radio advertising, and mass mailings. The cost of initiative campaigns has skyrocketed in recent decades, and the most expensive in U.S. history have taken place in California (see Table 3.2). It is not uncommon for supporters and opponents to spend between

Emotions ran high on both sides as the vote on Proposition 8, a measure banning same-sex marriage, neared. Voters narrowly approved it in November 2008, 52.3 percent to 47.7 percent. Supporters of same-sex marriage vowed to "bring it back to the ballot" again.

TABLE 3.2   Five Most Expensive Ballot Measure Campaigns

Proposition	Election year	Subject	Total spent*	Proponents	Opponents	Pass/fail (% margin)
87	2006	Alternative energy	$154,199,199	$61,251,188	$92,948,011	F (45/55)
5	1998	Indian gaming	$114,012,698	$81,316,570	$32,696,128	P (62/38)
8	2008	Same-sex marriage ban	$82,869,785	$38,766,260	$44,103,525	P (52/48)
86	2006	Tobacco tax	$82,748,301	$16,446,205	$66,302,096	F (48/52)
38	2000	School vouchers	$76,428,996	$37,489,136	$38,939,860	F (29/71)

Source: Proposition 8 figures from *Los Angeles Times*, http://theenvelope.latimes.com/la-moneymap,0,4156785. htmlstory. All other figures from *Democracy by Initiative*, 2nd ed. (Los Angeles: Center for Governmental Studies, 2008). Available at www.cgs.org/images/publications/cgs_dbi_full_book_f.pdf.

* Excluding Proposition 8, figures have been adjusted to 2006 dollars.

$50 million and $100 million combined on highly controversial measures; in 2008 approximately $83 million was spent on Proposition 8, a constitutional amendment banning same-sex marriage. Not surprisingly, more money tends to be spent when industries are directly affected in some way, whereas uncontroversial measures tend to attract little or no spending.

The Power of the Initiative Process

Only a simple majority is needed to pass an initiative or a recall, but supermajorities (two-thirds vote) are required for general obligation bonds and most school bonds (55 percent). Election results don't always settle issues, however. Opponents often file lawsuits as soon as the votes are counted, triggering expensive court battles over a measure's constitutionality or validity, battles that can last years and may result in partial or total invalidation of the measure. Public officials may also search for ways to get around laws they find objectionable, and there is always the likelihood that a contentious issue will be revisited in a future proposition both because new laws often have unintended consequences and losers always have another chance to prevail.

Initiative use has increased for other reasons. Aspiring politicians and lawmakers build their reputations by sponsoring propositions that can't get traction in the legislature. Corporations and special interest groups find them attractive because successful measures can translate into financial gain or more friendly regulation. Proponents and opponents frequently offer "dueling propositions" on the same

ballot. Only rarely do grassroots movements mushroom into initiative movements, and even those tend to be elite- or activist-driven affairs. Still, such movements can have enormous consequences for governing.

Today the power of the average voter has been eclipsed by industry initiative activity and special interest group imperatives. Voters endure campaigns waged by corporations with deep pockets and media barrages containing oversimplified messages. Armed only with these biased accounts, they must decide on complex policies frequently crafted without the benefit of compromise, and these policies may set rules that are difficult to amend later. Not surprisingly, most citizens believe there are too many propositions, that the ballot wording is too complicated, and that the process needs to be changed,[4] and confused voters tend to vote "no," especially when the ramifications of voting "yes" are not clear. Given California's history, it is only a matter of time before further reforms are made (see Box 3.1).

Referendum

Citizens may also reject or approve measures passed by the legislature. To prompt a referendum, petitioners must collect the same number of signatures required for initiatives (433,971) within three months. If it qualifies for the ballot, voters will decide whether a particular legislative act should be rejected. **Petition referendums** are rare; far more common are **bond measures** that are first approved by the legislature and then passed along to voters for approval. The constitution requires that voters approve state borrowing above $300,000. Bond measures authorize the state treasurer to sell bonds on the open market, which essentially are promises to pay back with interest any amounts loaned to the state. Bonds are typically used to finance multimillion- or billion-dollar projects ranging from water restoration to stem cell research to library renovation, and since 2000 the average bond has cost more than $5 billion (see chapter 8). Most generate little controversy and around 60 percent pass.

Recall

California is one of eighteen states allowing voters to remove and replace elected officials between regular elections. Nationwide, the majority of recall attempts are aimed at local officials such as justices, city council members, or school board members; state officials are frequently targeted, albeit unsuccessfully. Until 2003 only one governor had ever been recalled: Lynn Frazier of North Dakota in 1921. For state lawmakers or executive officers, low recall success rates are partly ensured through fairly high signature requirements; the threshold for the number of signatures is 20 percent of the votes cast in the last Assembly or Senate district election. The requirements are also high for recalling governors; in some states the threshold to bring a recall question to the ballot is as high as 25 percent of voters. Citizens wishing to recall a governor in California have 160 days to submit valid signatures equal to 12 percent of the votes cast during the previous gubernatorial election, or more than 1 million based on the 2006 election.

BOX 3.1 **Reforming the Initiative Process**

Is the initiative process ripe for reform? Californians overwhelmingly support their right to make laws alongside the state legislature, but many acknowledge the process isn't perfect. Its built-in biases have long been recognized, and resource-rich special interests have advantages over average citizens at every stage, a situation that contradicts the original intent of empowering the many at the expense of the few. Fixing these problems and others will require balancing individual power and free speech rights. Opinion is sharply divided over whether and how to address these complex issues and how effective any solutions would be.

Problems and Suggested Remedies

Problem: It is far easier for paid circulators to collect enough valid signatures than it is for volunteer-based groups; virtually anyone can qualify an initiative by paying a signature-gathering firm $1–$2+ million.

Remedy: Extend the signature-gathering period well past the current 150 days so that smaller groups have more time to spread their messages and volunteers throughout the state, or ban paid signature-gathering.

Problem: Big money dominates the initiative process.

Remedy: Limit campaign donations from groups and individuals. Disclose donor information as close as possible to the date a draft is titled and prominently display that information on initiative petitions and advertising throughout the campaign.

Problem: Ballot measures are confusing and complex.

Remedy: Hold legislative hearings to generate more substantive discussion about a measure's probable impacts. If two conflicting measures are being considered in the same election, group them together in the ballot pamphlet and explain which will prevail if both pass. In addition, direct voters to online resources to help them in their search for more comprehensive information.

Problem: There are too many initiatives.

Remedy: Require the legislature to vote on proposed laws first. After a public hearing on a measure, the legislature could vote to pass it, with or without any changes that the initiative's authors may approve or reject. Courts could be given a role in verifying that the legislature's version respects the authors' intent.

Problem: It is too difficult to revise initiatives once they become law. They cannot be changed except through a future ballot measure, even if flaws are discovered.

Remedy: Allow the legislature to amend measures after a certain amount of time, holding lawmakers to strict guidelines or further review.

Problem: The state constitution is cluttered with redundant and contradictory amendments.

Remedy: Enable more frequent, comprehensive reviews of the state constitution to weed out obsolete, unnecessary, or contradictory language. Alternatively, require a constitutional revision commission to meet periodically and make recommendations that voters or lawmakers may act upon.

Problem: Too many initiatives are declared unconstitutional.

Remedy: Require that a measure be reviewed at a legislative hearing or by a panel of active or retired judges to determine whether the proposed law is consistent with the California state constitution. Inform voters of any conflicts, and give authors the option to withdraw their measures.

For further reading, see *Democracy by Initiative*, 2nd ed. (Los Angeles: Center for Governmental Studies, 2008). Available at www.cgs.org/images/publications/cgs_dbi_full_book_f.pdf.

No specific grounds for removal are needed to launch a recall in California, but proponents must state their reasons on the petitions they circulate. Since 1913, 150 recalls have been made against state elected officials in California, but only nine of these qualified for the ballot and only five ultimately succeeded. The most dramatic of these was the 2003 recall of Gov. Gray Davis, discussed earlier in chapter 2. Ironically, it takes a majority vote to remove an incumbent, but the replacement wins by plurality vote (the most votes of all cast), so Schwarzenegger could have won with far less than the 48.7 percent he received.

Conclusion: Frustrating Collective Action

California's unique blend of representative and direct democracy creates winners who use public authority to establish their version of reform and their vision of "better policy" that reflects their values and interests. As political devices, the initiative, referendum, and recall do not encourage the compromises needed to solve dilemmas that frustrate collective action. Though voters make far fewer decisions at the ballot box than legislators make in a typical morning, the political, fiscal, and social impacts of initiatives and referendums can profoundly upset the status quo—frequently with unintended consequences. Yet direct democracy is sacred in California. According to a recent survey, citizens believe they make better public policy decisions than elected officials do,[5] and voters continually reshape their government with the goal of "making things work." Direct democracy doesn't ensure success, but its presence feeds citizens' hopes for it.

SAMPLE

STATEWIDE SPECIAL ELECTION - OCTOBER 7, 2003 - SAN DIEGO COUNTY
OFFICIAL BALLOT

STATE

VOTE YES OR NO ON THE RECALL MEASURE BELOW

| Shall **GRAY DAVIS** be recalled (removed) from the office of Governor? | 3 | YES ➡ ○ |
| | 4 | NO ➡ ○ |

THE CANDIDATES TO SUCCEED (REPLACE) GRAY DAVIS
IF HE IS RECALLED (REMOVED) ARE LISTED ON THIS PAGE
AND THE FOLLOWING 6 PAGES

FIGURE 3.2

2003 Governor Recall Measure Question on the Sample Ballot

Notes

1. The term "hybrid democracy" is attributed to Elizabeth Garrett, "Hybrid Democracy," *George Washington Law Review* 73 (August 2005): 1096.

2. Initiative and Referendum Institute, iandrinstitute.org.

3. Elisabeth Gerber et al., *Stealing the Initiative* (Upper Saddle River, N.J.: Prentice Hall, 2001), 12.

4. Public Policy Institute of California, November 2008, "Just the Facts: Californians and the Initiative Process." Polls conducted September 2008 (n = 2,002 adults) and October 2008 (2,004 adults). Fifty-nine percent agreed with the statement: "There are too many propositions on the state ballot." Seventy-eight percent agreed that "ballot wording for citizens' initiatives is often too complicated and confusing for voters to understand what happens if the initiative passes." A combined 64 percent believed that minor or major change is needed in the initiative process.

5. Public Policy Institute of California, November 2008.

OUTLINE

Design, Purpose, and Function of the Legislature

California Representatives at Work

Policymaking and Lawmaking

Annual Budgeting

Constituency Service and Outreach

Executive Branch Oversight

Leaders

Conclusion: Of the People, For the People

CHAPTER 4

The State Legislature

Should all dogs and cats be sterilized after they reach six months of age? Should oil companies pay higher taxes on the oil they extract? Should children receive medical care if their parents are too poor to pay for it? Legislators answer just such questions. Throughout the lawmaking process they are obligated to express the will of the citizens they represent, and they make decisions that touch almost every aspect of people's lives.

Design, Purpose, and Function of the Legislature

In California's system of separated powers, the legislature makes law or policy, the executive branch enforces or implements it, and the judicial branch interprets the other branches' actions. Chapters 2 and 3 discussed how the people also dabble in lawmaking through the initiative process, but legislators are primarily responsible for solving the state's problems, and they are better suited to the task: they work on issues year-round, assisted by professional staffs that analyze alternatives, costs, and outcomes of proposed laws.

California's legislature resembles the U.S. Congress in both structure and function. Like its federal counterpart, it is bicameral; that is, it is divided into two houses that check each other. Legislators in both the state's eighty-member lower house, called the **Assembly**, and the forty-member upper house, the **Senate**, represent districts that are among the most populous

BOX 4.1 FAST FACTS on the California Legislature

Lower house:	Assembly, 80 members
Upper house:	Senate, 40 members
Term length:	Assembly, 2 years; Senate 4 years
Term limits:	Assembly, 6 years; Senate 8 years
Majority party in Assembly and Senate:	Democrat
Leaders:	Speaker of the Assembly, President pro Tem of the Senate, Minority Leaders of the Assembly and Senate
Leaders' salaries:	$109,583.98,* plus a per diem of $173/day
Legislators' salaries:	$95,290.56,* plus a per diem of $173/day**

Source: California Citizens Compensation Commission. Available at www.dpa.ca.gov/cccc/salaries/main.htm.

*Effective December 2009; reflects a decrease of 18 percent, or more than $20,000 per legislator.

**Per the Senate Rules and Assembly Rules Committees, per diem amounts are set by the Victim Compensation and Government Claims Board and are intended to cover daily expenses associated with working away from home. Total amounts vary annually with the number of days in session and by chamber. In 2007–2008 senators could earn up to $38,804 annually, and Assembly members averaged $33,383 during the same period (four legislators do not accept per diem payments).

in the nation: based on the 2000 census, Assembly districts average 462,500 people, and Senate districts average nearly 847,000 residents.[1]

Unlike members of the U.S. Congress, however, California legislators are term-limited. In 1990 voters adopted Proposition 140, a term-limits initiative that restricts Assembly members to three two-year terms, for a total of six years, and senators to two four-year terms, or eight years total. Lifetime bans prohibit lawmakers from running for the same offices once they've reached those limits. Prop 140 has profoundly influenced individuals' perspectives and the way the legislature operates, a point revisited later in this chapter.

Legislators are elected from districts that are redrawn once a decade. Redrawing district boundaries has traditionally been a legislative responsibility, but Proposition 11 (passed in 2008) handed the mapmaking power over to an independent commission. Proponents hope this decision will increase party competitiveness and reduce the power of incumbents.

California Representatives at Work

California's legislature has come a long way from the days when allegiances to the Southern Pacific Railroad earned it the nicknames "the legislature of 1,000 steals" and "the legislature of 1,000 drinks." Today, members are the highest paid in the nation, earning more than $100,000 per year, including per diem payments. Special interests and their lobbyists still permeate Sacramento politics with their presence, money, and messages, but legislators' loyalties these days are splintered by district needs, statewide demands, and partisanship. Crammed schedules are split between their home districts and Sacramento.

Nowadays, term limits create large classes of freshman legislators every two years, pushing others into campaigns for the next office and year-round fund-raising. Nearly everyone is in a learning curve, anticipating the next election, and aware that the clock is ticking. Rigid ideological positioning has driven Democrats and Republicans to gridlock over raising taxes, cutting social programs, and balancing the budget. Often the air seems combustible.

In many ways the legislature is a microcosm of California. More than ever before the demographics of the Assembly and Senate resemble the state's population (see Figure 4.1). There are more women and ethnic minority members representing a wider range of ages and backgrounds, and more than one-third of Senate and Assembly members identify with an ethnic minority. The extent to which a legislature is a "portrait in miniature" of a constituency (as U.S. president John Adams put it) is a measure of **descriptive representation**. The extent to which members translate those outward features as well as their values into meaningful policies is **substantive representation**.

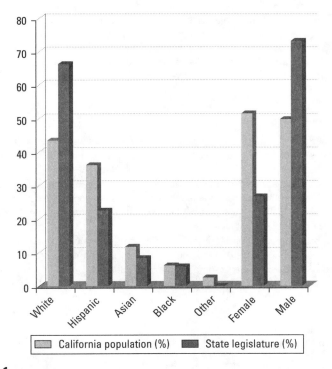

FIGURE 4.1

Profile of California's Population vs. California State Legislature

Sources: DOF Demographic Research Unit, March 2007 estimates (published January 2009); author's data, snapshot of legislature in April 2009.

BOX 4.2 **Term Limits: Political Earthquake**

Have term limits for legislators been good or bad? Both supporters and detractors can find ammunition in the findings. One thing neither side can deny, however, is that the reform has dramatically changed the rules and the environment in which legislators work.

Prior to the passage of Prop 140 in 1990, state legislators were condemned for being out-of-touch careerists who had developed cozy relationships with lobbyists. Stagnant rates of member turnover were pegged to lack of electoral competition, and the legislature was still reeking from an FBI sting two years earlier that had netted fourteen state officials for bribery, including three legislators who went to jail.

The electorate was ready for change when an initiative bill modeled after one passed shortly before in Oklahoma qualified for the ballot. Echoes of the early California Progressives were heard in proponents' sweeping promises to restore a "government of citizens representing their fellow citizens."* The measure quickly gained momentum and passed with just over 52 percent of the vote. Since then, support for term limits among Californians has solidified and increased, and twenty other states subsequently adopted similar measures, although these were invalidated or repealed in six states, bringing the current total number of states permitting initiatives to fifteen.

Term limits had an immediate impact. Long-term legislators were forced to campaign for other elected offices, and staff members were driven into private lobbying firms when Prop 140 slashed legislative budgets. Within a few years, Speaker Willie Brown was mayor of San Francisco, Assembly careers were ending for good, and sitting senators were anticipating their next move. Overall, the wide-ranging effects have touched virtually every aspect of legislative life, and they range from positive to negative.

Electoral Changes

- Competition has increased for political offices at all levels, from county boards of supervisors to seats in the U.S. Congress, as more termed-out legislators run for them.
- Open seat primary elections occur with regularity and can be ferociously competitive; open seat general elections in a handful of districts are competitive as well.
- Incumbents still have huge advantages—about 99 percent are reelected. Many cruise to victory, some without challengers.
- Nearly all senators are former members of the state Assembly, and some senators return to the Assembly to finish serving out a final term before reaching their lifetime limits (fourteen years: six in the Assembly, eight in the Senate).
- Intraparty competition has risen as members of the same party vie for the same seats—usually in the state Senate.

Membership Changes

- Far higher numbers of open seats have encouraged the candidacies and election of ethnic minority members—higher than would be expected through redistricting alone. More than a third of legislators are Latino, African American, or Asian American.

- Higher turnover has led to record numbers of female candidates for office since 1990, though their total percentage of membership follows a longer historical upward trend unconnected to term limits.
- More women are being elected to the Senate and occupy more leadership roles in both houses; these trends most favor women members of the Democratic Party.

Institutional Changes

- Newer legislators have recently experienced the effects of current laws in their districts and have fresh ideas about how to address problems arising from them.
- "Institutional memory" has drained away as career legislators and their staffs leave; members are less expert across a range of policy areas than in the past, and their knowledge of how state systems interrelate is poorer.
- The average senator has about two-and-a-half times as much legislative experience as the average Assembly member.
- Senate staff members tend to be more experienced than Assembly staff members and consider the upper house the "watchdog" of the more turnover-prone Assembly.
- Some lobbyists who represent powerful groups are experienced and well connected and can quickly establish relationships that exert undue influence over legislators. They must work harder to get to know those new members, however, as newer legislators are likely to regard lobbyists as a group with skepticism.
- Executive branch departments command informational resources and benefit from less frequent institutional turnover, rendering oversight by the legislature even more difficult than in the past.

Behavioral Changes

- "Lame duck" legislators lack electoral accountability to their current districts. Many look to their next possible constituency when considering how to vote; some feel less obligated to lobbyists in their last terms and more frequently feel free to "vote their conscience."
- Long-term, comprehensive lawmaking suffers as term-limited legislators lack the time and incentive to tackle many big projects or issues that will outlast their tenures. Smaller district-level projects are more attractive to term-limited legislators.
- There is a sense that "everyone is running for the next office."

Sources: Author's data. See also Bruce Cain, Thad Kousser, and Karl Kurtz, "California: A Professional Legislature after Term Limits," in *Governing California,* Gerald C. Lubenow, ed. (Berkeley: IGS Press, 2006).

*California Secretary of State, "Argument in Favor of Proposition 140," November 1990 ballot pamphlet.

Policymaking and Lawmaking

Assembly members and senators fulfill their representative functions chiefly through various aspects of **lawmaking**. To deal with the 6,000 or so bills introduced in a two-year session, they research issues between visiting sites like schools and inter-acting with community leaders and citizens to get a better sense of their districts. They introduce bills addressing problems that lobbyists or constituents bring to their attention. As members of committees (where the bulk of policymaking occurs), they help shape or amend legislation after fielding complaints, testimony, and predictions from witnesses who will be affected by potential changes. They deliberate and vote both in committee and later on the Assembly or Senate floor, where every member has a chance to vote on every bill. As all bills must be passed in identical form by both houses before the governor can veto or sign them, members also continue building support for or opposition to measures that are moving through the other house.

Each bill bears the imprint of a unique set of players, is shaped by the rules, and is affected by timing. More often than not, the concerns of important groups are accommodated to some degree, their input gathered throughout the bill pas-sage process. Legislators tend to be sensitive to the fears and threats expressed by well-financed, vocal, influential, and large organizations that support their party or are active in their districts. For instance, businesses that employ large numbers of

The Senate Rules Committee holds a hearing to consider the appointment of Mary Nichols to chair the California Air Resources Board (CARB). A former state Department of Resources secretary and chair of CARB under Jerry Brown from 1978–1983, she reassumed the post in 2007.

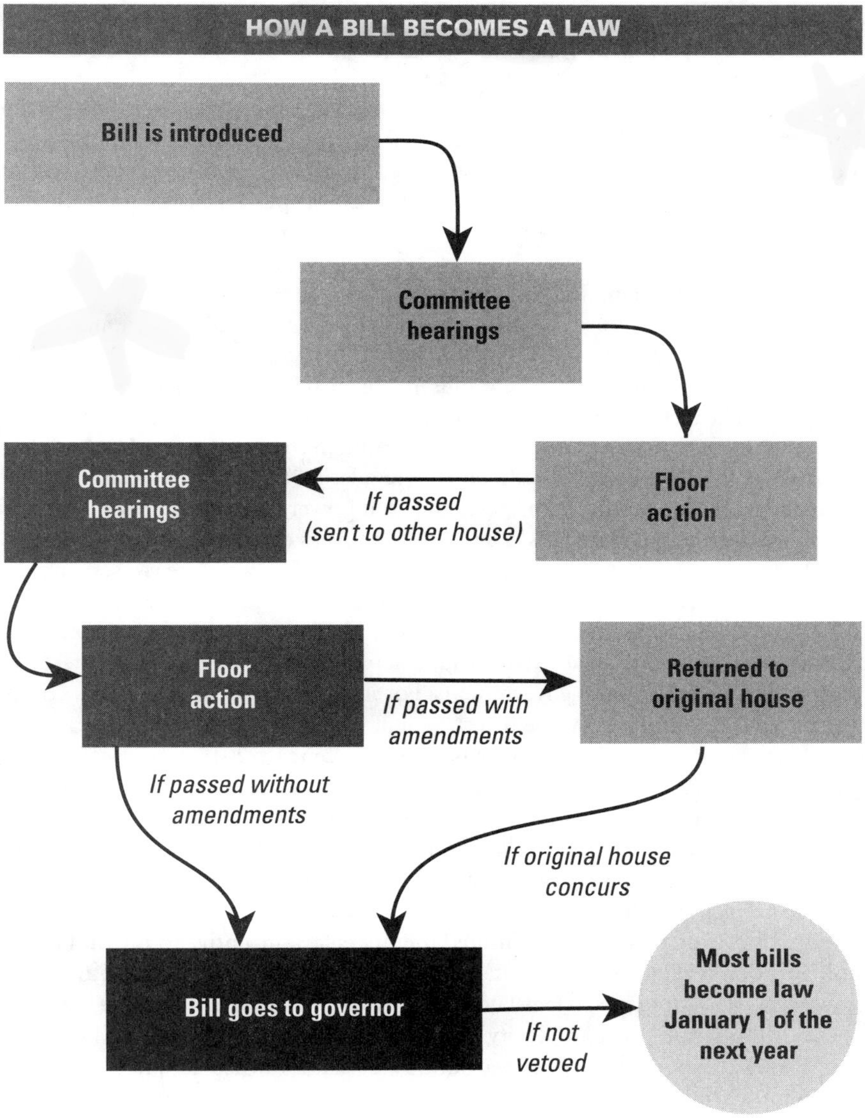
HOW A BILL BECOMES A LAW
Bill is introduced
Committee hearings
Floor action
If passed (sent to other house)
Committee hearings
Floor action
If passed with amendments
Returned to original house
If passed without amendments
If original house concurs
Bill goes to governor
If not vetoed
Most bills become law January 1 of the next year

FIGURE 4.2

How a Bill Becomes a Law

people in a legislator's district may be called upon to testify about bills or may be asked to provide feedback about pending legislation.

Relationships also matter. Partisans tend to support fellow partisans, but legislators who get to know others "across the aisle" tend to be more willing to support them legislatively. Because in the final analysis compromise is key, relationships among the players—from legislative staff to legislators to lobbyists to the governor's staff—help facilitate necessary give and take.

Bills vary in scope, cost, urgency, and significance and cover every imaginable topic, and most go no further than being referred to a committee. Of lesser scope and significance are simple resolutions passed to express the legislature's position on an issue. For example, in March 2009 the Assembly passed a resolution "memo-rializing its opposition to Proposition 8" on the grounds that the proposition improperly revised the state constitution. No Republican supported the resolution, but it was adopted by a majority vote of Democrats. Inexpensive "local bills," which deal with such concerns as creating a downtown redevelopment zone, may matter a lot to the people directly affected by the legislation but usually have only a minor impact on state government. Many bills relate to the administration of govern-ment and make technical changes or amendments to existing state law. These might impose mandates, or directions, on local governments or agencies, such as prohibit-ing counties from adopting an ordinance or regulation that affects the taking of fish and game from local nature areas, reserving that power for the state Fish and Game Commission instead. Other bills create new categories of crime, authorize commis-sion studies, or set up programs. It takes a law to establish a nature conservancy for the restoration and cleanup of environmentally sensitive areas, for example.

Legislators also introduce bills that at first glance may appear to make small changes, but which, if enacted into law, actually will have tangible effects on Californians and their local governments. For instance, as of 2000, city and county governments are supposed to be diverting half of the solid waste generated locally away from landfills; a proposal to make it 60 percent by 2015 would cause cities and counties to revisit this issue and devise new plans to deal with their waste, from imposing fees to further regulating businesses to trying to change household hab-its. Of major import are multimillion- or billion-dollar, long-range, complex bills that affect many different groups and usually require years of study and compro-mise. Examples include revising workers' compensation programs or regulating watersheds. Unfortunately, term-limited members lack incentive to unwind knotty problems that take years to understand and for which they will receive little credit, though this does not stop all legislators from trying to "make a difference."

Given the scope and complexity of the state's ongoing issues, legislators need help. Thousands of staff members working in legislators' offices and for committees assist with scheduling, constituent relations, research, and expert legislative analysis. The Senate, which has retained more veteran professional committee staff and more experienced legislators, tends to collectively view itself as having stronger filters for "bad ideas." Staff members are particularly invaluable players in analyzing the thou-sands of bills that cross legislators' desks during a two-year term.

Legislators also heavily depend on institutional housekeepers like the Assembly chief clerk's staff or the Senate's secretary to ensure that legislators follow standing rules and parliamentary procedures. The nonpartisan **Legislative Analyst's Office (LAO)** has been the so-called conscience and eyes and ears of the legislature since

TABLE 4.1   Day in the Life of Sen. Denise Ducheny

April 20, 2009
Monday

All Day	**GET BOARDING PASS FOR DMD AT 8:30 PM ON UNITED FOR TOMORROW**
9:30 AM–10:00 AM	**STAFF MEETING**
10:00 AM–10:15 AM	**DMD: Call DHCS Director David Maxwell Jolly. DMD TO CALL.**
11:00 AM–1:00 PM	**Sen. Approps – FILE ORDER – Capitol, Room 4203** SB 358, Native American Small Business Loan & Guarantee Prog SB 608, Dept of H & CD: bond fund expenditures 28.8
11:00 AM–12:00 PM	**Speak at Motorcycle/ABATE Rally (stop by anytime during this hour time frame)—Capitol, SOUTH STEPS**
12:00 PM–12:45 PM	**(MOVED UP) SESSION – Recognition for Consul General Bologna on the Floor (DMD INTRODUCE, PRESENT RESOLUTION, AND ANNOUNCE RECEPTION FOLLOWING SESSION IN ROOM 211).**
1:00 PM–1:45 PM	**SEN. PE & R HEARING—5 Bills only—Capitol, Room 2040**
1:30 PM–2:00 PM	**PAL (Police Activities League) groups from the district for Lobby Day**
1:30 PM–2:00 PM	**Sen. Environmental Quality Committee—FILE ORDER—Capitol, Room 112** SB 167, Waste Tire Recycling
2:30 PM–3:30 PM	**UI meeting with Pat Henning (EDD), Pamela Harris (Chief Deputy Director, EDD), Angie Wei and Emily Clayton (Labor Federation), Jason Schmelzer (CalChamber) and Cynthia Leon (CMTA).** ADDED: Dolores Duran Flores (CA School Employees Assn) and Libby Sanchez (Teamsters).
2:30 PM–3:00 PM	**Associated Students at CSU San Diego (2) Lobby Day**
3:00 PM–3:30 PM	**EQCA (Equality California) Lobby Day youth (7) re support for SB 572, Harvey Milk Day and SB 543, Minor Mental Health Consent.**
3:30 PM–4:00 PM	**Taxpayers for Improving Public Safety Lobby Day re prison crisis, impact of Prop 9, rehab. programs and recidivism.**
4:00 PM–5:00 PM	**(ADDED) FYI: Coffee (hosted by Sen. Steinberg & Speaker Bass) for Alex Rooker for Vice Chair of CA Demo. Party—Chicory—private room, 1131 11th St.**
4:30 PM–5:00 PM	**State Board of Equalization—Ray Hirsig (Exec. Dir.), Margaret Shedd (Leg. Counsel) and Elizabeth Houser (Deputy Dir., Administration Dept)—"Meet and Greet."**
5:00 PM–6:00 PM	**FYI: ACHD (Assn of CA Healthcare Districts) Meet and Greet Reception—Hyatt—15th Floor—Capitol View Room.**
5:30 PM–7:30 PM	**(TIME CHANGE) Delta Plan Working Group. MEMBERS ONLY. DINNER (PIZZA & SALAD) AVAILABLE FOR $6/PERSON—Willie Brown Conference Room** DWR Director Lester Snow will be making the presentation on state-wide water management (Goal 4) and Delta water infrastructure (Goal 5).

1941, providing fiscal and policy advice based on continuing, in-depth research of programs, bills, and the annual budget. Similarly, since 1913 the nonpartisan **Legislative Counsel** has acted as an in-house law firm, crafting legislators' proposals into formal bills, rendering legal opinions, and making bill information available electronically (www.leginfo.ca.gov).

It should also be noted that the majority party controls the fate of nearly all bills because simple majorities (41 in the Assembly; 21 in the Senate) are needed for passage, though a good number of bills are noncontroversial and pass unanimously. The bottom line: minority party Republicans are at the mercy of majority Democrats when it comes to lawmaking, and their bills rarely move out of committee. Democrats can safely ignore the minority unless they need Republican votes to pass fiscal measures that require a two-thirds supermajority.

Annual Budgeting

Democrats do need a few Republican votes to pass an annual budget. It takes more than half the year to work out an **annual budget** for the fiscal year (FY) that starts July 1. The process begins January 10, when the governor submits his version to the legislature, and it should end by June 15, when the budget is officially due—but long overdue budgets are the norm. To deal with the budget crisis in 2009, the legislature put aside the normal schedule and developed an unprecedented seventeen-month budget plan covering the remainder of FY2008–2009 and the subsequent FY2009–2010.

During the winter and spring of a normal fiscal year, the committees in both houses divvy up the work of determining how much money is needed to keep government programs running. Big-ticket items such as education are automatically funded, leaving a relatively small chunk of the budget pie for discretionary purposes; therefore, each legislator fights hard for the crumbs. The inherently partisan process is exacerbated by the rule that two-thirds of both the Senate and Assembly must approve the budget. This effectively grants tremendous power to a few at the expense of majority rule. As one former Democratic leader put it, "If you're in the minority you really control the budget," because those few members can arm-twist the majority into major concessions in exchange for needed votes. As Senate President pro Tem Darrell Steinberg has pointed out, "It makes no sense to completely thwart the will of the majority by empowering, in this instance, essentially nine [now six] people to dictate the outcome of the most important thing that California does."[2] California is one of only three states to impose such a high vote requirement for passing the budget (Rhode Island and Arkansas are the other two).

Constituency Service and Outreach

Constituency service entails "helping constituents navigate through the government system,"[3] particularly when their troubles stem from bureaucratic "red tape." Legislators hire caseworkers to help them respond quickly to requests, and these staff members spend their days tracking down CalTrans managers and scheduling appointments at state agencies for frustrated constituents, among other things. Legislators take constituency service seriously though it is nowhere mentioned in the state constitution. Many consider it "paramount to return every phone call, letter, and e-mail" and make government seem friendlier through personal contact.[2]

Most legislators try to communicate frequently with district residents via e-mail, Web sites, events, and franked mail pieces (correspondence paid for through office budgets). Other activities include addressing select groups like Rotary clubs or attending public events (store openings, groundbreakings for public facilities, etc.) at which milestones are commemorated. This kind of constituent outreach, or "**public relations**" as some members call it, helps educate constituents as well as provide incumbents with necessary ammunition for reelection by enhancing their name recognition and reputations.

Executive Branch Oversight

Who will monitor programs to ensure that a law is being carried out according to the legislature's intent? Ideally, Assembly members and their staff should be regularly questioning administrators and reviewing programs, but term-limited legislators

The Assembly floor is normally a beehive of activity when the Assembly is in session. Here, Gov. Arnold Schwarzenegger addresses a more subdued joint session of the legislature on June 2, 2009, telling members in regard to the state's financial situation, "Our wallet is empty. Our bank is closed. Our credit has dried up."

have little time or staff resources to determine if the laws they've created are being faithfully executed. In practice, they rely on investigative reports in the media, lobbyists, citizens, and administrators to sound the alarm about needed fixes. Once a problem is identified, the Assembly and Senate can rescue legislative intent by threatening to reduce program funding or eliminate the positions of uncooperative state employees. Senators also influence programs through the power to **confirm gubernatorial appointees** to boards and commissions, such as the Air Resources Board or the Department of Corrections.

Leaders

Aside from the governor, the **Speaker of the Assembly** and the **President pro Tem of the Senate** are among the most powerful figures in Sacramento. Along with the governor and the **minority leaders** of each house, these individuals form the **"Big Five"** of California government: the leaders who speak for all their fellow party members in their house and are ultimately responsible for cobbling together last-minute political bargains that clinch the budget or guarantee the signing of big bills.

A party leader's job is to keep his or her majority in power or to regain majority status. Nonstop fund-raising, policymaking, rule-making, and deal-making all serve that overarching objective. Party leaders oversee their *caucus* (all the members of a party in a house) and help shape the electorate's understanding of what it means to support a "Democratic" or "Republican" agenda. Still, institutional agendas are fluid and more often than not they emerge from commonalities among legislators' individual plans more than they are imposed by elites at the top. However, what leadership wants, leadership gets. Leaders' ability to obtain desired results rests on many factors, including having credible weapons such as removing members from choice committees, endorsing opponents, cutting off campaign funds, reducing office budgets midyear, and moving offices or parking spaces to undesirable locations.

The Speaker is the most visible member of the Assembly and its spokesperson at-large; he or she negotiates budgets, bills, and policies on behalf of the entire membership, curries a high profile with the press, and cultivates a distinct culture of discipline and institutional independence through a unique and personal leadership style. Campaign funds are a resource leaders actively use to reward faithful party members and punish traitors. The Senate's President pro Tem plays these same roles, and in a term-limited era when legislative experience is concentrated in the Senate, the Senate leader's visibility has increased relative to that of the Speaker.

Speakers appoint chairs and members to all Assembly committees, as does the President pro Tem through his or her chairing of the all-powerful, five-member Rules Committee. Given that most senators are former Assembly members,

Assembly Speaker Karen Bass confers with Senate Minority Leader Dave Cogdill. Cogdill's leadership was cut short by fellow Republican senators who denounced his tacit approval of a budget that included tax increases for sales, gas, and vehicle registrations. The more conservative Dennis Hollingsworth replaced Cogdill in February 2009.

committees in the upper house are chaired not by freshmen or sophomores with zero to five years' legislative experience but usually by members who have been in the legislature at least four years when seated. The President pro Tem also can use the Rules Committee's power over the governor's key administrative appointments as a bargaining chip in budget and bill negotiations—a tool the Speaker lacks.

These days neither the Speaker nor the Senate President pro Tem regularly leads floor sessions. Visitors catch glimpses of them as they crisscross the floor to privately speak with members in an effort to find support for bills and negotiate deals while normal business proceeds. More often than not an assistant "pro tem" guides floor proceedings.

Leaders never forget that they are elected by their colleagues and stay only as long as they can maintain the trust and confidence of those colleagues by meeting their political needs. This was as true for flashy former Speaker Willie Brown (1980–1995) as it is for Speakers today. No tyrants can survive, if only because so many potential replacements impatiently wait in the wings—and under term limits, they needn't wait long before the next opportunity arises. Brown presided over the Assembly for almost fifteen years. In the fifteen years since his departure there have been *nine* Speakers.

Influential Assembly Speakers in California History

Jesse Unruh

Willie Brown

Antonio Villaraigosa

Karen Bass

Conclusion: Of the People, For the People

Although the legislature's basic framework has changed little since the constitutional revision of 1879, major changes in electoral law, campaign finance rules, ethics law, redistricting, compensation levels, and terms of office have molded and remolded California's legislative environment. Initiatives continue to complicate the already difficult task of condensing a multitude of competing interests, opinions, backgrounds, values, expectations, and ideas into an effective decision-making body. Californians have been quick to alter the political rules to make their representatives resistant to what is generally regarded as the poisonous influence of partisanship, money, and power, yet they have done so with limited success.

Lawmaking is *supposed* to be hard, and an institution that features overlapping powers and shared responsibilities among many elected officials inevitably frustrates it. In California the policymaking process is further complicated by direct democracy and hyper-diversity. Bills bear the imprints of competing interest groups, parties, leaders, funding sources, personal ambitions, rules, history, and a host of other factors that influence choice and impede the easy resolution of issues. Short of creating a tyranny, no reform will change that.

The California state legislature comes closest to the U.S. Congress in form than any other in the nation. Perhaps that is one reason for its dismal approval ratings, but it also remains the best hope for each citizen to achieve a degree of representation that would be unimaginable under an unelected bureaucracy or a dictatorial governor. The lawmaking body is closer to the people than the other two branches could ever be: neither the elected executives nor judges can understand the needs and interests of California's communities as thoroughly as firmly anchored representatives can. Not enough attention is paid to the hundreds of public-spirited men and women who have served and are serving resolutely and honorably as California state legislators, individuals who work hard to sustain representative democracy.

Notes

1. The U.S. Census 2000 apportionment population in congressional districts is 646,952; California contains fifty-three districts. Data found at http://nationalatlas.gov/articles/boundaries/a_conApport.html.
2. Author's interview with freshman Assembly member, 1999.
3. Donald Lathbury, "Two-Thirds Majority Battle Still on Radar," The California Majority Report, September 22, 2008, www.camajorityreport.com/index.php?module=articles&func=display&ptid=9&aid=3581.

CHAPTER 5

OUTLINE

California's Plural Executive

California's Governor
   Head of State
   Chief Executive
   Legislative Powers
   Budgeting Power
   Chief of Security
   Party Leader
   Sources of Power

The Constitutional Executive Officers

Administrators and Regulators

Conclusion: Competition for Power

The Executive Branch

Question: Who is in charge of California's K–12 education system?

Answer: The *governor* guides education policy through budgetary changes or oversees bill proposals based on suggestions from his own appointed *secretary of education* (who manages a small *Office of Education,* at least until the 2009 budget crisis threw that operation into doubt)—not to be confused with the elected *state superintendent of public instruction,* the executive officer constitutionally mandated to head the state's education system who oversees the *Department of Education,* the agency through which the public school system is regulated and controlled as required by law and which also takes cues from the administration's powerful *State Board of Education,* also appointed by the governor but technically administered by the superintendent, who in turn implements the educational regulations of the State Board of Education . . . not to mention the *Assembly* and *Senate Education Committees* that steer education bills into law.

Confusing? A case of checks and balances gone awry? Somewhere among the governor's need to obtain information and make recommendations, the legislature's regulatory imperative, and the people's desire to elect at least one accountable officer, the system evolved into a tangled network of authority that even Education Department employees have difficulty explaining.

Number of executives:	8, plus a Board of Equalization (12 persons)
Elected executive offices:	Governor
	Lieutenant governor (LG)
	Attorney general (AG)
	Secretary of state
	Controller
	Treasurer
	Superintendent of public instruction
	Insurance commissioner
	Board of Equalization
Balance of political parties:	4 Republicans, 7 Democrats, 1 nonpartisan (2008 elections)
Governor's salary:	$173,979*
Salary for AG and superintendent:	$151,127
Salary for controller, treasurer, insurance commissioner:	$139,189
Salary for secretary of state, LG:	$130,490
Terms of office:	Four years
Term limits:	Two terms

Source: California Citizens Compensation Commission. Available at www.dpa.ca.gov/cccc/salaries/main.htm.

*Effective December 2009; reflects a decrease of 18 percent, an average of more than $30,000 per official. (Schwarzenegger does not draw a salary).

California's Plural Executive

The Founders of the U.S. Constitution rejected the notion that more than one person could effectively lead an executive branch. They argued that only one, the president, could bring energy to an office that would otherwise be fractured by competition and differences of opinion. What then are we to make of California's **plural executive**, comprised of eight constitutional executive officers plus a five-member board, sharing responsibility for administering state government—the longest list among the states? Or the fact that among them are both Republicans *and* Democrats?

Term limits on each office, two four-year terms under Proposition 140, also call into question executives' ability or desire to cooperate. As term-limited colleagues they are potential or actual rivals for each others' seats, driven from one elected position to the next as in a game of musical chairs. However, despite their responsibilities to lead the nation's most densely populated state jointly, like most elected officials they remain virtually anonymous to average residents.

The duty of an executive is to carry out laws and policies. Whereas federal administrators direct agencies in their departments to implement a coherent presidential

Under term limits individuals may only be elected to the same seat twice. Elected officials are usually looking for another job long before eight years are up, and open statewide offices are attractive options to those who have campaigned statewide and have run other aspects of state government. In a term-limited era, it's all about the "next" office.

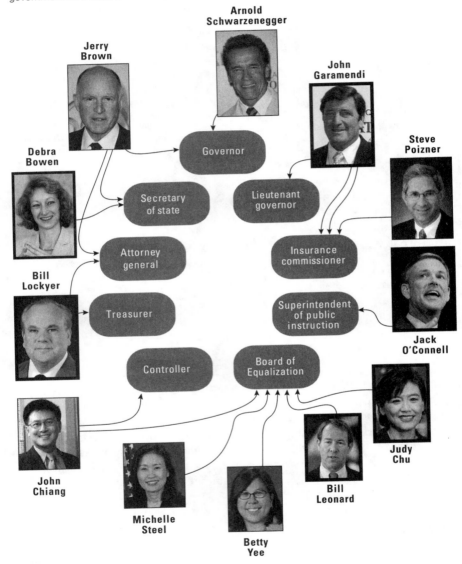

FIGURE 5.1

California Executives and Musical Chairs

These executives have held positions in the California legislature. They have served terms in both the Assembly and the Senate, except for Judy Chu, who has served only in the Assembly.

agenda, in California a large assortment of departments, agencies, and commissions serve different masters: the governor, other California executives, the legislature, the entities they are supposed to regulate, or a combination of any of the above. Years of legislative and administrative turf battles as well as citizen-driven initiatives have produced a thicket of offices, boards, agencies, and commissions, some of which retain independent regulatory power and many more of which follow the governor's lead. In theory the dispersion of power across several offices inoculates government against the worst effects of a single, inept leader, but a fragmented power structure works against the production of consistent government policy and counteracts accountability.

California's Governor

According to the state constitution, "The supreme executive power of this State is vested in the Governor," which places him or her first among equals—for none of the executive officers answer directly to the governor. As the most recognized and powerful figure in state government, his constitutional duties are like those of most state governors; what distinguishes him is both the size and hyper-diversity of his constituency and the resulting volume of conflicts to address.

The usual route to office is not through recall; only Gov. Arnold Schwarzenegger initially escaped both the primary and general election contests as well as an extended campaign. Strong partisans tend to survive the regular winnowing process and prior elected experience also tends to be favored—two qualities the atypical Schwarzenegger did not possess when he replaced Gov. Gray Davis in 2003.

Head of State

A governor has responsibilities both formal and informal. The role of **head of state** resonates with average citizens: the governor appears at official ceremonies and public events, summarizes California's outlook and his agenda in an annual "State of the State" address, receives and entertains foreign dignitaries, and speaks for Californians on the national political stage. He also functions as the state's official liaison to federal officials in Washington, D.C., and works with other state governors to advance causes nationally.

Chief Executive

Chief executive powers rest with the governor. He indirectly controls the bureaucracy through approximately 1,000 top-level appointments to his cabinet, key administrative posts, and his own staff, which numbers around 150 individuals. He also appoints members to 320 state boards and commissions with more than 2,250 slots to be filled. Appointments to about one hundred full-time administrative positions and seventy-five boards and commissions require Senate approval,

As head of state, a governor performs the ceremonial duty of appearing at important gatherings, events, or natural disaster sites. Here, Governor Schwarzenegger speaks in front of a fire command post in Beaumont, California, on October 29, 2006.

and overall, only a fraction of appointees serve at the governor's whim. For instance, civil service laws protect virtually all state employees, and roughly 99 percent are hired based on merit rather than nepotism, favoritism, or patronage.[1] Outside of this, on rare occasion the governor may name a replacement to an open U.S. Senate seat.

Legislative Powers

Legislatively, the governor plays a significant role by setting policy priorities for California not only through proposed laws but also through the budget. Combined with the power to call special legislative sessions and special elections, having long-term, permanent staff dedicated to research and program oversight gives the governor's office institutional advantages over the legislature.

Aides monitor bills at all stages of the legislative process, from proposing bills to participating in critical final negotiations over a bill's wording and price tag. They testify before Assembly or Senate committees about pending measures and help build coalitions of support or opposition among legislators and interest groups. They also advise the governor to **veto** or **sign** legislation, as a bill becomes law after twelve days without gubernatorial action. Like governors in four out of five states, the hand of the governor of California is strengthened by the **line-item veto**, the power to reduce or eliminate dollar amounts in bills or the budget. Veto overrides by the legislature are rarely attempted or successful. The governor may also issue **executive orders** directing state employees in how to implement the law, but Schwarzenegger's power falls short of forcing all executives to do his bidding.

Budgeting Power

Budgeting power arguably gives the administration a powerful advantage over the Assembly and Senate. The **Department of Finance (DOF),** a permanent clearing-house for state financial and demographic information, works in tandem with the governor to propose a budget in January each year and to revise it in May based on actual tax receipts. The nearly 440 of the DOF work year-round to prepare the following year's budget and enact the previous year's financial plan, and they also analyze any legislation that has a fiscal impact.

Chief of Security

The governor promotes security as **commander in chief** of the state's National Guard, which may be called on at short notice to, for example, deliver emergency services to victims of natural disasters. With few restraints the governor also can pardon, grant clemency, or commute sentences, even for death row inmates.

Party Leader

Finally, a typical governor symbolically heads his or her state **party**. The extent to which a governor can influence fellow party members in state government depends on the governor's commitment to core party principles, however; a conservative like Gov. Pete Wilson (1991–1999) exerted far greater leadership within the California Republican Party than a moderate Republican like Arnold Schwarzenegger ever could, as Schwarzenegger has alienated fellow partisans by working with Democrats and staking out policies that defy the state party's official platform.

Sources of Power

California governors resemble U.S. presidents but with important exceptions. The state's constitution limits their ability to live up to citizens' expectations. For exam-ple, the governor sets policy priorities as the most visible and accountable leader, yet he shares responsibility for day-to-day administration with the other executive officers who may choose not to follow his priorities. Further, governors are also subject to voters' whims at the ballot box. If one is to overcome those structural disadvantages, he or she must draw on other sources of power to be effective. Some will be institutional, such as whether the governor's party holds a majority in both the Assembly and Senate. Others are personal or informal: charisma, the power to persuade, the perception of having a mandate, or strategic use of the media can go a long way in enhancing a governor's power base.

The Constitutional Executive Officers

Should the governor leave the state at any time, the **lieutenant governor** takes temporary control; should the governor resign, retire early, die, become disabled, or be impeached, the lieutenant governor takes the oath of office. Topping the "LG's" lackluster list of duties is presiding over the Senate, which in practice means exercising a rare tie-breaking vote. The "governor-in-waiting" also sits on the State Lands Commission and several other boards *ex officio,* or by virtue of his or her position.

Second in power to the governor is actually the **attorney general**, known as the state's chief law enforcement officer. Through the state's Department of Justice, the "AG" employs district attorneys to help represent the people of California in court cases; provides legal counsel to state officials; and supervises all sheriffs, police chiefs, and state agencies to enforce the law "adequately and uniformly." The office is inherently political not only because the state's lead lawyer is elected and may use the position as a stepping stone to bigger and better offices (AG is also shorthand for "Aspiring Governor") but also because he or she privileges some causes above others. For example, an AG might step up lawsuits against repeat environmental polluters or sue cities to overturn local ordinances that violate state law.

The **secretary of state** acts as the chief elections officer, overseeing all aspects of federal and state elections—from registering voters to distributing ballot pamphlets in sixteen languages to printing ballots to certifying the integrity of voting machines—and from compiling election results to publishing them on the Web and in print. The office's Political Reform Division implements rules relating to proper disclosure of lobbying and campaign activity and makes that information available electronically (www.cal-access.ca.gov). As keeper of official historical records, the secretary of state also charters corporations and nonprofits, maintains business filings, and safeguards the state archives.

Fragmentation of authority is most evident in the three separate offices that regulate the flow of money through the state government. The prominent **controller** (known as comptroller in other states) pays the state's bills and continually monitors the state's financial situation. State employees and vendors who sell services or goods to the state might recognize the controller's signature on their checks. The controller sits on numerous advisory boards, including the Tax Franchise Board, which deals with income taxes, and more than sixty other commissions and organizations relating to state payouts, such as employee pensions and construction projects.

The second money officer is the **treasurer**, acting as the state's investment banker and bond manager. Every year the state borrows several billion dollars to finance huge projects such as the rebuilding of bridges or schools; this borrowing takes the form of bonds sold to investors (see chapter 8). The treasurer manages the state's mountainous debt by selling and repaying bonds to investors on an ongoing basis,

The most powerful executive officers in California: former governor–turned–attorney general Jerry Brown addresses a crowd with Gov. Arnold Schwarzenegger.

securing acceptable credit ratings that lead to lower loan interest rates, and maintaining the state's financial assets.

The **Board of Equalization** represents the third money office. Consisting of the controller and four other officials elected from districts containing more than 9 million Californians apiece, the board's job is to standardize the tax systems in the state, which bring in more than $50 billion per year—almost 35 percent of the state's entire revenue in 2005–2006.[2] Aided by fifty-eight elected county tax assessors, they ensure that residents pay fair rates on properties; they also collect state sales and use fees, as well as liquor, tobacco, and fuel excise taxes that fund essential state services. The board is the only one of its type elected in the fifty states.

In the same antitax spirit of Proposition 13, voters rebelled against spiraling auto insurance rates and elevated the **Office of Insurance Commissioner** from a governor-appointed subagency to a full-scale executive position in 1988. The elected commissioner is authorized to review and pre-approve rates for car and homeowners' insurance, grant licenses for agents and companies operating in California, investigate fraudulent practices, and enforce rulings against violators.

As noted in this chapter's opener, the **superintendent of public instruction** leads the Department of Education and advocates for student achievement as the state's only nonpartisan executive officer. The superintendent is the point person for testing and reporting, including implementation of the state's high school exit exams; statewide student testing; data collection on a range of education-related issues such as drop-out rates, yearly funding levels for K–12 and community college education, and achievement levels; and implementation of the federal No Child Left Behind Act.

Though these executive officers are free to consult each other and frequently find themselves in each other's company, at no point do they meet as a governing board, and no mechanism exists to centrally coordinate their work. Sometimes this arrangement makes for strange bedfellows, as Governor Schwarzenegger found in 2009 when he wrote an executive order closing state offices two Fridays per month, effectively furloughing all state workers, including those of his fellow executives. However, his mandate legally could not apply to his colleagues, who promptly ignored the order. Sharp disagreements over how to govern during a budget crisis have also surfaced between Schwarzenegger and the state's controller, John Chiang, over the issue of temporary pay cuts for state workers. Chiang refused to slash state worker pay to the federal minimum wage level at the governor's request, balking at the logistical nightmare of recalculating paychecks but also shying away from alienating employee unions, which vehemently opposed the cuts. The contest opened a legal battle over who has the authority to set state workers' pay, and it was ultimately resolved in the governor's favor. One lesson to be gleaned from this example is that an organizational structure that allows Democrats and Republicans to share executive power virtually guarantees that differences in governing philosophies and approaches will exist, but it usually takes a looming crisis to make those differences visible and put them to the test.

Administrators and Regulators

A great checkerboard of departments, administrative offices, boards, and agencies form the state's bureaucracy. Almost all are linked to the governor through the cabinet secretaries whom he or she designates to head each department. All the departments and state agencies these secretaries lead are organized either by statute or initiative and are designed to help the governor execute state law faithfully.

Bureaucratic reorganization occurs periodically, but Gov. Pat Brown's "superagency" scheme has stuck since the 1970s. These superagencies act as umbrella organizations for the smaller departments, boards, and commissions nested within them. The six superagencies include: (1) Business, Transportation, and Housing; (2) Resources; (3) Youth and Adult Corrections; (4) State and Consumer Services; (5) Health and Human Services; and (6) Environmental Protection (EPA). For example, the Business, Transportation, and Housing Department houses eight entities, including CalTrans, the DMV, and the state highway patrol. Secretaries of these six superagencies plus remaining departments, including three "superdepartments"—the Departments of

Finance; Food and Agriculture; and Industrial Relations (see Figure 5.2)—comprise the governor's cabinet. Working for them are more than 244,000 public employees who make up the state bureaucracy.[3]

The governor's stamp is also felt in membership appointments to some 320 commissions and boards that share regulatory authority with the governor. Among these are large entities, such as the University of California's Board of Regents and the State Lands Commission, and smaller ones like the boards overseeing professional licensing. Most boards consist of four or five members, but never is every seat vacated during a governor's term nor is every seat controlled by the governor; thus, competing ideological viewpoints are often represented on boards depending on who appointed whom. Together, these unelected authorities make rules affecting Californians in virtually every imaginable way, from making beaches accessible to determining trash dump locations.

Conclusion: Competition for Power

The Progressives' lack of faith in parties and mistrust of elected officials have left a legacy of many individuals at the top both sharing and competing for power. Ironically, although no single person is in charge, most Californians believe the governor is and blame him (or her) when things go awry. Perhaps not surprisingly, then, they are also unwilling to vest more power in that office, having twice recently rejected Governor Schwarzenegger's proposals to increase the office's budget-cutting powers (defeating Proposition 76 in January 2006 and Proposition 1A in May 2009).

What are we to make, then, of California's plural executive? In the first place, the splintering of authority among many offices may provide checks against the concentration of authority, but it also obscures accountability. Decentralized decision making means that voters cannot hold anyone but the governor accountable for decisions produced at the state level, even though he may not be the source of their discontent.

In the second place, no one is truly "in charge" of the state, and fragmented authority places limitations on the governor's ability to coordinate a political agenda. The governor may be vested with "supreme" administrative authority by the constitution, but he can no more tell the controller what to do than the secretary of state can. State executives are entitled to their own approaches, initiatives, and budgets, and they have little incentive to set aside their ideological differences. Coherent, consistent policy planning does not occur, and Republicans and Democrats continue their work in spite of each other.

For the most part, however, California's executive officers coexist in pursuit of the same basic goal: to keep the state afloat in times of economic crisis, and to advance its health during prosperity. Their inability to do so signals just how intractable California's problems are and how ungovernable the state has become.

CALIFORNIA STATE GOVERNMENT

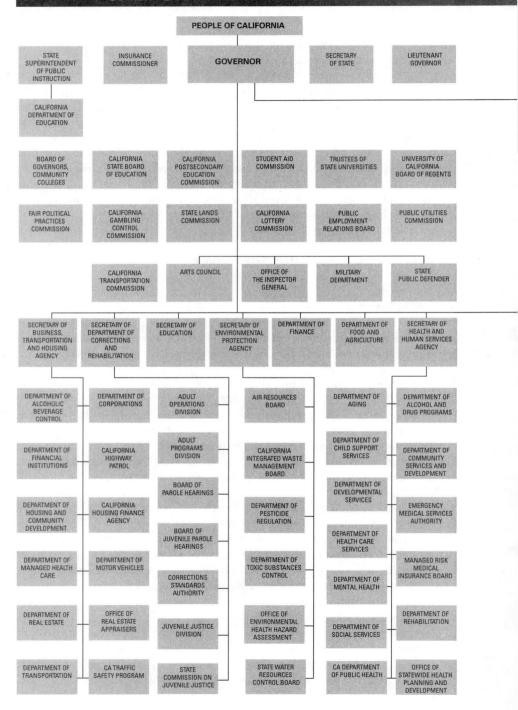

FIGURE 5.2
Organization Chart of California's Executive Branch

THE EXECUTIVE BRANCH

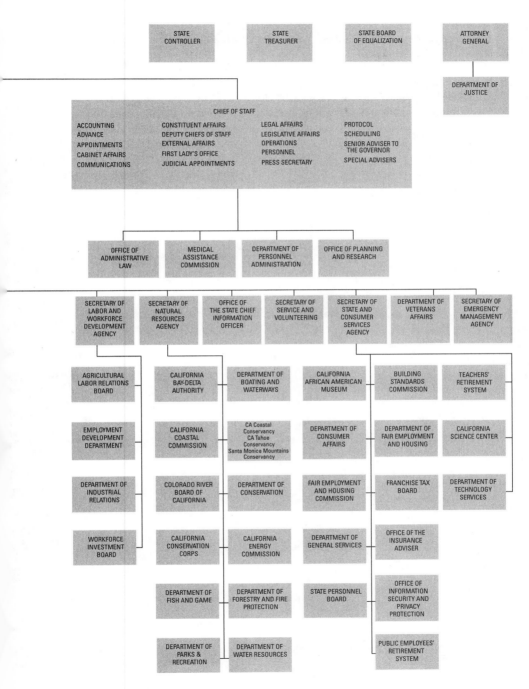

Source: Adapted from organizational chart found at www.cold.ca.gov/Ca_State_Gov_Orgchart.pdf.

Notes

1. Most state workers are members of the powerful union known as the California State Employees Association.

2. www.boe.ca.gov/info/agency_history.htm.

3. Total number is 244,061, including part-time workers and excluding institutions of the California State University system. Data taken from State Controller's Office, June 2009, www.sco.ca.gov/ppsd_empinfo_demo.html.

OUTLINE

The Three-Tiered Court
System

On and Off the Court

Court Administration

Juries

Criminal Justice

Conclusion: Administering
Justice

CHAPTER 6

The Court System

The state courts' place in a separated system of powers is to verify that the actions of the executive and legislative branches—and also popular will as expressed in initiatives—are lawful and, more generally, to provide "fair and equal access to justice for all Californians."[1] Impartiality forms the judicial system's core, but the branch is political nevertheless. Progressives realized this when they established nonpartisan elections for judges in 1911, but there was no avoiding the fact that judges are appointees who make policy through their interpretation of laws and their choices about how to apply them.

California's court system is the largest in the nation, with 2,000 judicial officers and 19,000 court employees handling approximately *9.5 million* cases annually. The state's constitution guarantees citizens the right to a jury trial for both criminal and civil cases, but chronic underfunding has led to overworked employees, shortages of judges, huge trial backlogs, and long delays for those who bring lawsuits—not to mention severe jail overcrowding. For those who can afford it, alternative dispute resolution (ADR), also known as mediation or legally binding arbitration, is a quicker way to decide cases. ADR relieves some pressure from the state's overall caseload but creates further divisions between those who can pay for high-priced mediators and those who must depend on state services.

The Three-Tiered Court System

As in the federal judicial system, California courts are organized into three tiers, and the legislature controls the number

The California Supreme Court hears arguments regarding the constitutionality of voter-approved Proposition 8, a measure defining marriage as between a man and a woman. The court decided in May 2009 to uphold the law, effectively denying homosexuals the right to wed, but ruled that the approximately 17,000 same-sex unions already performed in the state would remain legal.

of judgeships. At the lowest level are trial courts, also called **superior courts**, which are located in all fifty-eight counties. More than 1,600 judges and four hundred commissioners and referees work in the courts at this level. Virtually all 9.5 million cases begin here and are categorized as either **criminal** or **civil**. Individuals are tried for three types of crime: felonies, which are serious and possibly violent offenses; misdemeanors, or lesser crimes; and minor infractions for which fines are imposed, including traffic violations, which make up about 60 percent of the superior courts' docket.

Civil suits, on the other hand, involve disputes between individuals or organizations seeking monetary compensation for damages usually incurred through injuries, breaches of contract, or defective products. The huge number of civil lawsuits in the state, nearly 1.5 million annually,[2] reflects general acceptance of litigation as a "normal" way to resolve problems. The state attorney general can also bring civil cases against companies that break environmental, employment, or other types of state law.

Juvenile, family, and probate cases are also heard in superior court. A single judge or trial juries may decide cases at this level, and persons who cannot afford to pay an attorney are entitled to help with their defense in the form of a public defender.

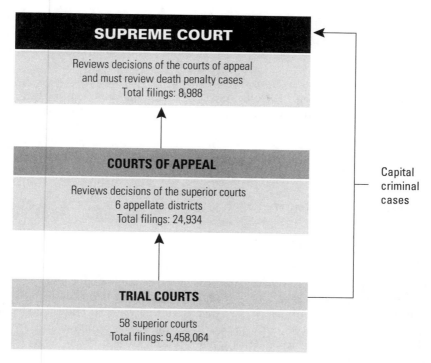

FIGURE 6.1

California Court System

Sources: www.courtinfo.ca.gov/courts/about.htm, and *Court Statistics Report 2008*, www.courtinfo.ca.gov/reference/3_stats.htm

If the losing party in a case believes the law was not applied properly, he or she may ask the next-higher district **court of appeal** to hear the case. There are no trials in district appellate courts, although three-judge panels may elect to hear lawyers argue a case. In six separate districts there are 105 appellate justices who review approximately 25,000 cases for errors, improprieties, or technicalities that could lead to a reversal of the lower court's judgment, though many are disposed of without a written opinion. On the whole, appellate court decisions clarify and actually establish government policy, as the state supreme court allows the great majority of these decisions to stand.

The highest judicial authority is vested in a seven-member **supreme court,** whose decisions are binding on all California courts. The justices mainly review cases appealed from the district courts of appeal, but they automatically review death row cases and exercise original jurisdiction over a few other types. Of roughly 9,000 cases appealed to it in 2005–2006, the court issued a mere 113 written opinions. Justices are not required to review all cases and therefore have wide discretion over case selection, concentrating mostly on those that either address important questions of law or promote uniform judgments across the system. Led by a chief justice, the court's reputation at a given time reflects policy decisions, both in the questions chosen to be addressed or ignored and the court's interpretation of a law's wording and intent.

Controversy often stems from the supreme court's review of initiatives, political measures that can only be ruled on after passage and are often overturned in whole or in part for violating the state constitution. In 2009, Proposition 8, a constitutional amendment that eliminated same-sex marriage by legalizing marriage between a man and a woman only, became a hot potato for the justices who were threatened with recall were they to overturn it. (They didn't.)

On and Off the Court

An attorney who has practiced law in California for at least ten years may become a judge, but these individuals usually enter the position through gubernatorial appointment rather than by first running for office. Interested applicants may apply through the governor's office. A governor has ample opportunity to shape the long-term ideological bent of the judiciary by selecting individuals whose partisanship and political principles are reflected in their judicial philosophy. When George Deukmejian (1982–1991) was asked why he was running for governor he replied, "Attorney generals don't appoint judges. Governors do." Gov. Arnold Schwarzenegger has been far less partisan with judicial appointments than his predecessors, with just over half Republican, about a third Democrat, and the remainder undeclared.[3] Governors also directly affect the demographic composition of the bench, which today remains disproportionately white, middle-class, and male— quite the opposite of the state's heavily ethnic prison population (see Table 6.1 and Box 6.1). Between October 2003 and July 2009 Governor Schwarzenegger made 437 appointments to the bench.

Superior court justices serve for six years without term limitations, and if they were first appointed to office and not elected, they must become nonpartisan candidates for their office when their term expires. Longer terms are intended to increase the judiciary's independence and consistency over time by reducing the frequency of distracting campaigns that can create potential conflicts of interest with campaign contributors. Contested elections are rare, and unopposed judges usually win.

Appointees to the six appellate courts and the supreme court also require the governor's nomination, but they must first be screened by the Commission on Judicial Nominees, a state agency whose members represent the legal profession, and then confirmed by the Commission on Judicial Appointments. Members of the latter include the attorney general, chief justice of the supreme court, presiding judge of the courts of appeal, and at-large members of the legal community who together evaluate appointees' fitness for office. Confirmation allows a justice to fulfill the remainder of his or her predecessor's twelve-year term, but the judge must participate in a nonpartisan "retention election" at the next gubernatorial election,

TABLE 6.1   Diversity of California's Justices and Judges

Court (persons reporting)	Female	Male	Black or African American	Hispanic or Latino	Asian	White	Native American/ Other/More than one	Information not provided
Supreme court (7)	42.9%	57.1%	0%	14.3%	14.3%	57.1%	14.3%	0%
Court of appeal (100)	29.0%	71.0%	4.0%	3.0%	3.0%	81%	8.0%	1.0%
Trial court (1,498)	28.7%	71.3%	5.1%	7.3%	4.7%	72.1%	5.0%	5.6%
Total	28.8%	71.2%	5.0%	7.1%	4.7%	72.6%	5.3%	5.3%

Source: Judicial Council of California, Administrative Office of the Courts.

Note: Supreme Court n = 7, Court of Appeal n = 100, Trial Court n = 1,498; demographic data reported December 31, 2008.

at which time voters are asked to vote "yes" or "no" on whether a judge should be retained in office. Judges may seek unlimited terms thereafter.

Voters rarely reject judges. Defeat requires public outrage fed by a well-publicized, media-driven campaign, as three supreme court justices found in 1986. Having earned reputations for being "soft on crime" at a time when rising crime rates were rattling the public, Chief Justice Rose Bird and two of her colleagues were targeted for their anti–death penalty judicial approach. For the first time in California history three justices lost their retention bids, with Gov. George Deukmejian replacing them with conservative justices.

Judges can also be dismissed for improper conduct or incompetence arising from a range of activities, among them bias, inappropriate humor, and substance abuse. Hundreds of complaints are filed each year with the Commission on Judicial Performance, the independent state agency that investigates allegations of judicial misconduct. The commission does not review a justice's record but focuses instead on personal behavior that may warrant a warning letter, formal censure, removal, or forced retirement. Only a tiny fraction of judges face disciplinary action; the great majority have internalized the norms of judicial propriety that are imparted through law school and the legal community.

Court Administration

A supporting cast of thousands helps run the court system. The chief justice of the supreme court directs the operation from his or her position as chair of the twenty-seven-member state **Judicial Council**, the public agency tasked with setting policy, rules, and procedures in accordance with ever-changing state law; making sure the court is accessible to citizens with diverse needs; and advising improvements to the system. The Judicial Council controls the judiciary's annual budget and reports to the legislature and responds to its mandates. With the help of administrative officers located at state courthouses, the council also manages the courts in a wide variety of ways; for instance, it makes information available to the public, keeps records, hires interpreters, schedules hearings, and assigns task forces to study issues such as foster care or domestic violence, among many other activities.

Juries

Barring a traffic violation, jury duty tends to be the average citizen's most direct link to the court system. Names of prospective jurors are randomly drawn from lists of registered voters and names provided by the Department of Motor Vehicles. Under the "one day–one trial" program, prospective jurors are excused from service at the end of the day if they have not been assigned to a trial, and they only need to respond to a summons once a year. If assigned to a trial, jurors consider questions of fact and weigh evidence to determine whether an accused person is guilty or not guilty. Convincing citizens to fulfill their duty isn't easy, and juries tend to overrepresent those who have relatively more time on their hands, such as the elderly, the unemployed, and the wealthy.

Grand juries are impaneled every year in every county to investigate the conduct of city and county government and their agencies. Each contains nineteen members, except for Los Angeles's grand jury, which has twenty-three members due to the city's large population. During one-year terms, grand jurors research claims of improper or wasteful practices, issue reports, recommend improvements to local programs, and sometimes indict political figures for misconduct, meaning they uncover sufficient evidence to warrant a trial.

Criminal Justice

About 90 percent of cases never make it to trial. High costs and delays associated with discovery, investigations, filings, and courtroom defense encourage out-of-court settlements and mediation, while the hope of receiving a lesser sentence for pleading guilty results in plea bargains. Nevertheless, California's prisons are bursting at the seams for a number of reasons.

Topping the list of culprits is California's "Three Strikes" initiative. In 1994 voters were appalled at the abduction and murder of twelve-year-old Polly Klaas, a crime perpetrated by a man with a long and violent record. Klaas's family lobbied vigorously for tougher sentencing of repeat offenders, culminating in the "three strikes and you're out" law: anyone convicted of a third felony is now sentenced to a mandatory twenty-five-years-to-life in prison without the possibility of parole, while penalties for second-strikers were also enhanced.

Prison populations have swelled under the Three Strikes and other mandatory sentencing laws, and so has spending on the 170,000 inmates in facilities designed to

BOX 6.1 FAST FACTS on California's Criminal Justice System

Proposed budget 2009–2010:	$10.6 billion
Cost per inmate:	$49,000
Staff:	63,050
Total number of inmates:	171,085
Lifers:	23,494
Prisoners on death row:	678
Parolees:	123,597
Average sentence:	49 months
Average time served:	24.9 months
Number of prisons:	33, including minimum to maximum security; plus 40 camps, 12 community correctional facilities, and 5 prisoner mother facilities
Number of escaped prisoners:	218
Gender of inmates:	93.3% male, 6.7% female

Racial composition of inmate population:

Category	Inmate population
White, Non-Hispanic	26%
Hispanic/Latino	39%
Black	29%
Other	6%

Source: California Department of Corrections and Rehabilitation, *Fourth Quarter 2008 Facts and Figures.*

hold 100,000. By comparison, in 1980 the entire prison population was 22,500, and in 1985 it cost less than $100 million to run the state's entire correctional system. Today, approximately 42,000 inmates are serving time for second and third strikes, most of which were nonviolent offenses.[4] At a yearly cost of $49,000 *per inmate*, spending on prisons and rehabilitation was nearly $10 billion for 2009–2010.

Longer sentences translate into an aging prison population with escalating health issues, and prisoners are constitutionally guaranteed a right to medical care—which is why a federal court put a federal official in control of regenerating the state's dysfunctional prison health care system when it was found to be unconstitutionally depriving inmates of guaranteed services and rights. The federal receiver in control of California's underfunded system subsequently demanded $8 billion for building and upgrading prison infrastructure to improve prison health care and relieve overcrowding. Short

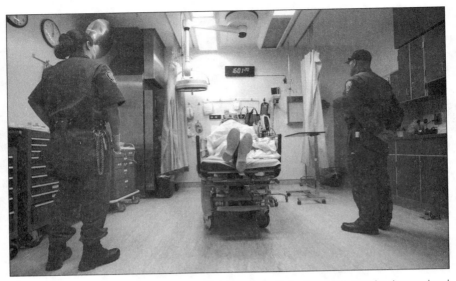

An aging inmate population has made prison health care a costly business. The state has been ordered by a federal receiver to spend billions more on upgrading sorely neglected facilities or risk being forced to release inmates early.

by a few billion to cover the gap, early prisoner releases have been identified as the only feasible option—and a highly controversial one at that.

Crime rates have fallen in California over the past decade, and many point to the Three Strikes law as the reason. Crime rates and prison population trends in states that lack a three strikes law are similar to California's, however, and researchers have shown the cause-and-effect relationship to be complicated by other variables. Yet voters believe it works. They have been unwilling to soften sentencing laws that boost state spending, as indicated by their rejection of Proposition 66 in 2004, which would have restricted Three Strikes sentencing to those who commit violent and serious offenses.

Conclusion: Administering Justice

Judges are expected to be independent arbiters of justice, yet they are held accountable to voters through retention and recall elections. They play significant policy-making roles through the cases they choose and their interpretations of the law, defining the boundaries of acceptable behavior for businesses, government, and citizens. Both the courts and criminal justice system mirror social ills such as poverty, lack of education, racism, unemployment, and homelessness, amplified in crimes ranging from minor to serious. By nature political, the system is subject to continual revision by voters through initiatives that influence the administration of justice.

Notes

1. www.courtinfo.ca.gov.

2. Administrative Office of the Courts, "2008 Court Statistics Report," IX, www.courtinfo.ca.gov/reference/3_stats.htm.

3. "Forum Sheds Light on How Judges Are Screened, Chosen," *San Jose Mercury News*, June 4, 2006.

4. Elizabeth Hill and Michael Genest, Letter to Edmund G. Brown, Attorney General (review of the proposed initiative cited as "The Three Strikes Reform Act of 2008"), November 29, 2007, www.lao.ca.gov/ballot/2007/070814.pdf.

CHAPTER 7

OUTLINE

Municipal Government

Special Districts

Regional Governments

Federalism

Tribal Governments

Conclusion: The State's
Interlocking Systems

Other Governments

The average Californian falls under the jurisdiction of many governments *within* the state's borders. Counties, cities, special districts, and regional governments share responsibility for delivering essential services that both protect and enhance residents' quality of life—from hiring police officers to making sure clean water flows beneath paved streets. Yet even in prosperous times these governments struggle to fund baseline operations with scarce taxpayer dollars. Demand for services outpaces voters' willingness to pay higher taxes for them.

The patchwork of subgovernments reflects historical demands for services along with the desire of communities for self-rule. Where one institution cannot or will not deliver, new entities have been created without regard to centralized planning. Bottom-up solutions are joined to state and federal mandates in a functionally segmented system, one that works with surprising efficiency for the number and scope of issues encompassed.

The revised state constitution of 1879 subdivided California into fifty-eight counties created to fulfill state government programs and mandates. All but three of these counties (Alpine, Mariposa, and Trinity) contain cities within their boundaries as well as "unincorporated areas" where more than 20 percent of Californians reside and for which county governments directly provide services and local political representation. San Francisco is the only combination city/county.

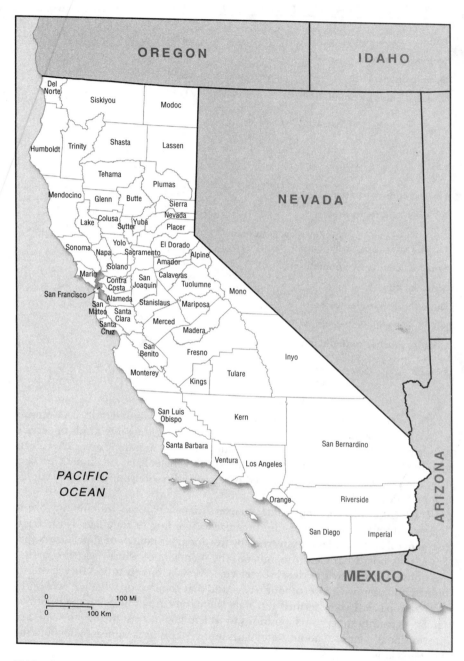

MAP 7.1

California's Fifty-eight Counties

BOX 7.1 FAST FACTS on California's Other Governments

Number of counties:	58
Number of cities:	480
Special districts:	3,400
5 largest cities by population:	Los Angeles, 4,065,585
	San Diego, 1,353,993
	San Jose, 1,006,892
	San Francisco, 845,559
	Fresno, 495,913
Largest county by area:	San Bernardino, 20,052 square miles
Smallest county by area:	San Francisco, 47 square miles (10,000 people per sq. mi.)
Largest county by population:	Los Angeles, pop. 9,862,049
Smallest county by population:	Alpine, pop. 1,200
Smallest city:	Vernon, pop. 95
Number of chartered cities:	112 (23%)
Number of general law cities:	368 (77%)
Number of cities with directly elected mayors:	147 (30%)

Sources: California Department of Finance, January 2009; U.S. Census Bureau; California League of Cities.

County lines drawn in 1879 bear no relation to population density or economic activity today, and all counties are expected to provide the same kinds of services to their constituents regardless of population size or geographic area. This means that the largest county by population, Los Angeles at 9,862,049, maintains the same baseline political departments, elected officials, and responsibilities as tiny Alpine, population 1,200.[1]

Thirteen counties organize under **charters** that allow some flexibility in governing structure; forty-five others are organized according to state law. These forty-five **general law** counties are governed by five-member **boards of supervisors** (San Francisco's board has eleven members), the members of which face nonpartisan elections every four years. Most are reelected overwhelmingly unless they are term-limited out after two, three, or four terms, and that depends on whether local initiatives have passed. Many termed-out state lawmakers are prolonging their political careers as county supervisors, positions to which they can put their knowledge and "institutional memory" about state issues and systems to good use by helping run the state's largest subgovernments.

Other elected county officials include the sheriff, district attorney, auditor/controller, treasurer/tax collector, and clerk/recorder, all of whom help the board supply basic but vital social and political services in many areas:

PUBLIC SAFETY: courts, jails, probation, public defense, juvenile detention, sheriff, fire, emergency services

PUBLIC ASSISTANCE: housing, homeless, food stamps, state welfare programs

ELECTIONS & VOTING: voting processes, voter registration

TAX COLLECTION: county, city, special districts, schools

ENVIRONMENT & RECREATION: parks, facilities, open space, waste removal and recycling, air quality, land use, water

PUBLIC HEALTH: hospitals, mental health clinics, drug rehabilitation programs

EDUCATION: libraries, schools

SOCIAL SERVICES: adoptions, children's foster care

TRANSIT: airports, bus and rail systems; bridges, road maintenance

VITAL RECORDS: birth, death, marriage certificates

Counties finance these operations by levying sales taxes and user fees and through state government funds, property taxes, and federal grants (see Figures 7.1 and 7.2). State budget crises stem the flow of revenue, forcing counties to lay off employees, cut services, raise fees, or a combination of these to cover losses.

Municipal Government

Communities in unincorporated areas of a county may want more control over land use in their neighborhoods, better services, or a formal identity. They can petition their state-chartered local agency formation commission, or LAFCO, to incorporate as a **city** or municipality if their residents generate enough tax revenues to support a local government.

Much like counties, cities provide essential public services in the areas of public safety and emergency services; sewage and sanitation; public health; public works, including street maintenance; parks and recreation; libraries and schools; and land-use planning. Sometimes these overlap or supplement county programs: for example, a city might maintain its own library and also contain two or three county library branches. If lacking their own facilities, cities can contract with counties for services, pool their resources in a joint-powers agreement, or contract with private firms.

More than 75 percent of California's 480 cities have incorporated under **general law,** meaning they follow state law in form and function. The remaining **charter cities** are creatures of local habits, formed through city constitutions that grant local government supreme authority over municipal affairs. This **"home rule" principle** permits municipal law to trump similar state laws.

A **council-manager system** exists in 70 percent of cities, an institutional legacy of Progressives who believed that efficient city management required technical expertise because "there is no partisan way to pave a street." A five-member city council is

Revenue

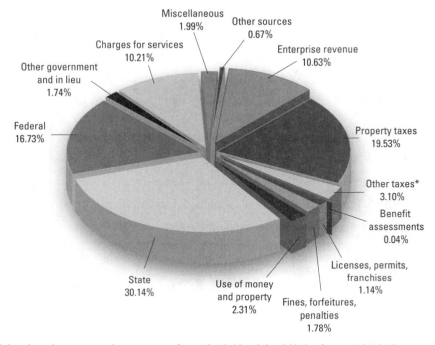

Miscellaneous 1.99%

Other sources 0.67%

Charges for services 10.21%

Enterprise revenue 10.63%

Other government and in lieu 1.74%

Federal 16.73%

Property taxes 19.53%

Other taxes* 3.10%

Benefit assessments 0.04%

Licenses, permits, franchises 1.14%

State 30.14%

Use of money and property 2.31%

Fines, forfeitures, penalties 1.78%

*Includes sales and use, transportation, property transfer, transient lodging, timber yield, aircraft, construction development, utility users, and other taxes.

Expenses

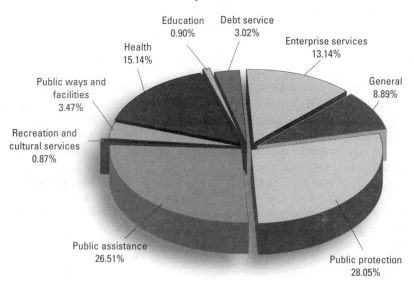

Education 0.90%

Debt service 3.02%

Health 15.14%

Enterprise services 13.14%

Public ways and facilities 3.47%

General 8.89%

Recreation and cultural services 0.87%

Public assistance 26.51%

Public protection 28.05%

FIGURE 7.1

County Revenues and Expenses, 2006–2007

The San Bernardino City Council debates a controversial 1996 proposal that would have made it unlawful for the city's landlords to rent to illegal immigrants and forced day laborers to prove legal resident status to employers. Other cities have approved or considered passing similar laws targeting undocumented persons; opponents have successfully stymied many of these efforts by challenging their constitutionality in court.

reelected every four years in nonpartisan elections, usually by the entire city's electorate in an **at-large election** rather than from separate districts, and many are subject to local voter-imposed term limits. If the mayor is not elected at-large, council members designate one among them to act as a ceremonial mayor, typically on a rotating basis, for one or two years at a time. Each city makes its own rules regarding how long and how often city council members can act as mayor and whether the appointment will be automatic, by acclamation, or by election. Automatic rotation creates opportunities for many young council members to assume the role of mayor, and twenty-something-year-old mayors are not altogether uncommon. Ceremonial mayors lack veto power, and their vote on the council is equal to that of their colleagues.

The 70 percent of California cities with city councils also have professional city managers to oversee the city budget and municipal operations. These individuals are hired by the city councils to budget for, manage, and oversee the day-to-day operations of a city. Executive and legislative powers blend in city councils, which concentrate on passing and implementing local laws, called **ordinances**. Boards and commissions help them recommend and set policy. All city and county governing institutions must abide by the **Brown Act**, which mandates advance notice of meetings, "open meetings," and full public disclosure of proceedings.

City managers wield great power behind the scenes. Alternatively, a directly elected chief executive can exercise those same managerial duties to enact a political agenda

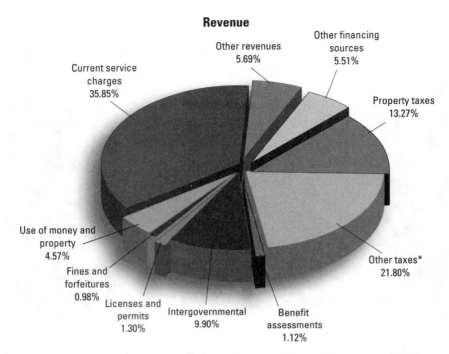

Revenue

Other revenues
5.69%

Other financing
sources
5.51%

Current service
charges
35.85%

Property taxes
13.27%

Use of money and
property
4.57%

Fines and
forfeitures
0.98%

Licenses and
permits
1.30%

Intergovernmental
9.90%

Benefit
assessments
1.12%

Other taxes*
21.80%

*Includes sales and use, transportation, transient lodging, franchises, business license, real property transfer, utility users, and other non-property taxes.

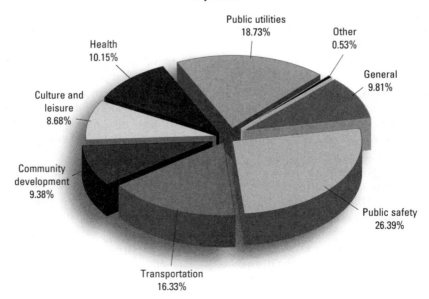

Expenses

Public utilities
18.73%

Other
0.53%

Health
10.15%

General
9.81%

Culture and
leisure
8.68%

Community
development
9.38%

Public safety
26.39%

Transportation
16.33%

FIGURE 7.2

City Revenues and Expenses, 2006–2007

Source: Cities Annual Report prepared March 30, 2009 by the State Controller's office.

and in doing so be held accountable by voters. As opposed to a council-manager system, a **strong mayor** form of government gives the mayor veto power over city council actions and substantial latitude over hiring and firing high-profile appointees. In some cities the police and fire chiefs are included in that list.

Cities depend heavily on taxes and fees to finance operations. Prior to Proposition 13, property taxes constituted 57 percent of combined city and county revenues annually; in 2006–2007 property taxes represented only 13 percent of the average city budget. The bulk of funding now comes from fines and developer fees; service charges for public utilities and transit; a variety of taxes on hotels, other businesses, and property; and state and federal agencies.

Assembly members and senators perform economic gymnastics to balance the state budget during hard times, and their routine includes yanking property taxes and other fees previously committed to cities to "backfill" the state's budget hole. In an effort to stop such state "raiding" of local funds, cities and counties sponsored a constitutional amendment to prevent the state from transferring locally generated property taxes, vehicle license fees, and sales taxes into the state's General Fund. Though voters approved Proposition 1A in 2004, the state has overridden some of those restrictions during fiscal crises, as it did for the 2009–2010 budget. Facing losses amounting to millions of dollars, cities (and counties) scramble to find substitute revenue sources. One popular strategy at the city level is to charge developers heavy fees for new construction projects or saddle them with the costs of constructing new streets, schools, sewers, or any infrastructure improvements related to population growth.

Another strategy is to base land-use decisions on a project's net fiscal impact, a phenomenon known as the **fiscalization of land use.** In practical terms this means that cities today have incentives to entice and keep retail businesses that can generate substantial sales taxes, as local governments receive 1 percent of state sales taxes collected in their jurisdictions. Auto dealerships, shopping malls, and big-box retailers like Wal-Mart are therefore favored over low-income housing and service-based industries that will further stress city resources—in other words, decisions are made without regard to the intrinsic value of or need for a project.

Redevelopment districts can also bring some measure of relief. These districts are created by designating economically distressed or "blighted" areas for revitalization; neglected buildings are torn down, refuse is cleared away, and new facilities are built. Property taxes are artificially capped within those zones, and cities are entitled to keep the additional property taxes that are paid after properties are improved. Approximately 80 percent of cities contain a redevelopment agency, or RDA, that oversees ongoing redevelopment activities.

Special Districts

Special districts are geographic areas governed by an elected board for a specific purpose, and they are arguably the most abundant power centers in California in that approximately 3,400 currently operate in the state. **School districts** are the most familiar of these: more than 1,350 districts provide K–12 education for about 6.3 million students attending almost 10,000 different schools; an additional seventy-two districts encompass 110 community colleges.[2] Created by state law, nonpartisan five-member boards of education (L.A.'s board has seven) govern their school districts by following the detailed operating instructions of the state's education code and heeding the State Board of Education's mandates. An appointed superintendent manages the local system, which may be responsible for more than 700,000 students—as is the case in the gargantuan L.A. system—or fewer than 20 students, which is the case in twenty-one districts. Governing boards handle issues relating to nearly every aspect of student life, from regulating students' cell phone use to meeting personal health needs to designing appropriate curricula, and they must consider the vocal parents and special interest groups trying to influence their decisions.

Proposition 98 dedicates approximately 40 percent of the state's general budget to education, yet this translates into only 61 percent of the money that schools receive. Additionally, just over 10 percent of education funds are federal dollars, and 21 percent come from property taxes that were previously directed to cities; miscellaneous sources supply the rest.

Virtually invisible, **special districts** proliferate because they are created to meet critical needs that cities and counties lack the will or capacity to address. A typical special district is single-purpose; that is, it specializes in one service such as street lighting, mosquito abatement, supplying irrigation water, or running an airport.

A Contra Costa County Mosquito and Vector Control District technician prepares to treat a mosquito-infested pool at a foreclosed home in Concord, California. Vector control districts protect public health by containing the spread of diseases such as malaria and West Nile Virus borne by mosquitoes and rats.

Of more than 3,400 special districts in the state, one-third are controlled by counties or cities through governing board appointments, whereas two-thirds (about 2,200) operate independently with their own elected boards of governors. The Southern California Metropolitan Water District (MWD) epitomizes this type: twenty-six cities and water districts coordinate their activities through the MWD to provide drinking water to 19 million residents in six counties, delivering nearly 1.7 billion gallons of water daily. The majority of special districts are paid for through property-related service charges or special assessments that initially require a two-thirds majority vote: in other words, the total fee per property owner will be a percentage of a property's assessed value.

Regional Governments

Regional governments plan, regulate, and coordinate land-use and development activities across counties and cities by providing a permanent forum in which local leaders can discuss ideas and exchange information. State law gives regional governments housing and transportation planning authority, but, in general, **councils of government** (COGs) plan for future populations across a wide spectrum of common infrastructure-related needs, including food and water availability, public safety, and environmental quality. There are twenty-five major COGs in California, plus six sub-COGs in the Southern California Association of Governments, or SCAG.

COGs coordinate rather than dictate because they cannot force decisions on local governments. Their governing boards are composed of mayors, city council members, and county supervisors, and they receive input from research specialists and advisers from federal departments, special districts, state agencies, and even Mexico. Their planning activities include reviewing federal grants-in-aid and proposing legislation. They do not deliver public services.

Regional government may also take the form of regulatory entities that set rules for environmentally sensitive activities. For instance, California's thirty-five "air districts" are dedicated to controlling pollution from stationary sources (Air Pollution Control Districts, or APCDs) and promoting air quality (Air Quality Management Districts, or AQMDs) by writing binding rules for their residents, monitoring air quality, researching issues, investigating complaints, and issuing special business permits.

Federalism

Whereas the state authorizes county governments, local jurisdictions, and special districts to perform necessary functions, the U.S. Constitution guarantees that states *share* governing power with the national government, although states' authority has diminished as both the federal purse and federal capacity have grown. The U.S. Congress discovered long ago that **funding** is a convenient instrument for enticing

BOX 7.2 The Feds vs. California on Air Quality

Noting that the federal government had neglected to address climate change for far too long, in an unprecedented move the state's majority-Democratic legislature joined Gov. Arnold Schwarzenegger in crafting the Global Warming Solutions Act of 2006, otherwise known as Assembly Bill 32 (AB32), the world's first law establishing a program of regulatory and market mechanisms to curb emissions of greenhouse gases. Importantly, the new law authorizes the state's Air Resources Board to:

- Set a statewide emissions cap for 2020, based on 1990 emissions levels.
- Adopt mandatory reporting rules for significant sources of greenhouse gases.
- Establish advisory boards to assist with planning.
- Advance a plan indicating how much emissions reduction will be achieved through regulations, market mechanisms, and other actions. Some of the major steps of the new plan include:
  - A state-administered cap-and-trade program. This market-based system sets an overall limit on greenhouse gas (GHG) emissions, and facilities that emit GHG will be granted a certain amount of allowances to emit those gases. Companies that emit less than their allowance will be able to sell or trade their credits to companies that exceed their allowances.
  - Setting fuel efficiency standards for new cars, trucks, and sport utility vehicles sold in California by 2012.

Passage of the act met fierce opposition from a tight coalition of automobile, manufacturing, and energy industries, which challenged the new law as going "too far" by setting stricter standards than the federal government—despite the fact that the Environmental Protection Agency (EPA) had never set a greenhouse gas emissions standard. Ruling that AB32 superseded federal authority to maintain clean air standards, the EPA under the George W. Bush administration denied California a waiver from adhering to lower national clean air standards set in the Federal Clean Air Act. On June 30, 2009, the EPA under the Barack Obama administration reversed the ruling, giving California the "green light" to proceed with implementation and enforcement of AB32. "This decision puts the law and science first," stated EPA administrator Lisa Jackson when announcing the decision that also affects the thirteen other states and District of Columbia that have followed California's lead. Schwarzenegger issued his own statement: "After being asleep at the wheel for over two decades, the federal government has finally stepped up and granted California its nation-leading tailpipe emissions waiver. . . . California's long battle to reduce pollution from passenger vehicles is over, and a greener, cleaner future has finally arrived." *

Source: California Air Resources Board.

*California Governor's Office, "Governor Applauds EPA Decision Granting California Authority to Reduce Greenhouse Gas Emissions," June 30, 2009, http://gov.ca.gov/issue/energy-environment.

states to adopt federal goals by granting or withholding monies in exchange for new state policy. In this way, highway funds have been exchanged for lower speed limits and setting the drinking age at twenty-one—issues that only the states can legislate.

California is also subject to **unfunded mandates**. These are federal laws that require the states to provide services but that do not budget federal funds to implement them. Such mandates amount to hundreds of millions of dollars in such areas as social services, transportation, education, health care, and maintaining or cleaning up the environment. For example, Gov. Arnold Schwarzenegger has stated that housing undocumented immigrants in state correctional facilities costs the state $180 million a year, and he has proposed turning over those inmates to federal authorities for incarceration in federal facilities.[3] Mandates also can take the form of **preemptive legislation,** which prohibits a state from passing certain laws; this has been done with some of California's progressive environmental rules and legislation.

California remains dependent on the federal government to balance its ledgers, receiving billions for major programs such as welfare and health coverage—$47 *billion* in 2007–2008 alone. Yet imbalances persist. Californians pay more in federal taxes than they receive: one source estimates that Californians receive $0.79 for every dollar paid in taxes. Governor Schwarzenegger swore to become "The Collectinator" by convincing Washington to send home the $50 billion or so that Californians overpay annually.[4] He has not been remarkably successful, despite the activity of fifty-three U.S. representatives and two powerful U.S. senators, the ascension of Californian Nancy Pelosi as Speaker of the House, and the appointment of Californians to chair powerful federal congressional committees.

Tribal Governments

Tribal governments operated in relative obscurity until recently. Isolated on 100,000 acres of remote and frequently inhospitable reservations throughout California, the state's 108 tribes had minimal impact on neighboring cities or state government. Native groups were defined politically by their interaction with the U.S. Congress and federal agencies as well as by prior case law that treated them as wards of the federal government rather than as fully sovereign nations. In the main, California governments could ignore them.

Gaming changed all that. As bingo halls flourished in the 1970s and blossomed into full-scale gambling enterprises by the late 1980s, states began looking for ways to limit, eliminate, tax, influence, or otherwise control this new growth industry, one whose environmental and social effects on surrounding communities were proving significant.

After the U.S. Supreme Court ruled in 1987 that tribes do indeed have the right to run gambling enterprises on their lands, Congress exercised its supreme lawmaking authority (to which tribes are subject) and wrote the **Indian Gaming Regulatory Act (IGRA),** a law that restricted the scope of gaming and deferred regulatory authority to the states. The IGRA also stipulated that tribes within a state and the state itself must enter into compacts to permit certain forms of gaming irrespective of tribal sovereignty.

No state can collect taxes from tribal nations, but California governor Gray Davis used this point as a bargaining chip with sixty-one tribes during their compact

The U.S. Constitution explicitly recognizes four sovereigns:

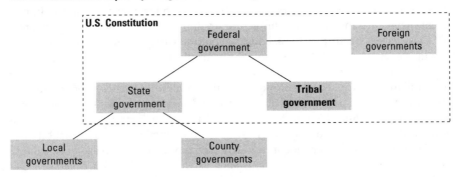

FIGURE 7.3

Tribes Are Recognized Sovereigns

Source: Reprinted with permission of the authors Kate Spilde, Kenneth Grant and Jonathan Taylor, "Commentary: Social and Economic Consequences of Indian Gaming in Oklahoma," *American Indian Culture and Research Journal* 28, no. 2 (Los Angeles: UCLA American Indian Studies Center, 2004).

negotiations. The final compact specified that in exchange for permitting Las Vegas–style gambling, tribes would participate in revenue-sharing with nongaming tribes and also contribute to a fund for reimbursing casino-related costs to cities and counties, such as those related to traffic congestion, public safety, and gambling addiction. California voters overwhelmingly approved this first compact as Proposition 5, which was superseded two years later by constitutional amendment Proposition 1A in 2000. Compacts that are renegotiated over time eventually take the form of referendums submitted to voters for approval. This recently occurred when several Southern California tribes negotiated a deal to add up to 17,000 slot machines to their casinos in exchange for an additional $122.6 million in annual state payments. The Native groups spent a combined $108.4 million to convince voters to approve four propositions in 2008, and each passed by at least 55.5 percent.[5]

Clearly, "tribal sovereignty" has limits with regard to both federal and state law. Tribes retain control over political activities within their reservation's borders, and their governments usually take the form of all-powerful tribal councils vested with executive, legislative, and judicial powers. Councils have full control over tribal membership, which is more than 50,000 registered individuals in California alone, and they implement federal programs and grants covering health care, education, and other social needs, amounting to about $100 million in funds per year.[6]

Gaming operations have laid the foundation for socioeconomic and political development in and around tribal territories. Relative prosperity has transformed tribal governments into fully staffed operations that have increasing institutional capacity to provide services that the state can't or won't. Tribes are now important participants in regional planning, and cities, counties, and the state benefit from their ability to obtain federal dollars for improvement projects, such as widening roads and building bridges where it is otherwise unaffordable. California tribes make themselves

The Morongo Casino Resort and Spa rises above the desert floor near the San Jacinto Mountains. The Morongo Band of Mission Indians in Cabazon, California, operates one of fifty-nine tribal gaming enterprises in the state. The fact that casinos must be located on existing tribal lands naturally limits their expansion. Gaming revenues have helped reduce the percentage of Native American families living in poverty, which still remained high in 2000 at 26 percent.

indispensible to state government by making annual payments to the General Fund, approximately $446.7 million out of a total estimated $8 billion in casino revenues in 2007–2008, figures that have dropped significantly with the economic downturn.[7]

Gaming enterprises have transformed tribal governments into major players at both the state and national levels, enabling them to lobby policies of interest to them and donate heavily to campaigns. Tribes nationwide contributed approximately $10.3 million to political campaigns in 2008, favoring Democrats by 75 percent.[8]

Conclusion: The State's Interlocking Systems

California's state government is much more than a mega-institution with a few major components. Instead, the state's government should be viewed as a complex organism, with approximately 5,500 identifiable working parts found in counties, cities, special districts, and regions, in addition to the state's courts, administration, and legislature. Each part contributes to the welfare of the whole, either singly or in conjunction with others, but never in isolation. When dissected, the system appears as a bewildering mess of overlapping boundary lines, yet these interlocking systems provide essential services that citizens need and will continue to demand.

Notes

1. Data taken from Department of Finance, January 2009 estimates.
2. Statistics are for 2006–2007, the most recent made public by the state's Department of Education in its 2008 *Fact Book*, www.cde.ca.gov/re/pn/fb.
3. Governor's speech, delivered May 20, 2009, http://gov.ca.gov/speech/12348.
4. Data compiled from the California Institute for Federal Policy Research, "California's Balance of Payments with the Federal Treasury, 1981–2004," www.calinst.org/index.html.
5. Vote results supplied by California Secretary of State. Data taken from followthemoney .org, Ballot Measure Summary for Propositions 94-97, www.followthemoney.org/database/ StateGlance/ballot.phtml?m=493.
6. Data taken from the U.S. Census Bureau, *Consolidated Federal Funds Report 2007*, http://harvester.census.gov/cffr/asp/Geography.asp.
7. Data taken from Opensecrets.org, Indian Gaming: Long-Term Contribution Trends, www.opensecrets.org/industries/indus.php?ind=G6550.
8. Data taken from the Governor's Budget 2008–2009, Revised Budget Summary, http:// 2008-09.archives.ebudget.ca.gov/Revised/BudgetSummary/LJE/32282142.html.TheNational Indian Gaming Commission reported that total revenues for fifty-nine gaming operations in California and Northern Nevada tribes was $7,363,493 in FY2008 and $7,796,488 for fifty-eight operations in FY 2007, http://64.38.12.138/docs/nigc/nigc060309.pdf.

OUTLINE

California Budgeting 101

Political Constraints

Mechanics of Budgeting: Revenue

Mechanics of Budgeting: Deficits and Expenditures

Tax Burden: Too High, Too Low?

The Budget Crisis and Beyond

Conclusion: Change the Rules?

CHAPTER 8

The California Budget Process

Question 1: How do you hide an $8 billion budget gap?

Answer: You ask Governor Davis to approve the California budget.

Question 2: How do you hide a $26 billion budget gap?

Answer: You don't.

Annual budgeting at the state level is a grueling process of translating social and political values into dollars, made all the more punishing by economic crises that make dollars disappear. A budget is also a statement of priorities, the result of intense bargaining, and the product of a sophisticated guessing game about future income and spending that provides risk-averse politicians with incentives to use accounting tricks and gimmicks to make things look rosier than they really are. But gargantuan deficits can't be papered over, and as California's government floundered while the economic emergency grew during the early 2000s, California's ungovernability made headlines ahead of the state's financial collapse.

Why can't lawmakers and governors effectively solve the state's budget problems, especially during economic crises when their solutions are most needed? "Why," many Californians ask, "do we pay so much in taxes but the state never has enough?" This chapter examines the budgeting process and explores the reasons for California's budgetary dilemmas—dilemmas that force representatives to make painful choices among alternatives.

California Budgeting 101

California's fiscal year (FY) begins July 1 and ends June 30. By law a new budget must be signed by July 1 or the state cannot pay for services that it hasn't yet authorized for the new cycle, but in spite of deadlines the budget is usually completed months late, injecting more uncertainty and panic into an already stressful process. Excluding delays, it takes at least eighteen months to construct the state's spending plan.

Advance work begins in the governor's **Department of Finance (DOF)**, which is staffed by professional analysts who continuously collect data about state operations. Each executive department itemizes its own budget needs, from operating expenses such as new vehicles to payouts such as teacher salaries. Their projections about how much money will be available through taxes and fees provide baselines for estimating how much *must* be spent on major existing programs and how much *can* be spent on new, desired programs or services. **Mandatory spending** absorbs most of the approximately $85–$100 billion annual budgets, leaving limited room for legislators to duke it out for the **discretionary** funds used to cover all other state services, from hiring new professors at state colleges to rehabilitating criminal offenders.

Guided by the governor's initiatives, political values, and stated objectives, the DOF prepares a budget by assigning dollar amounts to state programs and services. The governor submits his budget to the legislature by January 10, whereupon it is routed to the legislature's own **legislative analyst** for scrutiny. Heeding recommendations from the Legislative Analyst's Office (LAO) and anticipating the governor's updated version that takes into account actual tax receipts (the **May Revision**), throughout the spring the legislative budget committees and subcommittees work on the legislature's own competing version of the budget. State analysts testify before the committees, as do officials, lobbyists, and citizens representing every sector of society and government as they seek protection for existing benefits or beg for more.

Once the committees finalize their work and the legislature resolves its differences into a comprehensive budget bill, legislative leaders and their staffs begin negotiating with the governor and his staff to reach compromises. For example, will money be set aside for emergency spending in a "rainy day" fund? If so, will that money come from cuts to mental health programs or afterschool care? Negotiations among the top four legislative leaders and the governor, together known as the "**Big Five**," also hinge on the governor's line-item veto power (see chapter 5). Eventually, often after considerable debate and struggle, the budget is passed and signed into law, as are "**trailer bills**"—a package of omnibus or large bills that make the necessary policy changes to the state laws and codes outlined in the budget plan.

Political Constraints

The budgeting process is far more than a series of steps. By nature it is political, involving many factors that condition and constrain policymakers' ability to make

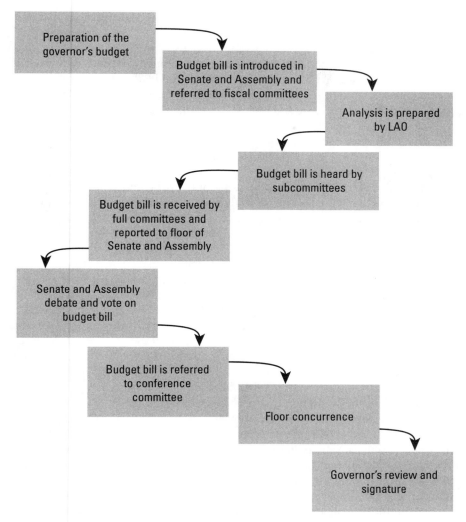

FIGURE 8.1

The Annual Budget Process

collective decisions. These factors help explain how budgets can be late and out-of-balance by billions of dollars within weeks of their passage.

Above all, the budget reflects the **larger economic climate**. All state governments suffer the same economic challenges when the U.S. economy falters. In California, however, budget deficits are **structural**—created by long-term commitments to programs that were initially paid for with temporary increases in revenues that have since disappeared. Deficits have been carried over from previous years, further widening budget gaps and underscoring the fact that every budget builds on the prior one.

The **political climate** also influences what kinds of programs receive funding and how much. Public opinion shifts over time, and public pressure causes some issues to gain political traction. In the 1990s crime dominated the political agenda; it could be education or health care in another year. To the extent that lawmakers know who the loyal voters are and respond to them, biases will result in their privileging some issues over others.

Special interests and their lobbyists also unduly prevail throughout the process. Not only do they actively "educate" legislators about the effects of proposed budget changes, they also threaten to use the initiative process to achieve what legislators may not deliver. Special interest groups are behind some of the **ballot-box budgeting** that impedes legislators' flexibility: several initiatives already guarantee funding levels for such areas as education (Proposition 98), and it was a coalition of local governments that forced changes in state budgeting practices (Proposition 1A).

Citizens' use of the ballot box has fundamentally reshaped budgeting practices throughout the state as well. **Proposition 13** is a case in point. Prior to 1978, cities, counties, and schools relied on property taxes to finance their budgets. When Prop 13 capped property taxes at 1 percent of a home or commercial building's purchase price and limited property assessment increases to no more than 2 percent per year, local governments were forced to look for other ways to pay for services (now mainly sales taxes and fees), and state government assumed responsibility for refilling local government accounts and funding schools. However, when times got tough, as they did in the early 1990s, the state substantially changed the way it allocated education funds, resulting in the redirection of yet more revenues away from local governments. Since then, state lawmakers have adopted the practice of occasionally "borrowing" property taxes from local jurisdictions to pay for schools or simply to plug large holes in the state budget. Thus, the burden of low property taxes has been shared by local governments, which have struggled to find alternative sources of revenue, and the state government, which cannot meet its obligations to fund local governments and schools when the General Fund is empty.

In all of this, rules matter. Majority party legislators hamstrung by the two-thirds vote requirement to raise taxes have opted to raise fees instead because those merely require a majority vote to pass. One rule matters most above all others, however: the **two-thirds supermajority** requirement for passing the budget. Unless the majority party has fifty-four Assembly members and twenty-seven senators willing to vote for the budget, it needs minority party votes to secure the budget's passage. Minority party members (Republicans since 1996) view the budget as their only opportunity to meaningfully influence public policy and force the majority to meet their demands. Long delays result from the parties' inability to reconcile fundamental political differences, compelled here by the minority Republicans' stand-pat refusal to compromise on tax increases and the majority Democrats' opposition to cutting services.

Gov. Arnold Schwarzenegger meets with three other members of the "Big Five" on May 20, 2009, to negotiate the state budget. Schwarzenegger is shown talking with Assembly Speaker Karen Bass as Senate Minority Leader Dennis Hollingsworth and Senate President pro Tem Darrell Steinberg (seated to the left of the governor) look on.

Mechanics of Budgeting: Revenue

A budget reflects the governor's and legislature's educated guesses about how much money the state will collect in taxes, fees, and federal grants during the coming year as well as the state's commitments to spending or saving what it collects. All budgets are built on economic data, assumptions, and formulas designed to produce accurate **forecasts** about dollar amounts and the numbers of people who will demand the services and products these dollar amounts pay for. Relatively small numerical shifts can equal hundreds of millions of dollars. For instance, the state controller reported that in June 2009 the state's three largest sources of revenue were 0.6 percent—just a bit more than a half a percentage point—below what had been predicted a *month* earlier in the May Revision, a difference equaling $499 million.

    Revenue is another word for income. The largest revenue streams are provided by **taxes** and **fees** for services, and in 2008–2009 these helped raise the state's total revenues to nearly $100 billion. The money is deposited into the state's General Fund or redistributed to county and local governments; special fuel taxes go into the Transportation Fund. A separate type of revenue, federal grant money, is funneled through the Federal Fund, and bond funds are designated for specific purposes. It should be noted that property taxes are raised at the local level and mainly used to fund schools; they do not augment the General Fund.

TABLE 8.1   General Obligation Bonds Passed, 2006–2008

2006	Bond	Cost	Purpose
Transportation	Proposition 1B	$19,900,000,000	Maintaining and expanding highways and roads, ports, passenger rail systems; bridge retrofitting
Natural resources	Proposition 84	$5,400,000,000	Water system planning; flood control; beach, bays, parks, and waterway protection
Education	Proposition 1D	$10,400,000,000	$7.3 billion for modernizing and expanding K–12 schools; $3.1 billion to UC, CSU, and community colleges
Natural resources	Proposition 1E	$4,100,000,000	Flood control
2008			
Transportation	Proposition 1A	$9,900,000,000	High-speed rail system
Children's hospitals	Proposition 3	$900,000,000	Constructing and improving children's hospitals
TOTAL 2006–2008		$50,600,000,000	

Source: Adapted from Dean Misczynski, "Just the Facts: California's Debt," February 2009, PPIC.org; www.ppic.org/content/pubs/jtf/JTF_CADebtJTF.pdf.

The state relies on several major categories of taxes, all of which are highly sensitive to larger economic trends: in other words, taxes rise and fall with the economy, creating unpredictable swings in tax collection. **Personal income taxes** contribute the greatest portion of state revenues, totaling more than $55 billion in FY 2007–2008, or more than a third of the state's total revenue. State personal income taxes are progressive, meaning that tax rates increase along with income so that people at the higher end of the income scale pay a greater percentage in taxes than those at the lower end. Current rates range from 1 to 10.3 percent (the top bracket applies to those making more than $1 million per year, what some call "soaking the rich"), though taxpayers can receive various exemptions and credits to offset the total they owe. **Corporate income taxes** contribute $11 billion, or just over 6 percent of the total collected, as do a variety of other sources, from underground storage tank fees to an energy resources surcharge.

Retail sales and use taxes account for nearly 20 percent of revenue, almost $35 billion in FY2007–2008, an amount based on the base state sales tax rate that the legislature raised by one cent in 2009 to help close the budget gap. It now stands at

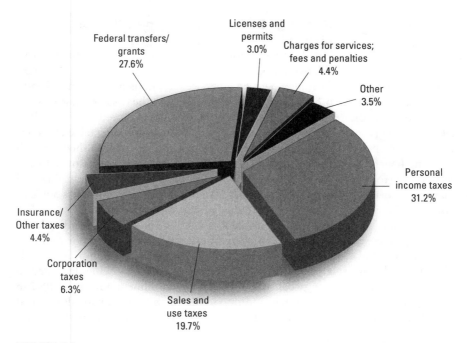

FIGURE 8.2

State Revenue, 2007–2008

Source: California State Controller.

8.25 percent, of which 6.25 percent goes to the General Fund and 2 percent is reallocated to local governments. The increased rate, the highest in the nation, expires in February 2010 because voters rejected a ballot measure to extend it. Consumer spending directly affects how much money is available to cover state expenses, and spending patterns during economic recessions have resulted in multibillion-dollar losses to state governments. This also applies to excise taxes for goods like fuel, the demand for which tends to decline as unemployment rates and fuel costs rise. The state also collects many smaller revenue-generating taxes placed on such items as alcohol and tobacco, vehicles, and insurance.

Apart from taxation, state **borrowing** to plug budget holes and to finance megaprojects has become so commonplace that the average bond measure is in the $5 billion range,[1] and the state now carries $89.1 billion in bonded debt. Most of the debt comes from voter-approved general obligation bonds dedicated to school construction and remodeling, public transportation projects (including a record-setting $19.9 billion omnibus transportation bill approved in 2006), and environmental and natural resource projects such as beach restoration and flood control. These measures veer sharply from the "pay-as-you-go" schemes typically used to finance large infrastructure projects in the past.

Mechanics of Budgeting: Deficits and Expenditures

The state commits to a spending plan before it knows how much will actually arrive in the state coffers. Legislative and Department of Finance analysts do their best to predict how much unemployment benefits, welfare, housing assistance, health coverage, and a host of other services will be demand, but the costs of these services depend on how the economic winds blow. When expenses exceed revenues, **deficits** result. Legislators and governors must return to the negotiating table to reconcile the differences, or "close the budget gap," which can be accomplished through reducing benefit checks, cutting salaries of state workers, eliminating or reducing services, borrowing, or a combination of any of these. Borrowing from financial markets to cover the deficit contributes to the state's **debt,** and the state has opted to borrow billions to cover portions of the state deficit during the 2000s.

What does the state pay for? **Education** dominates the budget, and funding levels for this area are typically locked in through initiatives and statutes. For example, except in times of fiscal emergency Proposition 98 mandates a minimum spending threshold that usually results in 40 percent of the budget's being dedicated to K–12 schools and community colleges. Total student enrollment during fall 2007 in K–12 schools neared 6.3 million, in addition to the 1.7 million individuals enrolled in 110 community colleges. Spending on the two major public university systems,

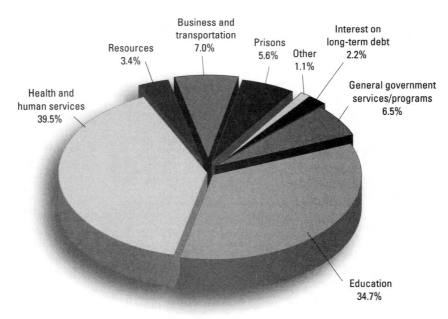

FIGURE 8.3

State Expenses, 2007–2008

Source: California State Controller.

When teachers speak, Democratic legislators—and sometimes the governor—listen. As the state's largest union, the California Teachers Association (CTA) exerts tremendous influence over education policy and funding. In response to Governor Schwarzenegger's proposal to cut education funding in 2009, the group spent millions airing television ads protesting his actions. Here, members are pictured marching to the governor's office to deliver petitions opposing his education policies.

If education was in the news this morning, chances are the powerful California Teachers Association (CTA) had something to do with it. As the state's largest professional employee organization, representing some 340,000 teachers, school counselors, and librarians, the union helps bargain for higher salaries and benefits in local districts and provides assistance in contract disputes. As an advocacy group the CTA is committed to "enhance the quality of education for students" and "advance the cause of free, universal, and quality public education"* through influencing state education policy.

Closely aligned with Democratic interests, the CTA participates at all stages of the bill passage process by writing bills, testifying before committees, shaping legislation through suggesting amendments, mobilizing citizens to support measures, and encouraging legislators either to support or oppose bills. Most of this work is done through lobbyists, but members also are highly active, holding public demonstrations in local districts and loud rallies at the state capitol, organizing massive postcard campaigns, calling legislators to voice their views, and contributing through the union both to state legislators' and initiative campaigns. In 2009 the union spent $2.1 million to get Proposition 1A passed; the measure would have guaranteed school funding from a newly created special reserve fund. When the governor proposed altering Proposition 98 to balance the budget in summer 2009, the CTA roared to life with a statewide ad campaign attacking the governor's plan to "rob millions of dollars from public schools."

*CTA, www.cta.org/about/who/Mission_statement.htm, and www.cta.org/about/who/CTA+Fact+Sheet.htm.

California State and University of California, is not included in Prop 98, and their funding dropped sharply with the 2009 budget crisis, though total enrollment over time has increased to more than 650,000. Ultimately, approximately $65 billion was spent on education in California in FY2007–2008.

Health and human services compete with education for the largest slice of the budget pie. This category encompasses a range of essential services, such as food stamps, residential care for the elderly, health care for children, and benefits for the unemployed and disabled. To help meet the state's needs, the federal government transfers $47 billion in welfare and other payments to the state, which are redistributed through state agencies, bringing the total spent by California to more than $74 billion (FY2007).

State government also incurs **general operational** costs: almost $12 billion is spent to run the state's court system, administrative departments, militia, and lottery, for instance. The state spends almost $15 billion on **business and transportation**, including the California Highway Patrol, and finally, at least another $10 billion goes to fund **prisons**, covering inmate medical care and rehabilitation programs as well as prison guard salaries and operating costs.

Tax Burden: Too High, Too Low?

It is a common complaint among Californians that they pay more in taxes than the average residents of other U.S. states. California's ranking in terms of overall state and local debt burden justifies that view: the state placed sixth among the fifty states in 2008.[2] However, if state and local revenues are considered as a share of economic wealth or income, the state's ranking is considerably lower.[3]

In combination with local sales taxes, the recent one-cent temporary increase to the state sales tax placed California ahead of all others in that category, but thanks to Proposition 13, individual property taxes remain relatively low and place the state near the bottom (43rd) in rankings in that category.[4] Corporate taxes and income taxes place it near the top, whereas comparatively low "sin" taxes on alcohol and tobacco once more place it near the bottom. For example, California ranks thirty-first in cigarette taxes, twenty-first in beer taxes ($0.20 per gallon), and forty-fifth for table wine taxes (also $0.20 per gallon).

On an individual basis, whether Californians pay more or less than taxpayers in other states depends greatly on which tax is being considered, how much a person earns, homeowner status, regional location, and what goods and services that person consumes. These also influence the perception of being overtaxed at least as much as a person's attitudes about public spending and the proper role of government do.

Yet when it comes to budgeting, not enough revenue has been collected to cover all that Californians seem to collectively want, and while spending outpaced population growth and inflation during the first half of the early 2000s, it was in alignment with overall economic growth. Politicians used higher revenues during those positive economic years to play catch-up with major programs that had been neglected or underfunded for years.

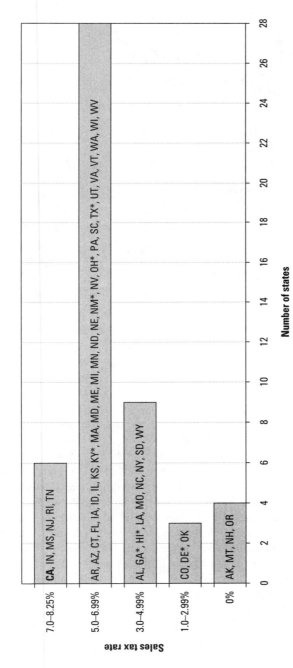

FIGURE 8.4

California's Sales Tax in Context

Source: Tax Foundation.

*Some states levy gross receipts taxes (GRTs), which are collected from firms rather than at the point of sale, and apply to a broader range of goods than retail end products. Some states levy only GRTs, and others levy both a GRT and a sales tax.

Gimmicks and tricks? The budget for 2009–2010 will force local governments to lend the state billions of dollars. County and local officials know that a promise of future repayments cannot compensate for the upfront losses and agonizing cuts to essential services.

The Budget Crisis and Beyond

The previous discussion contains a partial answer to the chapter's opening question about the inability of policymakers to effectively address budget crises. Their failings chiefly stem from economic triggers like compounding deficits resulting from severe and unanticipated drop-offs in tax revenues and no realistic way to immediately cut services without undermining the government's legal commitments. In one year, 2008 to 2009, collections for three major taxes—personal income, retail sales, and corporate—declined $12.1 *billion*.[5] Meanwhile, costs and demands kept increasing as unemployment rates rose, home foreclosures mounted, cost-of-living adjustments were enacted for major programs, and a federal receiver demanded billions for prison funding. Notably, the legislature and Gov. Arnold Schwarzenegger did act swiftly in February 2009 to cut about $10 billion and raise a projected $10 billion through new taxes. But it simply wasn't enough to staunch the bleeding.

The inability to act quickly and effectively also stems from political constraints—such as the rule requiring two-thirds of the legislature to approve the budget—as well as electoral concerns that lead legislators to support certain interests over others. Term limits also contribute to the tangle by filling the legislature with many neophytes who lack big-picture understanding of how systems in the state inter-relate and how cuts in one area will affect others.

Finally, the people's penchant for keeping taxes low has led to severely restricted revenue streams—property taxes capped at 1 percent of sale value by Proposition 13, a reduction of the vehicle license fee, and an emergency sales tax increase that will not be extended. All this despite relentless population growth and demands for services—services that become more critical in economic hard times. These imbalances translate into billions of dollars that policymakers cannot quickly replace.

Conclusion: Change the Rules?

As a U.S. state California faces most of the same basic challenges as the other forty-nine, but as one of the world's largest *countries*, its economy is intimately tied to global fortunes and its fiscal dilemmas are comparable in scope and depth. The sheer volume of issues generated by its more than 38 million residents is staggering, and the majority of those issues will be reflected, though not always resolved, in the state's annual budgets. As the 2009–2010 budget meltdown illustrates, effective governing demands rules that facilitate rather than obstruct compromise. Avoiding economic catastrophe depends on it.

Notes

1. Ellen Hanak, "Paying for Infrastructure: California's Choices," Public Policy Institute of California, January 2009.
2. Data taken from Tax Foundation, www.taxfoundation.org/files/state_various_sales_rates-20090701.pdf.
3. Tracy Gordon, "California Budget," Public Policy Institute of California, July 2009.
4. Tax Foundation, www.taxfoundation.org/taxdata/topic/9.html.
5. State Controller, www.sco.ca.gov/Press-Releases/2009/07–09summary.pdf.

CHAPTER 9

OUTLINE

A Weak Party State

Party in the California Electorate

Party in Government

The Party Organizations

Elections: Continuity and Change

California Campaigns

Major Voting Trends

Conclusion: A Complex Electorate

Political Parties, Elections, and Campaigns

Political scientist E. E. Schattschneider wrote in 1942 that "modern democracies are unthinkable save in terms of political parties." The same can be said of elections because through both diverse interests are voiced, aggregated, and translated into policy. Without parties, the scale and scope of conflict produced by countless, disorganized factions would be unmanageable. Without elections, citizens would lack the means to hold their representatives accountable.

Political communities define themselves by how they use parties and elections, and the patterns are telling across California. One of the most important developments worth noting upfront is an **east-west divide** that has opened along liberal-conservative lines, whereby the coastal regions are heavily liberal and Democratic and inland counties are conservative and Republican. Reasons for this trend are discussed in this chapter, along with the style of California parties, the character of elections, and the conduct of campaigns.

A Weak Party State

Historically speaking, political parties in California have struggled for survival, not prospered. Much of their troubles date to early twentieth-century Progressive reforms deliberately designed to strip them of their power. Idealizing politics

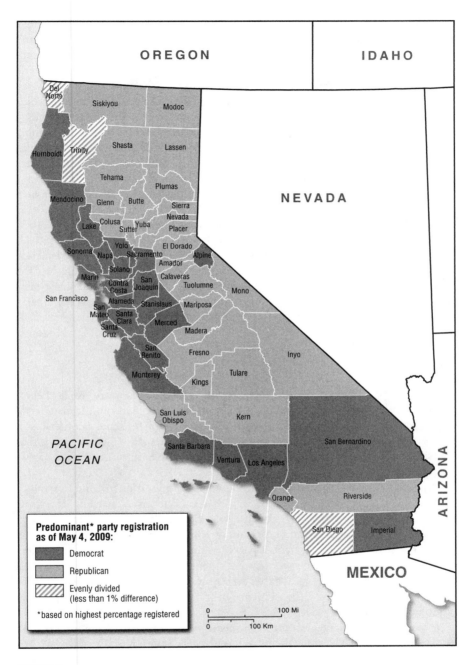

MAP 9.1

California's East-West Partisan Divide

without partisanship, Progressives overhauled election law by establishing new mechanisms for voters to bypass parties altogether: the initiative, referendum, and recall being foremost among these. Other innovations included nonpartisan elections for local elections and judges, and cross-filing at the state level for statewide elected officials (discussed in chapter 2). Through secret ballots, direct primaries, and banning parties from endorsing candidates prior to elections, party members would also be able to choose their nominees without the blessing of party bosses.

A good deal of the Progressives' antiparty program flourishes today. Cross-filing and pre-primary endorsements have been eliminated,[1] but the long-term consequences of the Progressives' attack on parties are still visible: voters split their tickets between Republicans and Democrats for different offices; state party organizations remain relatively weak; and candidates tend to self-select and draw on their own resources rather than those of their party. One of every five registered California voters is in the "Decline to State" category, having registered with no party at all.

Parties are far from ineffective in the state, however, and they continue to thrive within a government in which ideologically polarized representatives frequently refuse to compromise with the enemy. Yet, on balance, the evidence supports the judgment that California remains a weak party state. This can also be seen by examining more systematically the three interconnected parts of the party system: party *in the electorate, in government,* and *as an organization.*

Party in the California Electorate

In one respect, a political party is made up of members who share similar beliefs about the role government should play in their lives, but "party in the electorate" also refers to the generalized sentiment a party's members share about what it means to be a Republican, Democrat, or any other party. It is this sentiment that leads them to vote for certain officials and reinforces their attachment to the party's "brand name."

Three-quarters of registered California voters belong to one of the two major parties, Republican and Democrat, but that number is somewhat deceiving. According to a recent statewide survey, a majority of Californians think the state needs a third political party, and seven out of ten prefer to be unaffiliated with any party.[2] Furthermore, because neither party has majority status, independent voters provide the swing votes necessary to win in general elections. While California is commonly labeled a "blue state" based on registration statistics and statewide elections that favor Democrats, the influence of independents has turned its political complexion slightly purple.

In terms of party registration, California was a majority Democratic state between 1934 and 1989; since then this has been the state's plurality party, edging out Republicans by 13.5 percent in May 2009. Democrats today are first in registration numbers at 44.5 percent, Republicans take second at 31 percent, and third parties collectively hold third place with a combined membership of 4 percent.

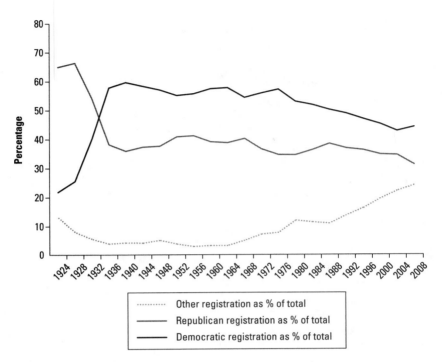

FIGURE 9.1

Party Registration in Presidential Election Years, 1924–2008

Source: California Secretary of State, Report of Registration, October 2008.

Note: The percentages reflect the statistics from the closing date for registration in the general election.

The largest and still-growing category of voters is Decline to State. These individuals affiliate with no party and constitute 20 percent of the state's electorate.[3]

Decline to State voters include people who consider themselves politically independent, although political scientists have found that those who "lean" toward one party or the other usually vote for that party. Historically, independents cast more votes for Democrats in California elections. Exit polls from the November 2008 presidential election found that among Democrats, 92 percent reported that they had voted for Obama, and 64 percent of "independents" had voted for him, whereas only 14 percent of Republicans had.[4]

Current members of the Democratic Party in California tend to be ethnically diverse, in the low-to-middle income bracket, and younger than in the past. One in three Democrats is Latino, black, or Asian, and 63 percent are white.[5] About a third of Democrats have household incomes of $40,000 or less per year, and a quarter of them are renters rather than homeowners. Women also prefer the

A political group can qualify officially as a political party in California either by petition or by registration. Petitioners need to gather 889,906 signatures, a number equal to 10 percent of the total number of people who voted in the previous statewide election, and file those petitions with several counties at least 135 days before the next election. Registration requires that 88,991 persons (1 percent) complete an affidavit of registration at least 154 days prior to the next election—a much harder task to coordinate statewide.

Registered Parties in California:

- American Independent: www.aipca.org
- Democratic: www.cadem.org
- Green: www.cagreens.org
- Libertarian: www.ca.lp.org
- Peace and Freedom: www.peaceandfreedom.org
- Republican: www.cagop.org

Parties That Have Failed to Qualify in the Past:

- Anarchy and Poverty
- California Moderate
- God, Truth, and Love
- Humanitarian
- Pot
- Reform
- Superhappy Party
- United Conscious Builders of the Dream
- Utopia Manifesto Party
- Whig

Source: California Secretary of State.

Democratic Party: approximately 14 percent more women than men registered as Democrats.

Republicans, meanwhile, tend to be white and middle- to upperclass, and they count more evangelical Christians among their ranks. In contrast to Democrats, 84 percent are white, and men outnumber women in Republican Party registration by eight points. Majorities in both parties are college graduates, and members tend to be fifty-four years of age or older (43 percent of Democrats, 44 percent of Republicans). By comparison, only 30 percent of independents are older than age fifty-four. On the whole, these statistics mirror nationwide trends in party registration.

Two out of three Republicans describe themselves as conservatives,[6] and for the most part, **California Republicans** tend to hold **conservative** views: they are more responsive to business than labor; generally want a government strictly limited in

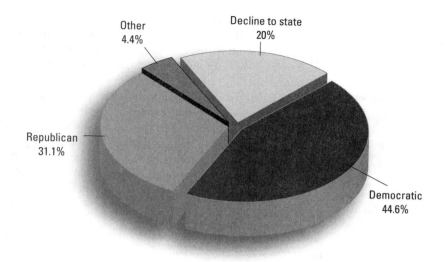

Other
4.4%

Decline to state
20%

Republican
31.1%

Democratic
44.6%

FIGURE 9.2

Registration by Political Party in California

size; do not believe in raising taxes; favor strong laws restricting illegal immigration; and believe that "individual destiny should be in the individual's hands."[7]

California Democrats, on the other hand, tend to hold **liberal** views: they place a premium on promoting social justice through government protection of civil liberties; they want the government to promote equal opportunity in education and the workplace and greater access to health care; they favor pro-choice laws; and they are more responsive to labor than business. Just over half of Democrats consider themselves liberals. In contrast, independents are distributed widely across the ideological spectrum: most (39 percent) describe themselves as middle-of-the-road, one-third consider themselves liberal, and the remaining third consider themselves conservative.[8]

Party in Government

Those most responsible for advancing a party's brand name through policymaking are current elected officials: the *party in government*. Approximately 20,000 officials in California hold elective office; of them, 132 hold statewide office and 55 represent Californians in the U.S. Congress. Governors, Assembly members, senators, representatives, and others not only pursue agenda items that become associated with a party's name, but they also fulfill their chief purpose: to *organize government* in order to achieve their policy aims.

Democrats have held the title of majority party for almost forty years in both legislative houses. The Assembly and Senate have been majority Democrat almost continuously since 1971, interrupted only by Republican rule in the Assembly from 1995 to 1996. A high degree of polarization pervades the capitol, especially with regard to taxation and spending: Democrats are more willing to raise certain taxes and fees (the annual tax paid on cars or cigarette taxes, for example), and Republicans are unwilling to raise them, period, and instead insist on cuts to social services.

This basic difference has exacerbated the parties' inability to pass budgets on time and is reflected in strong party solidarity and ideological rigidity. One explanation for that rigidity is found in uncompetitive districts that are drawn to ensure the election of a Democrat or a Republican. In most districts the "real" competition takes place during the primaries among candidates of the same party vying for the votes of strong partisan primary election voters. More extreme candidates tend to be favored under these circumstances. Virtually all districts in California are considered "Democrat" or "Republican" seats, and almost none switch parties from election to election (none did in November 2008).

Why are districts so uncompetitive? Reasons include *gerrymandering* and *natural sorting*. **Gerrymandering** refers to the act of manipulating district boundaries to include or exclude certain groups in order to benefit a party or an incumbent. What this means is that the redistricting processes during the past several decades produced maps that guaranteed a Democratic majority and few competitive seats. The partisan composition of Democratic districts virtually guarantees that Democrats win in those districts and that Republicans win in the state's Republican districts. Because state lawmakers—in actuality, the majority Democrats—were in charge of drawing their own boundaries for years, they managed to achieve the electoral outcomes they desired with minimal regard to competitiveness.

This is not unlike the process in the majority of states: twenty-nine states allow lawmakers to redraw their own boundaries, whereas another twelve hand redistricting authority to independent commissions.[9] Californians joined the latter category in 2008 through the passage of Proposition 11, which authorizes an independent commission to take control of the redistricting process. Party leaders and legislators will play no role in shaping their own districts following the 2010 census.

Yet it could be argued that the political geography of California reflects natural sorting: like-minded people tend to live near each other, and settlement patterns have produced a coastline that is more "blue" Democrat and an inland that is more "red" Republican. A less partisan redistricting process like the one promised by Prop 11 is unlikely to produce a slew of new competitive districts because mapmakers are still bound to draw districts containing numerically equal populations that are as compact as possible, respect city and county lines, and do not split communities of interest. These strictures pit practicality against ideals and, in the end, electoral competition suffers.

The Democrats' stronghold does not extend to the executive branch, where Republicans have held the governor's seat for almost fifty of the past sixty years since World War II. They have also managed to secure other statewide executive offices, preventing Democrats from monopolizing state administrative power.

TABLE 9.1   Modern Era California Governors by Party Affiliation

Term	Governor	Party affiliation
1943–1954	Earl Warren	Republican*
1955–1958	Goodwin Knight	Republican
1959–1966	Edmund "Pat" Brown	Democrat
1967–1974	Ronald Reagan	Republican
1975–1982	Edmund "Jerry" Brown Jr.	Democrat
1983–1990	George Deukmejian	Republican
1991–1998	Pete Wilson	Republican
1999–2003	Gray Davis	Democrat
2003–2006	Arnold Schwarzenegger	Republican

*Warren also received the nomination of the Democratic Party.

The Party Organizations

Finally, the concept of party encompasses organizational bodies and their rules. It should be noted that when citizens register to vote they actually become members of their *state* parties, organized according to election law in the fifty different states and the District of Columbia. The national organizations known as the Democratic National Committee and Republican National Committee have little to no control over the state parties.

Party organizations are well suited to fulfill another key party role: that of *nominating candidates for election and getting them elected*. At the top is the party **state central committee**, responsible for coordinating the local bodies that exist below it, for strategizing to win seats, and for assisting candidates with funding and other resources. These run the respective state conventions every year.

A state party chair acts as "CEO" of the party, and members of the state central committees include current statewide elected officials, nominees for statewide office, county-level party officials, and appointed and elected members from across the state. Democratic members of their state central committee number 2,900, evenly divided between men and women. There are 1,356 Republican members (no gender quotas) in the Republican state central committee. Beneath the major state party organs are fifty-eight **county central committees** for each party, also organized by the state election codes. Further down are volunteer local regional clubs that are home to a few activists but not many members.

Elections: Continuity and Change

Like political parties, elections continue to evolve in response to initiatives and reform movements that readjust the rules for citizens, parties, incumbents, and candidates. With term limits for elected state officials, for example, the game of political office "musical chairs" now extends to all levels of government: competition for "downticket" offices such as county boards of supervisors and big-city mayors has grown and so has rivalry for congressional seats. About two-thirds of all statewide officials will attempt to run for another office within two years of being termed-out, which adds to the pool of experienced candidates looking for a job. Term limits have not affected incumbents' chances for reelection, however; officeholders continue to be reelected at near-perfect rates.

Democratic senator Leland Yee joins supporters at the capitol in Sacramento to celebrate his election to the state Senate in 1996, the first Chinese American to serve in that chamber.

Special elections to fill vacant seats are also on the rise due to term limits, as politicians leave one office for another as they become available. This tends to create a "domino effect," which occurs when a state senator runs for an open U.S. Congress seat and a member of the Assembly then runs for the subsequently vacated state Senate seat, creating a third election needed to fill the empty Assembly seat and so on down the line. Governors or the legislature may also call special statewide elections so that voters can consider measures of great urgency. Governor Schwarzenegger has not found special elections to be a particularly helpful vehicle for building political support, however: an irritated electorate rejected every one of his proposals in special elections held in 2005 and 2009. Unfortunately for cash-strapped California, the average price tag for state special elections can approach $100 million, and voter turnout can be dismally low.[10] Barely 21 percent of eligible voters cast ballots in the special election held in May 2009—the lowest in state history.

In addition to term limits, at least two other significant reform efforts have recently affected California elections. First, the failings of punch-card systems laid bare by the 2000 presidential election between Vice President Al Gore and Texas governor George W. Bush prompted the U.S. Congress to pass the Help America Vote Act of 2002. Every state received millions of dollars to replace older voting equipment with more accurate touch-screen and optical scan machines. California's secretary of state, who has overseen the transition away from punch-card devices, continues monitoring the new

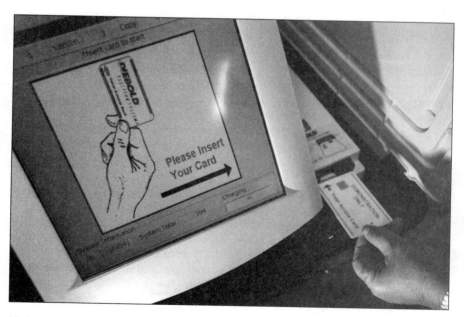

Modern touch-screen systems have been certified for use in every California county, though some counties use optical scan machines that require voters to fill in bubbles on a paper ballot that is electronically scanned.

equipment for software glitches and intentional mischief. All counties are now outfitted with advanced voting technology—the need for which is increasingly offset by the more than one-third of registered California voters who "vote by mail" or are "permanent absentee" voters—a figure that has doubled since 2004.

Second, for years reformers have tried to pry open primary elections to allow greater participation by the entire electorate. In **primary elections**, party members nominate candidates for various offices who then will go on to compete head to head with the other party's nominees in the general election. For instance, six Republicans may jump into an Assembly primary race, but only one will receive enough votes to become the Republican nominee for the Assembly seat, and incumbents invariably receive their party's renomination. That person will later face the Democratic nominee in the November **general election**.

Until 1996 the state had a **closed primary** system, meaning that only voters who declared their party affiliation prior to the election could participate in their own party's election. At the voting station a voter would receive a Republican or a Democratic ballot listing party candidates for each office. Independent or Decline to State voters could not participate in the nomination elections, though they could vote on statewide initiatives, local measures, or nonpartisan offices.

Proposition 198 (1996) changed the rules, but only temporarily. Californians had approved the **blanket primary**, in which all registered voters could vote for any candidate. In 1998 primary election voters were given a single ballot listing each office and every possible candidate for it, just as in a general election. Two years later the U.S. Supreme Court ruled the scheme an unconstitutional violation of political parties' First Amendment right to free association. A **modified primary** took its place: Decline to State voters may now have their votes counted if a party authorizes it. Today, the state has a modified closed primary system.

In June 2010 California voters will decide again whether to switch to an **open primary**. In exchange for his vote to pass the budget in 2009, Republican senator Abel Maldonado demanded the legislature place a constitutional amendment on the ballot creating a "top-two candidate" version in which any registered voter may select a top choice from among all candidates for office. The top two winners for each office would advance to the general election.

California Campaigns

Given parties' weak hold over Californians, the frequency of elections, a mobile population, and the immense size and density of districts, campaigns serve the important role of connecting citizens with candidates and incumbents. Across the state virtually all campaigners face the same basic challenges: raising huge sums of cash to buy access to potential voters and convincing enough of them to reject their opponents.

Assembly Speaker Jesse Unruh proclaimed, "Money is the mother's milk of politics." This is why incumbents cannot afford to stop raising money, waging what is known as the nonstop "permanent campaign." On average, a successful Assembly campaign costs more than $770,000 and a Senate campaign more than $1,00,000.[11] But those costs critically depend on how strong the competition is: incumbents running in a general election usually face "sacrificial lambs" who spend almost nothing in their defense, though some incumbents without serious challengers still spend in excess of $1.5 million "defending" their seats.

Open seat elections, created regularly now by term limits, require far higher sums. Candidates for open Assembly seats spend an average of $950,000; the most exorbitant legislative races can cost candidates nearly $3 million. Costs are also higher when there is a possibility that the other party could win the seat: more than $8.5 million was spent between two Senate candidates in 2008, and the winner squeaked by with 857 votes.

Among the largest contributors to campaigns are tribal governments, trade unions, energy companies, candidates who give to each other, the state parties, and business associations. Out-of-state contributors also donate multiple millions. All campaign fund-raising and expenditures must be reported to the California secretary of state's office, which makes fund-raising activity publicly available pursuant to Proposition 9 (see http://cal-access.ss.ca.gov).

Why do candidates require so much campaign funding? In districts as large as those found in California, paid media are the only ways to reach large swaths of potential voters. Most candidates in the state engage in **retail campaigning,** the kind of campaigning that takes place through television advertising and direct mail. These two types of retail activities dominate the statewide elections and are costly, particularly in urban media markets where the airwaves are crowded with competition from commercial advertisers. Professional campaign managers and consultants help candidates build efficient money-raising machines by coordinating other critical aspects of successful campaigns: access to donors, polling data, media buys, Web-based tools, a targeted message, and volunteers.

TABLE 9.2   Largest Campaign Contributors to State Campaigns by Industry, 2008

Industry	Contributions
Tribal governments:	$163,223,225
Public sector unions:	$37,892,448
Electric utilities:	$33,924,119
Candidate-to-candidate:	$28,261,485
Oil and gas:	$25,491,497
Party committees:	$23,936,653

Source: www.followthemoney.org; www.followthemoney.org/database/state_overview.phtml?s=CA&y=2008.

Danny Gilmore, the Republican candidate for the Thirtieth Assembly District, talks with potential constituents at a senior center in Bakersfield in 2008. Gilmore, a retired California Highway Patrol officer, squeaked by to win with 1,310 votes over Democratic city councilwoman Fran Florez in an open seat election. The two spent a combined $4.6 million in the state's second-most-expensive Assembly race; Gilmore was outspent by more than $1 million.

This is not to say that knocking on doors, attending community events, "pressing the flesh"—types of **wholesale** campaigning that require a comfortable pair of shoes rather than large amounts of campaign cash—are not also still important in modern campaigns. These are particularly beneficial in local contests in which friends and neighbors help turn out the vote.

Major Voting Trends

In representative democracy the act of voting provides a critical check on officeholders, offering not only a means to remove unresponsive representatives but also cues about what policies a constituency prefers. In a direct democracy the voters "check" each other through the act of voting, but the most votes still wins. For these reasons, who votes has profound implications for electoral outcomes, policymaking in the public interest, and, ultimately, the quality of representation.

The California electorate does not represent all Californians, nor does it reflect the population's size, growth, or diversity.[12] In other words, *voters, residents, and*

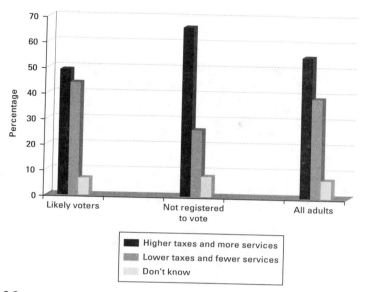

FIGURE 9.3

Differing Perceptions about the Role of Government

Source: Public Policy Institute of California Statewide Survey, May 2006.

citizens are not the same groups of people. Not all residents are citizens, about 25 percent of the eligible population doesn't register to vote, and not all eligible voters vote in every election. What's more, those who cast ballots generally hold very different views about the proper role of government than those who do not.

Immigration has changed the state's demography far more quickly than it has contributed to changes in the voting population. For instance, although whites now make up approximately 43 percent of California's resident population, they comprise 70 percent of all voters, who are in general also slightly older, native born, and more conservative than nonvoters. In contrast, one in three Californians is Latino, but only 15 percent are likely to turn out for elections.[13] Differences in turnout also are related to *age* (younger residents are more likely to be Latino and these groups vote at the lowest rates); *education* (higher education levels translate into higher turnout); *home ownership* (as well as length of residency, both are positively related to voting); *nativity* (native-born residents are more likely to vote than foreign-born citizens); and *income* (higher-income voters are more likely to vote). All of these characteristics are at least indirectly related to immigrant status, in that the "haves" out-shout the "have-nots" in elections.

It is also important to note that different combinations of voters produce different electoral outcomes. Voters grouped into Assembly districts choose candidates who tend to reflect their characteristics and preferences, and as a result, elected legislators resemble those localized voters. Initiative voters, on the other hand, hail

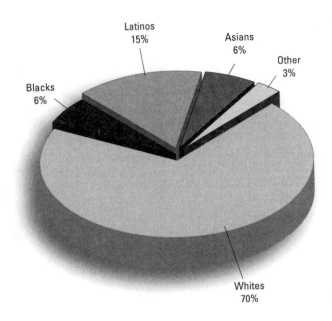

Latinos
15%

Asians
6%

Other
3%

Blacks
6%

Whites
70%

FIGURE 9.4

Ethnic Makeup of California's Likely Voters

Source: Public Policy Institute of California.

from the entire state, and their votes reflect a different set of characteristics and preferences.

Conclusion: A Complex Electorate

Parties, elections, and campaigns have been both the instruments of change and the targets of reform. Historical disdain for parties lingers in California's state election codes and permeates the conduct of elections, surfacing in initiatives that seek to empower individuals over organizations, such as that found in the movement to reform primaries. It is also manifested in weak party organizations, a growing number of independents, and in the candidate-centered nature of campaigning that requires extraordinary personal fund-raising muscle.

Though political participation encompasses categories of activities not discussed in this chapter, the focus on voting emphasizes its intrinsic value as a democratic exercise and its vital role in linking citizens to their representatives. Uneven levels of participation, including nonvoting among ethnic groups, contribute to the governing dilemmas of policymakers as they weigh their responsibilities to serve the greater public interests but also respond to those who actually cast their ballots. Until the electorate more accurately reflects the entirety of the state's population, elected officials' decisions will continue to reflect the political, cultural, geographic, and demographic biases of those who vote. Expanding the electorate is one way California's government might be made more accountable and representative in the search for greater governability.

Notes

1. Cross-filing was finally eliminated through legislative action in 1959, and pre-primary endorsements were found to be unconstitutional in 1989.

2. Mark Baldassare, "California's Post-Partisan Future," Public Policy Institute of California, January 2008, 2.

3. Data taken from the California Secretary of State, "15-Day Report of Registration, May 4, 2009," http://sos.ca.gov/elections/ror/ror-pages/15day-stwdsp-09/hist-reg-stats.pdf.

4. Data compiled from National Election Pool poll results, reported on CNN Election Center 2008, www.cnn.com/ELECTION/2008/results/polls/#val=CAP00p1.

5. Baldassare, "California's Post-Partisan Future," 2.

6. www.cagop.org.

7. Baldassare, "California's Post-Partisan Future," 5.

8. Ibid.

9. National Conference of State Legislatures, "Redistricting Commissions: Legislative Plans (Go16617)," www.ncsl.org.

10. Data compiled from the California Secretary of State's Election Division.

11. Based on 2008 data, www.followthemoney.org/database/state_overview.phtml?s=CA&y=2008.

12. Mark Baldassare, *California's Exclusive Electorate* (San Francisco: Public Policy Institute of California, 2006).

13. Public Policy Institute of California, "Just the Facts: Latino Voters in California," August 2008, 1. In 2008, when turnout reached its highest point since 1972, the *Los Angeles Times* reported that actual turnout among Latinos was 18 percent, whereas among whites it was 63 percent (National Election Pool, November 2008), www.latimes.com/news/politics/la-110608-me-superchart-g,0,7151660.graphic.

10

Concluding Thoughts: Political Paradoxes and Governability

Is California ungovernable? The state teeters on the edge of economic catastrophe, paralyzed by governmental indecision in the face of massive budget deficits extending into an uncertain future, with no long-term resolution in sight. The prognosis for fiscal year 2009–2010: near death, with an excruciatingly slow and painful recovery ahead.

Economic woes merely compound what is at best an impractical political situation. Having embraced the power of direct democracy, slices of California—that is, some percentage of eligible voters rather than all adult residents—make decisions for the entire state as a parallel lawmaking institution, one far less deliberative than its counterpart in Sacramento. In fact, what was supposed to be a stop-gap measure for keeping legislators in check is now an overworked policymaking machine whose gears are oiled by campaign donations and shifted by an electorate not fully representative of the state's diverse population. In a system dominated by special interests parading as public interests, meeting the state's actual needs becomes more difficult.

Direct democracy and representative democracy live in uneasy tension, and imbalances in the distribution of power between voters and policymakers are inevitable. This can be seen most clearly in voter-imposed rules that restrict legislators' budgeting power, such as guaranteed funding for big-ticket items like schools, but also practically unattainable thresholds for raising tax revenues (two-thirds voter approval for ballot measures and two-thirds of the legislature for revenue-raising bills and the annual state budget). California's hybrid democracy is an institutional paradox, a seemingly illogical development that calls the state's governability into question. So is the notion that Californians demand strong and efficient leadership from all elected officeholders, yet they choose to limit authorities' power and therefore the ability of these officials to perform efficiently and effectively.

California politics is riddled with other paradoxes that go a long way toward explaining the current state of affairs. For example, Californians generally distrust politicians and are averse to political conflict, so they continue to reach for ways to take politicians—and politics, for that matter—"out" of politics; they resort to passing initiatives like term limits and open primaries that will automatically remove people from office at prescribed intervals and will lessen party control. Disappointment and resentment in the body politic continue to grow, however, because political systems are by nature designed to expose conflicting interests in the struggle to reach consensus, and the people not only need politicians to govern what is effectively one of the largest countries in the world, they need to organize in order to win, and parties provide that reliable structure. Nevertheless, younger Californians are unconvinced that parties matter, and increasingly they are registering as Decline to State voters.

Historically speaking, Californians' choices also reflect unrealistic expectations about the capabilities of governing institutions. On the whole, for instance, Californians presume that rooting out government waste will offset necessary revenues for government services, as if saving millions of dollars could compensate for not raising billions.

Paradoxically, Californians also expect that their own personal needs and the public good will be simultaneously served. This may be possible with a government service like public education, a "good" that yields private gains with long-term public benefits, but it does not produce sustainable economic policies. To wit, Californians prefer to pay lower sales, income, and property taxes in the short term, creating chronic underfunding of local and state governments that are burdened with meeting basic sanitation, education, health, transportation, and safety needs. Moreover, this tendency has resulted in a shift away from policies that impose upfront costs and toward long-term bond debt that costs twice as much in the long run, generating interest payments that place stress on the General Fund by siphoning off money that could be used for other necessary budget items.

Quite apart from the institutional aspects of governing are socioeconomic and political issues that determine the state's political state of affairs—issues that involve more than 38 million people who place evolving demands on the state. It is estimated that California will be a majority Latino state in the next decade, and the population will grow to approximately 50 million people by 2025.[1] How will decision makers nurture the educated workforce that will be needed to drive the state's service-based economy? Will voters be willing to extend helping hands to those on the bottom end of the socioeconomic scale? One in seven Californians will be sixty-five years of age or older by that time: How will the state provide for a large elderly population that places the immense demands on health care systems? Already the state administration has estimated that to accommodate such growth, approximately $500 billion will be required to rebuild and expand aging transportation, school, water, and other systems in the next twenty years. How will Californians be able raise that kind of cash?[2]

In many ways, political reforms brought California to this point, and political reforms will help transform the future. Yet institutional reforms can only go so far. Rules set boundaries for decision making but do not determine the choices people make, and choices must be based on realistic understanding about government's capabilities if the state's policies and laws are to work. Voters' expectations and attitudes about government underscore California's governability.

Overall, California government faces the same challenges as other states; what makes it distinct are the scope and scale of its issues, a hybrid governing structure in which voters can change the rules of the game for representatives, and the large number of constraints placed on authorities' power. The issues are mostly the same across the nation, however, and they pose enormous challenges for state government now and for the foreseeable future. The extent to which these policy questions overwhelm competent elected officials is a measure of California's ungovernability:

- Education: Only an educated workforce can sustain a sophisticated, diverse, service-oriented, modern economy. Budget cuts threaten to destabilize the state's premier college and university systems by carving away funds for hiring the "best and brightest" who teach and prepare students for the workforce and who advance their disciplines through necessary research. California continues to spend less on its K–12 students than most other states, and hard economic times mean fewer days of instruction, lower pay for teachers, lack of instructional or supplementary materials, and shortages of reliable afterschool care and programs. The fastest growing segment of the population is Latino, but as a group these students lag behind in graduation rates and test scores. How will achievement gaps be closed? How will the state prepare its students to meet the state's changing economic needs?

- Immigration: California's immigrant population is the largest in the nation, with one in four current residents having been born elsewhere. Will voters be willing to extend the same public benefits to immigrant groups that many of them enjoy, and if not, how might a service economy–based state accommodate massive numbers of low-skilled, unemployed, low-educated groups that would require state services to fulfill basic needs, from food to housing to employment?

- Environment: Climate change threatens California's basic lifelines. Rising temperatures bring less rain and lighter snowpack as well as limited water supplies for thirsty farms, manufacturing plants, and homes. Lower rainfall increases the risk of wildfires in bone-dry areas and increases airborne fine particle pollution; wildlife unaccustomed to higher than average temperatures cannot quickly adjust, so biodiversity suffers. Rising sea levels threaten a densely populated coastline, and inland recreation and tourism patterns take a blow. Will California lawmakers go far enough to reduce the human-made greenhouse gas emissions directly contributing to these environmental changes, and will other states follow? Can the government adequately respond and the economy readjust when environmental crises like torrential rains and resulting mud slides, earthquakes, heat waves, extensive wildfires, and extended droughts hit in quick succession?

- Transportation: The nation's highest number of cars on roads and freeways travel California's roadways, the most congested in the United States. Combined with trucks, buses, and farm and construction equipment, California's motorized vehicles also create dirty air that causes major respiratory illnesses. California's airports, seaports, and railway systems contribute to pollution levels as well, an inevitable consequence of being a gateway to Asia and containing the nation's busiest port (Long Beach). Can lawmakers provide programs that improve California's air and travel systems, but also allow residents and businesses the mobility they desire? Can they ensure the safety of residents as those systems take on larger proportions?

Less than a generation ago California government was held up as a distinguished model of efficiency and planning. The state's fairly quick reversal of fortunes is a testament to the power of rapidly changing social, economic, and political circumstances; the cumulative force of historical decisions; the power of culture; the consequences of rules; and the importance of collective choices. These will continue to be at the heart of policymaking that defines California's future and its governability.

Notes

1. Ellen Hanak and Mark Baldassare, *California 2025: Taking on the Future* (San Francisco: Public Policy Institute of California, 2005).
2. Ibid, 1.

List of Counties, Including Median Income per County

County	Median household income
Alameda	$68,263
Alpine	$46,136
Amador	$54,903
Butte	$39,466
Calaveras	$51,447
Colusa	$43,882
Contra Costa	$76,317
Del Norte	$35,910
El Dorado	$64,256
Fresno	$46,547
Glenn	$38,521
Humboldt	$37,281
Imperial	$33,576
Inyo	$46,865
Kern	$46,639
Kings	$45,087
Lake	$38,113
Lassen	$47,676
Los Angeles	$53,494
Madera	$44,259
Marin	$83,910
Mariposa	$42,757
Mendocino	$42,329
Merced	$43,789
Modoc	$33,713
Mono	$54,174
Monterey	$56,668
Napa	$61,988
Nevada	$58,658
Orange	$73,107

County	Median household income
Placer	$69,667
Plumas	$45,516
Riverside	$57,736
Sacramento	$56,823
San Benito	$66,273
San Bernardino	$55,995
San Diego	$61,724
San Francisco	$67,333
San Joaquin	$51,874
San Luis Obispo	$55,942
San Mateo	$82,913
Santa Barbara	$57,741
Santa Clara	$84,265
Santa Cruz	$62,849
Shasta	$41,980
Sierra	$44,950
Siskiyou	$35,692
Solano	$66,575
Sonoma	$62,279
Stanislaus	$50,367
Sutter	$49,104
Tehama	$36,884
Trinity	$35,439
Tulare	$40,444
Tuolumne	$45,478
Ventura	$72,762
Yolo	$55,988
Yuba	$40,602

Sources: California Department of Finance, Financial and Economic Data, All County Profiles. Median income figures adapted from "County-Level Unemployment and Median Household Income for California, 2007," Economic Research Service, United States Department of Agriculture, April 21, 2009, www.ers.usda.gov/data/unemployment/RDList2.asp?ST=CA.

Current Constitutional Officers and Leaders of the Legislature, Including Salaries, July 2009

Constitutional Officers

Office	Officeholder	Salary***
Governor	Arnold Schwarzenegger (R)	*$212,170 ($173,979.40*)***
Lieutenant Governor	John Garamendi (D)	*$159,134 ($130,489.88*)*
Secretary of State	Debra Bowen (D)	*$159,134 ($130,489.88*)*
Attorney General	Jerry Brown (D)	*$184,301 ($151,126.82*)*
Treasurer	Bill Lockyer (D)	*$169,743 ($139,189.26*)*
Controller	John Chiang (D)	*$169,743 ($139,189.26*)*
Insurance Commissioner	Steve Poizner (R)	*$169,743 ($139,189.26*)*
Superintendent of Public Instruction	Jack O'Connell (D)	*$184,301 ($151,126.82*)*

Leaders of the Legislature

Senate position	Officeholder	Salary
President pro Tempore	Darrell Steinberg (D-Sacramento)	*$133,639 ($109,583.98*)*
Majority Leader	Dean Florez (D-Shafter)	*$124,923 ($102,436*)*
Minority Leader	Dennis Hollingsworth (R-Murrieta)	*$133,639 ($109,583.98*)*

Assembly position	Officeholder	Salary
Speaker	Karen Bass (D-Los Angeles)	$133,639 ($109,583.98*)
Speaker pro Tempore	Isadore Hall III (D-Compton)	$116,208 (95,209.56*)
Minority Floor Leader	Michal Blakeslee (R-San Luis Obispo)	$133,639 ($109,583.98*)

Sources: State of California and California Citizens Compensation Commission.

*Effective December 9, 2009, salaries for all statewide officials will decline by 18 percent. The starred salaries listed above reflect this reduction.

**Governor Schwarzenegger declines to take a salary.

*** All legislators are entitled to receive a per diem payment of $173 for each day they work while their house is in session. Per diem amounts are set by the Victim Compensation and Government Claims Board and are intended to cover daily expenses associated with working away from home. Total amounts vary annually with the number of days in session, and by chamber. In 2007–2008 senators could earn up to $38,804 annually, and Assembly members averaged $33,383 during the same period (four legislators do not accept per diem payments). This information taken from the Senate Rules Committee, Assembly Rules Committee.

Recent Governors, Senate Presidents pro Tempore, and Speakers of the Assembly

Governors of California, 1943–Present

Name	Party	Year(s)
Earl Warren	R	1943–1953
Goodwin J. Knight	R	1953–1959
Edmund G. Brown	D	1959–1967
Ronald Reagan	R	1967–1975
Edmund G. Brown Jr.	D	1975–1983
George Deukmejian	R	1983–1991
Pete Wilson	R	1991–1999
Gray Davis	D	1999–2003
Arnold Schwarzenegger	R	2003–

Presidents pro Tempore of the Senate, 1939–Present

Name	Party	Year(s)
Jerrold L. Seawell	R	1939–1947
Harold J. Powers	R	1947–1954
Clarence C. Ward	R	1954–1955
Ben Hulse	R	1955–1957
Hugh M. Burns	D	1957–1969
Howard Way	R	1969–1970
Jack Schrade	R	1970–1971
James R. Mills	D	1971–1981
David A. Roberti	D	1981–1994
Bill Lockyer	D	1994–1998
John L. Burton	D	1998–2004
Don Perata	D	2004–2009
Darrell Steinberg	D	2009–

Speakers of the Assembly, 1943–Present

Name	Party	Year(s)
Charles W. Lyon	R	1943–1946
Sam L. Collins	R	1947–1952
James W. Silliman	R	1953–1954
Luther H. Lincoln	R	1955–1958
Ralph M. Brown	D	1959–1961
Jesse M. Unruh	D	1961–1969
Robert T. Monagan	R	1969–1970
Bob Moretti	D	1971–1974
Leo T. McCarthy	D	1974–1980
Willie Brown	D	1980–1995
Doris Allen	R	1995
Brian Setencich	R	1995–1996
Curt Pringle	R	1996
Cruz M. Bustamante	D	1996–1998
Antonio Villaraigosa	D	1998–2000
Robert M. Hertzberg	D	2000–2002
Herb J. Wesson, Jr.	D	2002–2004
Fabian Núñez	D	2004–2008
Karen Bass	D	2008–

MOBILE PHONE BEHAVIOR

This book provides the first comprehensive introduction to the rapidly emerged science of mobile phone behavior. It presents the unexpected complexity of human mobile phone behavior through examining four basic aspects of mobile phone behavior (users, technologies, activities, and effects) and four major domains of such behavior (medicine, business, education, and everyday life). Chapters open with the common thoughts on mobile phone behavior of ordinary mobile phone users, then present a series of real-life cases, scientific studies, and synthesized knowledge, concluding in complex but highly readable summaries of each aspect of mobile phone behavior. Readers should achieve two intellectual goals: gaining a usable knowledge of the complexity of mobile phone behavior and developing the skills to analyze the complexity of mobile phone behavior.

ZHENG YAN is Associate Professor of Developmental Psychology at University at Albany. He has a doctoral degree from Harvard University and previously lectured at the Harvard University Graduate School of Education. His previous publications include the *Encyclopedia of Cyber Behavior* (2012) and the *Encyclopedia of Mobile Phone Behavior* (2015), and he has been a co-editor of the *International Journal of Cyber Behavior, Psychology and Learning* since 2012.

MOBILE PHONE BEHAVIOR

ZHENG YAN

University at Albany, State University of New York

CAMBRIDGE
UNIVERSITY PRESS

University Printing House, Cambridge CB2 8BS, United Kingdom

One Liberty Plaza, 20th Floor, New York, NY 10006, USA

477 Williamstown Road, Port Melbourne, VIC 3207, Australia

314–321, 3rd Floor, Plot 3, Splendor Forum, Jasola District Centre, New Delhi – 110025, India

79 Anson Road, #06–04/06, Singapore 079906

Cambridge University Press is part of the University of Cambridge.

It furthers the University's mission by disseminating knowledge in the pursuit of
education, learning, and research at the highest international levels of excellence.

www.cambridge.org
Information on this title: www.cambridge.org/9781107124554
DOI: 10.1017/9781316417584

© Zheng Yan 2018

First published 2018

Printed in the United States of America by Sheridan Books, Inc.

A catalogue record for this publication is available from the British Library.

Library of Congress Cataloging-in-Publication Data
NAMES: Yan, Zheng, 1958– author.
TITLE: Mobile phone behavior / Zheng Yan, University at Albany, State University of New York.
DESCRIPTION: New York : Cambridge University Press, 2017. |
Includes bibliographical references and index.
IDENTIFIERS: LCCN 2017009359 | ISBN 9781107124554 (Hardback) |
ISBN 9781107561946 (Paperback)
SUBJECTS: LCSH: Cell phones–Social aspects. | Mobile communication systems–Social aspects. |
Interpersonal communication–Technological innovations–Social aspects. |
CLASSIFICATION: LCC HE9713 .Y36 2017 | DDC 303.48/33–dc23
LC record available at https://lccn.loc.gov/2017009359

ISBN 978-1-107-12455-4 Hardback
ISBN 978-1-107-56194-6 Paperback

Contents

List of Figures   *page* vi
List of Tables   vii
About the Author   viii
Preface   ix

1   The Science of Mobile Phone Behavior   1

2   Mobile Phone Users   23

3   Mobile Phone Technologies   57

4   Mobile Phone Activities   85

5   Mobile Phone Effects   115

6   Mobile Phone Behavior in Medicine   146

7   Mobile Phone Behavior in Business   185

8   Mobile Phone Behavior in Education   215

9   Mobile Phone Behavior in Daily Life   242

10 The Complexity of Mobile Phone Behavior   270

Index   285

Figures

1.1 The Basic Relationship between Technologies and Humans *page* 9
1.2 The Four Basic Elements of Mobile Phone Behavior 10
1.3 Initial Search of Published Journal Articles on Mobile Phones 13
1.4 Initial Search of Published Journal Articles on Television 14
1.5 Initial Search of Published Journal Articles on Computers 14
1.6 Initial Search of Published Journal Articles on the Internet 15
1.7 The Overall Organization of the Book 20
2.1 A Summary Diagram of User-Based Mobile Phone Behavior 54
3.1 A Summary Diagram of Technology-Based Mobile Phone
     Behavior 83
4.1 A Summary Diagram of Activity-Based Mobile Phone Behavior 113
5.1 A Summary Diagram of Effect-Based Mobile Phone Behavior 143
6.1 Trend of Published Articles on Medical Mobile Phone Behavior
     Research 170
6.2 A Summary Diagram of Mobile Phone Behavior in Medicine 183
7.1 The Linear Growth Trend of Journal Article Publications
     on Mobile Phone Behavior in Business 204
7.2 A Summary Diagram of Mobile Phone Behavior in Business 212
8.1 A Summary Diagram of Mobile Phone Behavior in Education 240
9.1 A Summary Diagram of Mobile Phone Behavior in Daily Life 269
10.1 A Summary of the Complexity of Mobile Phone Behavior 274
10.2 Two Examples of the Summary Diagrams: (a) the Summary
      Diagram of Technology-Based Mobile Phone Behavior and (b)
      the Summary Diagram of Mobile Phone Behavior in Medicine 277
10.3 (a) The Four-Element Basic Model as a General Model for
      Structural Equation Modeling and (b) the Specific
      Hypothesized Model for Structural Equation Modeling 281
10.4 A Simple System Dynamics Model of Two Friends Sending
      or Receiving Text Messages Reciprocally and Developing
      Together over Time through Co-Construction 282

Tables

2.1 The *Encyclopedia* Chapters on User-Based Mobile Phone
Behavior   *page* 47

3.1 The *Encyclopedia* Chapters on Technology-Based Mobile
Phone Behavior   72

4.1 The *Encyclopedia* Chapters on Activity-Based Mobile Phone
Behavior   104

5.1 The *Encyclopedia* Chapters on Effect-Based Mobile Phone
Behavior   134

6.1 The *Encyclopedia* Chapters on Mobile Phone Behavior
in Medicine   171

6.2 Numbers of Journal Articles Published on Different
Technology Addictions   178

7.1 The *Encyclopedia* Chapters on Mobile Phone Behavior
in Business   205

8.1 The *Encyclopedia* Chapters on Mobile Phone Behavior in
Education   232

9.1 The *Encyclopedia* Chapters on Mobile Phone Behavior
in Daily Life   264

About the Author

ZHENG YAN is Associate Professor of Developmental and Educational Psychology at University at Albany since 2007. He graduated from Harvard University Graduate School of Education with a doctoral degree in Human Development and Psychology. His research mainly concerns dynamic and complex relations between contemporary technologies and human development as well as research methodology of human development, and specifically focuses on computer behavior, cyber behavior, and mobile phone behavior. He is the editor of *Encyclopedia of Cyber Behavior* and *Encyclopedia of Mobile Phone Behavior*. He is the co-editor of the *International Journal of Cyber Behavior, Psychology and Learning* and the guest editor/co-editor of special issues/sections on mobile technology and child and adolescent development; mobile computing behavior; children, adolescents, and the Internet; and the psychology of e-learning.

Preface

In October 2014, I finished editing the three volumes of the *Encyclopedia of Mobile Phone Behavior*. One of the follow-up projects I was thinking about was to write an introductory book on mobile phone behavior as a companion to the *Encyclopedia*. The reasons are quite simple: (1) the three-volume *Encyclopedia* is really comprehensive, but somehow hard for ordinary readers to learn quickly about mobile phone behavior; and (2) the *Encyclopedia* synthesizes the scientific literature really effectively, but it is somehow too technical for ordinary readers to really appreciate the complexity of mobile phone behavior easily. Cambridge University Press has successfully published multiple widely recognized books on the psychology of the Internet, such as: *The Psychology of the Internet*; *Psychology and the Internet: Intrapersonal, Interpersonal, and Transpersonal Implications*; *Cyberpsychology: An Introduction to Human–Computer Interaction*; and *Psychological Aspects of Cyberspace: Theory, Research, Applications*. Mobile phones are becoming the most ubiquitous technology in human history and mobile phone behavior is becoming one of the most important social phenomena of the twenty-first century. While the next major wave of the psychology of mobile phones is rapidly forming, Cambridge University Press should be leading the wave again. Thus, I sent my pre-proposal inquiry to Cambridge University Press in January 2015. After just two hours, I received an enthusiastic e-mail from Senior Editor David Repetto. This eemail led to the pleasant journey of completing this book in 2017.

Many excellent books on mobile phone behavior are already currently available, taking different perspectives, targeting different audiences, and presenting at different levels. These existing books can be grouped into the three major types: (1) scholarly monographs on specific topics of mobile phone behavior, such as Katz's *Perpetual Contact: Mobile Communication, Private Talk, Public Performance* and *Magic in the Air: Mobile Communication and the Transformation of Social Life*, Ling's *Taken for Grantedness:*

The Embedding of Mobile Communication into Society, Ling and Campbell's *Mobile Communication: Bringing Us Together and Tearing Us Apart*, Baron's *Always On: Language in an Online and Mobile World*, Goggin and Hjorth's *The Routledge Companion to Mobile Media*, and Carlo and Schram's *Cell Phones: Invisible Hazards in the Wireless Age*; (2) general references on mobile phone behavior, such as Katz's *Handbook of Mobile Communication Studies* and Dushinski's *The Mobile Marketing Handbook*; and (3) technology books on how to design and use mobile phones, such as Felkers' *Android Application Development for Dummies,* Muir's *iPhone for Seniors for Dummies,* and Meurling and Jeans' *The Mobile Phone Book: The Invention of the Mobile Telephone Industry.* In addition, there are new books in press or under development (e.g., the *Mobile Communication Research Series* which Ling and Campbell have been editing). All of these indicate that the field of mobile phone behavior has been growing exponentially. I highly recommend these excellent books in order for us to stand on the shoulders of giants. This is the broad intellectual context that a reader should know when using this book, which features introductory levels, comprehensive coverage, and interdisciplinary orientation.

Looking back at this pleasant journey, I would like to acknowledge those who have made invaluable contributions to the completion of this book.

Intellectually, the book was deeply influenced by a few great thinkers of our time: (1) Daniel Kahneman's theory is one of the primary analytic frameworks used in the book to analyze mobile phone behavior. A brief conversation with him on April 16, 2008 when he gave a series of talks at Harvard inspired and motivated me to study online judgements and mobile phone judgements as he indicated that it was an emerging area and the research was still limited. (2) The complex system theory by Yaneer Bar-Yam at New England Complexity Institute (my postdoctoral mentor) and the system dynamics by Jay Forrest and John Sterman at the MIT Sloan School of Management (the two instructors of multiple system dynamics courses I audited at Sloan) is another major analytic framework used in the book. (3) Donald Norman's ground-breaking book, *Psychology of Everyday Things*, taught me how extremely important it is to develop deep scientific insights from everyday observations to psychological research and how particularly useful it is to write a serious scientific book in a relaxing way. (4) Kurt Fischer and Catherine Snow, my mentors at Harvard Graduate School of Education, supported my ideas of examining modern technologies and human development from the very beginning. Without their encouragement, I might still be searching for a dream research topic in the darkness. (5) Martin Cooper, the Father of Mobile Phones, is a real role model to me, personally and professionally. In his fabulous Forward written for the *Encyclopedia of Mobile Phone Behavior*, he wrote a short story about a poor woman in an Indian village. The woman first borrowed some money to buy a mobile phone, and then lent it to other farmers to call the neighboring villages to find the best markets for their farm goods. For the first time in my life, I have learned how powerful a small story like this could be to help understand the complexity of mobile phone behavior.

I am a student of mobile phone behavior. My understanding of mobile phone behavior has been developing as a result of learning from many leading scholars in the field, including: Robert Atkinson, Naomi Baron, Joël Billieux, Karel Brookhuis, Jennings Bryant, Heidi Campbell, Scott Campbell, Elisabeth Cardis, Susan Carey, Judith Carta, Jonathan Donner, David Finkelhor, Xiaolan Fu, Cynthia Garcia Coll, Rui Gaspar, Susan Gelman, Patricia Greenfield, Mark Griffiths, Leslie Haddon, Lennart Hardell, Larissa Hjorth, Randi Hjorthol, Gwo-Jen Hwang, Reynol Junco, Sara Kiesler, Robert Kraut, Amanda Lenhart, Louis Leung, Sonia Livingstone, Jenny Radesky, Donald Redelmeier, Michael Repacholi, Eric Rice, Martin Röösli, Matthew Schneps, David Strayer, Kaveri Subrahmanyam, John Traxler, Marion Underwood, Patti Valkenburg, Dan Wang, Ellen Wartella, Janis Wolak, Clare Wood, Heng Xu, Kimberly Young, Tingshao Zhu, and especially James Katz at Boston University and Rich Ling at Nanyang Technical University, the two pioneering scholars in the field. To all of them, and to many others not listed here, I personally want to extend my heartfelt thanks.

I wish to express my profound appreciation to five anonymous reviewers for their first-class reviews of my book proposal. Their insightful reviews have shaped the book in multiple significant ways, from overall book designs to various technical details, which can be grouped into four categories: (1) The overall design. The reviewers stressed the importance of focusing the book on *behavioral* and psychological aspects of mobile phones rather than on "too much discussion of actual mobile phones." They recommended "packaging this area of research and theory from *a perspective that is new*" and expanding beyond the "usual suspects" of just putting together the edited collections in order to include more scholarly breadth in the materials available for teaching and research. They analyzed the *pros and cons* of developing and marketing the book as a textbook, a monograph, or a hybrid one. (2) The pedagogical features. The reviewers emphasized the importance of *pedagogical* features of a book to make the publication "an intuitive and educational read," with one consistent voice and various effective uses of introduction, diagrams, images, cases, and summaries. (3) The comparative perspective. The reviewers recommended *comparing* similarities and differences among different modern technologies and technology-based behavior (e.g., comparing the prevalence rates among all the modern technologies) in order to effectively address unique features of mobile phones and mobile phone behavior. (4) The technical treatment. The reviewers discussed possible treatment of various *technical* issues, such as how to accurately estimate the number of mobile phone users, what the logical starting point of mobile phone behavior should be, and how to include the important topic of privacy and security. I have taken all of these excellent recommendations to heart and worked hard to implement them as much as I can. If I find out who they are in the future, I will buy each of them a large beer!

I would like to thank many people at Cambridge University Press who contributed directly to the completion of the book: Alexandra Poreda, Jane Bowbrick, Joshua Penney, especially Dave Repetto for his extraordinary enthusiasm, trust, and wisdom, Bethany Johnson for her exceptional production management, and Sophie Rosinke for her outstanding editing abilities.

I must say a special thank you to my wonderful doctoral students: (1) Holly Meredith for her extremely careful proofreading and particularly insightful comments on the entire book. Without her meticulous corrections of many errors and mistakes, this book simply would have not been completed; (2) Samantha Bordoff for her assistance in completing the references and indexing; (3) Sung Yong Park for his excellent work in searching the existing literature on human behavior with telephones, television, computers, the Internet, and mobile phones; (4) Quan Chen for her inspiring studies on multitasking when driving and learning and for our collaborative work on the science of mobile phone behavior; (5) Fusun Sahin for our collaborative work on mobile assessment; (6) Dr. Lai-Lei Lou for our collaborative work on the possible links between mobile phones and brain cancers; as well as (7) Dr. Qiufeng Gao at Southern China Normal University for our collaborative work on mobile phone school policy. It is my true fortune to work with them and learn from them all.

I also want to thank many students, friends, and relatives for their quick responses to my questions about their understanding of mobile phone behavior. Their intuitive and authentic responses form the extremely useful baseline knowledge of ordinary people and an important part of the book.

Finally, I would like to thank my family, WQY, YAM, ZXS, ZKX, YY, YH, BJ, LK, and especially ZJK, Riv, and Sisi, for their support during the special process of finishing this book while fighting against unusual odds.

Zheng Yan
Newton
14 October 2016

CHAPTER I

The Science of Mobile Phone Behavior

Outline

1. *Surprising Responses*
2. *Mobile Phones*
   2.1 *Classic Mobile Phones*
   2.2 *Modern Mobile Phones*
   2.3 *Future Mobile Phones*
3. *Mobile Phone Behavior*
   3.1 *The Human Side*
   3.2 *A Special Human Behavior*
   3.3 *The Four Basic Elements*
   3.4 *The Four Complex Systems*
   3.5 *Diverse Contexts*
4. *The Science of Mobile Phone Behavior*
   4.1 *Mobile Phone Behavior Research*
   4.2 *The Intellectual Childhood (1991–2005)*
   4.3 *The Intellectual Adolescence (2005–2015)*
5. *Understanding Mobile Phone Behavior*
   5.1 *Target Readers*
   5.2 *Intellectual Goals and Content Organization*
   5.3 *The Style*

1. Surprising Responses

One afternoon in 2015, I received an email inviting me to give a talk to a group of graduate students about mobile phone behavior. This was the very first time I had received such an invitation to talk about mobile phone behavior. Since this is my current research focus, I accepted the invitation with great pleasure. In preparing for this talk, I found that I knew little about how much my audience would know about mobile phone behavior.

Thus, I started my talk by first asking participants whether they had mobile phones and whether they used them daily. Everyone immediately raised their hands, indicating that each of them had a mobile phone and used it daily. Then I asked them to quickly write down their initial thoughts about a few brief questions so that I could learn their initial knowledge about mobile phone behavior, adjust my speech plan based on their knowledge, and warm them up for my talk on mobile phone behavior.

The talk went well and we had an interesting discussion about mobile phone behavior research. After the talk, I read their responses again and summarized them as follows: (1) When they were asked to quickly write down two key features of mobile phones, the majority of them indicated calling and texting. (2) When they were asked to quickly list two to three examples of mobile phone behavior, the majority of them listed sending text messages, looking up emails, and using Facebook. (3) When they were asked to estimate how many journal articles have been published on mobile phone behavior, the majority of them came up with a number ranging from 6 to 500 with an average of 173.

These responses were both interesting and surprising to me for several reasons. First, although I have been studying mobile phone behavior for several years and at the time of my talk had just finished editing the *Encyclopedia of Mobile Phone Behavior*[1] a few weeks prior, this was the first time I was able to explicitly see what people's *intuitive* knowledge about mobile phone behavior actually looked like. Obviously, these were very quick and informal responses from a group of graduate students. However, these quick and informal responses delivered authentic and interesting information: how much ordinary people may intuitively know about mobile phones, mobile behavior, and mobile behavior research.

Second, although we all know that many people have their own mobile phones and they use their mobile phones every day, looking at these responses, I was quite surprised to see how *limited* the knowledge was that some ordinary people had about their mobile phones and their mobile phone behavior. They tended to substantially oversimplify the complexity of mobile phone behavior. As we will first discuss in this introduction chapter and throughout this book later on, modern mobile phones, mobile phone behavior, and mobile phone behavior research are much more complex than we thought. After the talk, I had several more opportunities to communicate with multiple institutions, groups, and individuals

---

[1] Yan, Z. (ed.). (2015). *Encyclopedia of Mobile Phone Behavior*. Hershey, PA: IGI Global.

informally about their intuitive knowledge about mobile phone behavior. The results remained quite similar: there is substantial oversimplification of the complexity of mobile phone behavior, despite the diverse backgrounds, needs, and knowledge that people have. This eventually became the primary motivation, central theme, and major goal of writing this book: to describe, analyze, synthesize, and explain the complexity of mobile phone behavior that is related to a pocket-sized mobile phone.

Third, now we might wonder *why* some people tend to oversimplify the complexity of mobile phone behavior. There could be different theories and speculations to explain this phenomenon. Based on the Nobel Laureate Daniel Kahneman's intuitive judgement theory:[2] (1) people think with two systems – intuitive thinking (System 1) and rational thinking (System 2); (2) intuitive thinking is limited due to various cognitive heuristics and biases; and (3) people tend to think intuitively in their daily lives often, but can think rationally only after making extra efforts or improving existing knowledge. In the context of mobile phone behavior, people may develop their intuitive thinking based on their daily use of mobile phones. However, their intuitive thinking about mobile phone behavior is limited due to various cognitive biases. Effortful learning and training is needed to develop rational thinking about mobile phone behavior in order to develop an understanding and appreciation of its unusual complexity. Thus, in this book, we will use the concepts of intuitive thinking (System 1) and rational thinking (System 2) as the main conceptual framework to analyze mobile phone behavior.

In the text that follows in this introductory chapter, we will briefly discuss some basic knowledge about mobile phones, mobile phone behavior, and mobile phone behavior research, and provide an overview of the book, including two primary goals to achieve after reading the book. This is to set the stage for further in-depth discussions of various topics in the entire book to reveal the complexity of mobile phone behavior.

2. Mobile Phones

In 490 BC, Pheidippides, a Greek professional courier, ran over 42 kilometers from the battlefield of Marathon to Athens to deliver a message of the Greek victory over Persia. At the end of his running, he said: "Joy to you, we've won!" Right after that, he collapsed and died.

---

[2] Kahneman, D. (2011). *Thinking, Fast and Slow.* New York: Farrar, Straus and Giroux.

In 1876, 2,366 years later, Alexander Graham Bell, an American inventor and then a professor of Vocal Physiology and Elocution at Boston University, sat in his laboratory and made the first successful telephone call to his research associate, Thomas Watson, and said: "Mr. Watson, come here, I want to see you." Since then, humans have used telephones to deliver voice messages across a long distance effectively and efficiently, rather than having someone run a long distance to deliver a message.

In 1973, almost 100 years later, Martin Cooper, another American inventor and then the head of Motorola's communications systems division, stood on the Sixth Avenue of Manhattan, New York, and made the first mobile phone call in public to Joel Engel, then the head of research at AT&T's Bell Labs, and said: "Joel, this is Marty. I'm calling you from a cell phone, a real handheld portable cell phone." After that, only forty-two years later, worldwide mobile phone subscriptions had grown to 7.1 billion, with a penetration rate of 96.8 per cent.[3]

The mobile phone held in the right hand of Martin Cooper was DynaTAC, one of the earliest classic mobile phones. Nowadays, mobile phones have remarkably wide variations. We hear various names, such as basic phones, feature phones, smartphones, cellular phones, cell phones, VoIP phones, satellite phones, or app phones. These names represent various features of mobile phones and can generally be used interchangeably. We see different brands on the market, such as Nokia 3310, Moto 360, iPhone 6, BlackBerry Passport, Samsung Galaxy, or Xiaomi Mi4. Each is made by different companies, such as Samsung, Nokia, Apple, LG, ZTE, and Huawei. We have mobile phones connecting with different cellular networks (e.g., 1G, 2G, 3G, 4G) or Wi-Fi networks (e.g., regular station-based Wi-Fi, campus-wide Wi-Fi, city-wide Wi-Fi, ad hoc Wi-Fi). We know millions of apps from the Apple App Store, Google Play, Windows Phone Store, or BlackBerry App World to perform unlimited specific functions, such as emailing, maintaining a calendar, looking up stock information, weather, and news, as well as apps for health care, finance, gaming, reading, cooking, banking, fitness, navigation, travel, task management, getting a taxi, and almost any kind of app we can imagine. To know what mobile phones are and what basic features mobile phones have, we should examine mobile phones at different stages of the mobile phone history and understand the similarities and differences between classic mobile phones and modern mobile phones.

---

[3] See www.itu.int/net/pressoffice/press_releases/2015/17.aspx#.V_j1rcm2LeY.

2.1   Classic Mobile Phones

Although such a wide variety of mobile phones exist, each and every classic mobile phone, frequently called basic phones, such as DynaTAC, Nokia 3310, and Moto 300, share two basic features.

The first feature can simply be called *phone* – the second part of the term *mobile phone*. That is, a mobile phone must have a function of communication, either voice-based like a traditional telephone or text-based like a traditional telegraph. In this regard, mobile phones are essentially a technology of communication.

The second feature can be called *mobile* – the other part of the term *mobile phone*. Mobile generally means that a mobile phone needs to be movable so that people can carry it with them and use it freely in a large area. This feature of mobility requires at least four elements: (1) it must be able to conveniently move with users themselves rather than with other moving objects such as a police car or an airplane; (2) it must be small and light enough for a user to carry it; (3) it must be able to have wireless access to both strong base stations and reliable cellular or Wi-Fi networks through sufficient and efficient radio frequency spectrums so that low-power radio signals can be sent or received by thousands of users even in peak use time; and (4) it must have a small but powerful battery to provide power for long-term use.

These two basic features are useful for distinguishing a mobile phone from other various relevant technologies (e.g., mobile phones vs. cordless phones), clarifying various existing confusions among ordinary mobile phone users (e.g., mobile phones vs. automobile phones), and providing a good conceptual base for further research and application (e.g., When should we consider the starting point of mobile phones to be? Should we include both mobile phones and cordless phones together to study the possible cancer-causing effects of mobile phones?).

For instance, DynaTAC is a mobile phone because it has the two basic features. However, a traditional landline phone is a phone but not a mobile phone because it is not mobile and wireless. A cordless phone is a wireless phone but not a mobile phone because it does not connect with the cellular networks or with the Internet and can only be used to make calls within a small area. Automobile phones that are used in police cars or ambulances are not mobile phones because these phones are only mobile in the sense that you can drive around with them, but they are actually fixed in the vehicle and are too large and heavy to put into a pocket. A desktop computer is not a mobile phone since it does not have the two basic features, despite it often having Internet access and the ability to send or receive emails. A pager is not a mobile phone because while it is portable, it does not really have the feature of voice or text communications. A television is neither mobile nor does it yet have a phone function, but it can actually become a feature of a mobile phone if it is integrated into a mobile phone, via various TV apps. A GPS device is not a mobile phone. While it is wirelessly connected to a satellite, its connection is one-way and is not interconnected with the public phone network. However, if it is integrated into a mobile phone, it becomes a feature of a mobile phone. A gaming console may be portable and interconnected to cellular networks (i.e., mobile gaming) or the Internet (e.g., online gaming), but its primary function is not for communication. However, if it is integrated into a mobile phone, it becomes a feature of mobile phone games. As for a computing tablet, it could be considered as a hybrid of a mobile phone and a computer. Given that a mobile phone normally has various computational functions (e.g., playing games) and a computer normally has various communicational functions (e.g., posting on Facebook), there is essentially no difference between a large mobile phone and a small tablet, as long as they meet the above two basic features.

2.2   *Modern Mobile Phones*

From DynaTAC or MicroTAC, the earliest classic mobile phones, to the iPhone 6 Plus or Samsung Galaxy S6 4G LTE, the most modern mobile phones, there are substantial differences. While modern mobile phones still share the two basic features, mobile and phone, they have been transformed into multi-functional, personal technologies.

According to Clayton Christensen,[4] the world's foremost authority on disruptive innovation, there exist four types of innovation: (1) Sustaining Innovation (it is expected and has no large effects, e.g., Microsoft produced Encarta as a digital encyclopedia to compete against *Encyclopædia Britannica* as the best print encyclopedia; (2) Evolutionary Innovation (it is expected and has large effects, e.g., fuel injection has become the current fuel delivery system in car engines to replace carburetors as the less efficient one); (3) Revolutionary Innovation (it is unexpected, but does not have large effects, e.g., the Concorde aircraft is supersonic, but ended its service

---

[4] Christensen, C. (2013). *The Innovator's Dilemma: When New Technologies Cause Great Firms to Fail.* Brighton, MA: Harvard Business Review Press.

in 2003); and (4) Disruptive Innovation (it is unexpected and has large effects, e.g., e-mail after postal mail, digital photography after chemical photography, and mobile phones after fixed line phones). Thus, we can consider that modern mobile phones are the new technology with two disruptive innovations.

First, *multi-function* technology. Due to the technology advancements, the modern mobile phones, often called smartphones, have become much more powerful than the classic mobile phones. This is achieved by (1) adding various new hardware devices such as cameras, GPS, and sensors, (2) having millions of new apps, and (3) linking with various new networks such as 4G or Wi-Fi. These so-called "smartphones" create additional capabilities besides the two basic functions. As a result, a small phone is no longer just a single voice-based communication tool with good mobility, but rather a strong technology that has multiple functions. It essentially integrates communicational technologies (e.g., a telephone from which one user can call or text to another), informational technologies (e.g., an Internet application that allows one user to browse the Internet), and computational technologies (e.g., a personal computer that allows one user to generate a file in Word) into a complex platform within a small size. Thus, a mobile phone may be able to identify its location using global positioning, may include a camera and various sensors, and may have substantial computing and memory abilities to make the device more useful to the user.

Second, *personal technology*. Along with the new feature of a multi-function technology, modern mobile phones become much more mobile in the sense that they do not limit the mobility of their users and eventually become much more personal. They have become cheaper, smaller, thinner, and faster, with a better interface. They are more useful and have more efficient batteries that can be recharged wirelessly. They have become much "smarter," with new sensors, new CPU chips, and new screens. Thus, mobile phone users start to build strong physical, cognitive, social, and emotional bonds with their mobile phones. Mobile phones can be used almost anywhere, at any time, by anyone, for anything.

As we can see, the two basic features of a classic mobile phone, *phone* and *mobile*, are closely related to the two advanced features of a modern mobile phone, *multi-function* and *personal*. It is extremely important for mobile phone users to know not only the basic features, but also the significant changes from the basic features to the advanced features. Mobile phones are no longer just mobile phones, but have evolved and transformed into a multi-function, personal technology. Knowing these core changes enables us to see the current status of mobile phone use, the latest developments of mobile phones, wide variations of the mobile phone, actual impacts on humans, and tremendous potentials for mobile phone use.

2.3 *Future Mobile Phones*

If classic mobile phones are a communication tool with mobility, and modern mobile phones are a powerful multi-function personal technology, we might wonder: What will be the key feature of future mobile phones?

Right now, at least two major features have emerged. First, mobile phones are becoming a powerful remote control or a command center for the Internet of Everything. Second, mobile phones are becoming more wearable. An iWatch is a good example. In the next fifty years or so, with mobile phones becoming much more powerful and much more wearable, future mobile phones might possibly become a powerful artificial organ or the second brain of human beings for the first time in human history. The human body has various biological organs such as ears, eyes, heart, brain, arms, and legs. Future mobile phones might be so seamlessly personalized with human bodies that they become a special organ, and so powerful for serving human needs that they become a highly complex artificial technology. They will build on the current multiple functions and personal technologies. They might have strong artificial cognitive intelligence, artificial social intelligence, and artificial emotional intelligence. They might have a wide variety of modern sensors to receive input seamlessly and automatically, develop more computational capacities and various apps to store and analyze big data, and become a command execution center to effectively and efficiently perform almost every function for humans. Wherever the future might lead humans, one thing is clear: mobile phones will no longer feature just two functions, calling and texting.

3. Mobile Phone Behavior

What we have discussed in the previous section is about what mobile phones are rather than what mobile phone behavior is or how humans interact with mobile phones or how mobile phones affect human life. What is mobile phone behavior? How are mobile phones and mobile phone behavior related to each other? Is it true that mobile phone behavior is simply about calling parents or texting friends, as shown in those informal responses from the graduate students? What are other kinds of mobile phone behavior? To answer these kinds of questions we might have, let us discuss five core concepts of mobile phone behavior in the following five subsections.

3.1   The Human Side

As mentioned earlier, the mobile phone DynaTAC used by Martin Cooper in 1973 is among the earliest mobile phones made by Motorola. Besides the mobile phone, there is much more involved in the first mobile phone call made in public in 1973, including the users of the mobile phone (the caller Martin Cooper to the invisible receiver Joel Engel), the action of making the call (e.g., dialing, walking while calling, purpose and content of the phone conversation), and the effect of the call (e.g., immediate and historical effects on human beings; possible cognitive, social, and emotional effects on Martin and Joel), as well as the context of the call (e.g., public relationships, media communications, research and development of mobile phones, the specific setting of Manhattan). These are all related to mobile phone use or mobile phone behavior, which is the human side of mobile phones rather than the technology side of mobile phones themselves.

As shown in Figure 1.1, the basic relationship between mobile phones and mobile phone behavior is analogous to that of a car and driving a car, a TV and watching a TV, a computer and using a computer. The former is about how an engineer invents and develops a technology – the technology side, and the latter is about how a user accesses and uses a technology – the human side. If the last section focuses on mobile phones as a powerful personal technology – the technology side of mobile phones, this section focuses on mobile phone use as a complex human behavior – the human side of mobile phones.

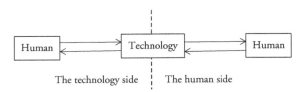

Figure 1.1   The Basic Relationship between Technologies and Humans

3.2   A Special Human Behavior

Researchers have studied various types of human behavior, such as health behavior, organization behavior, entrepreneurial behavior, violent behavior, economic behavior, sexual behavior, consumer behavior, social behavior, motor behavior, aggressive behavior, addictive behavior, machine behavior, cyber behavior (some of these are actually names or parts of names of academic journals). Behavioral science essentially is an interdisciplinary field that examines human behavior across various disciplines, including psychology, sociology, biology, medicine, law, business, education, criminology, neuroscience, psychiatry, economics, anthropology, and so forth.

As one specific type of human behavior, mobile phone behavior can broadly refer to any physical, cognitive, social, or emotional activity that humans engage in while using mobile phones. As observed in our daily lives and reported in the existing research literature, there exists a wide variety of mobile phone behavior, such as the use of mobile phones by people who are deaf or have dyslexia, sexting and its effects on children's social development, m-gaming, using mobile phones during disasters, mobile phones and sleep disturbances, m-consulting, mobile phones and brain tumors, calling and texting while driving, mobile phone distraction, mobile phone addiction, m-therapy, m-shopping, m-banking, m-learning, and m-voting. These types of mobile phone behavior will be systematically discussed in the subsequent nine chapters.

3.3   The Four Basic Elements

As shown in Figure 1.2, despite the extremely wide variety, mobile phone behavior primarily concerns four basic elements: mobile phone users, mobile phone technologies, mobile phone activities, and mobile phone effects. Based on the four elements, mobile phone behavior could be

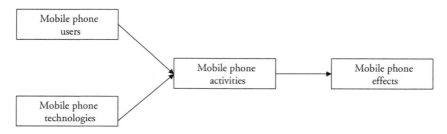

Figure 1.2   The Four Basic Elements of Mobile Phone Behavior

categorized into four general types: (1) user-based mobile phone behavior; (2) technology-based mobile phone behavior; (3) activity-based mobile phone behavior; and (4) effect-based mobile phone behavior. Extensive research has been conducted to study each of the four types of mobile phone behavior, accumulating scientific knowledge about mobile phone behavior, and revealing the extreme complexity of mobile phone behavior.

3.4   The Four Complex Systems

The four basic features actually concern four complex systems. In the real-life world, there exist different mobile phone users (e.g., ordinary users and people with special needs), different mobile phone technologies (e.g., text messenger, GPS, cameras, apps), different activities (e.g., m-learning, m-shopping, m-therapy), and different effects (e.g., positive and negative effects on human cognition or emotion). These four complex systems lead to a wide variety of mobile phone behavior among human beings. In this book, four specific chapters (i.e., Mobile Phone Users, Mobile Phone Technologies, Mobile Phone Activities, and Mobile Phone Effects) focus on the four types of mobile phone behavior (i.e., user-based, technology-based, activity-based, and effect-based mobile phone behavior).

3.5   Diverse Contexts

Mobile phone behavior always takes place in various contexts of human activities, such as daily settings, medicine, business, education, justice, agriculture, government, arts, and religions. Thus, the four complex systems (i.e., users, technologies, activities, and effects) apply to various contexts, generating an extremely wide variety of mobile phone behavior in the real world and making mobile phone behavior particularly complicated. In this book, four specific chapters focus on various types of mobile phone behavior in four contexts (i.e., mobile phone behavior in medicine, business, education, and daily life) as selected examples, illustrating complex mobile phone behavior in diverse contexts.

4.   The Science of Mobile Phone Behavior

4.1   Mobile Phone Behavior Research

Given the complexity of mobile phone behavior, how much do we know about it? As you may recall, the students responded to the question of how many journal articles have been published on mobile phone behavior and the majority of them came up with a number ranging from 6 to 500, with an average of 173. Is this correct? Is it important to know this question and how it is related to the science of mobile phone behavior? What is the science of mobile phone behavior? Is it a new and emerging field of study? These questions will be discussed below.

First, we can perform an initial database search to quickly estimate the general scope of the literature on mobile phone behavior. Among three excellent databases, PsycINFO, PubMed, and WOS, it is desirable to choose PubMed for the first search for two reasons. First, PsycINFO is produced by the American Psychological Association and focuses more on the psychology literature with nearly 3 million records, and thus it is a little too narrow. WOS is produced by Thomson Reuters and focuses more on the science, social science, arts, and humanities literature, with nearly 100 million records, and thus it is a little too broad. PubMed is produced by the National Institutes of Health and focuses on the life sciences and biomedical sciences, including the behavioral sciences, with 25 million records, relatively close to the interdisciplinary nature of the science of mobile phone behavior, especially given the particularly extensive literature on the impacts of mobile phones on human health. Second, besides the desirable coverage of PubMed, it also has a desirable technical feature to visually demonstrate the publication record change over years easily and quickly. This feature can be used to analyze and compare growth trends of given research areas.

As of April 2016, if we use the keyword of *mobile phone* to perform an initial search in the PubMed database, there are a total of 8,938 publications between 1992 and 2016, including 809 clinical trial articles and 671 review articles. Furthermore, as shown in Figure 1.3, based on the data from PubMed, the number of publications rapidly increased over the years, especially after 2010. Due to the publication lag and especially the database entry lag, the data of 2015 and 2016 are not complete and should be much more if we check the data after 2016 or 2017. It is clear that the students' estimation of 197 total publications is much lower than the 8,938 identified publications in PubMed, let alone the exponential growth trend in the past five years.

Second, the number of journal article publications is a basic and important indication of the development of a given field of study. Of course, there are other indicators, such as citation rates or impact factors. Bibliometrics or scientometrics are the methods often used by scholars to study various indications related to scientific publications. As a basic indicator of scientific research, the number of journal article publications

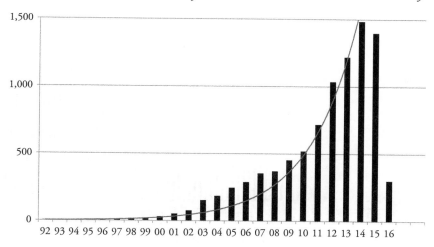

Figure 1.3   Initial Search of Published Journal Articles on Mobile Phones

on mobile phone behavior can be used to answer various interesting questions: How many researchers in the world have been studying mobile phone behavior? Who are the leading experts in the field? What topics have been heavily studied or hardly examined? What are the leading journals in the field? What are general and specific trends of scientific outcomes? One thing is very clear: if an area of study has only 197 publications, one would very likely conclude that this area of study is still in its infancy. However, if an area of study has 8,938 publications, one would very likely believe that this area of study is quite established.

To make a comparison, when we use the keyword *television* to perform an initial search in PubMed, 35,227 journal articles have been published since 1922, with 1,794 clinical trials and 1,339 review articles. This area of research is still growing, but shows some sign of slowing down in the past five years (see Figure 1.4).

When we use the keyword *computer*, an initial search in PubMed results in 644,634 journal articles having been published since 1922, with 22,216 clinical trials and 34,913 review articles. This area of research, as shown in PubMed, is still growing strongly (see Figure 1.5).

When we use the keyword *Internet*, an initial search in PubMed results in 79,171 journal articles having been published since 1947, with 3,169 clinical trials and 7,239 review articles. This area of research, shown in PubMed, started growing very strongly in 1995 and is still growing strongly (see Figure 1.6).

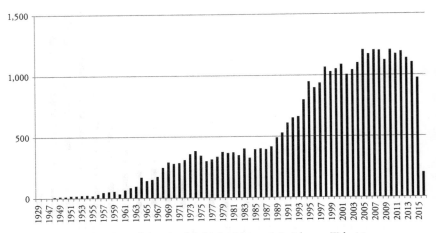

Figure 1.4   Initial Search of Published Journal Articles on Television

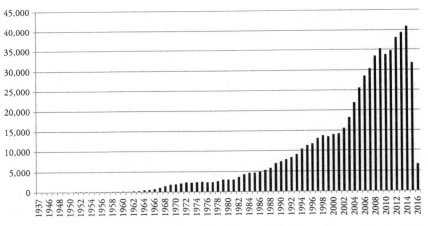

Figure 1.5   Initial Search of Published Journal Articles on Computers

While these comparisons are initial and rudimentary, we can make two basic observations from the figures of growth trends of the four areas of research regarding the behavior science literature of four modern technologies. First, the literature on mobile phone behavior is relatively young compared to the literature on televisions, computers, and the Internet. Second, the literature on mobile phone behavior already has a good knowledge foundation and has been growing particularly fast since 2010.

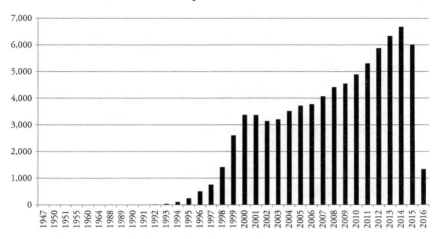

Figure 1.6   Initial Search of Published Journal Articles on the Internet

It is certainly not in its infancy with less than 200 articles, as estimated by some graduate students.

Third, to describe or analyze the science of mobile phone behavior, it is useful to do so from a historical perspective or developmental perspective.

A person's life generally consists of three major developmental stages: childhood, adolescence, and adulthood. Childhood (0–10 years old) is the initial stage of human development for individuals to develop fundamental physical, linguistic, cognitive, and social abilities. Adulthood (after 20 years old) is the final stage for individuals to perform independently in society with matured physical, cognitive, and social abilities. Adolescence (11–20 years old) is a transitional stage between childhood and adulthood. Taking the perspective of human development, metaphorically, we could consider the science of mobile phone behavior as growing from childhood into adolescence. This is because the field has developed a fundamental knowledge and methodology base in the past twenty-five years of its childhood (e.g., currently ten to twenty academic journals publishing mobile phone behavior articles), but has not yet fully matured intellectually and is not yet widely recognized as an independent field of research. For example, there is no one single entry covering mobile phone behavior among the 4,000 entries of the *International Encyclopedia of the Social & Behavioral Sciences.*[5]

---

[5] Smelser, N. J. and Baltes, P. B. (eds.). (2001). *International Encyclopedia of the Social & Behavioral Sciences.* Amsterdam: Elsevier.

And one entry was included in the second edition of the *International Encyclopedia of the Social & Behavioral Sciences* edited by James Wright and published in 2015.[6] The entry title is "The Mobile Communication" and was written by Rich Ling, a renowned scholar in the field. Thus, we would argue that the field is currently in the transitional stage of adolescence. One useful way to collect evidence and substantiate this assessment is to examine both quantitatively and qualitatively the current status of scholarly journals focusing on mobile phone behavior.

4.2   The Intellectual Childhood (1991–2005)

The science of mobile phone behavior has a history of nearly twenty-five years since Karel Brookhuis and his collaborators' article,[7] The effects of mobile telephoning on driving performance, was published in *Accident Analysis & Prevention*. Like Sherry Turkle's seminal book *Second Self*,[8] marking the beginning of cyber behavior research, Brookhuis's article is the first published study on mobile phone use from the perspective of the behavioral sciences. Twelve adults participated in this three-week study. Each of them drove 1 hour every weekday. They used two modified Volvos as well as multiple measures, including lane tracking for lateral position, event recorder for a keyboard input, electrocardiogram for cardiac inter-beat-intervals, a video camera for rearview mirror check, potentiometer, speed radar, and distance laser. By comparing driving with and without using mobile phones, they found: (1) differences in turn control for light traffic, but no difference for heavy traffic; (2) no difference in steering control for light traffic, but differences were found for heavy traffic; (3) no difference in rearview mirror checking for light traffic, but differences were found for heavy traffic; (4) no difference in car following for both light and heavy traffic, but there was a speed change delay of 600 ms and braking delay of 130 ms while using mobile phones; and (5) higher heart rate due to mental workload for both light and heavy traffic while using mobile phones. This first empirical study demonstrated two important features in the very beginning of mobile phone use research. First, it chose an urgent and timely issue. It focused on driving safety rather than other common topics such as daily usage. It was published as early as

---

[6] Wright, J. D. (2015). *International Encyclopedia of the Social and Behavioral Sciences* (2nd edn.). Amsterdam: Elsevier.

[7] Brookhuis, K. A., de Vries, G., and de Waard, D. (1991). The effects of mobile telephoning on driving performance. *Accident Analysis & Prevention*, 23(4): 309–316.

[8] Turkle, S. (2005). *The Second Self: Computers and the Human Spirit.* Cambridge, MA: MIT Press.

1991 when the mobile phone was just starting to be used by ordinary users in developed countries. Second, it used rigorous experimental methods to collect multiple data rather than questionnaire surveys or other commonly observed data collection methods.

4.3 The Intellectual Adolescence (2005–2015)

Since 2005, the science of mobile phone behavior has been growing exponentially. To further estimate the scope of the research literature in this field, a few years ago, we conducted a scoping review entitled "The science of cell phone use: Its past, present, and future."[9] In this review, we searched nineteen databases, including PsycINFO, PubMed, and ERIC. Keywords such as cell phone use, mobile phone use, cellular phone use, smartphone use, iPhone use, behavior, and behavioral science were searched in different variations and combinations. In addition, we also conducted a dialog search with senior university librarians to confirm our search results and contacted leading experts for their guidance and consultation. Based on several specific exclusion and inclusion criteria, we identified and confirmed a total of 3,305 publications from 1991 to 2013 that explicitly examined the use of mobile phones across various disciplines in the behavioral sciences, such as medicine, education, psychology, sociology, political science, and business. In 2011 alone, for example, 455 journal articles on mobile phone behavior were published. Major research journals that have published studies on mobile phone behavior include *Accident Analysis and Prevention, Human Factors, Traffic Injury Prevention, Computers in Human Behavior,* and *Computers and Education.* New journals exclusively publishing mobile phone behavior research are *Mobile Media & Communication,* the *International Journal of Mobile Communications, Wireless Communications and Mobile Computing,* and the *International Journal of Interactive Mobile Technologies.* On the basis of quality, quantity, and influence of their work, leading researchers in the field include James Katz at Boston University, David Strayer at the University of Utah, Naomi Baron at American University, Rich Ling at Telenor R&D and the University of Michigan, Scott Campbell at the University of Michigan, Nenagh Kemp at the University of Tasmania of Australia, Anne McCartt at the Insurance Institute for Highway Safety of the United

---

[9] Yan, Z., Chen, Q., and Yu, C. (2013). "The science of cell phone use: Its past, present, and future." *International Journal of Cyber Behavior, Psychology and Learning (IJCBPL),* 3(1): 7–18.

States, and Mike Sharples at the University of Birmingham of the United Kingdom.

For twenty-five years, researchers in ergonomics, medicine, sociology, education, psychology, and various other disciplines have been extensively examining how people use mobile phones and how mobile phone use influences people's lives. As a result, the science of mobile phone behavior has produced broad and profound social impacts and implications for a wide variety of areas, such as mobile phone use and brain tumors, phoning during driving, mobile phone distraction, mobile phone addiction, m-health, m-business, and m-learning.

The twenty-five-year-long history, current high productivity, and particularly promising future in the field of mobile phone behavior research justifies a multi-volume encyclopedia project that synthesizes significant contributions of mobile phone research to the behavioral sciences.

The *Encyclopedia of Mobile Phone Behavior* was published in 2015 by IGI Global. Nearly 300 authors from almost forty countries across five continental regions (Africa, the Americas, Asia, Europe, and Oceania) have contributed to the *Encyclopedia*. Among these authors, besides pioneering and leading experts, the majority of them are active researchers who have published their empirical research in some of the best journals in more than ten different scientific disciplines, such as psychology, medicine, business, education, communication, sociology, economics, political science, law, and computer science. Through this *Encyclopedia*, these researchers disseminated their research work to a worldwide readership and at the same time more readers across the world can really benefit from their wisdom, knowledge, and expertise. Readers will be able to know about both pioneering scholars and leading scholars of the science of mobile phone behavior and the new generation of promising researchers across the world.

The *Encyclopedia* is intended to produce a multi-volume authoritative reference to synthesize the accumulated knowledge of mobile phone behavior research. Specifically, it includes 120 chapters that are arranged alphabetically with twelve major category sections. It consists of four major parts: (1) an introduction to the science of mobile phone behavior (under the category of Discipline and Methodology); (2) four major sections (under the categories of Activities and Processes, Effects and Impacts, Technologies and Apps, and Users and Special Population) that focus on four fundamental elements involving mobile phone use (i.e., mobile technologies, mobile users, mobile processes, and mobile effects); (3) six major sections (under the categories of Business and Commerce,

Communication and Daily Life, Education and Pedagogy, Health Care and Medicine, Politics and Policy, Traffic and Transport) that focus on six domains of mobile phone behavior (i.e., mobile business, mobile communication, mobile education, mobile health, mobile policy, and mobile safety); and (4) a conclusion presenting mobile phone behavior across different countries in the mobile world (under the categories of Regions and Countries). With this overall content structure, the *Encyclopedia* provides a fundamental presentation of what the past, present, and future of the science of mobile phone behavior is and how complex human mobile phone behavior is.

It is foreseeable that the field will continue its exponential growth in the next decade due to both further fast development of mobile phone technologies and the unprecedentedly ubiquitous and profound influence of mobile phone use on human beings. Thus, we can state that mobile phone behavior research is an emerged field of study rather than an emerging one, and it is completing its energetic, intellectual adolescence and soon will start its even more prosperous adulthood.

5. Understanding Mobile Phone Behavior

5.1 Target Readers

The target readers of this book are individuals who are *interested* in knowing about the profound effects of mobile phones on human behavior. They perhaps have been using mobile phones for years or may not even own a mobile phone. They could be graduate and undergraduate students, academic specialists, industrial developers and researchers, business professionals, policy makers, or grandparents who just had their own mobile phones and are curious about various issues related to mobile phone use. They could be in the fields of behavioral sciences, such as psychology, communication, sociology, health care, business, or education, and are interested in studying more about technologies and media in general and mobile phone behavior in particular. Thus, given the wide readership, this book features introductory-level comprehensive coverage with an interdisciplinary orientation.

5.2 Intellectual Goals and Content Organization

Considering both our limited intuitive thinking shown in the informal survey presented at the outset of this chapter and the last twenty-five years of development in the science of mobile phone behavior presented thereafter, we will set up two primary intellectual goals for us to accomplish together after studying this book: readers will develop (1) a *usable knowledge* of the complexity of mobile phone behavior and (2) a *workable skill* to analyze the complexity of mobile phone behavior. The first goal sets the stage for the second goal by providing basic concepts and tools for the effective analysis of mobile phone behavior. The second goal will help to better achieve the first goal by deepening the knowledge.

To achieve these two goals, this book is organized into four major sections, as shown in Figure 1.7. In the first section, Chapter 1 introduces basic knowledge of mobile phones, mobile phone behavior, and mobile phone behavior research and specifies the two major goals. The second section consists of four chapters, each discussing the four basic elements of mobile phone behavior (users, technologies, activities, and effects) to develop the knowledge of the complexity of mobile phone behavior and the skill to analyze this complexity. The third section also has four chapters, presenting the four major domains of mobile phone behavior (medicine, business, education, and everyday life) to further develop readers' knowledge of the complexity of mobile phone behavior and readers' skill in analyzing this complexity. The last section summarizes the essential knowledge of the complexity of mobile phone behavior and the core skill of analyzing the complexity of mobile phone behavior, ending with two future goals of developing an advanced knowledge of the complexity of mobile phone behavior and an effective skill to analyze this complexity. The content is organized in this way to first introduce a basic knowledge of mobile phone behavior, then break down this behavior into four basic elements and apply them in major, real-life domains involving mobile phone behavior. It is hoped that the general sequence

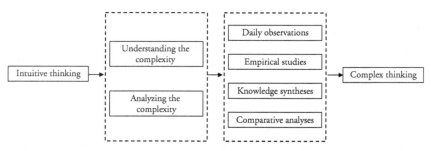

Figure 1.7   The Overall Organization of the Book

of moving from more basic issues to more complex topics will develop the usable conceptual knowledge and the workable analytic skill in understanding the complexity of mobile phone behavior.

In addition, in order to achieve the two major goals of this book, each of the main chapters from Chapter 2 to Chapter 9 follows a similar six-step sequence:

Intuitive Thinking ▶ Daily Observations ▶ Empirical Studies ▶ Knowledge Syntheses ▶ Comparative Analyses ▶Complex Thinking.

Each major chapter will (1) start with intuitive thinking shown in a mini-survey of actual real-life people I have met, then (2) present multiple real-life cases to show readers some observed mobile phone behavior in the real world, then (3) discuss multiple research articles to help readers see specific scientific evidence, then (4) provide readers with several literature reviews to show the real scope of the existing scientific knowledge, then (5) compare similar human behavior (e.g., users with disabilities or addictive behavior) with other different technologies (e.g., television, computer, and the Internet) to further expand readers' knowledge, and, finally, (6) end with a summary of complex thinking of the given topic of that chapter. This sequence is largely based on Daniel Kahneman's intuitive judgement theory. As we discussed earlier, this theory specified and explains two basic systems of human thinking – intuitive thinking and rational thinking. Intuitive thinking operates automatically with little effort and arises from heuristics and biases that lead to various human errors. Rational thinking operates deliberately with considerable effort and develops through learning, training, and education.

Note that this book will still use intuitive thinking, but will use *complex thinking* instead of rational thinking to discuss initial and developed knowledge of mobile phone behavior. This is because we consider complex thinking to be a special type of rational thinking that focuses on the ability to understand and analyze the complexity of a given object. In other words, this book aims to help readers develop their complex thinking about mobile phone behavior rather than their flawless or perfect understanding of mobile phone behavior. It is hoped that this sequence in each major chapter will help readers gradually develop from their intuitive thinking based on their daily experiences to their complex thinking based on the analysis and discussion of various kinds of materials presented in the chapters. In fact, the overall book also started with intuitive thinking that a group of graduate students had about mobile phone behavior and now ends with a summary of complex thinking about mobile phone behavior that readers are expected to achieve.

5.3   The Style

Given the rapid growth and genuine interdisciplinary nature of scientific knowledge of mobile phone behavior, deliberately, the book is not written in a style of a presumably very knowledgeable senior scholar standing in front of a group of students and giving a long lecture in a large lecture hall. Instead, by design, it is written in a style of a series of intellectual dialogs and discussions among a group of curious and analytic individuals who attend a graduate proseminar or a professional seminar. Everyone participates in and contributes to the intellectual dialogs and discussions. As a deliberative practice routine throughout the book, we will use *WE* as the intellectual group instead of *YOU* as the listeners and *I* as the speaker. It is my sincere hope that WE as a group work and grow together to develop a better understanding of the complexity of mobile phone behavior and to help millions of mobile phone users across the world benefit more from our scientific knowledge and complex thinking.

CHAPTER 2

Mobile Phone Users

Outline

1. *Initial Thinking: Responses from Three Graduate Students*
2. *Daily Observations: From the Tsarnaev Brothers to Jorma Ollila*
   2.1 *The Tsarnaev Brothers and the Farook Couple*
   2.2 *A 1-Year-Old Boy and a Group of Seniors*
   2.3 *Danny Bowman and Matthew Schneps*
   2.4 *Barack Obama and Bill Gates*
   2.5 *Martin Cooper and Jorma Ollila*
3. *Empirical Studies: From Penetration Rates to Multiple User Groups*
   3.1 *PEW and ITU: How Many Mobile Phone Users?*
   3.2 *Teens Sexting Explicit Sexual Images*
   3.3 *Young Australian Users*
   3.4 *Users with Different Personalities*
   3.5 *Users with Dyslexia*
   3.6 *Users Who Plan to Use Mobile Phones While Driving*
   3.7 *Multiple User Groups Involved in Mobile Phone School Policy*
4. *Knowledge Syntheses: From Users in Latin America to Problematic Users*
   4.1 Encyclopedia *Chapters: Users in Latin America and with Visual Impairment*
   4.2 *Review Articles: Young Users and Radiation Exposure, and Problematic Users*
5. *Comparative Analyses: From TV Viewers to Mobile Phone Users*
   5.1 *Reviewing Users of Four Technologies*
   5.2 *Comparing Users of Four Technologies*
6. *Complex Thinking: Diverse Users, Complex Behavior*

1. Initial Thinking: Responses from Three Graduate Students

"Who are the mobile phone users? Please give three to five short examples coming to your mind as quickly as you can." This is a simple question

I asked three graduate students to solicit their intuitive thoughts about mobile phone users. Below are the answers I received:

GRADUATE STUDENT A: Mobile phone users I think are adolescents, young adults, adults, and the elderly. I think all people except toddlers would be users of the mobile phone.

GRADUATE STUDENT B: I think everyone is a mobile phone user, they just may use it for different things. Even little kids use mobile phones to play games and for entertainment. At this point, I don't know a single person who does not own a mobile phone.

GRADUATE STUDENT C: I think almost everyone is a mobile phone user now (90% of US population?). Therefore, I think the difference should be who spends more time on mobile phones and who spends less time on mobile phones. People who spend more time on mobile phones: younger people, especially college students, business men (or any other job that requires extensive communication), people who travel a lot (spend a lot of time on the road, can't access a laptop), and less self-regulated people. People who spend less time on mobile phones: older age group (i.e., 65+) who were less educated, people in rural areas, low home income, office workers (can't use cell phone during working, i.e., 9:00 to 5:00), and busy housewives.

These responses, from relatively brief to relatively elaborated, are particularly interesting for at least two reasons. First, in terms of similarities, they all considered that mobile phone users are *everyone* or almost everyone. Responder A indicated that: "I think all people except toddlers would be users of the mobile phone." Responder B indicated that: "At this point, I don't know a single person who does not own a mobile phone." And Responder C indicated that: "I think almost everyone is a mobile phone user now (90% of US population?)." Second, in terms of differences, while they all agreed that almost everyone is a mobile phone user, each of them focused on different *aspects* of mobile phone users to categorize users. Responder A focused on the ages of different users, Responder B focused on the ways in which different users use mobile phones, and Responder C focused on amount of time spent on mobile phones by different users.

Looking at these responses, many of us might feel that these responses are quite good and that we ourselves might come up with similar answers. However, some of us might come up with more questions: e.g., What do the similarities and differences of these responses tell us? Do their responses represent correct, thoughtful, and comprehensive understanding of mobile phone users? Is it true that almost all people are mobile phone users? Is it true that almost all people are mobile phone users, but differ in ages, ways of use, or time spent?

In this chapter, we will address these questions and expand our initial understanding to a much more complex understanding of mobile phone users. Specifically, we will (1) discuss a few examples from real life, (2) analyze a few studies from the research literature, (3) synthesize the current knowledge in this area, and (4) compare users of different technologies (e.g., television, computer, and the Internet). By the end of the chapter, we should be able to see that our initial knowledge actually only covers a small portion of the current knowledge of mobile phone users, and mobile phone users perhaps are one of the most complex concepts for us to define, understand, study, and apply.

2. Daily Observations: From the Tsarnaev Brothers to Jorma Ollila

Mobile phone users could be easily and simply defined as anyone who owns or uses a mobile phone. However, from the real-life examples presented below, we might see that mobile phone users are much more complex than this simple definition suggests.

2.1 The Tsarnaev Brothers and the Farook Couple

In April 2013,[1] Tamerlan Tsarnaev and Dzhokhar Tsarnaev used their cell phones to detonate two pressure cooker bombs as improvised explosive devices near the finish line of the 117th Boston Marathon. This terrorist attack led to six deaths and 280 injuries. Based on the definition, the Tsarnaev brothers are mobile phone users. They purchased mobile phones, owned the phones, and used them for their daily communication and special ignition of bombs. Dzhokhar Tsarnaev, the younger brother, even deliberately smashed his cell phone to destroy possible critical information in it before he was arrested. However, they are not typical mobile phone users. They are *criminal mobile phone users*.

During this terrorist attack, there were actually various kinds of mobile phone users involved. For example, many marathon runners used their mobile phones to text a safe message to their families. Friends identified a victim who was a Chinese student after texting her but never receiving a

---

[1] See https://en.wikipedia.org/wiki/Boston_Marathon_bombing.

reply from her cell phone. The police decided to search for the Tsarnaev brothers in Watertown by tracking a cell phone belonging to Danny – a middle-aged man whose car was stolen by the brothers from a gas station and whose cell phone remained in his car when the brothers drove it away. Khairullozhon Matanov, a close friend of the brothers, deleted hundreds of documents and threw away his cell phone in order to hide his relationship with the brothers. In short, they were all mobile phone users, but differed significantly in many ways.

In December 2015,[2] Syed Rizwan Farook and Tashfeen Malik killed fourteen people and injured twenty-two in a terrorist attack in San Bernardino, California. During the terrorist attack, Farook coordinated the shooting with his wife via his cell phone and even tried to use it to ignite self-made bombs. The two killers later died in a shoot-out with police.

After the attack, the FBI asked San Bernardino County, who had issued the mobile phone to government employee Farook for his work, to reset the password to the shooter's iCloud account in order to acquire data from the iCloud backup. However, this rendered the phone unable to back up recent data to iCloud unless the original password was entered. After the attack, the police recovered the phone intact, but could not open it due to its password protection feature. All the data in the phone would be eliminated after ten failed password attempts. The FBI wanted Apple to create new software that would enable the FBI to unlock the iPhone 5C. Apple declined to create the software in order to protect the security of all other iPhone users. This became the well-known court case between the FBI and Apple.

Based on the typical definition of mobile phone users, Farook, the husband, might not be considered to be a mobile phone user because he did not own a mobile phone. He used an iPhone 5C, but this phone was issued by his governmental employer. During this terrorist attack, Farook tried to use it to ignite self-made bombs. Furthermore, what makes this case more complicated is that there are three major parties involved: San Bernardino County as the owner of the phone, who did not know the password; the FBI, who possessed the phone for criminal investigation but could not open it; and Apple, who were capable of opening and using the phone, but did not want to do so in order to protect the product security for all other iPhone users.

---

[2] See https://en.wikipedia.org/wiki/2015_San_Bernardino_attack.

2.2 A 1-Year-Old Boy and a Group of Seniors

One day, I observed a very young boy outside of a dance classroom. He took a mobile phone quickly from his mother, skillfully touched a few buttons on the screen, and played a children's game on the phone. His mother told me that her son was 1 year old and loved to play games on the phone. He did not own the phone, he might not have known how to use the phone well, but he knew exactly how to play his games on the mobile phone – his favorite toy.

Another day, I also saw a group of senior citizens, about 70 to 80 years old, in an Apple store. They had just purchased iPhones from the store and had not yet used them. Each of them held an iPhone in their hands and sat around a table and listened to a technician from the store about how to use their phones. I was very impressed by their desire and enthusiasm to learn how to use this new technology given their ages.

The 1-year-old boy should be considered a mobile phone user, even though he might only have known how to play games on the phone and did not own a mobile phone. The group of seniors should also be considered mobile phone users: they owned a mobile phone and were just learning how to use it. They might be among the newest mobile phone user groups. Thus, in terms of age differences, the boy might be among the youngest users and these seniors might be among the oldest users. Besides age, mobile phone users might have other important *demographic characteristics* such as gender, ethnicity, education, social class, religion, culture, and country origin.

2.3 Danny Bowman and Matthew Schneps

Danny Bowman[3] is a teenager from the United Kingdom who was extremely obsessed with selfies, a self-portrait photograph typically taken with a mobile phone camera and often shared on Facebook or Instagram. Danny had an iPhone and would spend 10 hours a day taking up to 200 photos of himself, constantly trying to take the perfect selfie. However, one day, he realized he could not achieve the perfect selfie and attempted to commit suicide. By definition, Danny is a typical mobile phone user because he owns and uses his mobile phone. However, his addiction to the selfie made him an atypical mobile phone user.

---

[3] See http://time.com/35701/selfie-addict-attempts-suicide.

Matthew Schneps is a Professor of Physics at Harvard University. He has been leading a group of researchers in his lab to study how to use technologies to help those with learning disabilities. He also has dyslexia, a reading disorder with various difficulties in spelling words, pronouncing words, reading proficiency, or understanding text. Thus, he developed a special way to read and text with his mobile phone. In recent years, he and his collaborators published several articles examining how mobile phones can help dyslexic people read better. By common definition, he is a mobile phone user, but he is a very special user with dyslexia who studies how to help other dyslexic mobile phone users.

Danny Bowman and Professor Matthew Schneps are two extremely special mobile phone users, one addicted to selfies and another with dyslexia. However, they share one common feature: they are special mobile phone users with psychological or behavioral differences. Across the world, mobile phone users could have a wide variety of *psychological differences* in physical, neurological, cognitive, social, moral, and behavioral aspects. Many of them are special mobile phone users, either with various disabilities (e.g., deaf, blind) or various talents or giftedness.

2.4   Barack Obama and Bill Gates

President Barack Obama is well known for using BlackBerry for over a decade. After becoming president in 2008, he had to use a highly secured Blackberry developed specifically by the National Security Agency (NSA) to protect national security. Other users of the highly secured mobile phones included Vice President Joe Biden, First Lady Michelle Obama, and Obama's top advisers. President Obama recently borrowed an iPhone from his staff back in 2015 and posted his first Twitter message: "Hello Twitter! This is Barack. Really!" President Obama was a user of three mobile phones: He owned a regular BlackBerry, he then used a very special highly secured BlackBerry, and he borrowed an iPhone for tweeting. As a political leader, he was a special phone user, like German President Angela Merkel, whose mobile phone was monitored by the NSA, or Chinese President Xi, who presents mobile phones made by China as gifts to his special guests. These political leaders in the world are all among *a special group of mobile phone users.*

As a world technology leader rather than a world political leader, the former Microsoft CEO Bill Gates used an iPhone 5s while traveling for his philanthropic endeavor. However, the Gates family has an informal family policy regarding mobile phones: their children, Jennifer Katharine (born in 1996), Rory John (born in 1999), and Phoebe Adele (born in 2002), were not allowed mobile phones until they were 13 years old.[4] Several IT CEOs in the United States also have a similar family policy regarding mobile phones for their children. Based on the typical definition, Gates is obviously a mobile phone user, but his children younger than 13 are not. Many other young children whose families do not allow them to have mobile phones too early are not typical mobile phone users. However, these children see other people using phones, are familiar with mobile phone use, and really want to have their own phones, and thus might be categorized as a *special group of mobile phone users*, the hidden or would-be mobile phone users, just like the Russian President Vladimir Putin, who is famous for claiming to have no mobile phone.

2.5   Martin Cooper and Jorma Ollila

Martin Cooper, often known as the father of mobile phones, is a mobile phone user. He used a Motorola DynaTac and made the first public mobile phone call in 1973. He probably is one of the earliest mobile phone users, in addition to being one of the earliest mobile phone developers. Similar to Martin Cooper, Jorma Jaakko Ollila is a Finnish entrepreneur and a mobile phone pioneer. He was chairman (1999–2012) and CEO (1992–2006) of Nokia Corporation and was credited with turning the company into the then world's largest handset maker. Again, he is a mobile phone user and mobile phone developer. Like Martin Cooper and Jorma Ollila, there are many special mobile phone users who are mobile phone designers, mobile phone engineers, and mobile phone entrepreneurs. They are the superstars of mobile phone users.

   To sum up, from these ten real-life examples briefly discussed above, we can see that the concept of mobile phone users is more complex than we might have earlier assumed. These examples can be used to show a general typology of mobile phone users: users who are bad vs. good; and users with different demographic, behavioral, and special characteristics. Compared with the three intuitive responses presented at the outset of this chapter, we can see substantial differences. First, it might be true that all people are mobile phone users in general, but it is important to be aware that these users can be good or bad users. None of the three student responders was clearly aware of this and generally and implicitly assumed that all mobile

---

[4] See http://betanews.com/2014/04/01/bill-gates-loves-his-new-iphone-5s-can-now-beat-bono-at-candy-crush/.

phone users are good. Second, age is one feature, but not all demographic features of users, such as gender, ethnicity, and social economic status, were considered by the graduate students. Third, whether a person uses a mobile phone or not is a natural feature of users, but it is more complex in real life: considering the examples of the FBI, Apple, and IT CEOs discussed above, users are much more complicated. Fourth, whether one spends a little or a lot of time using phones is an interesting observation, but it should not be a defining feature of mobile phone users. Finally, there are various special groups of users such as users with disabilities or political leaders such as President Obama.

3.   Empirical Studies: From Penetration Rates to Multiple User Groups

Having discussed some real-life examples of mobile phone users, let us now consider how researchers examine these users. In the field of the science of mobile phone behavior, researchers have been examining behavior among different users for years. There exists extensive literature on user-based mobile phone behavior. In this section, we will discuss five examples.

3.1   PEW and ITU: How Many Mobile Phone Users?

As presented at the beginning of this chapter, the three individuals all believed that everyone or almost everyone is a mobile phone user. Is this true? Is there any scientific evidence to support this? Where is the scientific evidence? Is it true that almost everyone is a mobile phone user in the United States? Is it true that almost everyone is a mobile phone user in the world? These questions should be among the first to address when we study mobile phone users.

In general, two of the best and most cited sources in estimating the number of mobile phone users are the International Telecommunication Union (ITU) and the Pew Research Center (PEW). Google Our Mobile Planet is another source that tends to provide detailed data, but does so inconsistently. Normally, the index commonly used is penetration rates of mobile phones. In the business literature, penetration rate is typically used to measure the performance of brand penetration or market penetration,[5] and generally means the percentage of the relevant population that has

---

[5] Ansoff, H. I. (1957). "Strategies for diversification," *Harvard Business Review*, 35(5): 113–124.

purchased a product or a service at least once in the time period under study.[6] For mobile phones, if a country has a 90 percent mobile phone penetration rate, that generally means 90 percent of the population in that country has used a mobile phone.

PEW reports on USA. The best estimation of the penetration rate of mobile phones in the United States is provided by the Pew Research Center. PEW was created in 2004 as a separate operating subsidiary of The Pew Charitable Trusts, an independent, non-profit organization founded in 1948 by the Pew family. It conducts policy analysis on public opinion polling, demographic research, media content analysis, and other empirical social science research. It is well known for its high-quality surveys on various important trends of technology use.

Based on PEW, in 2015, 92 percent of American adults owned a mobile phone of some kind. Although these mobile devices are ubiquitous today, the share of adults who own one has risen substantially since 2004, when PEW conducted its first poll on cell phone ownership. At that time, only 65 percent of Americans owned a cell phone.[7] The estimation of 92 percent penetration rate was based on two Pew Research Center surveys. The first survey was conducted in March through April, 2015, among a national sample of 1,907 adults, ages 18 and older, living in all fifty US states and the District of Columbia. A total of 672 respondents were interviewed on a landline telephone, and 1,235 were interviewed on a cell phone, including 730 who had no landline telephone. For the second survey, the smartphone ownership data were based on telephone interviews conducted in June through July, 2015, among a national sample of 2,001 adults, ages 18 and older, living in all fifty US states and the District of Columbia. A total of 701 respondents were interviewed on a landline telephone, and 1,300 were interviewed on a cell phone, including 709 who had no landline telephone.

PEW has used *ownership* to estimate the popularity of mobile phone behavior. In the interview, participants were asked to respond to a simple question: Do you have a cell phone? The main advantage of using ownership as a measure of mobile phone behavior is being able to quickly and simply see if one owns a phone or not. The main disadvantage is that ownership is not a direct estimation of the number of mobile phone users.

---

[6] See https://en.wikipedia.org/wiki/Market_penetration.

[7] PEW (factsheet). Monica Anderson, "Technology device ownership: 2015" (Pew Research Center, October 29, 2015), available at: www.pewinternet.org/2015/10/29/technology-device-ownership-2015.

ITU reports on the world. For the penetration rate of mobile phones in the world, the most comprehensive estimation is provided by ITU. ITU is a United Nations specialized agency for information and communication technologies. Its main mission is to allocate global radio spectrum and satellite orbits, develop the technical standards that ensure networks and technologies seamlessly interconnect, and strive to improve access to ICTs to underserved communities worldwide.

Based on ITU data, worldwide mobile phone subscriptions have grown to 7.1 billion, representing 96.8 percent of the world's population, compared with 14.5 percent for traditional telephones, 45.4 percent for computers at home, and 46.4 percent for Internet access at home (ITU, 2015).

Here, ITU used *subscription* rather than *ownership* to estimate the number of mobile phone users. Quite similar to traditional telephones, a mobile phone user needs to not only buy a mobile phone (e.g., an iPhone or Blackberry), but also subscribe to a mobile phone service provided by a mobile phone network company (e.g., T-Mobile or Verizon Wireless) to make the mobile phone *active* or *workable*. Based on World Bank data,[8] mobile subscriptions are subscriptions to a public mobile phone service that provides access to the public switched telephone network (PSTN) using cellular technology. Technically, PSTN is the underlying infrastructure network of all public telecommunication networks that are operated by national, regional, or local telecommunication companies across the world. It consists of telephone lines, fiber optic cables, microwave transmission links, cellular networks, communications satellites, and undersea telephone cables that are interconnected by switching centers to allow all mobile and fixed phones to communicate with each other.

Just like ownership, the number of mobile phone subscriptions is not exactly the same as the number of mobile phone users. Based on an estimation by Ericsson (February 2014),[9] there were 6.7 billion mobile subscriptions worldwide at the beginning of 2014, but there are only around 4.5 billion mobile users. This is because many users have several subscriptions for different devices. The main advantage of using subscriptions to estimate the number of mobile phone users is that it is related to current active use of mobile phones. However, the main disadvantage is that it is based on the number of service subscriptions rather than a direct estimation of mobile phone users.

---

[8] See http://data.worldbank.org/indicator/IT.CEL.SETS.P2.
[9] See www.ericsson.com/mobility-report.

In summary, penetration, ownership, and subscription rates are all relative approximations of the estimation of mobile phone users. It is a complex issue and a challenging task to accurately estimate the number of mobile phone users. However, two things are clear: mobile phones are extremely popular; and not everyone is a mobile phone user. In the United States, 92 percent of adults have a cell phone. Across the world, 98 percent of the population is actively subscribing to a mobile phone service. But exactly how many mobile phone users are in the United States or the world? This is still a mysterious and puzzling question that remains to be solved.

3.2   Teens Sexting Explicit Sexual Images

Having discussed the challenging issue surrounding how many mobile users there are in the world, let us now discuss some specific groups of mobile phone users.

The empirical article we will discuss is entitled "How often are teens arrested for sexting? Data from a national sample of police cases."[10] In the article, sexting was specifically defined as a behavior when youth created and distributed explicit sexual images that are legally considered to be child pornography. The data were based on a mail survey with heads of law enforcement agencies and a telephone interview with police officers in the United States. The authors are Janis Wolak, David Finkelhor, and Kimberly Mitchell, three well-established scholars in the area of crimes against children at the University of New Hampshire. The article was published in 2012 in *Pediatrics*, the official journal of the American Academy of Pediatrics and the most cited journal in the field of pediatrics.

In the study, the authors surveyed a nationally representative sample of 2,712 law enforcement agencies for sexting cases handled in 2008 to 2009 in the United States and then interviewed investigating police officers for 675 cases. Further analysis of these cases indicated the following major findings: (1) During 2008 to 2009, about 3,500 cases were handled by the law enforcement agencies. (2) 67 percent of these cases were serious because either adult offenders were involved or a youth's sexting behavior was intentionally harmful or really reckless. For instance, a girl, aged 13, sent a nude photo to her boyfriend. After they broke up, the boy, aged 14, used his cell phone to send the photo to about 200 students. (3) 33 percent

---

[10] Wolak, J., Finkelhor, D., and Mitchell, K. J. (2012). "How often are teens arrested for sexting? Data from a national sample of police cases," *Pediatrics*, 129(1): 4–12.

of the cases were experimental for romantic relationships or sexual attention seeking. For instance, a boy, aged 16, received a video of another boy masturbating. (4) Over 60 percent of young sexters are 13 to 15 years old. About 70 percent of the cases involved sexual images showing genitals or explicit sex acts. The majority of these sexual images were of themselves and taken and distributed by themselves. (4) For over 80 percent of the cases, the sexual images were sent to others through cell phones, but not posted onto the Internet.

This study shows the dark side of mobile phone users, especially young mobile phone users. First, the study focused only on youth-produced explicit sexual images, the heavy side of sexting behavior, rather than other types of sexting behavior (e.g., sexting verbal messages). Even for this heavy side of sexting behavior, the authors show two major types – severe and experimental, with seven subtypes. Thus, youth's sexting behavior is diverse and complex. Second, these 3,500 cases are only those that eventually came to the police. Many more cases, especially less serious ones, might have been unnoticed by adults or not handled by police. Third, mobile phones rather than stand-alone computers or stand-alone cameras are the dominant means for young sexters to produce, store, and distribute the sex images.

3.3   Young Australian Users

Age is the most often studied demographic feature of mobile phone users. So is the original country of users. For the demographic features of mobile users, we can use the article entitled "Over-connected? A qualitative exploration of the relationship between Australian youth and their mobile phones"[11] by Walsh and her collaborators as a good example to show the scientific evidence that reveals how young ages of users are associated with specific mobile phone behavior, i.e., mobile addiction. Walsh is an established counseling psychologist in Australia. She and her group have published a series of articles focusing on mobile phone use among Australian youth. Thus, we have reasons to believe that she is an experienced researcher before discussing the article.

In this study, the researchers aimed to find potential indicators of mobile phone addiction among Australian youth. To achieve this research

---

[11] Walsh, S. P., White, K. M., and Young, R. M. (2008). "Over-connected? A qualitative exploration of the relationship between Australian youth and their mobile phones," *Journal of Adolescence*, 31 (1): 77–92.

goal, they used a research design called focus groups (interviewing a specific group of individuals through natural conversations) to collect qualitative data of self-reported experiences. They then analyzed emerging themes and used specific addiction criteria as the framework for investigating addiction indicators.

Specifically, they recruited thirty-two participants, aged between 16 and 24 years old, with occupations ranging from first-year, full-time psychology students, to trade and office workers, to high-level white-collar workers. They formed six focus groups. Participants were required to use their mobile phone at least once per day. Participants used their phones between one to more than twenty-five times per day and the length of ownership varied from two months to eight years. They used a snowballing method to recruit participants, i.e., researchers sending an email to initial contacts and the initial contacts then forwarding the email to their own networks.

They developed a guide for focus group discussions that contained a series of discussion points and suggested questions. There were three types of suggested questions, including: (1) general questions about mobile phone use (e.g., What do you mainly use your mobile phone for?); (2) more specific situational questions (e.g., I'd like you to think of a situation where you are asked to turn your mobile phone off. What do you do with your phone in those situations?); and (3) questions related to problems arising from use (e.g., Have you experienced any problems from using your mobile phone? If so, can you explain what happened?) and addictive use (e.g., Thinking about addiction, do you think that there is a potential for people to become addicted to their phones? If so, what would be happening that would indicate its occurrence?). Clearly, the third type of question is most directly related to their research goal of finding potential indicators of mobile phone addiction.

The procedure for collecting the focus group data had several features: (1) The researcher moderated the entire focus group session. (2) The session lasted approximately 1 hour. (3) Each focus group was audio-recorded for further analysis. (4) Participants were invited to discuss each focus question within the group openly and honestly. The moderator probed for clarification if required and used validation comments. (5) At the conclusion of the discussion on each question, member checking was conducted. Participants' general comments and a summary of the discussion were stated. This process ensured that the researcher understood participants' perspectives, and allowed participants to clarify or confirm any ambiguous points. (6) Following the conclusion of each focus group, the researcher noted any questions that lacked clarity or resulted in new themes being uncovered. As a result of this process, questions were refined over the duration of the focus groups. Data collection ceased once no new themes emerged, indicating theoretical saturation had been reached.

From this study, there were two major findings. First, the Australian youth discussed numerous *beneficial functions* of using mobile phones to users (e.g., safety and convenience) as an intrinsic part of most young people's lives. For instance, a 16-year-old female said that her phone really becomes a part of her because it's with her more than anything else in the world. Second, potential indicators of mobile phone addiction emerged from the focus group discussion and some young people are extremely attached to their mobile phone with *early symptoms* of behavioral addiction. The most frequently mentioned early symptoms in participants' discussions include: (1) cognitive and behavioral *salience* (e.g., a female wakes up and checks her phone right away. Then after having a shower, she checks the phone again). (2) *Conflict* with other activities, but not interpersonal conflict (e.g., a participant said that if someone texts him, he stops what he is doing and texts back). (3) *Enthusiasm* and relief (e.g., a young girl discussed that when someone wants to talk to her she just feels anxious or excited and wants to answer it). (4) *Loss* of control or tolerance (e.g., a participant tells herself not to call anyone anymore, but she keeps calling others. She does not even know when she does it). (5) *Withdrawal* (e.g., a participant talked about if no one has contacted her she gets really depressed and feels that no one loves her). (6) *Relapse* and reinstatement (e.g., one young woman mentioned that when she has big phone bills she thinks about cutting down, but for years she has never gotten her bill much lower).

This study has multiple strengths. (1) It collects qualitative data about young users from Australia that are rich, unique, intriguing, and informative rather than often-observed general survey data. (2) It conducts a thoughtful and well-executed focus group study. (3) It used Brown's criteria as a framework to code the data and thus enhance its theoretical base.

It has also a few weaknesses. (1) The one-year requirement for participation in the study might be too short and should be longer, given that 93 percent of Australian youths use mobile phones and the research goal of the study is to find addictive precursors. (2) While using the specific addiction criteria is useful, the existing mobile phone addiction research and the existing Internet addiction research should be used to develop more specific questions rather than general questions. (3) The grounded theory approach, as the author pointed out, should be used to identify authentic themes from the data. (4) Given the as low as 3 to 5 percent Internet addiction rate, it might not be feasible to find true symptoms of addiction among regular populations or ordinary students. It is difficult to distinguish addiction from excessive behavior. For the current sample, it is not surprising to observe low levels of addiction indicators rather than the typical addiction level that meets the clinical standard of addiction. (5) Given the pilot nature of the study and the predetermined criteria, it is an overstatement to claim that "results will provide a solid foundation for developing a targeted investigation of mobile phone addiction using the specific indicators identified in this study." However, these weaknesses are understandable given that this qualitative study was conducted in 2008, relatively early for this type of study.

From the perspective of mobile phone users, there are two most inspiring contributions of the study. First, the study suggests that young Australian mobile phone users might experience a *dynamic process* between positive attachment and negative over-attachment to mobile phones. Young mobile phone use might start with a positive emotional attachment when using mobile phones, and then the positive attachment may develop into negative addiction. In other words, some of these young Australian mobile phone users are not mobile phone addicts right away when they have their mobile phones. Second, it provides detailed qualitative data about six types of early addiction symptoms of young Australian users rather than general survey data that we have seen too often in the literature. It is always useful to find the initial identification of symptoms of mobile phone addiction to investigate the precursors of mobile phone addiction in young people rather than to see the clinical symptoms so that prevention and intervention can take place in a timely manner. In summary, mobile phone users are diverse and complex, and this article enriches our understanding of mobile phone users by introducing two specific demographic features of users (i.e., younger Australian users in terms of age and country) and describing their six specific early symptoms of mobile phone addiction (e.g., withdrawal and relapse). Here, Bill Gates might be right to allow his children to have mobile phones after they turn 13 so that they can use the phones more appropriately.

3.4   *Users with Different Personalities*

The example discussed above focuses on demographic characteristics of mobile phone users. The next example we will discuss focuses on behavioral or psychological characteristics. In methodological terms, the former is about variables that are "fixed" and normally cannot be changed or modified, whereas the latter is about random variables that can be changed or modified through prevention and intervention.

The title of the article is "Correlating personality and actual phone usage: Evidence from psychoinformatics."[12] The lead author, Christian Montag, is a biological psychologist at the University of Ulm in Germany. His publications mainly focus on using genetics and neuroscience to study psychiatry such as depression and addiction to the Internet or games and his 2008 article is his first in studying mobile phone behavior.

In this study, the authors attempted to test a hypothesis that users with higher levels of extraversion should be associated with more frequent use of the mobile phone (e.g., incoming and outcoming calls, length of telephone calls, and the number of different persons directly contacted).

To test this hypothesis, the authors recruited forty-nine undergraduate students from Germany. The design of the study was straightforward. Each student had to have their own smartphone already. A special app called Menthal was installed on their phones to collect the mobile phone data automatically. They also asked the participating students to complete the German version of the Big Five Personality Questionnaire as another set of independent variables. In personality psychology, "The Big Five" typically refers to five personality traits, including openness to experience (e.g., a person who is quick to understand things), conscientiousness (e.g., a person who is always prepared), extraversion (e.g., a person who feels comfortable around people), agreeableness (e.g., a person who feels others' emotions), and neuroticism (e.g., a person who gets upset easily). They assessed these five personality factor scores as independent variables and ten types of mobile phone behavior (e.g., call in count, call out duration, SMS in participants, and SMS out length) as dependent variables. The study took five weeks to complete.

Their major findings include that: (1) All ten calling variables (e.g., call in count, call out count, and call miss count) are positively and significantly related to extraversion. Only two calling behaviors (call out duration and call total duration) are related to conscientiousness. Thus, certain personality characteristics such as extraversion and conscientiousness did make various kinds of mobile phone calls more often. (2) Different from

---

[12] Montag, C., Błaszkiewicz, K., Lachmann, B. *et al.* (2014). "Correlating personality and actual phone usage," *Journal of Individual Differences*, 35(3): 158–165.

calling behavior, seven texting behaviors (e.g., SMS in count, SMS out count, SMS total count, and SMS in length) are positively and significantly related to all the five personality factors. SMS in length and conscientiousness were related negatively.

This study has multiple strengths. (1) It pioneered a method to collect big data automatically via an app. (2) The unique data collection process is thoughtful and clearly presented, including recording, extracting, categorizing, and selecting. (3) The results are particularly informative in revealing the significant differences among five personality factors, especially extraversion, and the significant differences between calling behavior and texting behavior.

However, this study has several weaknesses. (1) The data analysis cannot test the hypothesis. It should have compared all the five personality factors to show why extraversion rather than the other four factors is particularly important to users' calling or texting behavior. (2) The regression analysis did not report model fit, used extraversion scores as the predictor based on the reason of technical inconvenience only, and justified using personality as the predictor, but actually used it as an outcome variable. This is partly due to the beginning stage of analyzing big data, where collecting data is strong, but analyzing data is weak. For the future, an effective method of analyzing a large number of outcomes should be developed and used.

However, despite these data analysis limitations, the study contributed to the current knowledge by using big data to show significant differences in how extraversion is related to calling and texting behavior. In other words, it is important to know how different personality factors play a role and how different types of mobile phone behavior, calling or texting, play their roles. From this study, we can develop a specific understanding of mobile phone users regarding different personalities rather than a general knowledge.

3.5 Users with Dyslexia

Mobile phone users are extremely diverse, given that nowadays almost everyone owns, uses, or plays on one or more than one mobile phone. They have different demographics (e.g., age, gender, race, SES, religion, education), different characteristics (e.g., personality, intelligence, attitude, motivation), and they show different types of mobile phone behavior. Among the existing empirical research on diverse mobile phone users is a particularly interesting experimental study conducted recently by Matthew Schneps and his collaborators. Its title is "Shorter lines facilitate reading in those who struggle."[13] Matthew Schneps is a Professor of Physics at Harvard University and an individual with dyslexia himself. Dyslexia generally refers to a neurological and genetically based reading disability. His current publications focus on how to use mobile devices to help dyslexic individuals read text.

In this study, the authors primarily asked one central research question: Is the smaller phone-sized screen of an iPod better than the larger book-sized screen of an iPad for individuals with dyslexia to read text? Mobile phones typically have a much smaller screen, and each line of text is much shorter; whereas computers or tablets typically have larger screens similar to a conventional book size, and each line of text is much longer. For individuals with dyslexia who have difficulties reading text, would it be a new challenge to further intervene with their reading struggles or a new opportunity to help them read text on the small screen of a mobile phone?

To answer this question empirically, the researchers recruited twenty-seven high-school students with lifelong histories of reading struggles at a school exclusively for students with language disabilities. The reading materials used in the study were sixteen non-fiction passages, each 208 words in total. In this meticulously and carefully designed experimental study, the authors used a regular within-subject design. Each student read the sixteen passages in two inter-letter spacing patterns (normal vs. spaced), two reading devices (iPod vs. iPad), and two hand positions (hand holding vs. without hand holding). To avoid the ordering effect, the order of the passages to read and the assignments to different conditions was arranged in the orthogonal Latin square sequence. This generated three independent variables: device, crowding, and hand-position. Students' reading was assessed based on seven aspects of their eye movement data recorded by eye tracking equipment, leading to seven dependent variables: reading speed in words per minutes (faster = better); number of fixations (less = better); number of regressive saccades (less = better); number of inefficient saccades (less = better); number of gaze motions up (lower = better); number of gaze motions down (lower = better); and number of gaze motions off-page (lower = better). In addition, each participant was asked to recall the details of the passages they read and assess for fidelity on a four-point scale (higher = better).

They used hierarchical linear modeling to analyze the data and found no hand-position effects, some text-spacing effects, and significant effects in

---

[13] Schneps, M. H., Thomson, J. M., Sonnert, G. *et al.* (2013). "Shorter lines facilitate reading in those who struggle," *PloS one*, 8(8): e71161.

seven out of eight reading performance variables, indicating the iPod condition leads to faster reading speed, more efficient eye movements, fewer reading errors, and better reading comprehension. Their major findings suggest that reading using a small screen resulted in substantial benefits in reading performance for students with dyslexia. This benefit could be due to the reason that short lines on the small screen reduce crowdedness or density in each line of the text to dyslexia students, which thus makes their reading process easier, quicker, and better.

Overall, this study has several strengths. (1) It used the within-subject experimental design rather than cross-sectional design that generates experimental evidence; (2) it used the mutually orthogonal Latin squares to deal with ordering effects; (3) it used multiple dependent variables to assess multiple aspects of reading rather than just one; (4) it collected eye movement data rather than often-observed, self-reported data; (5) it analyzed data by controlling for potential confounding variables such as visual attention span and previous reading abilities; and (6) it used experimental design to rule out other factors, such as line spacing, letter spacing, and line width. Its limitations include: (1) its relatively small sample size of twenty-seven students rather than multiple groups of dyslexic people; (2) lack of control groups; (3) lack of variations of line widths to estimate the line-widths effect; (4) not investigating attention and crowding in dyslexia under conditions of gaze motion; and (5) no different oral and written languages were tested.

Mobile reading among regular users is rapidly increasing, as part of the mobile reading revolution, and is becoming a particularly promising and emerging area of research, but the research on mobile reading for users with special needs is particularly sparse. It discovers benefits that we normally do not expect. Its implications indicate large potentials due to the flexibility afforded by mobile phones for providing a critical advantage: electronic text can easily adapt to the needs of individuals. Therefore, by reinventing reading in this mobile era, everyone may be able to gain, and impairments in reading may cease to be a barrier for many people with dyslexia. For these reasons, overall, this study provides a good example of m-user research, and made scientific contributions to the mobile phone behavior literature by pioneering the area of mobile phone reading (m-reading). It provided experimental evidence of how using iPods can improve multiple aspects of reading performance for dyslexic students, a special group of mobile phone users. In short, can readers with dyslexia use or benefit from mobile phones? Yes, they can, but benefits should be specific and complex rather than general and simple. Here, we can learn about mobile phone users from the perspective of disability, especially the unexpected unique benefits of using mobile phones for a special population.

3.6   Users Who Plan to Use Mobile Phones While Driving

Besides common demographic and general behavior characteristics, characteristics of special groups of mobile phone users such as those of drivers, patients, and politicians are widely studied. Here, we introduce an article entitled "An examination of the factors that influence drivers' willingness to use hand-held mobile phones."[14] It focuses on characteristics of a group of users who use mobile phones while driving. While there is little information about the first author as a student author, the corresponding author, Dr. Ioni Lewis, is a counseling/health psychologist in Australia. Her several publications focus on mobile phones and driving. The article was published in a journal with an unusual name called *Transportation Research Part F*. The journal of *Transportation Research* was one of the earliest and best journals that have been publishing strong research on calling while driving since 1980 and later was divided into six journals to focus on specific topics. These specific journals are: *Part A: Policy and Practice*; *Part B: Methodological Issues*; *Part C: Emerging Technologies*; *Part D: Transport and Environment*; *Part E: Logistics and Transportation Review*; and *Part F: Traffic Psychology and Behavior*.

In this study, the authors attempted to test three hypotheses about whether (1) situation-based external factors (e.g., urgency while driving), (2) intention-based internal factors (e.g., planned behavior), and (3) personality-based internal factors (e.g., extraversion) are related to willingness to use a mobile phone while driving. The research motivation is that hand-held mobile phone use while driving is illegal in Australia, yet many drivers persist with this behavior.

To test these hypotheses, the authors used a repeated measures design (i.e., testing the same participants multiple times) and developed a scenario-based survey (i.e., asking participants to respond to four different driving scenarios). They recruited 160 Australian undergraduate students. Hierarchical regression analyses were used to analyze the data. Specifically, the outcome variable is the willingness to use mobile phones while driving in the next three months. The predictors are time urgency while driving,

---

[14] Rozario, M., Lewis, I., and White, K. M. (2010). "An examination of the factors that influence drivers' willingness to use hand-held mobile phones," *Transportation Research Part F: Traffic Psychology and Behaviour*, 13(6): 365–376.

passenger presence while driving, planned behavior, extraversion, and neuroticism. The control variables included age and gender (included in the data analysis), traffic density, and weather conditions (included in the scenario instruction). The study was conducted in a scenario-based survey format in a classroom setting using the questionnaire consisting of the planned behavior scale and the personality scale under four scenarios.

The study found that, for this group of Australian undergraduate students who plan to use their own mobile phones while driving, multiple characteristics rather than one single characteristic are needed to identify them. Specifically, (1) these mobile phone users' beliefs regarding their favorable behavior, their social norms, and their ability to perform are significant predictors of drivers' willingness to use a mobile phone, (2) neuroticism and extraversion are not significant predictors of drivers' willingness to use a mobile phone, and (3) passenger presence, but not time urgency, are significant moderators with three planned behavior variables (i.e., favorable behavior, social norms, and ability to perform), but not two personality variables (i.e., neuroticism and extraversion).

The study has several strengths. (1) This is a well-designed, well-executed, and well-written study. (2) It uses a repeated measures design which is better than simple cross-sectional, survey-based studies. (3) It controls several potential confounding factors. (4) Its data analysis is careful. (5) Hierarchical regression analysis is appropriate and effective. (6) It uses the scenarios-based survey. (7) It uses a counterbalanced sequence to run experiments. (8) It draws on two theoretical models – the Theory of Planned Behavior and the Prototype Willingness Model. (9) It distinguished between spontaneous behavior, habitual behavior, and planned behavior.

Its weaknesses include that: (1) it focuses on willingness, but not actual behavior; and (2) it still relies on using the self-reported data rather than objective observational data. Although the research questions match the research design, it is not real-life, true observation, and thus less authentic in order to have good ecological validity.

From the perspective of user-based mobile phone behavior, this study shows another aspect of its complexity. First, it concerns a *special group* of mobile phone users: Australian undergraduate students who plan to use their own mobile phones while driving. It is not easy to use one single common demographic or behavioral characteristic (e.g., age or intelligence) to label them. Second, a complex combination of *multiple characteristics* is needed to identify them. These characteristics might include their behavioral tendencies and personality traits and might be directly or indirectly related to their demographic features such as age and gender and their reactions to specific situations such as passenger presence, time urgency, traffic density, and weather conditions.

3.7 *Multiple User Groups Involved in Mobile Phone School Policy*

All the examples we discussed above essentially come from a perspective of an individual mobile phone user (e.g., a user with different personality characteristics or with dyslexia) or a single user group (e.g., young users who might use mobile phones while driving). However, in real life, mobile phone users might form different user groups and have to play multiple roles or might have multiple indirect relationships to other mobile phone users at the same time. Here, we will discuss a good research example about multiple user groups. The title is "Three different roles, five different aspects: Differences and similarities in viewing school mobile phone policies among teachers, parents, and students."[15] The first author, Dr. Qiufang Gao, is a young researcher at Shenzhen University of China and this is her second article co-authoring with me as her mentor on mobile phone school policy.

In this study, researchers aimed to address four research questions, examining the different views of teachers, parents, and students on (1) motivation, (2) implementation, (3) evaluation, and (4) improvement of mobile phone school policy. To address these questions, the study surveyed 435 elementary, middle-school, and high-school students in a city of China, 435 parents of these students, and 356 teachers of these students. The survey had three similar versions for students, parents, and teachers, each consisting of a twenty-five-item questionnaire with 5-point Likert scale items (1 = strongly disagree and 5 = strongly agree), assessing perceptions of mobile phone use policies at school. The major findings include that students, parents, and teachers have significantly different views on: (1) reasons to use mobile phones (e.g., does mobile phone use help students' learning?); (2) policy content regarding the use of mobile phones (e.g., should mobile phones be allowed during classes and exams?); (3) implementation details regarding the use of mobile phones (e.g., should the school's mobile phone policies be emphasized at parent–teacher conferences?); (4) evaluation regarding the use of mobile phones (e.g., are

---

[15] Gao, Q., Yan, Z., Wei, C. *et al.* (2017). "Three different roles, five different aspects: Differences and similarities in viewing school mobile phone policies among teachers, parents, and students," *Computers & Education*, 106: 13–25.

the existing policies effective?); and (5) improvement regarding the use of mobile phones (e.g., should the school increase the number of public telephones for safety on campus?) – all five findings with the largest difference being between students and teachers (the most positive view from the students and the most negative view from teachers).

The study has several strengths. (1) It used three user groups in one single study to compare the perception differences regarding the mobile phone school policy. (2) It had a relatively large sample size and a well-tested questionnaire with three versions for three groups. (3) Its data analysis was well performed, starting with overall analysis of variance (ANOVA) and then with follow-up ANOVA. The weaknesses include: (1) the teachers, parents, and students are partially, not fully matched; and (2) it focuses on users' views rather than users' actual behavior. Future research can be undertaken to examine the matched triple of teacher–parent–student by using hierarchical linear modeling.

From the perspective of user-based mobile phone behavior, students, parents, and teachers are all mobile phone users in a broad sense and all involved in the mobile phone school policy process. However, these three user groups play different roles: teachers are usually school policy makers, students are mobile phone users regulated directly by the school policy, and parents perhaps could be supporters/attackers of the school policy or monitors of students' mobile phone use. These three user groups form a complex relationship. For various reasons, these three groups differ in various important ways and consequently show different views toward the policy. Eventually, they may have different behaviors toward the policy, leading to varying effectiveness of the policy.

To sum up the section on empirical studies, we have discussed the two reports and six articles in this section. From these studies, we can see scientific evidence of various mobile phone users, including users in the United States, users throughout the world, users charged for sexting, young users addicted to mobile phones, users with different personalities, users with dyslexia, users who engage in distracted driving, and multiple users in different relationships with each other. The empirical literature indicates that: (1) not everyone is a mobile phone user; (2) mobile phone users are a complex concept involving different types of users with diverse demographical, behavioral, and special characteristics; and (3) different users are associated with different mobile phone behaviors (e.g., sexting, mobile reading, or distracted driving), which is the most important aspect that we care about in studying and understanding mobile phone users.

Now, after our discussions on intuitive thoughts, everyday observations, and scientific research on mobile phone users, thoughtful and interested readers might become more eager to learn how much we know about mobile phone users overall and how we can develop a comprehensive knowledge about mobile phone users in order to develop an understanding of their complexity and their mobile phone behavior. The next section addresses these two questions.

4.   Knowledge Syntheses: From Users in Latin America to Problematic Users

There are two particularly useful ways to develop comprehensive know-ledge of a given area of research: reading handbook/encyclopedia chapters and reading review articles. Of course, for any given research, there must be substantial literature accumulated over time, and there must be scholars to synthesize the literature and publish the synthesized work in hand-books/encyclopedias or journals. Thus, whether a given area of study is emerging, emerged, or well established, the review literature rather than the empirical literature should be a quick indication. Below, we will discuss these two types of knowledge synthesis literature, the encyclopedia chapters and published review articles, on mobile phone users.

4.1   Encyclopedia *Chapters: Users in Latin America and with Visual Impairment*

As shown in Table 2.1, about thirty chapters in the *Encyclopedia of Mobile Phone Behavior* focus on different mobile phone users and relevant mobile phone behavior. About half of these present mobile phone users with different demographic and behavior characteristics, and about another half deal with mobile phone users in health care, education, and everyday settings. These chapters vividly show the unusual diversity of mobile phone users in the world. For instance, the chapter on Mexican mobile phone use indicates that the mobile phone network has provided new service to those poor people who were previously excluded from the world of technology and has transformed the lives of the poor. However, the mobile broadband penetration in Latin American countries is still low, averaging 17 percent. For another example, the chapter on mobile phone users with visual impairment indicates that smartphones with touch screens present new challenges for this group of users because the flat screen does not have visually perceptible features for them. However, researchers have developed

Table 2.1 *The* Encyclopedia *Chapters on User-Based Mobile Phone Behavior*

Feature	Chapter Title
Age	Children, risks and the mobile Internet
Age	Teenage sexting: Sexual expression meets mobile technology
Age	Keitai and Japanese adolescents
Age	Textism use and language ability in children
Age	Adolescent text messaging
Country	Generation Y and mobile marketing in India
Country	Mobile internet use in Japan: Text-message dependency and social relationships
Country	Social impacts of mobile phones on the life of the Chinese people
Country	Focus on text messages: A review of studies in French
Country	Mobile communications in Mexico in the Latin American context
Country	Mobile phones' influence on journalism practice in Africa
Country	Mobile screen media practices in Korea
Country	Mobile user behaviors in China
Disable	Deaf adolescents' textisms
Disable	Mobile phone technology for ALL: Towards reducing the digital divide
Disable	Use of mobile phones by individuals with visual impairments
Disable	Mobile phone: Repurposed assistive technology for individuals with disabilities
Disability	Mobile phones as assistive and accessible technology for people with disabilities
Disability	The use of mobile phone technology to support people with autism spectrum disorders
Education	Exploring the use of mobile devices to support teacher education
Education	Mobile phone use by middle school students
Medicine	Mobile health in emergency care
Medicine	Use of mobile phones to help prevent child maltreatment
Medicine	Students hurting students: Cyberbullying as a mobile phone behavior
Medicine	mHealth in maternal, newborn, and child health programs around the world
Everyday	The role of mobile phones in romantic relationships
Everyday	Divorced coparents' use of communication technology
Everyday	Portable social groups

different ways to overcome this problem, including clear sound, perceptible feedback, synthetic speech, voice command, and gesture-based input.

4.2 Review Articles: Young Users and Radiation Exposure, and Problematic Users

The empirical literature on mobile phone users is substantial. However, the number of published review articles is limited. If searching the database of PsycINFO using the two keywords, cell phones and literature review, we might find only about five relevant reviews. You might find 222 reviews in the database of WOS, but very few directly focus on users and most are on medical research on brain cancers and addiction. Here, we will discuss two relatively recent and quite informative examples: "Mobile phone use and exposures in children" by Joachim Schüz (2005)[16] and "Problematic use of the mobile phone: A literature review and a pathways model" by Joël Billieux (2012).[17]

Schüz pointed out that the main difference in radio wave exposures concerning the use of mobile phones between today's children and adults is (1) the *longer* lifetime exposure of children when they grow older, due to starting to use mobile phones at an early age, and (2) *higher* frequency of use among children, including higher popularity of mobile phones and features specifically designed to attract children. The review indicates that the prevalence of mobile phone users is already as high as 90 percent among adolescents in some countries. For children, mobile phones are dominant sources of radio wave exposure and relevant sources of extremely low frequency magnetic fields. Children will have a much higher cumulative exposure to radio waves than today's adults when they were at the same age. Radio wave exposure of children may be estimated more easily, because the variety of exposure sources is smaller than for adults. It concludes that as long as adverse health effects cannot be ruled out, it is appropriate to instruct children and their parents about careful use of mobile phones.

Billieux defined problematic use of the mobile phone as an inability to regulate mobile phone use, leading to negative impacts on mobile phone users' daily life. He reviewed the existing literature on risk factors for problematic mobile phone use. Based on his review, the risk factors are associated with three types of characteristics of mobile phone users. The first type is demographic characteristics. Mobile phone users' gender and age but not educational level and socioeconomic status are related to problematic mobile phone use. The second type is personality traits. Mobile phone users' neuroticism (i.e., the tendency to be emotionally unstable) and extraversion (i.e., the tendency to be sociable), but not other personality traits (e.g., agreeableness, consciousness), and impulsivity are related to problematic mobile phone use. The last type is mobile phone users' low self-esteem, which is related to problematic mobile phone use.

---

[16] Schüz, J. (2005). "Mobile phone use and exposures in children," *Bioelectromagnetics*, 26(S7): S45–S50.
[17] Billieux, J. (2012). "Problematic use of the mobile phone: A literature review and a pathways model," *Current Psychiatry Reviews*, 8(4): 299–307.

These two reviews present in-depth, specific, synthesized knowledge about two specific topics – young users' risk of radiation exposure and users' characteristics related to addiction. It helps us understand the complexity of mobile phone users related to two adverse aspects. However, these are specific narrative reviews rather than systematic or scoping reviews and thus do not provide a comprehensive knowledge about mobile phone users in general.

In summary, similar to the scientific research, the scientific synthesis of the literature still focuses on specific features of mobile phone users (e.g., demographic features such as age or region or behavioral features such as addiction or visual impairment). However, it focused on various studies rather than on one so that we can see specific aspects of the complexity of users in a relatively broad way (e.g., diverse findings about mobile phone users and various needs of mobile phone users).

5. Comparative Analyses: From TV Viewers to Mobile Phone Users

After considering the real-life observations, scientific research, and research synthesis about mobile phone users, it is natural for us to wonder whether and how users of mobile phones differ from those of other technologies, such as television, computers, and the Internet. Due to the methodological challenges in comparison, the complexity of this topic, and the space limitation, here we will only be able to briefly compare users of different technologies by discussing four reviews that touch on a few key issues of users of different technologies.

5.1 Reviewing Users of Four Technologies

TV viewers. The first review is a meta-analysis, a special type of review based on quantitative data. It is entitled "Relationships between media use, body fatness and physical activity in children and youth: A meta-analysis" by Simon Marshall and his three collaborators.[18] An expert panel stated in 1996 that youth's obesity is related to their increased hours of viewing TV and decreased physical activities. Thus, one of the primary goals of the meta-analysis was to review the published English journal articles from 1985 to 2004 and to verify the above expert statement. The relevant major

---

[18] Marshall, S. J., Biddle, S. J., Gorely, T. *et al.* (2004). "Relationships between media use, body fatness and physical activity in children and youth: A meta-analysis," *International Journal of Obesity*, 28(10): 1238–1246.

findings based on over thirty studies include: (1) The relationship between TV viewing and body fatness is positive and statistically significant, but the effect size is small (Pearson r = .084, p < .005). Some age-based difference was found among three age groups (0–6, 7–12, 13–18), but no gender difference was found. (2) The relationship between TV viewing and physical activity is negative and statistically significant, but the effect size is small (Pearson r = −.129 p < .005). Some age difference was found among three age groups (0–6, 7–12, 13–18), but no gender difference was found.

Computer users. The second review is also a meta-analysis, entitled "Computer anxiety and its correlates: A meta-analysis" by Siew Lian Chua and his two co-authors.[19] Computer anxiety was defined in the study as an emotional fear of computers when individuals use computers or consider using computers. Since computer anxiety leads to computer user avoidance, the authors attempted to examine whether computer anxiety is related to gender, age, and computer experiences, the three most commonly considered correlates. The meta-analysis of thirty-six relevant articles suggests the following: (1) Gender is significantly related to computer anxiety among undergraduate students. Female students had higher levels of computer anxiety than male students. (2) Computer experience is significantly related to computer anxiety among undergraduate students. Students with less computer experience had higher levels of computer anxiety than students with more computer experience. (3) No sufficient studies examining age differences were available for meta-analysis.

Internet surfers. The third review is, again, a meta-analysis. Its title is "Internet use and psychological well-being: A meta-analysis" by Chiung-jung Huang.[20] The effect of Internet use on well-being is the most popular topic in Internet behavior research. The author aimed to synthesize the existing studies and find meta-analytic evidence on this topic. The author identified forty relevant studies, yielding forty-three samples, nearly 22,000 participants. The major findings include: (1) a small negative relationship exists between Internet use and well-being; and (2) no consistent and inclusive evidence shows significant age or gender difference.

Mobile phone users. The last review is a regular narrative review, entitled "The sensitivity of children to electromagnetic fields" by Leeka

[19] Chua, S. L., Chen, D. T., and Wong, A. F. (1999). "Computer anxiety and its correlates: A meta-analysis," *Computers in Human Behavior*, 15(5): 609–623.

[20] Huang, C. (2010). "Internet use and psychological well-being: A meta-analysis," *Cyberpsychology, Behavior, and Social Networking*, 13(3): 241–249.

Kheifets at UCLA and her collaborators from WHO.[21] Mobile phones and brain cancers has been one of the most studied topics in mobile phone behavior research. However, no meta-analysis has been published in synthesizing effects of mobile phones on brains of young mobile phone users. One primary reason is that specific empirical research is rapidly emerging, but this has not been sufficiently accumulated for a meta-analysis. In this review, the authors pointed out multiple important issues: (1) Children have a longer time of *exposure* to radio frequency energy from mobile phones than the childhood of adults today. (2) Children may be biologically *vulnerable* to radio frequency energy from mobile phones. Their brain tissue is more conductive than that of adults and thus has greater absorption of radio frequency energy. (3) Children's vulnerability to radio frequency energy might be greater and have longer impacts during certain *critical* time periods, such as the prenatal period. (4) *Residential* exposure (e.g., television signals and Wi-Fi at home) and *parental* exposure (e.g., mobile phone use by mothers with infants) are two major exposure resources for young children. More children often use their parents' mobile phones and more adolescents will have their own mobile phones at home and at school. (5) Potential health *risks* to children from radio frequency fields include an increase of temperature in body tissues, blood circulation of the fetus and the mother during pregnancy, changes in the formation of proteins, and development of brain tumors.

5.2 Comparing Users of Four Technologies

What can we learn from these four articles regarding users of different technologies? First, in general, studies of users of different technologies always further examine similar *characteristics* of users, either as demographic background variables or independent and moderating variables. For TV viewers, in the meta-analysis of over thirty students, age and gender were further examined as two independent variables to see if TV viewing will influence fatness and physical activity for TV viewers with different ages and genders. Similarly, for PC users, in the meta-analysis of thirty-six students, age and computer experience were also examined as two independent variables and significant gender differences and experience-based differences in computer anxiety were found. For Internet users, in the meta-analysis of forty studies, age and gender were further

---

[21] Kheifets, L., Repacholi, M., Saunders, R., and Van Deventer, E. (2005). "The sensitivity of children to electromagnetic fields," *Pediatrics*, 116(2): e303–e313.

examined as two moderators. No consistent and inclusive evidence was found for the observed small negative relationship between Internet use and well-being and this changed among different age groups and different genders. For mobile phone users, children at young ages are considered to be more vulnerable than adults, biologically, developmentally, and environmentally, to radio frequency energy from mobile phones.

Second, different technology users might face unique *challenges* and thus draw from extensive research as the empirical base for meta-analysis studies. For instance, as indicated in the three meta-analyses and one review, television viewers might face a challenge of decreasing physical activities, computer users (especially female college students) might face a challenge of computer anxiety, Internet users might face a challenge concerning psychological well-being, and mobile phone users might face radiation exposure problems.

Third, it is extremely *difficult*, if it is possible at all, to have a direct, straightforward comparison of users of different technologies. One of the reasons is that mobile phones *integrate* different technologies. Thus, mobile phone users can be television viewers (e.g., via mobile TV), computer users (e.g., calculating arithmetic problems), or Internet users (e.g., using smartphones going online) at the same time. Another reason is that different technologies are going through different *stages* of adoption and diffusion of their own history. Television public viewing might have about eighty years of history since the 1940s, personal computer use might have about fifty years of history since the 1970s, popular Internet use might have twenty years of history since the 1990s, and pervasive mobile phone use has about thirty years of history since the 1980s. It is difficult to compare users of different technologies in their different stages at the same time. The third reason is that *unit* of use differs for the different technologies. Television viewers are related to households rather than individuals. Computer users are attached to different computers at home or at work. Internet users are attached with Internet accessibility at home and at work. However, mobile phones are attached with each individual user.

Thus, it is hard to compare users of different technologies, even for the most basic issues about *how many users* there are of different technologies. Recall that the three graduate students' intuitive responses indicated that everyone is a mobile phone user. Is this also similar for television viewers, computer users, and Internet surfers? To make the comparison simple and feasible, let us look at the situation of using different technologies at home. Certainly, everyone can be a television viewer as long as the television set is there and people have the capacity to view it. Television can be viewed alone, but is often shared by multiple viewers. Typically, one home might have one or two television sets. At home, adults usually have their personal computers, older kids have a desktop or a laptop, and young kids might have a laptop or a tablet. Each family member will access the Internet. Typically, one home will have one Internet service line. As for a mobile phone, the major difference is that it becomes a personal device. Typically, each family member will have their own mobile phone and hardly share them with each other. In addition, many functions of previous technologies, such as television, computers, and Internet, are included in modern mobile phones. Based on ITU data, worldwide mobile phone subscriptions have grown to 7.1 billion, representing 96.8 percent of the world's population, compared with 14.5 percent for traditional telephones, 45.4 percent for computers at home, and 46.4 percent for Internet access at home. These figures are more related to the number of *technologies* (i.e., computers or Internet) rather than actual technology *users* (e.g., people who actually use, play, or share mobile phones). In short, given the lack of good statistical reports, it is difficult to state that users of one technology are more or less than those of another technology, which makes the scientific comparison of penetration rates of different technologies in the world almost impossible at present. Nevertheless, it is much needed in the near future to conduct innovative and rigorous comparative studies of users of different technologies so that we can better understand the mobile users as well as other technological users based on scientific comparisons.

6. Complex Thinking: Diverse Users, Complex Behavior

At the beginning of this chapter, we discussed intuitive responses about mobile phone users from three graduate students. These three graduate students all considered that mobile phone users are everyone or almost everyone, but each of them focused on different aspects of mobile phone users (e.g., their ages, their ways of using mobile phones, and their amount of time spent on mobile phones). After reading this chapter, we should be able to easily and clearly see that their intuitive knowledge is authentic, but not deep, broad, and sophisticated enough. To reflect on what we have discussed and learned from this chapter: (1) Perhaps we now have realized that mobile phone users do not necessarily have to be mobile phone owners. Mobile phone users as a concept is much broader and more complex than the owners. (2) Perhaps we now understand that mobile phone users are a key element of mobile phone behavior. We should always look at the users first when we study mobile phone behavior. (3)

Perhaps we know much more about the users by being familiar with the substantial literature on mobile phone behavior among different mobile phone users with diverse demographical, behavioral, and special characteristics, and even the complex relationship among different users. These pieces of knowledge are more scientific rather than intuitive, and research-based rather than perception-based.

Figure 2.1 provides a brief summary of this chapter. It shows that this chapter presents mobile phone users and relevant mobile phone behavior from four major dimensions, the good-vs.-bad dimension, demographic characteristics, behavioral characteristics, and special characteristics, and reveals the complexity of user-based mobile phone behavior. For *bad* users, we discussed the cases of the Tsarnaev brothers and the Farook couple and the studies of teens arrested for sexting and addicted users. For *demographical* characteristics, we discussed the cases of a 1-year-old boy playing a mobile game, several seniors learning to use mobile phones, and studies of young Australian users with early symptoms of addiction. For *behavior* characteristics, we discussed the cases of Danny Bowman and Professor Matthew Schneps and studies of users with different personalities, users with dyslexia, users who use mobile phones while driving, and problematic users. For *special* characteristics, we discussed the cases of Barack Obama,

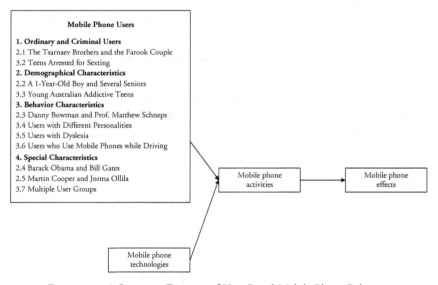

Figure 2.1   A Summary Diagram of User-Based Mobile Phone Behavior

Bill Gates, Martin Cooper, and Jorma Ollila, and for special users, we discussed the study on user relationships among students, teachers, and parents. Toward the end of the chapter, we compared TV viewers, computer users, Internet surfers, and mobile phone users in terms of technology users and human behavior in using different technologies. We know now that: mobile phone users are particularly diverse; user-based mobile phone behavior is particularly complex; and the research on user-based mobile phone behavior is particularly extensive. As a result, we should always consider who uses mobile phones first when we examine various mobile phone behaviors in the real-life world and in the scientific world.

Previous research always inspires and motivates future research. It can be predicted that, in the next five to ten years, we will and should see some major breakthroughs in mobile phone user research. Several particularly important topics should be examined more proactively in future research and will make timely and important contributions to the field of mobile phone behavior.

First, for the *bad* mobile phone users, we need to know more about the mobile phone behavior of criminal users. With cyber safety and cyber security becoming a serious global concern, we need to examine criminal users, including their behavioral characteristics and their mobile phone behavior. Furthermore, we need to study criminal users and victim users as a pair together to better understand the complex interaction between them.

Second, for the users with different *demographic* characteristics, we need to know more about mobile phone behavior of users younger than the age of 10, users older than 70, and female users. Currently, the most studied population is college students, one of the most active groups of mobile phone users. However, with the global penetration rate of mobile phones approaching 100 percent, the numbers of younger users, older users, and female users are rapidly increasing. Thus, their mobile phone behavior is in particular worth further research.

Third, for the users with different *behavioral* characteristics, we need to know more about the mobile phone behavior of criminal users. The current research has examined personality traits, attitudes, perceptions, and other behavioral characteristics of ordinary users. We need to know more about gifted or talented users. The current research has examined various users with special needs. While this line of research should continue and be expanded, we should start to develop strong research programs to study gifted or talented users, especially young, older, and female talented users. The current positive psychology movement across the world suggests that talented user research will advance knowledge not only about what the extraordinary strengths of talented users are, but also about how ordinary users, including users with disabilities, can learn from these extraordinary strengths.

Fourth, for the users with *special* characteristics, we need to know more about several groups of users and their mobile phone behavior. Such groups of users include users in business settings, clinic patient users, and users from special cultures. The current research focuses more on individual users and their mobile phone behavior. It is time for the mobile phone behavior research community to identify, describe, analyze, and support many more groups of users. In addition, we need to know more about romantic partners, intergenerational users, and multi-task users. The current research focuses more on users on their own. We should study users in more complex relationships with other users or non-users. This line of research will help us to understand complex mobile phone behavior in the real world.

We have discussed some examples of future research. However, it is neither an exhaustive list nor a fixed one. If we continue and accelerate our research efforts, after five or ten years, we will have a much better understanding of mobile phone users and the related mobile phone behavior. As a result, more mobile phone users will benefit more from the research.

CHAPTER 3

Mobile Phone Technologies

Outline

1. *Intuitive Thinking: Words from Sunny*
2. *Daily Observations: From Signature Touch to the Right to Know*
   2.1 *Mobile Phones: Signature Touch and Freedom 251*
   2.2 *Mobile Phone Features: Flight 93 and Ferry Sewol*
   2.3 *Mobile Phone Software and Hardware: Leo Grand and Vincent*
   2.4 *Mobile Phone Batteries and Chargers: Galaxy S4 and Energous*
   2.5 *Mobile Phone Networks: Wi-Fi in Nanjing and Li-Fi in Dubai*
3. *Empirical Studies: From Apps to Base Stations*
   3.1 *Smartphone Apps: Users in Korea*
   3.2 *Calling vs. Texting: Adolescents' Decisions*
   3.3 *Mobile Cameras: Patients with Nasal Bone Injuries*
   3.4 *Base Stations: Childhood Cancers*
   3.5 *GPS: Children's Mobility*
4. *Knowledge Syntheses: From Mobile Security to Battery Explosion*
   4.1 *Mobile Devices: Security*
   4.2 *Mobile Texting: Positive and Negative Sides*
   4.3 *Mobile Apps: Health-Care Implications*
   4.4 *Mobile Sensing: Ubiquitous, Complex, and Fast Growing*
   4.5 *Mobile Phone Batteries: Fire and Explosion*
5. *Comparative Analyses: From Closed Captions to Texting*
   5.1 *Study 1: Closed Captions*
   5.2 *Study 2: Microsoft Word*
   5.3 *Study 3: E-mail*
   5.4 *Study 4: Texting*
6. *Complex Thinking: Diverse Technologies, Complex Behavior*

1. Intuitive Thinking: Words from Sunny

Sunny is a Korean man who is technology savvy and has several mobile phones. I know this because a thief broke into his apartment at midnight and took all of his mobile phones. Mobile phone theft and robbery, privacy protection of lost phones, and localization and self-destruction of lost phones are interesting issues of mobile phone behavior that we will discuss in later chapters. One day, half out of curiosity and half challenging him, I asked Sunny for his intuitive thoughts about mobile phone technologies: What technologies are mobile phone technologies? What technologies are not mobile phone technologies? Please give three to five quick examples of mobile phone technologies. His quick answers are as follows: First, mobile payment. The mobile phone allows us to pay or transfer money easily and safely. Second, GPS. Mobile phones, especially smartphones, provide us with GPS services such as Google maps, enabling us to find a location easily and quickly. Third, text messenger. Nowadays, there are many types of messenger apps such as KakaoTalk and WeChat that are embedded in the mobile phone, allowing us to communicate with others efficiently. In addition, mobile phones may be used for accessing social networking sites (SNS), watching movies, recording sound and video, listening to music, taking pictures, and more. It is difficult to actually identify what technologies are not mobile phone technologies as most technologies can be embedded in the mobile phone.

Sunny's intuitive responses outlined above are interesting. What can we learn from his intuitive responses about mobile phone technologies? We can learn at least four points. First, from his three examples of mobile phone technologies, mobile payment, GPS, and text messenger, we can say that Sunny knows mobile phone technologies pretty well in terms of software and hardware. He knows mobile apps such as the one used to make his mobile payments; he knows mobile phone hardware such as GPS. Second, from his brief description, we can also say that he knows why and how to use these hardware and software. He has a great deal of knowledge about different features or functions of mobile phones, such as watching movies, recording, listening to music, and taking pictures, based on his own experience. Third, he has had experience using KakaoTalk and WeChat, two specific programs that are widely used in Korea. Fourth, he is obviously aware of technology embeddedness or the technology integration of mobile phone technologies, believing that most technologies can be embedded in the mobile phone.

Clearly, Sunny's knowledge focuses on various features of mobile phones, but does he have comprehensive knowledge about mobile phone technologies? Of course, I specifically asked him about mobile phone technologies rather than about mobile phone behavior, but does he have a strong awareness of mobile phone behavior that is related to various mobile technologies? After studying this chapter, we should have a relatively clear answer to these two questions. Now, we will use his initial thoughts as a starting point for further understanding the content of this chapter. The goal of the chapter is to understand the complexity of mobile phone behavior that is specifically related to mobile phone technologies. To achieve this goal, we will use four strategies: daily observations, empirical studies, knowledge syntheses, and comparative analyses, each of which represents the four major sections of this chapter. Let us work together to achieve this goal.

2. Daily Observations: From Signature Touch to the Right to Know

2.1 *Mobile Phones: Signature Touch and Freedom 251*

In October 2015,[1] Vertu, a British manufacturer and retailer of luxury mobile phones, announced that their latest flagship model, the 2015 Signature Touch, would hit the market, with a price of nearly $15,000, about thirty times more expensive than an iPhone. It is generally considered to be one of the most luxurious phones on the market. This model has multiple luxury features, from handcrafted parts, a wireless charger, a sapphire glass screen, robust speakers, an integrated calf leather case, and a personalized concierge service for the annual fee of nearly $8,000.

In February 2016,[2] Ringing Bells, a little-known Indian company, launched the world's cheapest smartphone, called Freedom 251, for a price of 251 Indian Rupee (about $3.73). This smartphone is a dual-SIM, 3G-capable phone, equipped with multiple fancy technical features, including a 4-inch WVGA resolution display, a 1.3 Ghz quad-core processor, 1GB RAM, 8GB total storage space, a 3.2 megapixel camera on the back, 0.3 megapixel camera on the front, and a 1,450 mAh battery. How much does an Indian earn per day on an average? By one estimate it is also around 251 Indian Rupee!

---

[1] See www.digitaltrends.com/android/vertu-new-signature-touch-hands-on/#:S3pTKJuEofrfzA.
[2] See http://indianexpress.com/article/technology/mobile-tabs/india-cheapest-smartphone-rs-500-make-in-india-ringing-bells/.

These two observations underline the complexity of mobile phones, as well as the complexity of mobile phone behavior. First, when we talk about mobile phone technologies, one of the first issues that we will naturally consider is mobile phones themselves as a technology product. There are various software and hardware in a mobile phone, but first and foremost, the mobile phone is a whole handset. Sunny, the Korean man we discussed at the beginning of this chapter, did not explicitly mention what kinds of mobile phones he was referring to. From his initial responses, he might very likely be referring to Samsung or LG smartphones, two of the most popular Korean mobile phone brands.

Second, mobile phones as a high-tech product are particularly complex. From the perspective of the mobile phone industry's history, there is a long list of various types of mobile phones produced by more than twenty major companies, from the Motorola Personal Phone and Nokia, released in 1992, to Apple's iPhone 3G and Samsung Tocco released in 2008, to the Samsung Galaxy S III and Xiaomi Mi 2 released in 2012. Generally, low-end phones are called basic phones, whereas high-end phones are called smartphones. But in the real world, with extremely fast developments of mobile phone technologies, this general categorization might not work very well. Vertu's Signature Touch and Ringing Bells' Freedom 251 are just two unique examples among hundreds of mobile phones that have been produced throughout mobile phone history.

Third, different mobile phones are associated with different types of mobile phone behavior. The significant difference in price between Signature Touch and Freedom 251 is obvious. But more importantly, these two types of mobile phones are owned by users with different social and economic statuses (e.g., a wealthy businessman vs. a poor farmer), and are used for different types of activities (e.g., showing it off at a celebrity party in Paris vs. using it for phone calls in a remote Indian farm market) that lead to different types of effects on people's lives (e.g., having a personal phone number of a famous celebrity or paying $1 for a good deal in the farm market).

2.2   Mobile Phone Features: Flight 93 and Ferry Sewol

On September 11, 2011,[3] United Airlines Flight 93 was hijacked by four terrorists. After the hijackers took control of the plane, several passengers and flight attendants were able to make about thirty-seven phone calls to

---

[3] See https://en.wikipedia.org/wiki/United_Airlines_Flight_93.

airplane officials using airplane phones and to family members using personal mobile phones. Tom Burnett, one passenger on the flight, successfully made several phone calls to his wife Deena Burnett. He told his wife that the plane had been hijacked and learned from his wife about the attacks on the World Trade Center in New York City. He ended his last call by saying, "Don't worry, we're going to do something." Jeremy Glick, another passenger, was also luckily able to have a 20-minute phone conversation with his wife Elizabeth Glick and her parents. Jeremy told his wife that he loved her and to take good care of their 12-week-old daughter Emmy. Tom Burnett, Jeremy Glick, and other passengers bravely stepped up to fight against the hijackers' plan to crash the plane into the White House or Capitol Building. To prevent the passengers from regaining control of the plane, the hijackers crashed it in a Pennsylvania field, killing all forty-four people on board.

On April 16, 2014,[4] a Korean ferry named *Sewol* capsized and sank in a disaster. There were 476 people on that boat – only 172 survived and 304 died. Most of the victims were students of Danwon High School on a field trip. After 9 months, a heartbroken father missed his young son who lost his life so much that he sent a text message to his son's mobile phone via KakaoTalk. To his surprise, he received a text reply from his son's phone, saying how much he loved the father, telling the father to take care of himself, and asking the father to pass his greetings to other family members. In the end, it was found that another young Korean boy bought a mobile phone and the previous owner's phone number was assigned to the phone. This boy knew of the disaster and tried to comfort the father.

The features or functions of mobile phones refer to the set of technical capabilities, carrier services, hardware devices, and software applications that they offer to their users. Generally speaking, mobile phone features can be grouped into three basic types: communication (e.g., making a phone call), information (surfing the Internet), and computation (playing a mobile game such as *Angry Birds*). We can learn a few important points about mobile phone features from the two cases presented above. First, calling and texting are two of the most common features of communication with mobile phones. Different software and hardware have to work together in a mobile phone to make calls or send texts. The two cases highlight two features of mobile phone communication respectively – calling and texting. Second, these basic features of mobile phones can be associated with some of the most uncommon mobile phone behaviors.

---

[4] See https://en.wikipedia.org/wiki/Sinking_of_MV_Sewol.

The two cases show two emotional behaviors – fighting against terrorists and missing a deceased, beloved son. There are many more technical features related to common mobile phone behavior, e.g., sharing photos via Instagram, contacting friends via Facebook, locating your current position using GPS, monitoring personal health with health apps, and having password protection via pupil recognition.

2.3   Mobile Phone Software and Hardware: Leo Grand and Vincent

Leo Grand[5] was a homeless African American man living in Manhattan, New York after losing his job at MetLife in 2011. In August 2013, after two years of homeless life, he met Patrick McConlogue, a computer programmer. Patrick asked him to choose between receiving $100 or learning how to code. Leo chose to learn how to write code. Patrick then provided him with books on programming, a cheap but durable laptop, and daily lessons every morning. After only four months of learning with Patrick, Leo wrote an app by himself called *Trees for Cars*, a ride-sharing app. The app cost $0.99 to download and had two features: (1) The app will suggest nearby riders who may want to share a ride for interested drivers. (2) The app tracks how much carbon dioxide emission was prevented by the shared riding. After only a few weeks of releasing the app, he had made about $10,000. This case has drawn wide attention from the media and on the Internet.

Vincent Quigg[6] is a young man from California. He has a special skill of repairing iPhones for less than $80 within 45 minutes. He often repairs broken screens. He founded a company called TechWorld in 2012. He first diagnoses problems and then repairs or replaces the cracked screens. At the time he started his phone-repair business, he was only 18 years old, raised by a single mother. Quigg says he fixes up to ten phones per week and makes about $1,500 in sales per month. He has hired two employees as his company expanded. He attributes his knowledge for fixing iPhones to watching lots of video tutorials and says Steve Jobs is his idol. He was hired at Best Buy when he was 16, working there for two years selling HDTVs and computers, but had always been involved with the iPhone ecosystem. People referred to him as the iPhone guy. So he decided to use his acquired knowledge from Best Buy to create what he originally called "iRepair," an iPhone repair business. In addition to his excellent

---

[5] See www.businessinsider.com/leo-the-homeless-coder-2014-5.
[6] See www.voanews.com/content/young-entrepreneur-specilizes-in-iphones/1558629.html.

technology and business talents, he is also a skilful basketball player. He started playing basketball at the YMCA when he was 3 years old and played for his high school varsity basketball team as a point guard for four years. This is also a case receiving wide media attention.

What can we learn from these two real-life cases? (1) Mobile phone technologies consist of millions of apps and hundreds of hardware. (2) Leo wrote a software app for mobile phones and Vincent repaired the hardware. (3) The software and hardware technologies involve interesting mobile phone behavior: sharing car driving and protecting the environment in Leo's case and fixing the broken phones and earning money to help support his single-parent household in Vincent's case. (3) Even novice people can create apps or fix hardware within a short period of time and with limited or no formal training.

2.4 *Mobile Phone Batteries and Chargers: Galaxy S4 and Energous*

In July 2013,[7] Mr. Du, a 47-year-old resident in Hong Kong, was charging his newly purchased Samsung Galaxy S4 while playing with it in his living room. Suddenly, the phone exploded in his hand. He was scared and dropped the phone on the sofa. The phone began to burst into flames, burning the sofa and window curtain before rapidly spreading to the entire room. He and his wife escaped out of the apartment with their dog and only minor hand injuries. Their neighbors were also able to escape. The fire was eventually put out by firefighters. The apartment they bought in 2003 for 780,000 Hong Kong dollars and all the furniture inside was totally damaged. The phone and the charger were completely burned. The phone, charger, and battery were all made originally by Samsung. Three surprisingly similar cases of a Samsung phone bursting into flames were reported in a 9-day period that month.

In May 2016,[8] Energous announced a joint development agreement with a leading commercial and industrial supply company to further develop industrial and commercial applications for the full-size WattUp, which enables wire-free charging at distances of up to 15 feet. This might remove the need for continual battery replacement or dedicated power cable runs. Developed by Energous, WattUp is a revolutionary radio-frequency-based wireless charger that delivers scalable power via the same

---

[7] See http://orientaldaily.on.cc/cnt/news/20130727/00174_001.html.
[8] See www.marketwired.com/press-release/energous-partners-bring-wire-free-charging-industry-leading-commercial-industrial-supply-nasdaq-watt-2129703.htm.

radio bands as a Wi-Fi router. WattUp differs from current wireless charging systems in that it will deliver contained, useable power, at a distance, to multiple devices, resulting in a wire-free experience that saves users from having to remember to plug in their devices.

We can take away a few things from these two cases presented above. First, batteries and chargers are generally considered to be accessories of mobile phones. However, they can be technically complicated (e.g., a new wireless charger of WattUp). Second, although these are just accessories rather than the main handsets, these can lead to life-threating outcomes or even death (e.g., the exposure of Galaxy S4). Third, these accessories are related to real users, real processes, and real effects, leading to various mobile phone behaviors (e.g., the Hong Kong man charged his new mobile phone and the phone exploded). Fourth, while there are always negative problems emerging (e.g., mobile phone battery explosion), there will always be a motivation to develop new solutions to address these problems. For example, we might see that a new type of wireless charger perhaps might become a surprising solution to the battery explosion issue.

2.5   Mobile Phone Networks: Wi-Fi in Nanjing and Li-Fi in Dubai

In April 2014,[9] the quiet and normal life of residents in a building in Nanjing, China was disturbed by a series of knocking sounds on apartment doors. An old man was knocking on the doors of each apartment in the building to ask if the people living there had a Wi-Fi router and, if so, begged them not to use it. The old man had a daughter-in-law who was pregnant and he believed that the Wi-Fi router would hurt the health of the mother and future baby. In one day, it was told that he knocked on the door of one of his neighbors fourteen times to make sure the Wi-Fi router would not be used.

In July 2011, Harald Haas, who teaches at the University of Edinburgh in the United Kingdom, coined the term "Li-Fi" at his TED Global Talk, where he introduced the idea of "wireless data from every light." At TED Global, Harald Haas demonstrated, for the first time, a device that could do exactly that. By flickering the light from a single LED light, a change too quick for the human eye to detect, he can transmit far more data than a cellular tower and do it in a way that is more efficient, secure, and widespread. In April 2016,[10] five years after Harald Haas' TED talk,

---

[9] See http://news.ifeng.com/a/20140415/35763506_0.shtml.
[10] See www.indiatimes.com/news/world/dubai-to-roll-out-high-speed-li-fi-this-year-where-internet-will-flow-through-city-s-streetlights-254055.html.

Dubai announced its plan to roll out public high speed Li-Fi this year where Internet will flow through the city's streetlights. This is part of the first-phase plan for creating a Dubai smart city. Internet users in Dubai will soon switch to the next generation technology for data transfer, aka Li-Fi, dubbed as the next generation of high-speed Internet and 100 times faster than Wi-Fi. If so, Dubai will be the first city in the world to get the Li-Fi service. What is even more interesting is that the Li-Fi service will be transmitted through the city's streetlights. Each of these high-end design lamps will cost around $1,000. While Wi-Fi transmits data using radio waves, Li-Fi transmits data through LED light bulbs. With visible light, Li-Fi is able to transmit much more information at much higher speeds.

These two cases indicate the following: (1) Mobile phone networks are an important part of mobile technologies. Without cellular, Wi-Fi, and various other networks, a mobile phone is just a handset in our hands. (2) One major concern related to the networks is the effects of radiation on human health. It was this concern that caused the Chinese man in Nanjing to knock on the door of his neighbors. (3) The mobile network technologies have gone through major revolutions, G1, G2, G2.5, G3, and G4. One of the latest developments is Li-Fi, as shown in Dubai. (4) Besides the large concern about Wi-Fi and the good news about Dubai's streetlights delivering Li-Fi, there are various other behavior issues related to the networks, such as the satisfaction with network services and switching among different networks.

To end our discussion in this section of daily observations of technology-related mobile phone behavior, let us quickly compare Sunny's initial responses and the ten observations presented above. One easy and immediate finding is that while Sunny did show strong knowledge about mobile phone features and mobile phone software and hardware, his knowledge about mobile phone technologies is actually quite narrow. The ten observations reveal that mobile phone technologies are much broader and much more diverse and concern at least five major types: (1) mobile phones as handsets (e.g., Signature Touch vs. Freedom 251); (2) mobile phone features (e.g., calling vs. texting); (3) mobile phone hardware (e.g. broken screen repair) and software (e.g., Leo's app of *Trees for Cars*); (4) mobile phone networks (e.g., Wi-Fi vs. Li-Fi); and (5) mobile phone accessories (e.g., batteries and chargers).

The second finding is that the five major types of mobile phone technologies are associated with complex mobile behavior, with diverse mobile phone users (e.g., Leo and Vincent), mobile phone activities (e.g., the phone conversation on Flight 93 and decision making regarding texting or calling), and mobile phone effects (e.g., battery explosion). Nevertheless, these daily observations are essentially anecdotal evidence rather than robust evidence of scientific research. After studying and analyzing a series of daily observations, let us study and analyze a few examples of empirical studies on technology-centered mobile phone behavior in the next section.

3. Empirical Studies: From Apps to Base Stations

3.1 Smartphone Apps: Users in Korea

The first article we will discuss is entitled "Differential innovation of smartphone and application use by sociodemographics and personality" published in *Computers in Human Behavior* by Yeolib Kim, Daniel A. Briley, and Melissa Ocepek from the University of Texas in Austin.[11] The two major reasons to choose this article for our first discussion in this section are that this article presents details of use of smartphone applications (very few studies were published) and examines demographic and behavioral characteristics of smartphone users (many studies were published). The first author, Yeolib Kim, was a doctoral student in the School of Information at the University of Texas at the time the article was written. He completed his dissertation entitled "A meta-analysis of online trust: Examining main and moderating effects" in 2015. He has published four articles on technology use based on a quick search in Webs of Science. The second author has published eighteen articles on behavioral genetics and the third author has published twenty-one articles on information behavior based on Research Gate.

The article presents a survey study that was completed in Korea in 2012 with 9,482 participants. Measures included a series of survey questions on media use, demographics, and an adapted scale of a version of the Ten-Item Personality Inventory. The major findings include the following: (1) About half of the participants were smartphone users. These mobile phone users used five major types of apps: relational applications such as instant messaging and social networking; entertainment applications such as games, music/video/pictures, and sports; information applications such as lifestyle and news; e-commerce applications such as finance and

---

[11] Kim, Y., Briley, D. A., and Ocepek, M. G. (2015). "Differential innovation of smartphone and application use by sociodemographics and personality," *Computers in Human Behavior*, 44: 141–147.

shopping; and literacy applications such as books, education, and reference management. (2) Participants who were male, younger, more educated, and had a higher income were more likely to use smartphones and participants with openness, extraversion, and conscientiousness were also more likely to use smartphones. (3) Gender, education, openness, conscientiousness, and emotional stability in particular play an important role in using different types of smartphone applications.

We can analyze these results in several ways. First, from the perspective of mobile phone technologies, this article presents self-report evidence of the five types of smartphone applications that are used in Korea, rather than listing all the thousands of mobile phone applications. Second, from the perspective of mobile phone behavior, this article provides initial evidence of how ordinary smartphone users in Korea are associated with certain types of smartphone applications and how often smartphone activities are implemented, although there was not much information about effects of mobile phone behavior in the study.

3.2   *Calling vs. Texting: Adolescents' Decisions*

The second article we will discuss is "Cell phone decision making: Adolescents' perceptions of how and why they make the choice to text or call" by Bethany Blair, Anne Fletcher, and Erin Gaskin.[12] Bethany Blair is from the Department of Human Development and Family Studies at the University of North Carolina in Greensboro. The article was published in *Youth & Society*, a well-established, peer-reviewed journal focusing on the social, contextual, and political issues that have influenced development of the 10- to 24-year-old population since 1969. We chose this article to discuss in this section because it is one of the few studies available examining how and why teenagers choose to call or text their friends/family rather than how often they call or text, which is much more widely studied. In addition, this article uses a qualitative method rather than the frequently used survey method so we can see how qualitative data can generate empirical evidence.

This study is a particularly thoughtful interview study with forty-one high-school students in North Carolina. During the interview, the researchers asked two types of open-ended questions about how and why the students decide to call or text, and what the content of the

---

[12] Blair, B. L., Fletcher, A. C., and Gaskin, E. R. (2013). "Cell phone decision making: Adolescents' perceptions of how and why they make the choice to text or call," *Youth & Society*, 47(3): 395–411.

conversation is when they call or text. They used the grounded theory method to analyze the interview data. The grounded theory was appropriate to be used in this study because this method allows researchers to develop their own theory based on the data rather than start with research-based hypotheses and then confirm or reject them with the collected quantitative data. The major findings are as follows: (1) All adolescents strongly preferred texting over calling, but five factors (restraints, urgency, emotionality, content, and perceived efficiency) influenced how they chose between the two. (2) Adolescents repeatedly used words such as "easier," "faster," and "more convenient" to explain why they chose texting over calling. (3) There were three specific reasons for choosing texting: maximizing multitasking, minimizing forethought, and accommodating peers.

There are at least two ideas that we can learn from this article. First, texting and calling are two of the most common communication features of mobile phones. From the technology history perspective, calling is related to the most basic voice-based function of a telephone and texting is related to the most basic text-based function of a telegraph. However, from the mobile phone behavior perspective, it has become more complicated. The major finding of the study shows that, for adolescents, they prefer to use texting rather than calling. Second, the decision-making process involves all four basic elements of mobile phone behavior: mobile phone users (e.g., teenagers, peers), technologies (e.g., technical restraints, asynchronized methods), activities (e.g., engaging in easy rather than hard tasks, activity efficiency, urgent activities, multitasking processes), and effects (e.g., feeling comfortable and meeting emotional challenges). The mobile phone behavior involved in this decision-making process is much more complex than just knowing about calling vs. texting, the two common features for communicating with mobile phones.

3.3   Mobile Cameras: Patients with Nasal Bone Injuries

Here, let us discuss another article, "The use of a camera-enabled mobile phone to triage patients with nasal bone injuries," by Taleb Barghouthi and others.[13] One of the reasons to discuss this study is that it focuses on a common mobile phone hardware, an iPhone camera, with a very simple design to address a very simple question. The article was published in

---

[13] Barghouthi, T., Glynn, F., Speaker, R. B., and Walsh, M. (2012). "The use of a camera-enabled mobile phone to triage patients with nasal bone injuries," *Telemedicine and E-Health*, 18(2): 150–152.

2012 in *Telemedicine and E-Health*. This journal has been one of the two official journals of The American Telemedicine Association for twenty-two years since 1995. It is the leading international peer-reviewed journal covering the full spectrum of advances and clinical applications of tele-medicine and management of electronic health records. It places special emphasis on the outcome and impact of telemedicine on the quality, cost effectiveness, and access to health care. The second journal, *Journal of Telemedicine and Telecare,* focuses on high quality scientific work and provides excellent coverage of developments in telemedicine and e-health, with a focus on clinical trials of telemedicine applications.

This is a very simple study reporting whether a camera is useful and accurate in diagnosing patients with nasal bone injuries. Fifty-five patients participated in the study. A total of 50 percent required and underwent nasal bone manipulation, whereas the remaining 50 percent required no intervention. There was no control group. Instead, to examine the effect-iveness, the study compared the diagnosis results of the same patients with the mobile camera method to the results of the regular examination method. It was found that twenty-five patients received a needed interven-tion based on both the camera and actual examination with no missing cases; twenty-two patients were correctly discharged from the clinic with-out intervention, but three cases should have had an intervention and did not receive one. Clearly, the new diagnosis method of using mobile cameras has achieved effectiveness similar to that of the regular method.

How can this study help us understand mobile phone behavior related to mobile technologies? First, a mobile camera is a common hardware installed in mobile phones. Instead of using traditional X-rays, a good-quality mobile camera can now be used in emergency rooms for accurately determining the priority of patients' treatments based on the severity of their condition of nasal bone injuries. Second, doctors as mobile phone users can use this common mobile technology to engage in the new diagnosis process of nasal bone injuries and achieve positive results.

3.4   Base Stations: Childhood Cancers

Now, we will discuss another article entitled "Mobile phone base stations and early childhood cancers: Case-control study."[14] The first and corres-ponding author is Paul Elliott, a professor of epidemiology and public

---

[14] Elliott, P., Toledano, M. B., Bennett, J. *et al.* (2010). "Mobile phone base stations and early childhood cancers: Case-control study," *British Medical Journal*, 340: c3077.

health medicine at Imperial College in London. The article was published in the *British Medical Journal* in 2010.

This is a case-control study. The object was to investigate the risk of early childhood cancers associated with the mother's exposure to radio frequency from mobile phone base stations (a cell tower installed at a fixed location to provide the connection between mobile phones and wider cellular networks) during pregnancy. To achieve this, the researchers reviewed 1,397 cases of cancer in children aged 0 to 4 from the UK national cancer registry between 1999 and 2001 to compare with 5,588 birth records which served as the control cases from the UK national birth registry. The three dependent variables were distance, exposure, and density of radiation of base stations at the birth address. The independent variables were the number of cases of cancer and leukemia. The major finding was that no association was found between exposure and cancer.

What does this study help us to understand about the complexity of mobile phone behavior? First, mobile phone technologies include more than just the phones themselves and the hardware or software in them. Our understanding of what mobile phone technologies are needs to be expanded to include base stations, cellular networks, or Wi-Fi *networks*, as they are important parts of the entire array of mobile phone technologies. Second, in the case of the base station, various *technical* issues such as distance, exposure, and density of radiation of base stations are involved. Third, base stations are not just about technical issues, but have a lot to do with mobile phone *behavior*. They are related to the potential risk of various possible complex health concerns (e.g., cancers) on various users (e.g., children or pregnant women) via various activities (e.g., outside or indoor activities). Fourth, although this study did not find an association, the scientific investigation is still needed, and many *other* researchers have been studying this line of research.

3.5   GPS: Children's Mobility

The next article we will introduce is entitled "Is children's independent mobility really independent? A study of children's mobility combining ethnography and GPS/mobile phone technologies."[15] The two authors are Miguel Romero Mikkelsen from the University of Copenhagen and Pia

---

[15] Mikkelsen, M. R. and Christensen, P. (2009). "Is children's independent mobility really independent? A study of children's mobility combining ethnography and GPS/mobile phone technologies 1," *Mobilities*, 4(1): 37–58.

Christensen from the University of Warwick. It was published in 2009 in a journal called *Mobilities*. I've chosen this article for discussion because it focuses on GPS, one common feature of a mobile phone related to the aspect of hardware.

The article reports a qualitative study. The main goal of the study was to examine the impact of the physical and the social environment on children's mobility by using GPS in their mobile phones. The participants were forty children, aged 10 to 13, from one suburban area and one rural area of Demark. The study started in 2003 and lasted for over one year. Besides ethnographic fieldwork and a mobile phone survey, the researchers used GPS to collect quantitative mobility data and created two maps of both where the children go and how long it took them to get there using a special software called ArcGIS to show location and duration of children's everyday mobility movement patterns. The finding relevant to the GPS component of the study suggests that the suburban children's daily mobility is largely related to their friends rather than mainly traveling by their own independently. Moving around on their own is not children's first priority. Moving around based on the physical environment is also not their preferred activity. Instead, children's everyday mobility shows strong social characteristics.

What can we learn from this study from the perspective of mobile phone behavior? First, as one common mobile phone technology, GPS can be used not only to guide people when traveling, but also to collect empirical data about how children move around. This is an *innovative* use of GPS in scientific research. Second, this study shows the *complexity* of mobile phone behavior in two types of ways occurring almost simultaneously. This small group of Danish children carried mobile phones with them when moving around daily for one week. At the same time, a few researchers as another group of mobile phone users in this case used GPS in the same mobile phones the children were carrying to track children's mobility and found specific patterns for their research. Third, the data collected through GPS in the mobile phone can effectively lead to visualization of adolescents' daily mobility patterns. Thus, it makes the graphic data analysis possible.

4. Knowledge Syntheses: From Mobile Security to Battery Explosion

After examining multiple everyday observations and empirical studies on mobile phone technologies, it is time for us to view the forest of the

Table 3.1 *The* Encyclopedia *Chapters on Technology-Based Mobile Phone Behavior*

Feature	Chapter Title
Smartphone	Using smartphones in the college classroom
Smartphone	Predicting psychological characteristics by smartphone usage behaviors
Smartphone	Smartphone health applications
Text	Texting: Its uses, misuses and effects
Text	Adolescent text messaging
Text	Focus on text messages: A review of studies in French
Text	Text messaging in social protests
Text	Texting and Christian practice
App	Branded mobile apps: Possibilities for advertising in an emergent mobile channel
App	The usage and applications of mobile apps
App	3D talking-head mobile app
Sensor	Cognitive phone for sensing human behavior
Sensor	Mobile phone sensing in scientific research
Sensor	Mobile phones as ubiquitous social and environmental geo-sensors
Medicine	Healthcare applications for smartphones
Medicine	Mobile technology and cyberbullying
Medicine	Mobile phones for plastic surgery and burns: Current practice
Business	Human resource recruiting and selection using cellphone apps
Education	Educational potentials of SMS technology
Education	Mobile games and learning
Education	Exploring the use of mobile devices to support teacher education
Daily	Cell-phones, distracted driving, bans and fatalities
Daily	Mobile phones and driving
Daily	Mobile technology and social identity

scientific knowledge in this area. There are about twenty-five chapters in the *Encyclopedia of Mobile Phone Behavior* that synthesize the scientific knowledge about mobile phone behavior specifically related to diverse mobile phone technologies. As shown in Table 3.1, these chapters summarize two sets of mobile phone technologies: (1) various technical features, such as smartphones, text technology, apps, and sensors; and (2) various technologies used in different contexts, such as those in medicine, business, education, and daily life.

In addition to the *Encyclopedia* chapters, published review articles are another efficient way to access the synthesized knowledge about mobile phone technologies. There are about twenty published reviews. Let us focus on five good reviews as examples on five topics – security, texting, apps, sensors, and batteries.

4.1 Mobile Devices: Security

The first review article focuses on mobile devices or smartphones, especially on an important issue for smartphones, mobile security, from a technical perspective. It is entitled "Survey on security for mobile devices" and was published in 2013 in *IEEE Communications Surveys & Tutorial* by two Italian researchers and one UK researcher, Mariantonietta La Polla, Fabio Martinelli, and Daniele Sgandurra.[16] The first author is from the Institute for Informatics and Telematics at the National Research Council in Pisa, Italy, and has published multiple articles on security, data mining, computer and society, and computer security and IT forensics. *IEEE Communications Surveys & Tutorials* is a free online journal published by the IEEE Communications Society for tutorials and surveys covering all aspects of the communications field.

This twenty-six-page long review has seven major highlights related to mobile security for smartphones. (1) Smartphones are becoming an ideal target for security attacks for three major reasons: more people use smartphones to access the Internet via various networks, more malware programs have been produced by security attackers, and more users download third-party apps into their smartphones without knowing they are rapidly spreading malware. (2) Compared with computer security, smartphones have more major security concerns due to mobility (e.g., being tampered with easily), personalization (e.g., taking personal pictures), connectivity (e.g., doing online banking any time), and multiplicity (e.g., having multiple Internet apps). (3) As of 2011, over 500 distinct kinds of malware have been identified. There are five major types of malware based on methods of malware infection, including virus (replicating malware itself, e.g., Dust), worm (replicating malware from one device to another, e.g., Cabir), Trojan (hiding malware inside a regular program, e.g., Liberty Crack), rootkit (hiding malware inside an operating system, e.g., Locknut), and botnot (allowing attackers to remotely control a device, e.g., Yxes). (4) Malware creates multiple security threats on privacy, intellectual property, classified information, financial assets, devices and services, and other aspects through ten types of attacks, including data leakage, unintentional disclosure of data, phishing attacks, spyware attacks, surveillance attacks, and financial malware attack. (5) There are two major types of technical solutions to mobile security, including detecting intrusions in smartphones

---

[16] La Polla, M., Martinelli, F., and Sgandurra, D. (2013). "A survey on security for mobile devices," *IEEE Communications Surveys & Tutorials*, 15(1): 446–471.

(e.g., identifying smartphones' abnormal behavior, such as higher power consumption) and building trusted smartphones by measuring, storing, reporting, and remedying malware programs (e.g., running a mandatory procedure of secure booting while starting a smartphone).

4.2   Mobile Texting: Positive and Negative Sides

The second review we will discuss is a chapter from the *Encyclopedia of Mobile Phone Behavior*. It is entitled "Texting: Its use, misuse, and effects" and is by Paola Pascual-Ferra from Loyola University in Maryland. She is an Assistant Professor of Communication who has published several articles on text-based communication and research methods. Although she is still a junior researcher, her review on texting is comprehensive, balanced, thoughtful, and interesting, and it is one of the outstanding chapters of the *Encyclopedia* in synthesizing the current knowledge in a given topic.

There are five highlights in this review. First, this chapter clarifies a few related terms. Texting is the short term for text messaging, referring to receiving and sending text messages via mobile phones. It differs from instant messaging, which is related to an application via the Internet rather than via mobile phones. It also differs from multi-media messaging services that use multiple media (e.g., pictures and video) rather than text. Second, the chapter specifies multiple leading scholars, such as Chrispin Thurlow, Naomi Baron, Clare Wood, and Scott Campbell, in the area of texting, but it should also have included Larry Rosen. It will be particularly useful for students and young researchers to stand on the shoulders of these giants in future research. Third, the chapter analyzes both negative and positive sides of texting behavior. Fourth, the chapter reviews seven major areas of texting behavior: education, health, language, privacy, relationships, bullying, and traffic safety. Fifth, it specifies future research directions, including the extension of the current research on privacy, bullying, safety, and linguistic creativity, and the development of future research on new applications such as Whatsapp and WeChat.

4.3   Mobile Apps: Health-Care Implications

Apps generally refer to mobile software applications. The *Encyclopedia of Mobile Phone Behavior* includes multiple chapters on behavior related to apps in (1) medicine (e.g., "Healthcare applications for smartphones," "Smartphone health applications") and (2) business ("The usage and applications of mobile apps," "Branded mobile apps: Possibilities for advertising in an emergent mobile channel," "Human resource recruiting and selection using cellphone apps"). The chapter entitled "Healthcare applications for smartphones" provides an excellent review of mobile apps and is briefly summarized below.

Relevant highlights of this review include the following: (1) the healthcare system is highly mobile in nature and the adaptation rates among health professionals are about 45 to 85 percent in 2005 in some countries; (2) apps are used by three major groups of users: professionals, students, and patients; (3) for professionals, there are seven major types of apps: diagnosis, drug references, medical calculation, literature search, clinic communication, hospital information system, and medical training; and (4) three important future research directions include identification of the best set of apps, use in developing countries, creation of quality control and improvement, and standardization of the use of Bluetooth.

4.4 Mobile Sensing: Ubiquitous, Complex, and Fast Growing

The third review work we will discuss is "A survey of mobile phone sensing."[17] There are a wide variety of mobile sensors installed in a mobile phone, e.g., accelerometer, pedometer, light sensor, thermometer, air humidity sensor, heart rate monitor, fingerprint sensors, and radiation sensor. This review effectively synthesizes the basic knowledge of mobile sensing, an important and fast-growing feature of mobile phones. Since 2010, it has been cited 357 times and is rated as a *highly cited paper* based on Web of Science (WOS). The authors are all researchers at the Mobile Sensing Group at Dartmouth College. The first four authors, Nicholas Lane, Emiliano Miluzzo, Hong Lu, and Daniel Peebles, are PhD students, and the last two, Tanzeem Choudhury and Andrew Campbell, are senior scientists and faculty members in computer science, while Dr. Campbell leads the Mobile Sensing Group. The first author has published eight articles on mobile sensing based on an initial search on WOS. The article was published in *IEEE Communications Magazine*. The articles published in this journal normally cover the latest advances in communication technologies and are written by leading experts in a tutorial style. This journal is the most popular among various important journals such as *IEEE Wireless Communications* and *IEEE Internet Computing Magazine*

---

[17] Lane, N. D., Miluzzo, E., Lu, H. *et al.* (2010). "A survey of mobile phone sensing," *IEEE Communications Magazine*, 48(9): 140–150.

published by the IEEE (Institute of Electrical and Electronics Engineers) Communications Society – an independent society with over 8,800 members. Note that IEEE journals are typically labelled as *magazines* or *transactions* (e.g., *IEEE Transactions on Cognitive Communications and Networking, IEEE Transactions on Communications*), but the contents are research-oriented and the quality is particularly high. Based on the initial screening presented above, we have reasons to believe that this article should be trustworthy and readable.

The review has seven major sections and synthesizes various important topics about mobile sensing, such as various sensors, various apps, major sensing scales (individual sensing, group sensing, and community sensing), and mobile sensing architecture. There are seven major ideas highly relevant to mobile phone behavior research and analysis: (1) Sensors are often invisible to ordinary users, but are extremely ubiquitous hardware within a sensor-enabled mobile phone. Various powerful yet embedded sensors in a mobile phone include a digital compass, gyroscope, GPS, microphone, camera, and an accelerometer, and even more will be added in the future. (2) There are extensive applications available in various areas, including business, health care, social networks, environmental monitoring, and transportation. (3) Various applications are used for different purposes of collecting, analyzing, and sharing simple and complex sensor data. (4) Each major smartphone vendor has an app store (e.g., Apple AppStore, Android Market, and Microsoft Mobile Marketplace). (5) Mobile sensing can be used on three major scales: personal (e.g., personal fitness), group (e.g., friend network), and community (e.g., an urban area) sensing. (5) The process of data analysis and interpretation includes three general steps: capturing raw sensor data from mobile phones; extracting key features using learning algorithms; and identifying classes of human behavior (e.g., driving, in conversation, making coffee). (6) There are two major ways for users to be involved: participatory sensing – where the user actively engages in the data collection activity and manually determines how, when, what, and where to collect sensing data; and opportunistic sensing – where the data collection is fully automated with no direct control by users. (7) Users' privacy is currently a major concern.

What can we learn from this technical review? From the mobile phone behavior perspective, we can learn at least three ideas: (1) Sensors are ubiquitous, complex, promising, and fast-growing technologies with broad implications for modern human life. (2) Mobile phone sensors lead to various unique, sensor-based mobile phone behaviors. (3) Sensors can be used to study and modify human behavior effectively and efficiently.

4.5   Mobile Phone Batteries: Fire and Explosion

The last review is entitled "Thermal runaway caused fire and explosion of lithium ion battery" by Qingsong Wang, Ping Ping, Xuejuan Zhao, Guanquan Chu, Jinhua Sun, and Chunhua Chen, a group of researchers from State Key Laboratory of Fire Science at the University of Science and Technology in China.[18] The article was cited 280 times based on Google Scholar. Qingsong Wang is an Associate Professor of Fire Safety and has published multiple articles on lithium battery safety. The review was published in the *Journal of Power Sources*, an international journal on the science and technology of electrochemical energy systems, including primary and secondary batteries, fuel cells, supercapacitors, and photo-electrochemical cells since 1976.

Batteries provide the power source for the mobile phone functions. Without batteries, mobile phones cannot work. Historically, batteries have been the bottleneck of mobile phone development. The battery is essentially a device to store energy to make using a mobile device possible. There is a large demand but slow progress for developing batteries. The generations of batteries have moved from zinc-based, lead-based, nickel-based, and now lithium-based. The lithium-ion battery is currently the predominant power source for mobile phones, laptop computers, and many other portable electronic devices, and is being used increasingly in electric vehicles. Various battery problems are related to overcharging it, charging it too fast, misuse, and malfunctions.

This is a very technical review involving substantial mathematical and electrochemical background and thus it is not an easy read. There is no good review available on mobile batteries and mobile phone behavior. However, this review offers the following insights relevant to mobile phone batteries: (1) The current mobile phones most often have lithium-ion batteries, with a few other types of batteries. The energy of a lithium-ion battery is generated through an electrochemical process. It involves three primary functional components – anode, cathode, and electrolyte. (2) Fires and explosions of mobile phones or laptop computers have been widely reported in the public media and many large companies recalled their batteries. However, research data indicate the probability of battery fires or explosions is much lower than ordinary people initially thought, with a probability of only one incidence in 1 to 10 million batteries. (3) The main

---

[18] Wang, Q., Ping, P., Zhao, X. *et al.* (2012). "Thermal runaway caused fire and explosion of lithium ion battery," *Journal of Power Sources*, 208: 210–224.

cause of fires or explosions is overheated temperature or circuit short-cutting in the battery. The large current flows through the battery in a short time period generate heat, trigger thermal runaways, and eventually lead to fires and explosions. (4) Technically, for the lithium-ion battery, it is so-called *thermal runaway* that causes fires or explosions. Generally, thermal runaway occurs as a chain reaction, like the process of an atom bomb. When an exothermic reaction as a heat-related chemical process in a battery goes out of control, an increase in temperature causes the reaction rate to increase, which causes a further increase in temperature and hence a further increase in the reaction rate, which possibly results in an explosion. (5) More specifically, usually, some rise in temperature is normal, as long as the heat balance is made. The temperature of a lithium-ion cell is determined by the heat balance between the amount of heat generated and that dissipated in the cell. The heat generation follows the exponential function and the heat dissipation keeps the linear function. When a cell is heated above a certain temperature (usually above 130 to 150 degrees Celsius), a chemical reaction between the electrodes and electrolyte occurs, raising the internal temperature within the cell. If the cell can dissipate this heat, its temperature will not rise abnormally. However, if the heat generated is more than the amount that can be dissipated, the cell's temperature will increase rapidly. The rising temperature will further accelerate the chemical reactions, causing even more heat to be produced, eventually resulting in thermal runaway. (6) Two ways to enhance the safety of batteries is either to have better materials and better safety designs for the lithium-ion battery or to find a way to release high pressure and heat before thermal runaway occurs. New battery safety features such as safety vents, thermal fuse, shutdown separators, and special battery man-agement systems have been developed and tested.

In summary, the five reviews published either in several technology journals or in the *Encyclopedia of Mobile Phone Behavior* synthesize the existing research literature on how different mobile phone technologies are related to different types of mobile phone behavior. Specifically, we can develop a much broader view of: (1) how smartphones are vulnerable to potential mobile security attacks; (2) how a common feature of mobile phones, texting, can have both negative and positive behavior in education, health, language, or traffic safety; (3) how health-care apps are used by professionals for diagnosis, drug references, medical calculation, literature search, clinic communication, hospital information system, and medical training; (4) how a common hardware in mobile phones, sensors, can be used in business, health care, social networks, environmental monitoring, and transportation; and (5) how a basic accessory of mobile phones, batteries, are related to various overcharging battery problems, including fire and explosion.

5. Comparative Analyses: From Closed Captions to Texting

Televisions, computers, the Internet, and mobile phones are all modern technologies for communication, information, and/or computation. However, these technologies have distinct technical features and serve different functions. An initial comparison of how these technologies are related to human behavior will help us further understand mobile phone behavior that is related to mobile phone technologies.

Historically, televisions became a popular device in the 1970s, computers in the 1980s, the Internet and mobile phones in the 1990s. Considering different technologies, one might think that the earlier technologies (e.g., televisions) are simpler than the more current ones (e.g., smartphones). However, it is much more complicated in the real-life world because each technology involves unique or similar technical features, has always improved over time substantially, and is often integrated with other technologies.

Consider technology-related human behavior. One might think that each technology has its own set of features and thus each must be related to a distinct set of human behavior. The existing literature indicates, however, that for various technologies, their technical features and behavioral features interact with each other in complex ways due to diverse users, diverse activities, and diverse effects. Below are four examples of text-related technology applications, i.e., closed captioning for television, Microsoft Word for computers, e-mail for the Internet, and text messaging for mobile phones.

5.1 Study 1: Closed Captions

The first example relates to "On-screen print: The role of captions as a supplemental literacy tool" by Deborah Linebarger and Jessica Taylor Piotrowski from the Annenberg School for Communication at the University of Pennsylvania.[19] It was published in 2010 in the *Journal of Research in Reading*. The study was an experimental one. The participants were seventy-two elementary students in the United States, many of whom spoke English as their second language. They were randomly placed in the intervention group

---

[19] Linebarger, D., Piotrowski, J. T., and Greenwood, C. R. (2010). "On screen print: The role of captions as a supplemental literacy tool," *Journal of Research in Reading*, 33(2): 148–167.

watching six 30-minute television programs with on-screen closed captions and the control group doing so without on-screen closed captions. After viewing each clip, students were assessed on word recognition and comprehension, as well as six general literacy and reading skills. The intervention group was found to perform significantly or nearly significantly better in all tasks than the control group.

5.2   Study 2: Microsoft Word

Another example concerns "Comparative study between two ESL writing approaches: Computer processing Microsoft Word vs. hand writing of two freshmen college Saudi student groups." This comparative study was a dissertation study. It investigated the effectiveness of two writing methods, hand writing (using paper and pencil) and computer processing (using Microsoft Word), in improving the English writing of freshmen students at two colleges in Saudi Arabia. One hundred students studying English from two colleges in Saudi Arabia were selected. One group of students was designated to write using Microsoft Word and the other wrote by hand using paper and pencil. Their writing quality was assessed twice. Three dependent variables were measured: overall writing quality, writing apprehension, and attitudes toward writing with a computer. They were based on two independent variables: gender and writing method. The research was designed to assess whether students actually wrote better using word-processing software than they did when writing with paper and pencil. The results showed that: (1) for overall writing quality, the students using Word wrote significantly better than the students using paper and pencil; (2) for writing apprehension, no significant differences were found between the students using Word and the students using paper and pencil; and (3) for attitudes toward writing with a computer, again, no significant differences were found between the students using Word and the students using paper and pencil.

5.3   Study 3: E-mail

The third article we will briefly introduce is "An exploratory study of e-mail application on FL writing performance" by Hui-Fang Shang,[20] a Professor of Applied English at I-Shou University in Taiwan who has multiple publications on teaching English as a foreign language and

---

[20] Shang, H. F. (2007). "An exploratory study of e-mail application on FL writing performance," *Computer Assisted Language Learning*, 20(1): 79–96.

curriculum/instructional design. This article was published in 2007 in *Computer Assisted Language Learning*, a journal that has focused on the use of computers in first and second language learning, teaching, and testing for twenty-nine years since 1990. In the study, the main objective is to examine the overall effects for non-traditional students of using electronic mail on the improvement of syntactic complexity, grammatical accuracy, and lexical density.

The participants were forty freshmen students enrolled in an English reading course. The students were asked to e-mail their initial writing to a peer for feedback and then submit their final writing. Two computer programs, Wordsmith Tools and Word Perfect Grammatik, were used to assess the writing quality – an innovative approach. The major findings were that significant improvements were found for the writing in all three aspects – syntactic complexity, grammatical accuracy, and lexical density.

5.4   Study 4: Texting

The last article is entitled "Supporting mobile learners: An action research project."[21] The authors are two researchers from Auckland University in New Zealand: Krassie Petrova, a Senior Lecturer in Information Systems and Information Technology who has published extensively on mobile learning, and Chun Li, an innovations specialist. This article was published in the *International Journal of Web-Based Learning and Teaching Technologies*, a relatively new journal of eleven years, launched in 2006. It is among the few that have examined how to use texting/SMS to help students who speak English as their second language. Twenty international undergraduates participated in the study for eight weeks. Students first learned new words in a class. After the class, the researcher texted students a test question based on the new words learned in the class, the students answered, and then the researcher provided feedback. At the end of the study, students were given an overall vocabulary test and an interview. For the second cycle, the procedure was modified by asking students questions about new words first and ending with a survey. The study found that: (1) students' vocabulary test scores improved significantly after they actively engaged in text-based learning; and (2) students reported that the text-based learning was a useful experience.

---

[21] Petrova, K. and Li, C. (2011). "Supporting mobile learners: An action research project," *Web-Based and Blended Educational Tools and Innovations*, 6(3): 46–65.

To summarize this section on comparative analyses, we can think about what we can learn from them in better understanding the complexity of technology-focused mobile phone behavior. First, one might intuitively consider television-related behavior, computer-related behavior, Internet-related behavior, and mobile phone-related behavior separately. However, comparative analysis helps us to see the integration and interrelationship of behavior, just like the integration of technology. We might call respecting each technology and appreciating each technology-related behavior the *diversity principle*. Second, the four study examples discussed above (i.e., closed captions, Microsoft Word, e-mail, and texting) suggest two basic ways to use text-based technologies to help ESL students. One is to use the technology to promote English as second language learning directly (see the first study on reading and the second study on writing) or indirectly (see the third study on peer review and the fourth study on after-class exercises and tests). Third, despite the specific focus on texting and ESL deliberately chosen in this section to compare relatively similar cases, there is still a wide variety of dimensions and aspects of mobile phone behavior. For instance, Study 1 on closed captions focused on difficult word recognition for young readers, Study 2 on Microsoft Word focused on English class writing with college students, Study 3 on e-mail focused on Taiwanese adult students and writing complexity, and Study 4 on texting focused on New Zealand college international students learning new words. Fourth, it has been widely discussed that the medium is the message (i.e., the form of a medium influences how the message is perceived)[22] and technological affordances are important (i.e., we should understand inherent and perceived potentials that a new technology can offer).[23] Mobile phone technologies are rich, diverse, and integrative. Thus, mobile phone behavior involves more technology options than traditional TV, PC, and Internet, while each technology offers unique features in relation to mobile phones (e.g., mobile TV, tablet computer, and mobile Internet).

6.   Complex Thinking: Diverse Technologies, Complex Behavior

At the beginning of this chapter, we saw Sunny's quick responses about mobile phone technologies. Now it should be clear to us the strengths and limitations of his intuitive knowledge. First, his responses focused on

---

[22] Marshall, M. and Fiore, Q. (1967). *The Medium is the Message. An Inventory of Effects*. New York: Bantam Books.
[23] Norman, D. A. (1988). *The Psychology of Everyday Things*. New York: Basic Books.

features, hardware, and apps – three components of mobile phone technologies. This is, of course, useful and important. Second, his responses concerned only a small part of the diverse mobile technologies. Mobile phones, networks, and accessories are all important components, as we can see from the ten cases, the five studies, and the four review articles discussed above. Third, although he was not asked about how mobile phone behavior is related to mobile technologies, this chapter shows that different technologies will connect with different users and form different activities, leading to different effects.

In contrast to Sunny's intuitive responses, Figure 3.1, as a summary of the entire chapter, shows how diverse mobile phone technologies are and how these technologies are related to complex mobile phone behavior. The ten daily observations reveal a typology of mobile phone technologies, mobile phone handsets, features, hardware and software, network services, and accessories such as batteries and chargers. The five studies show how smartphones, apps, features, GPS, cameras, and base stations are related to various users, activities, and effects, resulting in various mobile phone behaviors. Five review articles or chapters synthesized five areas of research on mobile phone behavior related to security, texting, apps, sensors, and batteries. Four articles were used to show comparative similarities and differences in using text to help ESL individuals through televisions, personal computers, the Internet, and mobile phones.

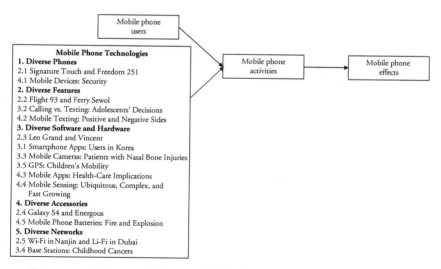

Figure 3.1 A Summary Diagram of Technology-Based Mobile Phone Behavior

Of course, more effects are needed to further understand the complexity of mobile phone behavior related to diverse technologies. Among various future directions, two are important. First, how should we keep up with new advances in mobile phone technologies and deal with new mobile-phone-related behavior? Getting familiar with various core journals by the IEEE, publishing good reviews, receiving continuing education, and timely updating and briefing are useful. Second, how should we handle the diversity in medicine, education, business, and other domains? The knowledge and efforts are unevenly distributed across domains. Thus, interdisciplinary research communications and collaborations are useful.

CHAPTER 4

Mobile Phone Activities

Outline

1. *Intuitive Thinking: Elizabeth's Thoughtful Responses*
2. *Everyday Observations: From Draining a Pond to Recycling Mobile Phones*
    2.1 *Access: Draining a Pond*
    2.2 *Use: Greeting the Pope and Dining without Smartphone*
    2.3 *Action: Hacking into Mark's Accounts and Hacking into SS7*
    2.4 *Reuse: Collecting 500 Mobile Phones*
3. *Empirical Studies: From Accepting Services to Managing Waste*
    3.1 *Access: Accepting Advanced Services*
    3.2 *Use: Using Mobile Phones in Africa and Misusing at the Workplace*
    3.3 *Action: Sexting and Gaming*
    3.4 *Reuse: Recycling in China*
4. *Knowledge Syntheses: From Complex Access to WEEE Management*
    4.1 *Four Kinds of Access*
    4.2 *Three Areas of Use*
    4.3 *Three Types of Gaming*
    4.4 *Four Trends of Recycling*
5. *Comparative Analyses: From Screen Time to Tweeting Difference*
    5.1 *Screen Time*
    5.2 *Tweeting*
6. *Complex Thinking: Diverse Activities, Complex Behavior*

1. Intuitive Thinking: Elizabeth's Thoughtful Responses

Elizabeth is a talented graduate student. When I asked her about what kinds of human activities are involved with the use of mobile phones and to give three to five quick examples, she gave very detailed responses, the kind that an outstanding student would give in a final exam. Her detailed responses are as follows: (1) Connecting with each other through mobile phones in different ways: making phone calls, sending WeChat voice messages, using FaceTime, making video calls, texting, using WeChat word messages, using Facebook messenger, and using QQ messenger. (2) Sharing and gathering information/thoughts: posting on Facebook/Instagram/Twitter/Weibo/ WeChat within friendship circles, posting in public forums, using Google search, using LinkedIn for job postings, and using Google maps. (3) Entertainment: shopping (Amazon, Taobao, Walmart, Target . . . all have smartphone apps), watching videos/listening to music/the radio (YouTube, mobile phone games). (4) Banking: using Bank of America, Chase, or Discover apps. (5) Travelling: booking hotels, buying tickets, etc. via Priceline app or calling taxi/car rental (e.g., Uber). (6) Health monitoring: keeping track of heart rate, walking distance, and sleeping quality.

In her responses above, Elizabeth presented six major types of mobile phone activities, from interpersonal communications to information sharing, entertainment, banking, travelling, and health monitoring. She also offered various specific examples, such as making video calls, posting on Instagram, shopping with a Walmart app, and using Uber to get taxis. Nobody perhaps would criticize that her responses are too narrow or too general. Nobody would deny that her knowledge about mobile phone activities is comprehensive and specific. If it were in a final exam, such thoughtful responses would likely receive a perfect score.

What can we learn from these responses from the perspective of mobile phone activities? First, Elizabeth specified various mobile phone activities. *Mobile phone activities* refer to various interactions between mobile phone users and mobile phone technologies. Casually, this concept might be confusing to some people. For example, they might think that mobile phone activities are equivalent to or synonymous with mobile phone behavior. By the definition made in this book, however, *mobile phone behavior* consists of four basic elements (users, technologies, activities, and effects), with mobile phone activities being the third basic element. In a real-life process, mobile phone users interact with mobile technologies to generate mobile phone activities, resulting in mobile phone effects. Consider a mobile phone user (e.g., a teenager) and a mobile phone technology (e.g., an iPhone). The teenager interacts with the iPhone to generate a mobile phone activity (e.g., texting a friend), which yields a mobile phone effect (e.g., an existing friendship bond is enhanced). In other words, a user and a phone need to connect and interact with each other to develop a meaningful activity that eventually leads to a certain type of effect. These four elements in a sequence form various types of mobile phone behavior. That is why we need to study mobile phone activities, after studying mobile phone users and mobile phone technologies, and before studying mobile phone effects.

Second, although Elizabeth's responses were quite thoughtful, the activities she discussed were generally on the positive side (e.g., communicating with good friends or conveniently banking through an app) rather than on the negative side (e.g., bullying among classmates or hacking into a bank). We should not always automatically assume that every mobile phone activity we are experiencing is useful and beneficial to everyone at all times.

Third, despite the fact that Elizabeth's knowledge about mobile phone behavior is comprehensive, her six types of activities and dozens of examples generally focus on a typical aspect, that is, *mobile phone use* across different contents and domains. These two concepts, mobile phone use and mobile phone activity, are often used interchangeably. However, while regular mobile phone use is indeed an important part of mobile phone activities, it is not all of them. We should look at mobile phone activities even more broadly and comprehensively, from the very beginning when mobile users start to interact with mobile phones (e.g., buying a phone) to the very end when mobile users stop interacting with mobile phones (e.g., updating to a new phone), rather than focus only on mobile phone use. In other words, it is important to explore the two ends of mobile phone activities rather than focus just on the in-between.

After discussing mobile phone users and mobile phone technologies in previous chapters, this chapter focuses specifically on mobile phone activities. Our learning goals are to appreciate the complexity of mobile phone behavior more broadly and deeply and to analyze the complexity of mobile phone behavior more effectively and efficiently from the perspective of mobile phone activities such as mobile learning and mobile gaming. After reading this chapter, we should develop better scientific knowledge about mobile phone activities than Elizabeth's initial ones.

2. Everyday Observations: From Draining a Pond to Recycling Mobile Phones

2.1 Access: Draining a Pond

In August 2014,[1] a 16-year-old German boy was fishing with his friends in a small pond owned by a fishing club. He accidentally dropped his iPhone

---

[1] See http://metro.co.uk/2014/08/02/german-schoolboy-drops-phone-on-fishing-trip-drains-entire-pond-to-look-for-it-4819315/?iframe=true&preview=true.

from his fishing boat into the pond. He loved his phone, especially since it had all of the phone numbers, pictures, and videos of many good friends stored on it. Thus, he tried to get his phone from the bottom of the pond. First, he asked the fishing club to loan him a diving suit but the club refused to do so. Then, he found a powerful water pump from somewhere, went back to the pond that evening, and attempted to drain all of the water out of the small pond. He hooked the pump up to a nearby toilet in the club, but the toilet was not connected to a sewer line. All of the drained water came out of the toilet and turned the club's parking lot into a little swimming pool. Eventually, the club owner found out what had caused the water problem in the parking lot and called the police. This German boy was required to pay for the toilet damage, clean up the mess, and refill the pond. Reflecting on this accident, the boy only regretted that he could have made his plan work and found his iPhone if he had brought two powerful pumps rather than just one.

We do not know whether or not this stubborn German teenager eventually got his iPhone back from the bottom of the pond, but what can this funny story tell us about mobile phone activities? First, this story illustrates beautifully that phone ownership is not equal to phone *accessibility*. By dropping the phone into the pond, this teenager, while still being the owner of the phone, could not access his phone. Users must need access to the phone after buying it and before using it. Thus, accessibility is the starting point for mobile phone activities and interactions.

The second point we can take away from the German boy's story is that phone accessibility could be related to various *sophisticated issues* of mobile phone behavior. For the German boy, he took several ridiculous actions in order to regain accessibility to his mobile phone. Other similar accessibility issues include mobile phone theft, phone power shutdown, skills to use mobile phones, privacy information protection, and password set-up procedures.

Third, the German boy's story shows that phone accessibility has *two sides* – the positive side (e.g., how to increase accessibility) and the negative side (e.g., when one loses accessibility). Ordinary users will face various challenges of losing or decreasing accessibility to mobile phones in daily life rather than always gaining it. Often, losing accessibility, like the German boy dropping his phone into the pond, may be even more devastating for him than gaining accessibility (e.g., buying a new phone). In other special cases, like Dzhokhar Tsarnaev, the younger of the Tsarnaev brothers who was responsible for the terrorist attack during the Boston marathon, he was the owner of his mobile phone, but really wanted to destroy the phone so that police could not regain accessibility to find evidence of his criminal behavior in his phone. Thus, we might need to pay more attention to the negative side of accessibility.

Lastly, besides the story about the German boy draining the water out of the pond to find his iPhone, many *similar stories* about people going to great lengths to avoid losing access to their phones have been reported. For instance, after a Chinese farmer dropped his phone into a large septic tank, he jumped into it and lost consciousness due to the strong chemical smell. A few of his family members then jumped into the tank to try and save him but everyone ended up dying. An American girl refused to give her new iPhone to a street robber in the evening and almost got killed. An Asian boy addicted to his mobile phone tried to poison his grandma after she hid his phone. Of course, one of the largest and most controversial cases of mobile phone accessibility was when the FBI wanted to hack into the iPhone belonging to the 2015 San Bernardino shooter in California and demanded that Apple unlock the phone. Thus, we need to understand more about this issue of phone accessibility.

2.2 Use: Greeting the Pope and Dining without Smartphone

In February 2016,[2] Pope Francis visited Mexico for the first time. A member of the organizing committee for the visit announced at a news conference that Mexican worshipers wanted to receive the Holy Father with a special wall, a wall of light and prayer. After Pope Francis landed at the airport, he took the bulletproof Popemobile to the Vatican's diplomatic mansion in Mexico City. The road he had to travel on is about 12 miles long. Most Mexican people own mobile phones, so thousands of worshipers lined the roadside holding up their mobile phones to form the special wall of light for Pope Francis.

Before his Mexican visit, on November 16, 2015,[3] Pope Francis actually talked about mobile phone use at St. Peter's Square in the Vatican. He commented that a family that rarely eats together or just looks at smartphones or watches television without good conversations is not much of a family. The Pope felt that the family meal is a great symbol of togetherness, but is disappearing in some societies. He advised people to not use their phones at the family dinner table. This was not the first time the Pope spoke

---

[2] See www.theguardian.com/world/2016/feb/08/pope-francis-to-be-greeted-by-19km-of-mobile-phone-lights-on-mexico-city-visit.

[3] See www.romereports.com/2015/11/11/pope-put-down-your-cell-phones-and-talk-to-one-another.

out against the misuse of mobile phones. In August 2014, he warned that while the Internet and smartphones can simplify and improve quality of life, they may distract attention away from what is really important.

These small stories about Pope Francis vividly illustrate the second issue related to mobile phone activities, the issue of mobile phone use. First, it is easy to see through the story of the Mexican wall of mobile phones how *popular* mobile phone use is right now, even in developing countries like Mexico. It may not have been possible to create the Mexican wall of mobile phone lights as little as five years ago, but now mobile phones are a common part of everyday life. Second, while mobile phones can be used in a wide variety of conventional ways, such as calling, texting, gaming, and sharing, as Elizabeth pointed out rightfully, they can also be used for various *special* purposes. The Mexican wall of mobile phones represents one of the very special mobile phone activities that Mexican people used to creatively express their extraordinary enthusiasm for the Pope's visit. Lastly, we can take away from the stories about the Pope that while mobile phones can be used in normal and even positive, creative ways, there can be a *negative* side of mobile phone use, from non-use, to misuse, excessive use, problematic use, and pathological use. Pope Francis' advice of eating with your family but not with your mobile phones pointed out the adverse impact of mobile phone misuse on family life and the fact that he had to address it shows how pervasive this issue has become. Thus, like the issue of accessibility we discussed in the previous section, we should always look at mobile phone use from both sides, positive and negative, rather than just one side.

2.3   Action: Hacking into Mark's Accounts and Hacking into SS7

On June 6, 2016,[4] Facebook founder Mark Zuckerberg's social media accounts, including Twitter, Instagram, and Pinterest, were hacked by a hacker group called OurMine. They found that Mark used a very simple password, "dadada," for all of his accounts. To prove their hacking success, OurMine posted a screenshot on the Internet, claiming that they knew Mark's password through a leaked LinkedIn database, gained access to his Twitter, Instagram, and Pinterest accounts, and wanted to test the security of his accounts and sound the alert about the security flaws that existed in Mark's accounts. It is not the first time that hackers have reported

---

[4] See www.nbcnews.com/tech/tech-news/zuckerberg-s-social-media-accounts-hacked-password-revealed-dadada-n586286.

accessing Mark's accounts. On August 20, 2013, his Facebook account was hacked by a Pakistani hacker who successfully posted his own message on Facebook CEO Mark Zuckerberg's official page.

On April 17, 2016,[5] the television program *60 Minutes* on ABC aired a report called *Hacking Your Phone*. In this report, Sharyn Alfonsi interviewed Karsten Nohl, a top German hacker, who demonstrated how to actually hack into the phone of Representative Ted Lieu, a congressman from California with strong knowledge about cyber security and a Stanford graduate with a computer science degree. During the interview, Nohl specified that his team had the ability to exploit a security flaw they discovered in Signaling System Seven (SS7), a vital global network that connects various phone carriers. Nohl and his team were legally granted access to SS7 by several international cell phone carriers. In exchange, the carriers wanted Nohl to test the network's vulnerability to attack.

These two stories share a key similarity. They both involve hacking activities related to mobile phones, OurMine hacking into Mark Zuckerberg's accounts and Karsten Nohl's team hacking into SS7. From the mobile phone activity perspective, these two stories show that the hundreds of mobile phone interactions include not only many typical ones such as learning, banking, shopping, and gaming, but also some atypical ones such as hacking, stealing, and robbing mobile phones. On the other hand, these two stories have one important difference. OurMine hacked into Mark Zuckerberg's accounts without his consent for the purposes of drawing attention to his security and privacy setting flaws while showing off their hacking skills. In comparison, companies actually hired and paid Karsten Nohl to hack into SS7 with their consent in order to find system vulnerabilities they should then improve on. Overall, even for the atypical activity of hacking, there are differences in positive or negative intentions and influences of these activities. Again, it is important to always be aware that mobile phone activities can have both positive and negative sides. However, this key issue was not mentioned at all in Elizabeth's intuitive responses as presented at the beginning of this chapter.

2.4   *Reuse: Collecting 500 Mobile Phones*

James Maturo is a resident of Paulsboro, New Jersey. Since 2007,[6] he has been collecting old mobile phones and then donating them to community

---

[5] See www.cbsnews.com/news/60-minutes-hacking-your-phone/.
[6] See www.911cellphonebank.org/press-coverage.asp.

service organizations. For example, he donated 250 phones to the Red Cross, which distributed them to Hurricane Katrina victims. He also donated another 250 phones to the 911 Cell Phone Bank, which was founded in 2004 and has provided thousands of emergency cell phones to victims' services organizations nationwide. These old phones have been used for senior citizens, abused or battered women, and disabled veterans for 911 communication. In case of emergencies, people can dial 911 even without a proper cell phone plan. One such phone was given to a woman in Las Vegas who had been abused by a man who was in and out of prison. One night, the abuser showed up at the victim's house after he cut the victim's landline phone so she could not call for help. The victim grabbed the emergency phone provided to her by the 911 Cell Phone Bank, ran into a locked bedroom, and was able to call for help. As a result, the abuser was caught, arrested, and the victim is alive today. After that, James Maturo received a letter from the 911 Cell Phone Bank thanking him for collecting and donating the old phone.

This is a very interesting story for two major reasons. First, while millions of new mobile phones are sold, thousands of old, used phones retire every year. How to handle these old phones leads to one special mobile phone activity, the mobile phone *recycling activity*. In general, we can consider mobile phone recycling as the end point of mobile phone interaction for mobile phone users and mobile phone technologies, while mobile phone accessing is the beginning of the interaction. Second, mobile phone recycling can further lead to *different results*, from accumulating a large amount of electronic waste and seriously polluting the environment to recycling old phones. James Maturo and the 911 Cell Phone Bank maximized mobile phone donations and their behavior not only helps reduce electronic waste and protects the environment, it also helps offer special social services and support to many of those, like the abused woman in Las Vegas, who might otherwise not be able to access a phone for emergencies. There are many other good stories like these.[7] We should not ignore this type of mobile phone activity.

To end this section, we can compare Elizabeth's initial responses with the stories discussed here. Elizabeth's responses covered various typical, positive mobile phone activities, like communicating, banking, and gaming. The cases that followed further indicate two important points. First, mobile phone activities have both positive and negative sides rather than a positive side only. Elizabeth listed typical positive everyday phone

[7] See www.911cellphonebank.org/press-coverage.asp.

activities such as collecting and donating old phones and the other stories pointed out atypical negative activities such as hacking into people's accounts. Second, mobile phone activities concern various time points, from the starting point of mobile phone accessibility to the end point of mobile phone recycling, rather than just mobile phone use and actions. In other words, there is a life cycle of mobile phone interactions between mobile users and mobile technologies, and while we tend to think about and focus on use and activities in the middle of the life cycle, we should not ignore the beginning and end points where equally important activities occur. Clearly, these stories create a much more complex picture of mobile phone activities by deepening (e.g., considering the negative side) and broadening (e.g., considering the recycling) Elizabeth's intuitive responses. The next section will present mobile phone activities in the research world rather than in the real-life world.

3. Empirical Studies: From Accepting Services to Managing Waste

3.1 Access: Accepting Advanced Services

The first article we will discuss is called "An assessment of advanced mobile services acceptance: Contributions from TAM and diffusion theory models."[8] It uses two well-known theories, TAM and diffusion theory, to examine how people accept new mobile services for banking, gaming, or parking rather than traditional mobile services for calling and texting. Developed by Fred Davis,[9] the technology acceptance model (TAM) suggests that when users are presented with a new technology, important factors (e.g., perceived usefulness and perceived ease of use) influence their decision about how and when they will accept it. Advanced by Everett Rogers,[10] the diffusion of innovations theory describes and explains the process of adaptation of new technologies. The article has been widely cited 382 times according to Google Scholar. The authors are two Spanish researchers, Carolina López-Nicolás and Francisco Molina-Castillo, and one Dutch researcher, Harry Bouwman. The first author Carolina López-Nicolás, is an Assistant Professor in the Department of Management and

---

[8] López-Nicolás, C., Molina-Castillo, F. J., and Bouwman, H. (2008). "An assessment of advanced mobile services acceptance: Contributions from TAM and diffusion theory models," *Information & Management*, **45**(6): 359–364.

[9] Davis, F. D. (1989). "Perceived usefulness, perceived ease of use, and user acceptance of information technology," *MIS Quarterly*, **13** (3): 319–340.

[10] Rogers, E. M. (2003). *Diffusion of Innovations* (5th edn.). New York: Free Press.

Finance at the University of Murcia, Spain. She has published about forty articles on knowledge management, information systems, and mobile communications based on information on ResearchGate. The article we will be discussing was published in 2007 in *Information & Management*, which has published articles on designing, implementing, and managing information systems applications (e.g., training and education, managerial policies and activities) since 1977. The fact that this article has been cited 382 times, the author's forty publication records, and established journal reputation gives us a good impression about its credibility.

In the study, the authors chose a representative sample of 542 Dutch residents to participate in a survey. The researchers attempted to test how behavioral intention is associated with seven variables, such as media influence (e.g., advertisements suggest people should use advanced mobile services), social influence (e.g., people around us think we should use advanced mobile services), perceived flexibility benefits (e.g., people can use mobile services anytime and anywhere), and perceived status benefits (e.g., using advanced mobile services is valuable). Structural equation modeling was used to analyze the data. It was found that: (1) media influence impacts social influence; and (2) social influence impacts all five remaining mediating variables (e.g., perceived flexibility benefits and perceived status benefits) related to behavioral intention.

This is a typical study that we frequently see on the topic of behavioral intention in various journals. What can we learn about the complexity of activity-related mobile phone behavior from this study? First, a number of issues, such as mobile phone services, advanced mobile phone services, intention to use these services, and switching between different services are real-life, complex, and important issues related to accessing mobile phones rather than just issues related to mobile phones alone. Without basic and advanced services, mobile phones will not be able to work and mobile phone behavior will not be able to occur. Second, related to the first point, users' acceptance, adoption, attitude, or intentions of using mobile phones and mobile phone services all concern mobile phone access and are the very beginning of mobile phone activity. Only after users first decide to use a certain mobile phone or a certain service will we be able to see how they will use mobile phones for various purposes and functions such as calling, texting, gaming, or learning. Third, besides many other factors such as product/service price and technical features, media influence and social influence play an important role in influencing users' acceptance of a given mobile phone service. Fourth, multiple other factors also influence users' intended action after media influence and social influence. Therefore, we can conclude that the process of determining how and why to use a phone or a service is complex rather than simple, involving multiple factors through multiple pathways.

3.2 Use: Using Mobile Phones in Africa and Misusing at the Workplace

Now we will examine a research report released by the Pew Research Center in 2015. As we introduced in Chapter 2, the Pew Research Center, or Pew, is an internationally well-known research firm or *fact tank* (a research institution for producing fact-based information rather than one for generating idea-based solutions, or a so-called think tank) that has published a series of highly regarded reports on trends of using media, the Internet, and mobile phones for decades. The title of the report we will be discussing is "Cell phones in Africa: Communication lifeline." It addresses the current status of mobile phone use in Africa.[11] This report was produced by a team of more than fifteen researchers, with the lead researcher being Jacob Poushter. Jacob Poushter is a senior researcher at the Pew Research Center and has written multiple research reports on international public opinions, including "Internet usage in the emerging and developing world." While the "Cell Phones in Africa" report is not a typical journal article having gone through the peer-review process, it was produced by a group of researchers and methodologists at Pew and should pass our initial trustworthiness screening.

The report presents a survey study examining mobile phone use in seven sub-Saharan African nations, namely: South Africa, Nigeria, Senegal, Kenya, Ghana, Tanzania, and Uganda. Roughly 1,000 residents from each of the seven countries participated in a survey with a sampling method called "multi-stage cluster sampling" and stratified by certain features such as region and urbanicity. A total of 7,052 face-to-face interviews with adults were conducted from April 11 to June 5, 2014. The results were from multiple survey items in the 2014 Spring Pew Global Attitudes Survey (e.g., Question #68: Do you own a cell phone? Question #74b: In the past 12 months, have you used your cell phone to do any of the following things? b. take pictures or video.).

The major findings include that: (1) 65 to 89 percent of the participants reported owning mobile phones, and this penetration rate of mobile phones (i.e., the percentage of the population in a given area that has purchased or owned a mobile phone) in South Africa and Nigeria was the

---

[11] See www.pewresearch.org.

same as in the United States, while more than 94 percent did not have a working landline telephone at home; (2) 80, 53, and 30 percent of the participants reported using their mobile phones for sending text messages, taking pictures or video, and doing mobile banking as the top three most popular activities respectively; (3) educated (e.g., 35 percent in Nigeria), younger (e.g., 34 percent in Nigeria), and English-speaking Africans (e.g., 33 percent in Nigeria) own smartphones; and (4) substantial variations in mobile phone use exist among the seven countries, with South Africa and Nigeria at the high end and Tanzania and Uganda at the low end (e.g., 34 percent of the participants in South Africa had smartphones, compared with only 5 percent in Uganda). What do these results mean and why are they important? These findings provide a general picture of mobile phone use as well as mobile phone ownership in Africa, with variations being a key feature.

After seeing what happened with mobile phone use in Africa, now let us discuss a different topic: mobile phone *misuse* rather than regular mobile phone *use*. The article we will examine is entitled "Managing mobile phones: A work/non-work collision in small business,"[12] which looks at mobile phone use for work and non-work purposes in the small business setting. This article has been cited twenty-two times by researchers studying work–life balance in using mobile phones based on Google Scholar. The authors are Keith Townsend and Lyn Batchelor. The first author, Keith Townsend, is an Associate Professor in the Department of Employment Relations and Human Resources at Griffith University of Australia and has published several articles on mobile phone use at work in his early career. This article was published in 2005 in *New Technology, Work and Employment*, an established Wiley journal publishing research on technological changes in the workplace for thirty-one years.

This article reports two case studies. The first is about a small real estate firm with ten employees. The researchers interviewed one manager and four employees from the real estate firm in 2002. The second case study is about a retail business store that also had ten full-time workers. The researchers interviewed two managers and three employees from the store in 2005. Interviews were transcribed and analyzed to find emerging themes of work/non-work interactions and control and technology. A major difference was found between these two small business units. The real estate firm actually provided mobile phones to their employees, who used them

---

[12] Townsend, K. and Batchelor, L. (2005). "Managing mobile phones: A work/non-work collision in small business," *New Technology, Work and Employment*, 20(3): 259–267.

for business and personal matters. In contrast, the retail store did not even allow employees to use phones at work unless it was an emergency. However, some store employees complained about the no mobile phone use policy and still often used them for personal matters when their bosses were not there. So, in the setting of the real estate firm, mobile phone use was typical and even encouraged, whereas in the setting of the retail store, it was considered misuse.

Comparing the two articles, we can learn several ideas. First, after mobile phone accessibility, we need to consider mobile phone use as the second major theme of mobile phone activities. If one accesses a mobile phone but never uses it, then mobile phone behavior cannot possibly occur. If we know how one can own or access a mobile phone (i.e., ownership rate or penetration rate), what one does with one's phone (i.e., use), how frequently one uses the phone (i.e., use frequency), or how long one uses the phone at one time (i.e., use duration), we can further our knowledge of various types of mobile phone behavior. However, mobile phone use is complex. Besides the rapid growth of mobile phone use (e.g., the current pervasive use in Africa) and mobile phone misuse (e.g., the misuse in the retail store of Australia), we might encounter various use-related topics, including overuse, abuse, excessive use, addictive use, multitasking use, hidden use, and non-use. Second, different types of use or misuse of mobile phones by different users (e.g., realtors or retail salespeople) with different technologies (e.g., texting or calling) might lead to different effects (e.g., increasing sales or reducing productivity). The article on mobile phone use in the workplace in the real estate firm vs. the retail store illustrates the positive and negative effects. In other words, mobile phone use, like accessibility, also has two sides, the positive and negative, rather than just one.

3.3 Action: Sexting and Gaming

Now we will study another article related to mobile phone activities. The article is entitled "Sexting among young adults"[13] and examines how young mobile phone users send or receive sexually explicit text, pictures, or video messages. It has been cited ninety-three times by multiple established scholars such as Michelle Drouin, Christopher Ferguson, Shelley Walker, and Kimberly Mitchel based on Google Scholar. The four

---

[13] Gordon-Messer, D., Bauermeister, J. A., Grodzinski, A., and Zimmerman, M. (2013). "Sexting among young adults," *Journal of Adolescent Health*, 52(3): 301–306.

authors are public health researchers from the University of Michigan, with the first author, Deborah Gordon-Messer, having published several articles on adolescent health behavior. The article was published in 2013 in the Elsevier *Journal of Adolescent Health*, the official publication of the *Society for Adolescent Health and Medicine*, which has been publishing research on adolescent medicine and health topics ranging from the basic biological and behavioral sciences to public health and policy since 1980. One piece of useful information is that at the end of the article, the authors acknowledged their funding sources (e.g., the National Institute of Drug Abuse research challenge grant and the National Institutes of Health Career Development Award). This type of information gives people interested in this area of research a good idea of some of the grants that are available and where to apply for them.

In this study, 3,447 American young adults participated in a survey. To determine these young adults' sexting behavior statuses, the researchers asked the participants two questions: (1) whether they had ever *sent* a nude photo or video of themselves to someone else using their cell phones; and (2) whether they had ever *received* a nude photo or video of someone on their cell phones. Based on the responses to these two questions, the researchers determined four types or statuses of lifetime sexting behavior: (1) non-sexters who have never sent or received sext messages; (2) senders who have only ever sent sext messages; (3) receivers who have only ever received sext messages; and (4) two-way sexters who have both sent and received sext messages. These four types of sexters were then used as the independent variable of the study. The major dependent variables were individuals' sexual behavior and depression. It was found that: (1) a total of 57 percent of the respondents were non-sexters, 28.2 percent were two-way sexters, 12.6 percent were receivers, and 2 percent were senders; and (2) after excluding the senders who were only 2 percent of the sample, sexting was significantly related to risky sexual behavior or depression among the remaining three types of sexters.

We can learn a few points about mobile phone activities from this article. First, texting or sending a text message is a common mobile phone activity. Ordinary people send texts frequently in everyday life. It is particularly popular among young users to text rather than call each other. However, sexting or sending or receiving sexually explicit cell phone text or picture messages is a serious social concern. The study we just discussed indicates that, just in terms of sending or receiving a nude photo or video, 28.2 percent of young adults were two-way sexters, 12.6 percent were sext receivers, and 2 percent were sext senders, totalling about 43 percent of

3,447 participants. Given that the study used young adults' self-report data and focused only on nude photos or videos and excluded sexually explicit text messages, we might consider that an even higher percentage of young adults are involved in general sexting. Second, while this study found significant associations between sexting behavior and sexual risks and depression in this specific sample, further studies are needed to identify the potential serious effects of sexting behavior among various subgroups of sexters, especially sext receivers and two-way sexters, and among various types of populations with different ages, genders, social classes, or cultures.

While one of the most common mobile phone activities, texting, could involve a popular yet negative activity – sexting, another common mobile phone activity, mobile gaming, could lead to unexpected yet useful activities. The next article we will discuss provides a good example and is entitled "Caring for mobile phone-based virtual pets can influence youth eating behaviors."[14] It illustrates how a mobile phone game where players take care of virtual pets can be used to improve how children actually eat their breakfast in real life. A group of seven authors from Cornell University contributed to the article, and the first author is Sahara Byrne, an Associate Professor who has published multiple articles on health communication. The virtual pets article was published in 2011 in the *Journal of Children and Media*, a peer-reviewed Taylor & Francis journal publishing studies of media in the lives of children and adolescents since 2007.

In the virtual pets study, thirty-nine middle-school students were randomly assigned to three groups who received different types of feedback, i.e., positive and negative, positive only, and no feedback as a control. Each student was given an iPhone that had a game on it where they had to care for a virtual pet of their choice for nine days. For each of these nine days, students received a breakfast reminder message on their iPhone from their virtual pet, requiring them to send a photo of themselves eating breakfast in real life to their pet. Students then received three types of feedback from their pets depending on their group assignment. The main result was amazing: the average percentage of breakfasts eaten in the nine days for the group receiving both positive and negative feedback was 52 percent, while it was only 27 percent for the group receiving only positive feedback, and 20 percent for the control group who received no feedback. The percentage differences between the first and second groups and between the second and third groups were significantly different. In other words,

[14] Byrne, S., Gay, G., Pollack, J. P. *et al.* (2012). "Caring for mobile phone-based virtual pets can influence youth eating behaviors," *Journal of Children and Media*, 6(1): 83–99.

students who received both positive and negative feedback from their virtual pets were more likely to eat breakfast than students who received positive feedback only or no feedback at all. Therefore, it is critically important to provide specific and appropriate feedback, both positive and negative, and doing so through the pet care mobile phone game can actually improve real-life breakfast-eating habits.

This article is interesting from the perspective of mobile phone activities for a few reasons. First, this study provides experimental evidence rather than survey-based, self-reported data. Through the true experiment design, researchers were able to examine the real causal effect of feedback methods through a mobile phone game on adolescents' breakfast-eating behavior. Second, while many studies focus on the negative effects of gaming (e.g., violence and aggression), this study shows some positive effects of mobile gaming on eating habits. We hope to see more studies of this type, i.e., studies investigating the positive effects of mobile gaming, as advocated in the current positive psychology movement. Third, from the mobile phone activity perspective, we see a good example of activity-based mobile phone behavior: a small group of adolescents used a relatively simple mobile game and a mobile camera to take care of virtual pets. With different types of feedback from the pets, this pet care gaming activity in nine days will lead to different patterns of adolescent breakfast-eating habits in real life.

3.4 Reuse: Recycling in China

The next article we will discuss is entitled "Survey and analysis of consumers' behaviour of waste mobile phone recycling in China."[15] The authors are Jianfeng Yin, Yingnan Gao, both from Nankai University of China, and He Xua from the Policy Research Center for Environment and Economy in Ministry of Environmental Protection. The publication record of these authors cannot be found. The article was published in 2013 in the *Journal of Cleaner Production*, one of the two journals extensively publishing studies on mobile phone recycling by Elsevier since 1993. The other journal is called *Waste Management*. Note that *Cleaner Production* in the journal name is a concept that goes beyond *pollution control*, involving not only active research and development of new structures, but also educational, training, management, and technical assistance programs to accelerate the adoption of cleaner production and sustainability.

---

[15] Yin, J., Gao, Y., and Xu, H. (2014). "Survey and analysis of consumers' behaviour of waste mobile phone recycling in China," *Journal of Cleaner Production*, 65: 517–525.

This is a survey study that was conducted in 2011 in China. A nationally representative sample of 1,064 individuals was obtained with stratified random sampling. The Likert-scale questionnaire used in the study consists of three major sections: (1) consumers' behavior and attitudes on recycling and treatment of waste mobile phones; (2) the consumers' environmental awareness of waste mobile phones, recycling, and treatment; and (3) consumers' willingness to pay for recycling and treatment of waste mobile phones. The major findings include: (1) 58 percent of the participants reported that the service life of their mobile phone was generally less than two to three years, and the major reasons that most consumers replaced their mobile phones were that their phones were damaged (43.8 percent) or their phones were unfashionable (37.1 percent). (2) Participants had five ways of dealing with waste mobile phones: 47 percent reported storing them at home; 24 percent reported giving them away or they were stolen; 19 percent participated in the paid recycling "Green Box Program"; 7 percent threw their phones away; and 2 percent participated in the free recycle "Old-for-New" program. (3) The main reasons why many waste mobile phones were not recycled were that most participants did not know where to send the phones (45.9 percent) or they would rather give their phones to family or friends (28.3 percent). Moreover, 17.7 percent of participants were afraid of privacy disclosure and 8.1 percent used waste mobile phones purely as data storage equipment. (4) A total of 33.4 percent of participants indicated that the main reason for the low recycling rate was the absence of a sound recycling system. Approximately 23.8, 15.7, and 15.2 percent believed the prime element behind the low rate was weak environmental awareness, the absence of government management, and the absence of laws and regulations, respectively. (5) In terms of participants' environmental awareness, they reported having some knowledge about waste mobile phones containing toxic and hazardous substances (e.g., lead, mercury, or arsenic) and recyclable precious metal substances (e.g., gold, silver, or palladium), and having little knowledge about the "Green Box Environmental Protection Program" proposed jointly by China Mobile, Motorola, and Nokia in 2005, Extended Producer Responsibility (EPR) stipulated in electric waste management laws, and the meaning of Extended Producer Responsibility.

From the perspective of mobile phone behavior, we can learn a few useful points from this study. First, it is helpful to know that a regular mobile phone will normally have two to three years of life. Thus, it is not a trivial issue we can ignore. Instead, it is now important to learn how to deal effectively with old mobile phones as well. How to handle old phones should be as important as how to access new phones. Second, ordinary people have various ways of treating old phones, whether it is storing them at home, giving them to relatives, recycling them through certain programs, or simply throwing them away. Third, multiple sophisticated factors are involved in influencing people's attitude and behavior of treating old phones, even including increasing concerns about security and privacy. Fourth, many ordinary mobile phone users might have very limited awareness of sophisticated environmental and social issues behind the treatment of old phones.

In summary, this section presents and discusses six empirical studies related to mobile phone activities and activity-based mobile phone behavior. As we discussed before, Elizabeth's initial thinking focused on several common mobile phone activities such as shopping and gaming; and the six everyday life observations presented after Elizabeth's responses further illustrate the breadth of mobile phone activities and activity-based mobile phone behavior (e.g., draining the pond or donating old phones). The seven journal articles illustrate various specific aspects of mobile phone activities, from gaining access to new services, to switching networks, using phones in Africa, employees struggling to use phones when they are not allowed, American young users' sexting, middle-school students' gaming with virtual pets, and ordinary Chinese people's behavior, attitudes, and knowledge about recycling mobile phones. This should further deepen and broaden our scientific knowledge about the complexity of mobile phone behavior from the mobile activities perspective. We can learn at least two major lessons: (1) mobile phone activities have both positive and negative sides rather than either positive only or negative only; and (2) mobile phone activities have a wide spectrum, starting with accessibility and ending with recycling, with various concerns of mobile phone use and various mobile phone functions in between.

4. Knowledge Syntheses: From Complex Access to WEEE Management

Mobile phone users can use mobile phones to engage in a wide variety of mobile phone activities, such as accepting, adopting, advising, assessing, worshiping, bullying, communicating, campaigning, connecting, consuming, controlling, coordinating, developing, gaming, information-seeking, intervening, learning, marketing, practicing, preventing, protesting, recruiting, recycling, sexting, socializing, studying, multitasking, teaching, or texting, to name just a few. Because mobile phone activities are extremely diverse, we can classify them in multiple ways. First, the activities can be organized in terms of four different stages of interactions between users and mobile phones (access, use, action, and reuse). Second, mobile phone activities can be grouped on the basis of different domains (medical, education, business, and daily). Third, another simple way of categorization is to base activities on different effects (physical, cognitive, social, and emotional). Fourth, we can group the activities simply based on whether it is a single activity or multiple activities (learning, gaming, calling while driving, texting while learning). Fifth, we can group the activities based on three major technologies – those relating to computation, communication, and information. In addition to the top-down approach, we can use a bottom-up approach to group the activities simply by actual everyday real-life observations or accumulated empirical research, like a ground theory approach. These typologies can further help us understand the complexity of mobile phone activities in particular and the complexity of mobile phone behavior in general.

Clearly, this chapter uses the first classification system based on the interaction stages to describe mobile phone activities. One of the major reasons for this is that both people's attention (like Elizabeth) and research effects (e.g., gaming to care for virtual pets) tend to normally focus on the middle stages, the stages of using and functioning, but it is important to examine the starting and end points as well, the starting stage of accessing and the end stage of recycling, in order to have a complete picture of how mobile phone users and mobile phone technologies interact with each other to generate various mobile phone activities.

Extensive literature exists on major issues of mobile phone activities. The *Encyclopedia of Mobile Phone Behavior*, especially the chapters in the section on mobile phone activities and processes, provides a good synthesis of the existing body of the literature. Nearly fifty chapters address various topics of mobile phone activities and can be organized into four themes: access, use, action, and reuse. Table 4.1 presents a brief summary.

Instead of covering all the topics on mobile phone activities, we will discuss a few published review articles and *Encyclopedia* chapters to illustrate the breadth and depth of the current literature on mobile phone activities.

4.1   Four Kinds of Access

The first article is "The digital divide as a complex and dynamic phenomenon."[16] The concept of the digital divide generally means inequalities in

---

[16] Van Dijk, J. and Hacker, K. (2003). "The digital divide as a complex and dynamic phenomenon," *The Information Society*, 19(4): 315–326.

Table 4.1 *The* Encyclopedia *Chapters on Activity-Based Mobile Phone Behavior*

Feature	Chapter Title
Access	Consumer acceptance of the mobile internet
Access	Mobile coupons: Adoption and use
Access	Consumer adoption of mobile e-WOM messages
Use	Using mobile phones for educational assessment
Use	The conceptualization and assessment of problematic mobile phone use
Use	Religious use of mobile phones
Use	Divorced coparents' use of communication technology
Use	Textism use and language ability in children
Use	Emoticon use in mobile communications :-)
Use	Positive technology: Using mobile phones for psychosocial interventions
Use	Use of mobile phones to help prevent child maltreatment
Use	Using mobile phones to control social interactions
Use	Mobile phone use enhances social connectedness
Use	Exploring the use of mobile devices to support teacher education
Use	Texting and Christian practice
Use	Mobile health in emergency care
Use	Mobile phones for plastic surgery and burns: Current practice
Use	The use of mobile phone technology to support people with autism spectrum disorders
Action	Sex, cyberbullying and the mobile phone
Action	Students hurting students: Cyberbullying as a mobile phone behavior
Action	Connecting 'round the clock: Mobile phones and adolescents' experiences of intimacy
Action	Cell phone conversation while driving
Action	Cell-phones, distracted driving, bans and fatalities
Action	Cellular phones' contribution to dangerous driving
Action	Mobile phone and driving
Action	Waste time or lose life: Assessing the risk of phoning while driving
Action	Mobile games and learning
Action	Mobile seamless learning from the perspective of self-regulated learning
Action	Mobile phone use and children's literacy learning
Action	Microlearning and mobile learning
Action	Mobile learning
Action	Science learning games for mobile platforms
Action	Mobile communication tools as morality-building devices
Action	Text messaging in social protests
Action	Human resource recruiting and selection using cellphone apps
Action	Teenage sexting: Sexual expression meets mobile technology
Action	Mobile phone multitasking and learning
Action	Adolescent text messaging
Action	Mobile tracking for mental health and wellbeing
Reuse	Sustainability of the use of mobile phones
Reuse	Generation, collection and recycling of used and end-of-life mobile phones

accessing digital technologies. The article is well cited perhaps due to its thorough analysis of the concept of the digital divide based on a thoughtful typology. The authors are Jan van Dijk and Kenneth Hacker. The first author, Jan van Dijk, is a Professor of Communication at the University of Twente in the Netherlands, who has published extensively on the social aspects of information and communication technology, especially on the digital divide. The article was published in 2003 in *The Information Society*, an established Taylor & Francis journal publishing studies on relationships between technological change and social change since 1981.

This article can be called a theoretical or position article rather than a typical review article. It uses both an effective analytical framework and existing survey data from the Netherlands and the United States to analyze the complexity and dynamics of the concept of the so-called "digital divide." It mainly focuses on information and communication technologies (computers and the Internet) broadly rather than mobile phones exclusively. There are at least eight major points we can learn from this article about accessibility. First, as one of two major themes of the article, the authors consider the issue of accessibility as a *complex* concept with four aspects: (1) mental access (whether individuals have interest, computer anxiety, or are attracted to the new technology); (2) material access (whether individuals possess computers and network connections); (3) skill access (whether individuals obtain digital skills); and (4) usage access (whether individuals have significant usage opportunities). Next, as the second central theme, the authors consider the four types of access as a *dynamic* sequence that changes substantially over time, usually with the first two accesses (mental and material accesses) improving gradually and with the second two accesses (skill and usage accesses) facing more challenges later on. Third, for mental access, the authors specified that about as many as *36 percent* of the Dutch users in the study lacked computer use skills due to substantial technology anxiety, negative attitude, and low-level motivation. Fourth, for material access, the technology possession gap *increased* over time between groups that differed by age, gender, education, income, and race. This is often due to a saturation effect – an effect that the group with a higher level of material access will remain at the same level, but the group with a lower level of material access will fall behind further. Fifth, for skill access, the digital divide will be observed not only in instrumental skills (how to use hardware and software), but more importantly in informational skills (how to search for information) and strategic skills (how to apply skills in personal careers or development). Sixth, for usage access, a usage gap will emerge. While some individuals take full advantage of and benefit more from a wide variety of advanced technologies, other individuals might only be able to use some simple technologies (e.g., people mainly use technologies at home for basic word processing and gaming). This article helps us further understand the complexity of mobile phone activities, especially accessibility and the digital divide, in two important ways. First, it categorizes the issue of accessibility into four major types: mental access, material access, skill access, and usage access. This comprehensive conceptual framework helps us appreciate the complexity of accessibility. In other words, there are four different kinds of digital divide rather than just one. For mobile phones, the digital divides in mental and material access might not be major concerns; however, there may be concerns about the digital divides in skill access (e.g., how to use mobile phones for searching medical or business information) and usage access (e.g., how to benefit most from the latest advances in mobile phone technologies in health care and learning). Second, although this conceptual framework was presented almost fifteen years ago, we can still use it to see or find a wide variety of specific research findings on various topics. These findings help us appreciate the richness of accessibility. While Elizabeth's initial responses do not touch on the issue of accessibility at all, and the everyday real-life observations and empirical studies demonstrate the breadth and depth of the issue of accessibility, this review article opens a large door into the enormous literature on accessibility.

4.2   Three Areas of Use

The second review is entitled "Research approaches to mobile use in the developing world: A review of the literature," and is written by Jonathan Donner.[17] Although this title sounds like a research methodological review, it actually is a typical review article of the literature on mobile phone use in developing countries, a timely, important, and much-needed research topic. Jonathan Donner is a researcher at Microsoft Research and has published extensively on mobile use in developing countries, including his recent book *After Access*,[18] which examines major

---

[17] Donner, J. (2008). "Research approaches to mobile use in the developing world: A review of the literature," *The Information Society*, 24(3): 140–159.
[18] Donner, J. (2015). *After Access: Inclusion, Development, and a More Mobile Internet*. Cambridge, MA: MIT Press.

implications of mobile internet in developing counties. The review we will be discussing was published in 2008 in *The Information Society*, the same journal in which the article discussed in the previous section was published.

This review article takes a broad approach to information and communication technologies and development (ICTD) to review nearly 200 relevant publications. There are at least five major points we can learn about mobile phone use in developing countries. First, the existing literature has concentrated on three areas: mobile phone adoption, mobile phone impacts, and the interrelationship between users and mobile phones. Second, for mobile phone adoption, there are three specific areas of research: patterns of mobile phone adaptation in different developing countries based on different theories, such as the diffusion theory, the technology acceptance theory, or the reasoned action theory; various policy issues regulating mobile phone services in different developing countries; and the new unique nature of digital divides or access gaps in mobile phone access. Third, for mobile phone impacts, various research findings indicate the economic impacts of mobile phones, showing the close association between increase of penetration rates and improvements in gross domestic product, inflows of foreign direct investment, small business start-ups, and fishing product sales. It also reports that mobile phones have other positive non-economic impacts on e-learning, health care, emergency, and family relationships. Fourth, for the phone-user interrelationship, the review synthesized four specific areas of research: modernization and globalization with mobile phone use; daily-life changes with mobile phone use; technological design changes with mobile phone use; and community sharing with mobile phone use.

This review broadens the traditional conceptualization of mobile phone use. Instead of just focusing on penetration rates or diffusion processes of mobile phones, mobile phone use in developing countries involves many more issues regarding new meanings of the digital divide, broad impacts on economic development, and various changes in human development. This is not something that Elizabeth thought about, as shown in her initial responses.

4.3   Three Types of Gaming

Mobile gaming is an interesting and common mobile phone activity. A chapter of the *Encyclopedia of Mobile Phone Behavior*, entitled "Mobile games," offers a good synthesis. The authors are two scholars from Australia, Ingrid Richardson and Larissa Hjorth, who have both published extensively on mobile games from epistemological and ethnographical perspectives.

Quite different from a typical review, this *Encyclopedia* chapter intended to offer a critical review of three types of mobile games. First, it starts with the *popularity* of mobile games, pointing out that between 2012 and 2013, 75 percent of all mobile phone downloads were games. *Angry Birds* alone, for example, since its release in 2009, was downloaded over 1 billion times in 2012 and over 2 billion times in 2015. Second, it presents the app-based mobile games, the first of the three major types of mobile game. Traditionally, games are categorized into two groups, casual games that involve brief, simple, and non-skill-demanded gameplay and hardcore games that concern long, complex, and skill-demanded gameplay. However, *app-based* mobile phone games really make the casual-vs.-hardcore classification almost unworkable because gamers now can play any downloadable mobile game anytime and anywhere. Current app-based mobile games (e.g., *Bad Piggies*) are not only different from traditional portable or handheld games (e.g., Nintendo's GameBoy), but also from early mobile phone games (e.g., Nokia's *NGage*). They are so much more flexible, complex, and dynamic that they become *assemblages* in which game elements and rules are flexible and dynamic rather than typical games with fixed game elements and rules. Third, the chapter discussed *location-based* mobile phone games (e.g., Geocaching), the second of the three major types of mobile game. Traditional location-based games (e.g., *MyTown*) include urban games, big games, pervasive games, and mixed reality games. Since smartphones have GPS as a common feature, when gamers play location-based games, they themselves can integrate their immediate real-life perception, GPS location information, and augmented and networked game situations all together, thus creating a special hybrid gaming experience that mixes the real world with the virtual world. Fourth, the last type of mobile game is the social-media-based game (e.g., *Words with Friends* or *I Love Coffee*). Social media games are embedded within social media websites such as Facebook, YouTube, Twitter, and Kakao so that social interactions and gameplays become almost seamless. Fifth, through their review and discussion of mobile phone games, the authors stress several important concepts in mobile games, such as assemblage (featuring flexible, dynamic, and complex gaming activities) and gamification (making non-game applications game-like, fun-oriented activities). These will eventually make mobile gaming behavior more rich, diverse, and complex.

4.4 Four Trends of Recycling

The last review article we will discuss is entitled, "How are WEEE doing? A global review of the management of electrical and electronic wastes."[19] The "WEEE" specified in the title is an acronym that stands for waste electrical and electronic equipment, or equipment that is being thrown away. This review is well cited (365 times based on Google Scholar). The authors are three UK researchers, Francis Ongondo, Ian Williams, and Tom Cherrett. The first author, Francis Ongondo, has published multiple articles on mobile phone reuse, while the second author, Ian Williams, is Ongondo's mentor and an expert on waste and environmental issues. This review was published in 2011 in *Waste Management*.

This review offers a comprehensive overview of global trends in managing waste electrical and electronic equipment in the world. Major points include the following: (1) *Geologically*, the quantities of WEEE generated are high and/or increasing in Africa, in the poorer regions of Asia, and in Latin and South America, but not in Europe. (2) For *regulations*, informational technologies and telecommunications equipment seem to be the dominant WEEE being generated, and many countries lack or are slow in initiating, drafting, and adopting WEEE regulations. (3) For *management strategies*, repairing and reusing within a largely informal recycling sector is typical in developing countries, landfilling is still used in both developed and developing nations, and stockpiling of unwanted electrical and electronic products is common in both the United States and less developed economies. (4) Four common *priority* areas are resource depletion, ethical concerns, health and environmental issues, and WEEE take-back strategies. (5) The four *future* trends of WEEE management are that: (a) global amounts of WEEE will continue to increase due to emerging new technologies and affordable electronics; (b) informal recycling in developing nations will play an important role in WEEE management; (c) the pace of initiating and enacting WEEE-specific legislation will be very slow across the globe; and (d) there will be a large need for more accurate and current data on amounts and types of WEEE.

From this review, we can further expand our knowledge of mobile phone reuse in at least four aspects. First, there is an imbalance in WEEE accumulation between developing vs. developed countries. Second, there is an imbalance between the rapid increase in WEEE and the slow response

---

[19] Ongondo, F. O., Williams, I. D., and Cherrett, T. J. (2011). "How are WEEE doing? A global review of the management of electrical and electronic wastes," *Waste Management*, 31(4): 714–730.

in managing it. Third, there is an imbalance of having relatively strong technological and policy programs in place, but relatively weak study and encouragement of individuals' awareness, adaptation, and assessment of WEEE. Fourth, there is an imbalance of formal and informal channels in managing WEEE.

5. Comparative Analyses: From Screen Time to Tweeting Difference

There are at least two ways to compare human behavior with different technologies. One, as used in the previous chapters, is to compare them across studies, e.g., comparing human behavior with televisions, computers, the Internet, and mobile phones across four different studies. One of the advantages of this approach is the flexibility to choose different studies. One of the disadvantages is that different studies have different designs, samples, instruments, and data analyses, making the comparison difficult. Another way is to compare them within studies, e.g., comparing human behavior with televisions, computers, the Internet, and mobile phones all within the same study. One of the advantages of the second approach is that the studies use similar designs, samples, instruments, and data analyses, making the comparison easy. One of the disadvantages is that it is hard to identify such studies comparing all these technologies at once. In this section, we will show two examples of mobile phone activity and related behavior within one study.

5.1 Screen Time

The first study comparing media use is entitled "Young children's screen time: The complex role of parent and child factors." It was published in 2015 by Alexis Lauricella, Ellen Wartella, and Victoria Rideout in the *Journal of Applied Developmental Psychology*.[20] The existing literature indicates that higher parent television use is associated with higher levels of child television time, but is it still true with other types of technology? In this study, a nationally representative sample of more than 2,300 American parents who had children aged 8 years and under participated in a 20-minute survey. Major measures included access to technologies at home, parent attitude toward technologies (positive or negative), parent time of

[20] Lauricella, A. R., Wartella, E., and Rideout, V. J. (2015). "Young children's screen time: The complex role of parent and child factors," *Journal of Applied Developmental Psychology*, 36: 11–17.

using technologies (low, medium, and high), and children's time of using technologies (low, medium, and high, based on parents' report). Technologies covered in the study were television, computers, smartphones, and tablet computers. It was found that children's screen time with the four technologies was significantly related to both parent screen time with the four technologies and parent attitude toward the four technologies.

5.2   Tweeting

The second study is entitled "Do we tweet differently from our mobile devices? A study of language differences on mobile and web-based twitter platforms."[21] It was published by Dhiraj Murthy, Sawyer Bowman, Alexander Gross, and Marisa McGarry in 2015 in the *Journal of Communication*. In this study, researchers collected over 235 million tweets over the course of six weeks in the summer of 2013 by using Twitter's Application Programming Interface (API), which allows automatic collection of a stream of sampled tweets from the overall flow of all global tweets at any given time. For the independent variable, researchers classified collected tweets in English as either mobile (e.g., Twitter for iPhone or Twitter for Android) or non-mobile (e.g., Twitter for desktop-based Web or Tweet-Button, where mobile tweet button usage is rare). For the dependent variables, the researchers coded n-grams (a series of unbroken characters or words in tweets) in four language styles: self style, gender style, emotional style, and agentic and communal style. Their major findings were as follows: (1) mobile tweets are more egocentric in language than non-mobile tweets; (2) no gender style difference exists; both mobile tweets and non-mobile tweets use words traditionally associated with the masculine; (3) no difference exists in negative and positive language use; both mobile tweets and non-mobile tweets have equal amounts of negative and positive language; and (4) no difference exists in agentic behavior; both mobile and non-mobile tweets employed language associated with communal behavior.

These two studies further expand our understanding of the complexity of mobile phone activities and behavior. First, for young children aged 8 years and under, their use of different technologies (television, computers, smartphones, and tablet computers) was strongly associated with

---

[21] Murthy, D., Bowman, S., Gross, A. J., and McGarry, M. (2015). "Do we tweet differently from our mobile devices? A study of language differences on mobile and web-based twitter platforms," *Journal of Communication*, 65(5): 816–837.

parent technology use and parent technology attitude. In short, parent behavior always matters. Second, the use of Twitter across different platforms leads to different types of language behavior; tweeting with mobile phones leads to more egocentric language, while tweeting through non-mobile means like a desktop-based website does not. Users tweet differently in several aspects, depending on using mobile devices or non-mobile web devices. Mobile tweeting is forming new behaviors, attitudes, and linguistic styles online. In short, the technology does matter since it plays a role in mobile phone behavior; the medium is indeed the message[22] since it allows features for new mobile phone behavior.

6. Complex Thinking: Diverse Activities, Complex Behavior

Now, after reading this chapter, we should much more easily see the strengths and limitations of Elizabeth's intuitive responses. We should have a much more sophisticated knowledge about the complexity of mobile phone activities. The breadth and depth of our previous under-standing should have expanded. Mobile phone activities are not just simply calling a parent or texting a friend. Instead, they are much more rich, dynamic, and complex due to diverse users, diverse technologies, diverse activities, and diverse effects. But, most importantly, we should consider them from the positive side to the negative side of the entire spectrum and from the beginning point to the end point of the entire process.

Specifically, as shown in the summary diagram in Figure 4.1, we should examine the mobile phone activities from four aspects: access, use, action, and reuse, from both positive and negative perspectives. First, mobile phone access should be considered the *beginning* point of mobile phone interactions or activities. Access involves various specific issues such as adopting, accepting, switching, discontinuing, and terminating in both positive and negative ways. We discussed the story of the 16-year-old German boy draining a pond, the empirical study on how Dutch residents accepted advanced services, and the review about four aspects of the digital divide (i.e., mental, material, skill, and usage access).

Second, mobile phone use may be a common topic, but it involves various complex issues such as innovative use (e.g., using mobile phones to

---

[22] Author's note: "The medium is the message" is a widely accepted statement, arguing that, besides the content of a medium, the form of a medium itself also delivers specific messages. McLuhan, M. (1994). *Understanding Media: The Extensions of Man*. Cambridge, MA: MIT Press.

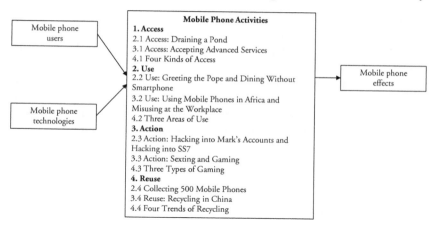

Mobile Phone Activities
1. **Access**
2.1 Access: Draining a Pond
3.1 Access: Accepting Advanced Services
4.1 Four Kinds of Access
2. **Use**
2.2 Use: Greeting the Pope and Dining Without Smartphone
3.2 Use: Using Mobile Phones in Africa and Misusing at the Workplace
4.2 Three Areas of Use
3. **Action**
2.3 Action: Hacking into Mark's Accounts and Hacking into SS7
3.3 Action: Sexting and Gaming
4.3 Three Types of Gaming
4. **Reuse**
2.4 Collecting 500 Mobile Phones
3.4 Reuse: Recycling in China
4.4 Four Trends of Recycling

Mobile phone users

Mobile phone technologies

Mobile phone effects

Figure 4.1   A Summary Diagram of Activity-Based Mobile Phone Behavior

greet the Pope), non-use (e.g., avoiding mobile phone use for religious reasons), semi-use, misuse, overuse, excessive use, and addictive use. Specific examples we discussed include the two stories of Pope Francis (using mobile phones to welcome the Pope, and the Pope recommending eating dinner as a family with no phone use), the two studies of mobile phone use in Africa and misuse at work, the review on mobile phone use in developing countries, and the comparative study of parental influence on the use of different technologies.

Third, mobile phone action such as mobile learning, mobile banking, and mobile gaming is the most common among mobile phone activities. However, we can see its complexity, especially the positive and negative sides, from different examples, including the story of negative hacking without consent vs. "positive" hacking with consent, the two studies on youths' sexting behavior and adolescents' mobile gaming with pets, the review on the three unique types of mobile games, and the comparison of Tweeting between mobile phones and non-mobile websites.

Fourth, mobile phone reuse can be considered the end point of mobile phone activities from both the positive and negative aspects. The examples we have discussed include the story of donating used mobile phones by James Maturo, the empirical study on recycling behavior in China, and the comprehensive review about global recycling behavior.

We need to further advance our scientific understanding of mobile phone activities. The future directions of mobile phone activity research are largely determined by the practical need of the mobile phone users and the scientific demand of mobile phone activity research. For instance, in the real-life world, people are using mobile phones while simultaneously engaging in other activities such as driving and learning. Thus, future research efforts should be made to identify and examine more multiple activities besides the multitasking research and the calling while driving research. In addition, in the scientific world, a large proportion of the current research is using simple survey methods to collect self-report data. Future research should develop and encourage complex survey methods such as experimental surveys and story-based surveys to study mobile phone activities. Furthermore, other innovative methods such as the big data method and the sensor-based method should be used to collect large, high-quality data over time. Finally, research on mobile phone recycling behavior, rather than programs or policies, should be enhanced to really promote and advocate the recycling programs effectively and efficiently. Successful macro-level policy decisions on mobile phone recycling really depends on effective micro-level psychological processes of individual users' mobile phone recycling behavior as the ideal starting point (e.g., a need assessment) and the desirable end point (e.g., an outcome assessment).

CHAPTER 5

Mobile Phone Effects

Outline

1. *Intuitive Thinking: Frances' Quick Responses*
2. *Daily Observations: From Jennifer Lawrence to Ebola Outbreak*
    2.1 *Negative and Positive Effects: Jennifer Lawrence and Tao Liu*
    2.2 *Health Effects: Simon Park and Jenny Fry*
    2.3 *Psychological Effects: Barack Obama and Valerie Kusler*
    2.4 *Social Effects: Sit-Down Protest and Ebola Outbreak*
3. *Empirical Studies: From Mobile Phone Allergy to Crime Rate Drop*
    3.1 *Health Effect: Sources of Metallic Allergy from Mobile Phones*
    3.2 *Health Effect: Significant Bacterial Contamination in Patients' Mobile Phones*
    3.3 *Psychological Effect: Phantom Vibration Syndrome among Medical Workers*
    3.4 *Social Effect: Crime Rate Drop in the 1990s*
4. *Knowledge Syntheses: From Mobile Phone Allergy to Child Maltreatment Prevention*
    4.1 *Various Mobile Phone Effects*
    4.2 *Consistent Mobile Phone Dermatitis*
    4.3 *Risky Bacterial Infections within Hospitals*
    4.4 *Debatable Phantom Vibration Syndrome*
5. *Comparative Analyses: From Device Allergy to Device Bacterial Contamination*
    5.1 *Device Contact Dermatitis*
    5.2 *Device Bacterial Contamination*
6. *Complex Thinking: A Complex Double-Edged Sword*

1. Intuitive Thinking: Frances' Quick Responses

Frances is a faculty member at a university in China. I asked her: What are the effects of mobile phones on human beings? I specifically asked her to give three to five ideas with three to five short examples that came to mind as quickly as she could.

Here are her responses: (1) Mobile phones make broader interactions and collaborations: With the use of the app Weixin, you can quickly know what is happening with your friends. (2) Mobile phones help you share various resources, such as cloud services, online classrooms, online shopping, online counseling, or using Uber or DiDi to get a taxi. (3) Mobile phones provide easy and efficient information services, such as no need to use paper-based newspapers and books to get information. (4) Mobile phones make payment extremely easy, such as making payments through Weixin or Zifubao (i.e., Alipay) and you can order anything from flight tickets to drinks, even in rural areas. (5) Most importantly, mobile phones can be used anytime and anywhere, such as using mobile Internet.

Are Frances' quick responses good? We would say that Frances' quick responses are pretty good. First, her responses are *broad*, concerning various effects related to social interacting, resource sharing, information seeking, personal financing, and living everyday life. Second, her responses include various *specific* examples, such as Weixin, Uber, and mobile Internet. Third, her responses stress the *core* feature of mobile phones – the ability to use them anytime and anywhere. Clearly, these are major strengths. However, her quick responses reveal some problems. First, her responses focus on the *positive* effects without mentioning anything about the negative effects. Second, understandably, her responses are *narrowly* based on her experience in China, including her examples such as Weixin, Didi, and Zifubao. Note that Uber is an American company, but is operating in China, and has been competing with Zifubao since 2015. Clearly, these are some limitations. Nevertheless, these are some mobile phone effects, but certainly not all of the effects. Mobile phone effects are much more complicated than we thought and they are the last element in the basic model of mobile phone behavior.

Now, some of us might think: This discussion on mobile phone effects seems similar to the discussion in the previous chapter on mobile phone activities. What is the difference between mobile phone activities and mobile phone effects? How do mobile phone effects fit into the basic model of mobile phone behavior? These questions are important and timely for us to better understand not only mobile phone effects, but also the basic element model of mobile phone behavior.

Let us briefly address them by looking at an example. Frances' first response consisted of a general statement: "Mobile phones make broader interactions and collaborations," and one specific example, "With the use of the app Weixin, you can quickly know what is happening with your friends." First, mobile phone activities refer to the interactions between users and mobile phones, whereas mobile phone effects are the results of the mobile phone activities. In Frances' first response, she mentioned one general mobile phone activity, *interactions and collaborations*, and one specific mobile phone activity, *using the app Weixin*. She also indicated one general mobile phone effect, *make broader* interactions and collaborations, and one specific mobile phone effect, *quickly know what is happening with your friends*. Here, we can see that the mobile phone activities and mobile phone effects are both logically related to each other, but conceptually different from each other. Second, based on the basic element model, mobile phone behavior consists of four elements: users, technologies, activities, and effects. Mobile users interact with mobile phones to generate mobile phone activities, leading to mobile phone effects. Frances' first response implicitly suggests one general mobile phone behavior: mobile users interact with mobile phones to generate mobile phone activities, i.e., interactions and collaborations, resulting in mobile phone effects, i.e., making broader interactions and collaborations. She also explicitly described one specific mobile phone behavior, you (user) interact with Weixin (the app) and generate an activity (using Weixin), resulting in an effect (quickly knowing what is happening with your friends). Now we might see more clearly two key points in understanding the diversity and complexity of mobile phone behavior. First, it is useful to *always* study mobile phone behavior as a basic unit based on its four basic elements and their sequential relationship. We follow this approach throughout the book. Second, it is also useful to *sometimes* analyze mobile phone behavior by focusing on one element at a time with a specific angle. This is why we use the four chapters to analyze mobile phone behavior from the perspective of mobile phone users, mobile phone technologies, mobile phone activities, and mobile phone effects individually and sequentially. Because these chapters talk about mobile phone behavior while emphasizing an element such as users or mobile phone effects, the chapter titles could be called user-emphasized mobile phone behavior or effect-emphasized mobile phone behavior. So, even though the chapters are focusing on one element in particular, the chapters are still about mobile phone behavior.

In this chapter, we will carefully and systematically examine mobile phone effects to further understand the complexity of mobile phone behavior. First, we will examine multiple everyday observations to see what types of mobile effects there are and try to broaden our knowledge about mobile phone effects. Second, we will examine details of scientific evidence from multiple studies and try to deepen our knowledge about mobile phone effects. Third, we will study a few reviews to help us view the big picture of this research area. Fourth, we will compare the similarities and differences of different technologies and their effects to further understand mobile phone effects. As always, we will end the chapter with a summary.

2.   Daily Observations: From Jennifer Lawrence to Ebola Outbreak

2.1   Negative and Positive Effects: Jennifer Lawrence and Tao Liu

In August 2014,[1] more than fifty nude pictures of actress Jennifer Lawrence and dozens of other famous female celebrities were stolen and posted on websites which rapidly spread on the Internet. These private pictures of Lawrence were taken on her personal iPhone and automatically uploaded in and downloaded from iCloud. The hackers had been targeting Jennifer and other celebrities systematically and eventually hacked into iCloud to steal these pictures. After 40 hours of investigation, Apple announced that they did not find any breaches in Apple's network systems, including iCloud or the Find My iPhone service that resulted in the leaking of these pictures. However, they did find that someone accessed celebrities' accounts using the celebrities' user names, passwords, and security questions. It was likely that the hackers used a hacking program such as iBrute that can repeatedly try different combinations of letters and numbers to find possible passwords. The hacker might have figured out the password of Apple's Find My iPhone service and then used that to get the iCloud password via Find My iPhone, and eventually was able to open and take images and other data stored in that iCloud account. After over a year, Lawrence was finally able to talk publicly about her experience: "I felt angry at websites reposting them . . . I can't really describe to you the feeling that took a very long time to go away . . . It was an unshakable, really awful feeling that after it healed a little bit made me incredibly angry."

To understand what happened with this case, we need to know a few key technical terms. (1) Cloud or Cloud computing is a new kind of Internet computing system that provides shared processing resources and data to computers and other devices on demand. It is like the electricity grid over a network to achieve economy and efficiency. The metaphor of *cloud* implies that all the network elements representing the

---

[1]   See www.npr.org/sections/thetwo-way/2014/09/02/345250421/celebrity-photo-leak-puts-spotlight-on-the-cloud-and-security.

provider-rendered services are invisible, but at the same time accessible for a user, as if a Greek mythological hero has a super power in the heavens, but is hidden behind a cloud. It differs from a traditional network system in a few important ways. It is a model for enabling ubiquitous *demand-based* access, instead of delivery-based access, to a *shared* pool instead of a designated system of configurable computing resources (e.g., networks, servers, storage, applications, and services), which can be rapidly provisioned and released with minimal management effort. Cloud computing and storage solutions provide users with various capabilities to store and process their data in third-party data centers. This allows users to store data in the cloud and free up space on mobile phones while providing the flexibility to still access their data from anywhere that you can access the cloud. (2) iCloud is a cloud storage and computing service released in 2011 by Apple. By linking an iPhone to iCloud, users can wirelessly store their data such as documents, photos, and music, download the data to iOS, Macintosh, or Windows devices, share the data with other users, manage their Apple devices if lost or stolen, and back up iOS devices directly to iCloud. It is a service for which users pay extra money per month if they want additional storage space. Access requires passwords via iPhones. Cloud computing in general and iCloud in particular are new technologies and can have various positive effects on users, but will also lead to some unexpected negative effects, like the case of Jennifer Lawrence, whose iCloud account was hacked.

In December 2015,[2] Tao Liu, a Chinese movie/TV star, perhaps as popular in China as Jennifer Lawrence is in the United States, visited Demark. However, one day when she came back to her luxury hotel room in Copenhagen, she discovered that all her property, jewelry, and money, worth 4 million Chinese Yuan (equivalent to $600,000), had disappeared. She did not know what to do. She used her iPhone 5s and sent her friends a text message asking for urgent help. Surprisingly, her text message spread out widely and quickly on social media through an app called Weixin. Within a few hours, she received 28,807 responses and her text was forwarded 65,158 times, and got 141,870 likes/supports. First, people suggested that the Danish Embassy in China could provide assistance in this matter. Second, people recommended reporting the loss to the hotel, meeting with senior hotel managers, and checking hotel cameras for evidence. Third, the embassy contacted the Danish

---

[2] See http://blog.sina.com.cn/s/blog_774682f90102wacp.html?tj=1.

Government, notified the police in Copenhagen to start an investigation, and contacted the Bureau of Policy and Bureau of Tourism Affairs. Shortly thereafter, police posted a tweet and announced that they arrested a 33-year-old suspect from Poland at the border with Tao Liu's jewelry, her expensive Bvlgari watch, and her Tiffany diamond ring. A Danish local newspaper reported the investigation. Within 17 hours, all of Tao Liu's property was returned. After the ordeal came to an end, she did not forget to text everyone: "This trip to Demark, felt cold in one day, but warm in the entire process. Thank all friends [sic], everything is fine now and I will come back to China soon."

From observing these two real-life cases, we can learn a few important points. First, the effects of mobile phones can be *positive* or *negative* and, often, an initial negative effect might turn into a positive one or, vice versa, an initial positive effect might turn into a negative one. If our property is unfortunately stolen, we can use mobile phones to ask for help. Fortunately, our stolen property can be returned to us, as experienced by the Chinese actress Miss Liu in Denmark. However, while new devices or services of mobile phones give us convenience, enjoyment, or excitement, they might lead to various harsh and even severe or permanent damage to ourselves, like in the case of Jennifer Lawrence.

Second, mobile phone effects may be *intentional* or *unintentional*. For example, some grandparents want to use mobile phones to get daily updates about their beloved grandsons and granddaughters thousands of miles away. However, in many cases, various mobile phone effects are not what we expected, like the negative effect of the Jennifer Lawrence case and the positive effect of the Tao Liu case.

Lastly, the four-element model can be used to describe the *effect-focused* mobile phone behavior related to the two observations of Lawrence and Liu. For Jennifer Lawrence, initially, she (the user) used her iPhone camera (the technology) to take her own pictures (the activity), and then her pictures were automatically stored in iCloud (the effect). Something unexpected then happened to Lawrence. The hackers (the user) used iBrute (the technology) to hack into her iCloud (the activity) and stole and posted the pictures online, causing emotional distress for the actress (the effect). For Tao Liu, she (the user) used her iPhone 5s (the technology) to text her friends for help after personal possessions were stolen (the activity) and the news spread rapidly (the effect). This devastating story then had an unexpected happy ending. Her friends (the user) used a mobile app Weixin (the technology) to share cues and solutions (the activity) and all of her lost property was returned within 17 hours (the effect).

2.2   Health Effects: Simon Park and Jenny Fry

In February 2015,[3] Dr. Simon Park, a senior lecturer in molecular biology at the University of Surrey in the United Kingdom, did an experiment with his students in his class of Practical and Biomedical Bacteriology. He asked his undergraduate students to imprint their mobile phones onto Petri dishes to study bacteriological growth. Note that a Petri dish was named after the German bacteriologist Julius Richard Petri. It is a shallow, cylindrical, glass or plastic lidded dish, partially filled with warm liquid containing agar and a mixture of specific ingredients. Biologists use the Petri dish to culture cells, such as bacteria. After three days, his students were shocked to see the phone-shaped pattern of development of various bacteria in the dish. Many of the bacteria found were harmless, but some of those present, like staphylococcus aureus, cause diseases. Dr. Park notes that bacteria can utilize many different things to promote their transmission. Insects, water, food, coughs and sneezes, sexual contact, and rain are just a few examples. Now the mobile phone is another mechanism for carrying invisible bacteria. It might be eighteen times dirtier than a toilet.

On June 11, 2015,[4] Jenny Fry, a 15-year-old British girl, committed suicide near her home by hanging herself from a tree. Since 2011, she suffered from irritation, headaches, fatigue, and other symptoms. Her mother Debra believed that her symptoms were due to her allergy to WiFi signals, known as electromagnetic hypersensitivity (EHS). Her family had removed the WiFi router from their home. However, her school still had WiFi routers, so Jenny still always felt the effects. She felt better only when she was away from WiFi. Thus, she always tried to leave classrooms to find a place on campus far away from WiFi to do her school work. Her school administrator did not believe that WiFi caused her symptoms and gave her detention for her "strange" behavior. After texting her friend to say she could no longer cope with her WiFi allergies, Fry ended her young life. Now her family wants to raise awareness of EHS and is campaigning to remove wireless technology from nurseries and schools. However, Simon Duffy, the head teacher of Fry's former school, indicated that the school needs WiFi to enable it to operate effectively and the installed WiFi complies with the relevant regulations and the school will ensure that this continues.

---

[3] See   www.news.com.au/world/europe/study-reveals-just-how-dirty-your-phone-could-be/news-story/dbeeb48c67e9a1a0a883039809181 6d4.

[4] See www.independent.co.uk/news/uk/home-news/school-girl-found-hanged-after-suffering-from-allergy-to-wifi-a6755401.html.

These two cases highlight one dimension of mobile phone effects – the effects on physical and mental health. Dr. Park's experiment shows possible bacterial contamination from mobile phones. The Jenny Fry case shows a possible physical reaction or allergy to the WiFi network of mobile phones. Whether these problems are proved scientifically is one matter that we will discuss in the chapter on mobile phones in medicine, but the potential consequences might be severe (e.g., Fry's death). Furthermore, mobile phone effects have multiple dimensions. Besides the positive and negative effects on human health, mobile phones might have positive or negative impacts on human cognition, social ability, emotional experience, and moral behavior, as we will discuss later in this chapter. Lastly, these two effect-focused mobile phone behaviors can be summarized based on the four-element model. For Dr. Park, his students (the user) took their mobile phones (the technology) and imprinted them onto Petri dishes (the activity) and various bacteria were observed (the effect). For Jenny Fry, she (the user) was exposed to WiFi signals (the technology) and felt the unusual pain of WiFi allergy (the activity) and eventually committed suicide (the effect).

2.3   Psychological Effects: Barack Obama and Valerie Kusler

On November 21, 2014,[5] President Barack Obama left the Oval Office and boarded Marine One on the South Lawn of the White House for a scheduled presidential trip. However, shortly after boarding, he hurried off Marine One and returned to the White House. When he came outside again, he held his BlackBerry in his hand, waved it in the air, and told reporters gathering at the White House: "Didn't you guys ever forget something?" Everyone then realized that President Obama had forgotten his BlackBerry and needed to get it before setting off on the trip.

Note that Marine One is the US Marine Corps aircraft carrying the President of the United States. It usually denotes a helicopter operated by Marine Helicopter Squadron One. Whenever the President has an important trip, he needs to first take Marine One from the White House and then take Air Force One from Andrews Air Force Base.

This incident reveals two important aspects of what researchers are now calling "nomophobia" (or, no-mobile-phone-phobia): (1) the feelings of anxiety or distress that some people experience when not having their

---

[5] See   www.dailymail.co.uk/news/article-2844398/Obama-keeps-Marine-One-waiting-heads-White-House-saying-s-forgotten-Blackberry.html.

phone; and (2) the degree to which we depend on mobile phones to complete basic tasks and to fulfill important needs. President Obama felt the need to hurry off Marine One and return to the White House, indicating that he might experience certain anxiety when his BlackBerry was not with him. Afterwards, he must have experienced certain pleasure when he got his BlackBerry and waved it in his hand since he could then use it for his everyday communication.

In September 2013,[6] Valerie Kusler, a woman working on a large cattle ranch in Tennessee, was interviewed by National Public Radio reporter Elise Hu about her experience of phantom vibration syndrome, a phenomenon where you think your phone is vibrating when it is not. She said that she does experience phantom vibration syndrome, especially when many cows make a deep sound of lowing or mooing and she is confused as to whether it is the deep and low sound of cows or the sound of her mobile phone vibrating. To deal with this phantom vibration syndrome, she is setting a personal goal to have a better boundary between her work life and her mobile phone.

As we will quite often come across various types of frequency in reading about mobile phone behavior, a few brief notes on this topic follow here: (1) In science, frequency refers to the number of occurrences of a repeating event in a unit of time. The common unit is hertz, meaning the number of cycles per second. For instance, the frequency of the alternating current in household electrical outlets is 50 to 60 hertz. In other words, the alternating current repeats its cycle 50 to 60 times per second. (2) Different sounds have different frequencies. People perceive frequency of sound waves as pitch (e.g., low or high pitch). When cows make a deep sound of mooing, the frequency of the sound ranges between 150 and 180 hertz. Coincidently, the frequency of vibration alerts used in mobile phones is also in that range (e.g., the default vibration frequency of an iPhone is around 180 hertz). The similar frequency between the mooing of cows and the vibration of phones is just one reason why our brains could trick us into thinking our phone is vibrating when it is not. (3) Mobile phones receive signals from and send signals to mobile phone networks. These signals involve a certain form of electromagnetic radiation waves. Typically, most cellular networks worldwide use portions of the frequency in the electromagnetic spectrum, so-called radio frequency, between 450 and 1,800 megahertz for the transmission and reception of signals. This is why many

---

[6] See www.npr.org/sections/alltechconsidered/2013/09/30/226820044/phantom-phone-vibrations-so-common-they-ve-changed-our-brains.

people now worry about the negative impacts of the electromagnetic radiation emission from mobile phones on users' health, a topic that we will discuss in detail in the chapter on mobile phone behavior in medicine.

From these two cases, we can learn two relevant psychological phenomena. The Obama case is related to nomophobia and the Kusler case is related to phantom vibration syndrome. More importantly, besides both nomophobia and phantom vibration syndrome, these two cases suggest another important dimension of mobile phone effects, the psychological or behavioral effects. In other words, mobile phone use might impact various aspects of users' behavior, including cognition skills (e.g., memory), social interactions (e.g., friendship), emotional status (e.g., addiction), and moral behavior (e.g., bullying). These effects can be negative or positive, intended or unintended, severe or mild, and short-term or long-term.

2.4   Social Effects: Sit-Down Protest and Ebola Outbreak

In June 2016,[7] a group of democratic congress representatives participated in a sit-down protest in the House of Representatives, seeking a vote on gun control measures after the 2016 Orlando nightclub shooting. A series of unexpected events then occurred. First, the group wanted their protest to be known to the nation. The first media responder would normally be C-SPAN, but this was impossible because the C-SPAN cameras in the galleries above the House floor are actually controlled by Republicans in the House. Second, Republican House Speaker Paul Ryan declared the House in recess. As a result, all of the cameras went black and could not capture the drama playing out. Third, the protesting House Democrats decided to use their own smartphones to document their protest. Suddenly, instant video feeds afforded by Periscope and Facebook Live started to show the protest. Note that Periscope is a company solely hosting live videos posted by anyone and viewed by anyone so that we can see a collection of live broadcasts from around the world with no account sign-up needed. Fourth, C-SPAN ended up showing video made by these House members on their smartphones – so did the major commercial cable news channels. In the end, this sit-down protest, led by the legendary civil rights leader and Representative John Lewis, had the live streams from the House floor and won great publicity online and on cable television.

---

[7] See www.npr.org/sections/alltechconsidered/2016/06/23/483205687/house-democrats-deliver-sit-in-via-digital-platforms.

In December 2013, the first case of Ebola occurred in a forested area of Guinea. As of January 26, 2016, 28,637 cases and 11,315 deaths have been reported worldwide, with the vast majority of them being in Guinea, Liberia, and Sierra Leone. This is the largest outbreak of Ebola in history that West Africa has ever experienced. At the height of the Ebola crisis, the Sierra Leone Government turned to mobile wallets, a way to pay with a mobile phone that stores credit card or debit card information in it, to make fast, accurate, and secure payments to emergency workers. Before digitization, cash payments were slow and inaccurate. The mobile wallet accomplished multiple achievements: (1) Mobile payments to emergency workers dramatically shortened payment times, from over one month to around one week, putting an end to many payment-related strikes by emergency workers and thereby allowing for more people to be treated by emergency workers. (2) Mobile payments stopped double payments and streamlined payments, saving the country more than $10 million. (3) Mobile payments transfer the money directly to the bank account of emergency workers, reducing fraud, removing the costs of physical cash transportation and security, and cutting travel costs for response workers. This Sierra Leone experience shows that governments in developing countries can use mobile payments to strengthen their capacity to contain the Ebola disease, treat those infected, and ultimately save lives.

These two cases present other aspects of mobile phone effects. First, these two cases concern *social* effects or political and economic effects, whereas the previous cases concerned physical and mental health effects (e.g., mobile phone allergy, bacterial contamination, phantom vibration syndrome, or nomophobia). Second, these two cases concern *macro-level* mobile phone effects rather than micro-level effects. The cases discussed earlier are primarily related to micro-level individual activities (e.g., Jennifer Lawrence's privacy, Jenny Fry's allergy to mobile phone WiFi signals, Valerie Kusler's experience with phantom vibration syndrome, Obama's attachment to his BlackBerry as a sign of nomophobia). In contrast, the sit-down protest and Ebola cases are mainly related to macro-level state affairs: the mobile phone users are congressmen and governmental leaders, and their activities impact on society.

Let us briefly summarize this section. The eight cases presented here expand our knowledge about mobile phone effects in the real world. Mobile phone effects have both positive and negative *directions*. Furthermore, mobile phone effects have different *dimensions*, such as health, psychological, behavioral, and social effects. Often, mobile phone effects can occur at a micro-level affecting only one individual or at a macro-level affecting the larger society. However, these cases are merely media head-lines and anecdotal news. Do we trust them? Are they true? Have research-ers found solid evidence to support these cases? To answer these questions, we should examine some research articles to find out exactly what research-ers have found and what scientific knowledge tells us about mobile phone effects.

3. Empirical Studies: From Mobile Phone Allergy to Crime Rate Drop

3.1 Health Effect: Sources of Metallic Allergy from Mobile Phones

In the previous section, we discussed the Jenny Fry case. While various other complex factors were related to Fry's death (e.g., her depression and her school environment), allergy to WiFi signals was certainly a potential major factor. We might then have one question: Is there any scientific evidence of allergy to mobile phones or mobile phone networks? Let us now examine one journal article that provides empirical evidence of the possible allergic effects of mobile phones, entitled "Mobile phones: Poten-tial sources of nickel and cobalt exposure for metal allergic patients."[8] It was written by a group of American medical doctors, Marcella Aquino, Tania Mucci, Melanie Chong, Mark Davis Lorton, and Luz Fonacier. It was published in 2013 in *Pediatric Allergy, Immunology, and Pulmonology*, an established research journal by Mary Ann Liebert since 1987.

In this study, metal allergic patients in a New York hospital who were over 18 years old and owned mobile phones were invited to the study. They were asked to contribute one or more of their phones to test whether they contained any nickel and cobalt, which have been known to cause skin inflammation (e.g., redness, swelling, itching, or blistering). Note that, by design, the researchers did not collect data of both these patients' clinical history and their mobile phone use history to directly determine the causal relation between mobile phone use and contact allergy. Popular brands of mobile phones (e.g., Apple, Samsung, and LG) were selected. A total of seventy-two mobile phones from seven different manufacturers were tested. The test program is common but has a very long name, called the Reveal and Conceal Nickel and Cobalt Spot Test Kits made by

[8] Aquino, M., Mucci, T., Chong, M. *et al.* (2013). "Mobile phones: Potential sources of nickel and cobalt exposure for metal allergic patients," *Pediatric Allergy, Immunology, and Pulmonology*, 26(4): 181–186.

SmartPractice. Five areas of these phones were tested, including the camera, keypad, metal logo, side panels, and speakers. Each area was swabbed first with the nickel cotton-tipped plastic applicator for 30 to 60 seconds. A known nickel-containing coin was used as a positive control, and a non-nickel-containing plastic case served as a negative control. The nickel spot test was followed by the cobalt spot test. It was found that twenty-four out of seventy-two mobile phones (33 percent) tested positive for nickel and ten out of seventy-two mobile phones (14 percent) tested positive for cobalt. The researchers concluded that patients with a known nickel or cobalt allergy may consider their mobile phones as a potential source of exposure and further studies are needed to determine the direct relationship between specific metal contents in mobile phones and specific metal allergy symptoms.

The story we discussed before about Jenny Fry was an everyday observation. In contrast, the research article we discuss here demonstrates how a carefully designed experimental study can generate scientific evidence about potential sources for allergy to mobile phones. Of course, an allergy to mobile phones such as iPhone or Blackberry due to users' contact with nickel and cobalt is different in many ways from an allergy to mobile phone networks such as cellular networks or WiFi networks due to electromagnetic radiofrequency radiation from mobile phone signals. While we have seen empirical evidence that certain mobile phones contain nickel and cobalt that might lead to certain allergies, the research evidence does exist[9] indicating that individuals like Jenny Fry might indeed be allergic to mobile phone network signals and we should work to prevent such a tragedy from happening to other users in the future.

3.2 Health Effect: Significant Bacterial Contamination in Patients' Mobile Phones

In the previous section, we also discussed the case where a professor showed his students how much bacteria their phones could be contaminated with. Is there any scientific evidence for this? Actually, there is extensive literature on contamination of mobile phones among medical

---

[9] Hedendahl, L., Carlberg, M., and Hardell, L. (2015). "Electromagnetic hypersensitivity – an increasing challenge to the medical profession," *Reviews on Environmental Health*, 30(4): 209–215; Carpenter, D. O. (2015). "The microwave syndrome or electro-hypersensitivity: Historical background," *Reviews on Environmental Health*, 30(4): 217–222; Hillert, L. and Kolmodin-Hedman, B. (1997). "Hypersensitivity to electricity: Sense or sensibility?" *Journal of Psychosomatic Research*, 42(5): 427–432; and De Graaff, M. B. and Bröer, C. (2012). "'We are the canary in a coal mine': Establishing a disease category and a new health risk," *Health, Risk & Society*, 14(2): 129–147.

workers, but the next article we will discuss is a unique one. The title is "The mobile phone technology and hospitalized patients: A cross-sectional surveillance study of bacterial colonization, and patient opinions and behaviours."[10] It examines how much bacteria are on mobile phones used by patients, as opposed to doctors as in many other research studies, in the hospital setting. Note that there are two public health terms in the title: (1) "colonization" means the development of a bacterial infection on an individual, as demonstrated by a positive culture;[11] and (2) "public health surveillance" is also known as epidemiological surveillance, clinical surveillance, or syndromic surveillance. It is, according to the World Health Organization (WHO), "the continuous, systematic collection, analysis and interpretation of health-related data needed for the planning, implementation, and evaluation of public health practice."[12]

The article was cited forty-nine times based on Google Scholar, one of the highest among the research articles on this topic. The authors are a group of researchers from two UK hospitals. It was published in 2011 in *Clinical Microbiology and Infection*, an established Wiley journal since 1995 (which has transferred to Elsevier as of January 2015) with a quite high impact factor of 5.197. A specialty journal like this one typically has an impact factor of lower than 3, whereas a general journal like *Science* or *The Lancet* usually has an impact factor of higher than 10. It was associated with the European Society of Clinical Microbiology and Infectious Diseases and has an open access version called *New Microbes and New Infections*.

In the study, 102 participating adults were patients from the surgical/urological departments of the Western General Hospital, in Edinburgh, in the United Kingdom. The study consisted of four steps. First, patients completed a survey of their demographics and opinions and utilization of mobile phones. Second, patients were asked to give their mobile phones to the investigators. The investigators used a moist germ-free swab/pad to sample the phones' keypad areas in a uniform fashion. Third, a separate sterile swab was used to sample patients' anterior nares (openings or passages leading out of the nose or nasal cavity) in a uniform fashion. Fourth, both the phone swabs and nasal swabs were inoculated and incubated in the medical lab. These swabs were examined daily and any microorganisms present were identified using standard laboratory procedures.

---

[10] Brady, R. R., Hunt, A. C., Visvanathan, A. *et al.* (2011). "Mobile phone technology and hospitalized patients: A cross-sectional surveillance study of bacterial colonization, and patient opinions and behaviours," *Clinical Microbiology and Infection*, 17(6): 830–835.

[11] See http://medical-dictionary.thefreedictionary.com/colonization.

[12] See https://en.wikipedia.org/wiki/Public_health_surveillance.

The findings are summarized as follows: (1) Ninety-eight patients (67.6 percent) owned one mobile phone, sixteen patients (11.0 percent) owned two mobile phones, and four patients (2.8 percent) owned three or more mobile phones. Most of the patients who owned a phone brought it into the hospital. (2) A majority of respondents (92.4 percent) supported the lifting of restrictions on inpatient use of mobile phones; 93.8 percent of respondents supported the use of mobile phones by medical staff. (3) Thirty-nine patients (38.2 percent) felt that the lifting of restrictions would make no difference and sixty-two (60.8 percent) said that it would negatively affect their inpatient experience. (4) Seventy-two patients (70.6 percent) charged their phone using their own charger plugged into the hospital ward/bedside power sockets/points. Twenty-seven (26.5 percent) stated that they or their relatives had charged their phone prior to admission, but three (3.0 percent) stated that they had borrowed a fellow patient's charger during this inpatient stay to charge their own phone. (5) Many used the phone daily, two to four times per day. About 5 percent regularly shared their own phones with another person outside of the hospital and nearly 50 percent were happy to share with other patients. (6) A total of 102 respondents (70.3 percent) were aware that phones could carry harmful bacteria. Fifty-two (50.9 percent) of those presenting phones stated that they had never cleaned their phone outside the hospital. (7) Seventeen phones (16.6 percent) demonstrated no microbial growth, sixty-six phones (64.7 percent) grew one bacterial species, twelve phones (11.8 percent) grew two species, and seven phones (6.9 percent) grew three or more species. (8) The most common group of isolated bacteria was coagulase-negative staphylococci, a bacterium that typically occurs in clusters resembling grapes, normally inhabits the skin and mucous membranes, and may cause disease. These bacteria commonly infect the skin, eyes, and urinary tract, and some produce toxins responsible for septicemia and food poisoning. (9) Coagulase-negative staphylococci were found on seventy-eight mobile phones (76.5 percent) and twelve mobile phones (11.8 percent) demonstrated growth of other pathogenic bacterial species (i.e., bacteria likely to cause infection in a variety of situations, such as skin wounds and urinary catheters).

What can we learn from this study? First, this is one of the few studies focusing on inpatients rather than medical workers. It has a strong design and follows standard clinical procedures to collect and examine the samples. Second, the bacterial contamination rate is over 87 percent, meaning a majority of phones used by inpatients had bacteria on them, compared to only 5 to 21 percent of the clinic workers' phones. Third, the

United Kingdom lifted the restriction of using mobile phones in hospitals, but a few risky attitudes and behaviors remain, such as sharing phones in and outside of hospitals, sharing chargers, and hand–phone co-contamination. Lastly, we can see one type of effect-focused mobile phone behavior: 120 British inpatients (the users) brought in their own mobile phones (the technology) and frequently used them during their stay in hospital (the activity), resulting in bacterial contamination from and to their mobile phones (the effect).

3.3   Psychological Effect: Phantom Vibration Syndrome among Medical Workers

The article we will discuss next is entitled "Phantom vibration syndrome among medical staff: A cross sectional survey."[13] It was written by a group of American medical researchers: Michael Rothberg, Ashish Arora, Jodie Hermann, Reva Kleppel, Peter St. Marie, and Paul Visintainer. It was published in 2010 in the *British Medical Journal*, one of the best medical research journals.

This study had two goals: establishing the prevalence of phantom vibrations among medical staff and identifying potential risk factors associated with experiencing phantom vibrations. A total of 176 medical staff completed an online questionnaire via SurveyMonkey (76 percent of the 232 people invited) in 2010, including internal medicine physicians, medical students, nurses, nurse practitioners, translators, and medical assistants who were in the hospital paging system. Measurements were self-developed, consisting of seventeen questions about demographics, device use, phantom vibrations experienced, and attempts to stop them. The dependent variable was whether the respondent had experienced phantom vibrations and independent variables were age, sex, occupation, the type of device used, whether the device was used in vibration mode, where it was worn, and how frequently it rang.

Major findings include the following: (1) A total of 68 percent of respondents reported having experienced phantom vibrations. (2) Phantom vibrations were equally common with pagers and mobile phones (68 vs. 69 percent). (3) Most respondents (61 percent) began experiencing phantom vibrations after carrying the device for between one month and one year. (4) Most respondents (87 percent) experienced the phantom

---

[13] Rothberg, M. B., Arora, A., Hermann, J. *et al.* (2010). "Phantom vibration syndrome among medical staff: A cross sectional survey," *British Medical Journal*, 341: c6914.

vibrations either weekly or monthly, but 13 percent experienced them on a daily basis. (3) Five factors were associated with experiencing phantom vibrations: age, occupation, device location, hours worn per day, and how often the device was used in vibrate mode. (4) Most respondents (93 percent) who experienced phantom vibrations found the sensation to be not at all or only a little bothersome. However, only 7 percent of respondents found the sensation to be bothersome or very bothersome.

What does this study tell us? First, this lends empirical support to Valerie Kusler's case where she experienced phantom vibration syndrome. Second, we can develop a general picture: among medical staff members who carry devices in their daily work, there is self-reported evidence of the relevance of the mobile phone effect of experiencing phantom vibrations. A total of 68 percent of the medical workers reported having experienced phantom vibrations, and most respondents (97 out of 111, or 87 percent) experienced the phantom vibrations either weekly or monthly, but fourteen respondents (13 percent) experienced them on a daily basis. Phantom vibration syndrome is a real phenomenon and frequently experienced among medical staff workers. Third, we now know multiple specific details about mobile devices and phantom vibrations, including the fact that there were no differences in using pagers vs. mobile phones; no major differences in vibration experience depending on how long people used their phones; only occupation (or age), device location, and how often the device was in vibrate mode remained significantly associated with phantom vibrations; most people do not feel bothered by the phantom vibrations; and many can find ways to stop them. In summary, this study illustrates another interesting type of effect-focused mobile phone behavior: 176 medical workers as mobile users (the users) frequently use their phones in vibrate mode (the technology) in their daily work at the medical center (the activities), resulting in the frequent experience of phantom vibration syndrome (the effect), but the majority of them do not feel bothered by said syndrome.

3.4   Social Effect: Crime Rate Drop in the 1990s

The next study is a popular law article.[14] Its title is "Mobile Phones and Crime Deterrence: An Underappreciated Link," and it is one of the first

[14] Klick, J., MacDonald, J., and Stratmann, T. (2012). "Mobile phones and crime deterrence: An underappreciated link," in Alon Harel and Keith N. Hylton (eds.), *Research Handbook on the Economics of Criminal Law*. Cheltenham, UK and Northampton, MA: Edward Elgar, pp. 12–33.

articles examining the relationship between the growth of mobile phone use and the decrease of crime rate in the United States. It was cited fifteen times on Google Scholar. The three authors are American law school professors, Klick, MacDonald, and Stratmann. It was published as a chapter in the *Research Handbook on the Economics of Criminal Law*.

This study is essentially a secondary data analysis. Using the existing data rather than collecting new data, the authors attempted to explain the fall in crime rates in the 1990s in the United States, a particularly popular modern criminal phenomenon. The study is based on two theories: (1) the Becker framework, predicting that an individual will commit a crime if the expected benefits of the crime exceed the costs; and (2) the routine activities theory, predicting that crime will increase if suitable targets of crime, potential offenders, and the lack of capable guardians increase. The mobile phone data are from the Federal Communications Commission, the Bureau of Justice Statistics, and the Bureau of Economic Analysis. The crime rate data are from the FBI's Uniform Crime Report between 1999 and 2007. The independent variables were (1) the number of mobile phone subscriptions (indicating how many people subscribe to mobile network services) and (2) the mobile phone penetration rate in the state population (indicating how many people own mobile phones). The dependent variables were violent crime rate, rape rate, assault rate, and property crime rate. The control variables were gross domestic product (GDP), per capita spending on police, and per capita spending on corrections. The regression analysis indicated that mobile phone subscription and mobile phone penetration rate were significantly but negatively related to violent crime rate, rape rate, assault rate, and property crime rate. The results were confirmed by robust tests after controlling for GDP, per capita spending on police, per capita spending on corrections, and other potential biases.

What can we learn from this study? (1) Although the study was not able to determine any causal effects, mobile phones might play a positive and important role in decreasing the crime rate. For example, mobile phones can be used to report to police immediately, mobile phone cameras can record and help identify criminals, bystanders can use mobile phones to report their observations to police, and criminals' phones can be used to collect criminal evidence. (2) The study illustrates another type of effect-based mobile phone behavior: victims use mobile phones during a crime and are better able to protect themselves and report to police and record evidence. This is then associated with the decline of crime rates in property crime, rape, assault, and violent crime.

4. **Knowledge Syntheses: From Mobile Phone Allergy to Child Maltreatment Prevention**

So far, we have discussed several everyday life scenarios and a few empirical examples. We now move on to talk about the review of the literature. Our goal here is to see what knowledge has been synthesized on mobile phone effects and to broaden our understanding of the complexity of mobile phone behavior from the perspective of mobile phone effects.

Compared to mobile users, mobile technologies, and mobile activities, mobile effects have been studied most extensively. Understandably, it is what the general public and scientific researchers care about most and thus the existing literature in this area is the largest. Two topics in particular stand out, compared to various positive and negative mobile effects with different dimensions (e.g., physical and cognitive ones) in different domains (e.g., medicine and education) at either macro- or micro-levels. The first is the links between mobile phone use and *brain cancers*. This has produced the largest amount of research literature and drawn the widest media attention. The second largest literature topic concerns *distracted driving* while using mobile phones. These two effects will be discussed in the two upcoming chapters on mobile phone behavior in medicine and on mobile phone behavior in daily life. This arrangement will allow this section of knowledge synthesis to cover other topics and avoid too much overlapping among different chapters.

4.1   Various Mobile Phone Effects

To access the synthesized literature on mobile phone effects efficiently, we might start with the *Encyclopedia of Mobile Phone Behavior*. The *Encyclopedia* has extensive coverage of mobile phone effects (see Table 5.1). First, some interesting chapters focus on negative effects, such as mobile phone addiction and mobile phone bullying, while other chapters focus on positive effects, such as effects on mobile presidential elections, psychosocial intervention effects, effects of supporting people with autism spectrum disorders, and effects of preventing child maltreatment. Second, besides the directions of mobile phone effects, these chapters also present four major types of mobile effects, behavioral (e.g., effects of calling while driving on car crash risk), health (e.g., effects of long-term mobile phone use on the brain in terms of cancer), psychological (effects of science learning games on cognition), and social (effects of mobile phone use on culture).

Table 5.1 *The* Encyclopedia *Chapters on Effect-Based Mobile Phone Behavior*

Direction	Dimension	Chapter Title
Negative	Behavioral	Cell phone conversation and relative crash risk
Negative	Behavioral	Cell-phones, distracted driving, bans and fatalities
Negative	Behavioral	Cellular phones' contribution to dangerous driving
Negative	Behavioral	Road safety and mobile phone behaviors
Negative	Behavioral	The role of mobile phones in real world motor vehicle crashes
Negative	Behavioral	Children, risks and the mobile internet
Negative	Behavioral	Mobile phone-related behaviors and problems in Japan
Negative	Behavioral	Students hurting students: Cyberbullying as a mobile phone behavior
Positive	Behavioral	Mobile phone: Repurposed assistive technology for individuals with disabilities
Positive	Behavioral	Use of mobile phones to help prevent child maltreatment
Negative	Medicine	Long term mobile phone use leads to brain tumors
Negative	Medicine	Mobile phone addiction
Negative	Medicine	Mobile phones-like electromagnetic fields effects on human psychomotor performance
Negative	Medicine	Internet and mobile phone addiction
Positive	Medicine	mHealth in maternal, newborn, and child health programs around the world
Positive	Medicine	Mobile health in emergency care
Positive	Medicine	Mobile phones for plastic surgery and burns: Current practice
Positive	Medicine	Mobile phones in haematology
Positive	Psychological	Science learning games for mobile platforms
Positive	Psychological	Digital mobile games in education
Positive	Psychological	Mobile phone behavior in the college classroom: Effects on student learning and implications for students and teachers
Positive	Psychological	Mobile tracking for mental health and wellbeing
Positive	Psychological	Positive technology: Using mobile phones for psychosocial interventions
Positive	Psychological	The impact of mobile phones on teenagers' socialization and emancipation
Positive	Social	Mobile phone use enhances social connectedness
Positive	Social	Using mobile phones to control social interactions
Positive	Social	Mobile phone culture: The impacts of mobile phone use
Positive	Social	Mundane mobile maintenance, entrapment, and hyper-coordination
Positive	Social	Portable social groups
Positive	Social	Social impacts of mobile phones on the life of the Chinese people
Positive	Social	The mobile presidential election

For example, a particularly readable and informative chapter is "Use of mobile phones to help prevent child maltreatment," by four researchers from Georgia State University – Katelyn Guastaferro, Matthew Jackson, Shannon Self-Brown, and John Lutzker – and Julie Jabaley from Craddock Center of Georgia.[15] The authors specified several pioneers and leaders such as Kathy Bigelow and Judith Carta at the University of Kansas, Jenn LeFever at the University of Notre Dame, and Julie Gazmararian at Emory University. In particular, four mobile-phone-based prevention programs were highlighted, including parent–child activities interview via mobile phones, parent–child interactions via texting, national intervention for pregnant and postpartum women via Text4baby, and home safety via iPhones. They summarize major positive effects of these programs for child maltreatment prevention and intervention as well as various advantages (e.g., less expensive than the landline phones for poor parents and less prohibitive for parents to spend time with their children during the study).

We will not discuss these chapters in detail. Instead, we will spend more time discussing three review articles on mobile phone allergy, mobile phone bacterial contamination, and phantom vibration syndrome in the following sections.

4.2   Consistent Mobile Phone Dermatitis

The first review we will discuss is "Mobile phone dermatitis in children and adults: A review of the literature."[16] This is a well-written, concise, and effective summary of mobile phone dermatitis, i.e., skin inflammation due to mobile phone use. The authors are Clare Richardson, Carsten Hamann, Dathan Hamann, and Jacob Thyssen, a group of medical researchers from the United States and Demark. It was published in 2014 in *Pediatric Allergy, Immunology, and Pulmonology*, a well-established journal published by Mary Ann Liebert since 1987, known for publishing journals in biomedical research, and expanding its journal publications to other areas (e.g., *Cyberpsychology, Behavior and Social Networking* and *Games for Health Journal*).

---

[15] Guastaferro, K. M., Jackson, M. C., Self-Brown, S. *et al.* (2015). "Use of mobile phones to help prevent child maltreatment," in Z. Yan (ed.), *Encyclopedia of Mobile Phone Behavior*. Hershey, PA: Information Science Reference, pp. 906–922.

[16] Richardson, C., Hamann, C. R., Hamann, D., and Thyssen, J. P. (2014). "Mobile phone dermatitis in children and adults: A review of the literature," *Pediatric Allergy, Immunology, and Pulmonology*, 27(2): 60–69.

There are a few important points we can learn from this review. (1) Allergic contact dermatitis is a form of skin inflammation due to an allergic response caused by contact with a substance. In general, it is relatively common in women and children. One of the reasons is that nickel, the most common metal cause of allergic contact dermatitis, is released from jewelry, belt buckles, buttons, glasses, coins, keys, and recently mobile phones, laptops, video game controllers, and technology accessories. Women and children are often exposed to these items. (2) The first two cases of mobile phone dermatitis were reported in Italy in 2000. (3) The researchers found that there have been thirty-seven case reports and only six research studies specifically related to mobile phone dermatitis between 2000 and 2013. Thus, this area of research is still limited. (4) The majority of the literature is concerned with a nickel allergy, but a few have also investigated cobalt and chromium allergies. (5) The allergic skin areas of interest include the face, cheek, chin, hands, forearms, abdomen, wrists, thighs, chest, and breasts. The parts of phones usually tested include the phone's front and back frames, headset, screen, menu button, power button, metal bar, side and front buttons, keypad, ear speaker, and cover. (6) Similar prevalence of mobile phone dermatitis exists between adults and children, and between those who have expensive phones vs. those who have cheaper ones. Those who have unusual habits (e.g., tucking the phone into a bra), use the phone frequently for occupational use, or have a new phone are more susceptible to mobile phone dermatitis. (8) This is a growing area of research, with reported publications increasing from two cases in 2000, to twenty-seven cases by 2010, and thirty-seven cases by 2012.

We can learn a few important points from this review regarding mobile phone allergy. First, this review offers a comprehensive picture of mobile phone dermatitis or mobile phone allergy and provides much broader coverage than the Jenny Fry case and the empirical study by Brady and his collaborators in 2011 discussed in the previous two sections. If Jenny Fry knew and went to see a specialist of allergology or dermatology, she might have been able to receive a timely and appropriate diagnosis and treatment to avoid tragedy. Second, with the rapid growth of new mobile phone production and the rapid increase of diverse mobile phone users, existing symptoms might become more complicated and new symptoms might appear. Thus, further research is needed to better understand the complexity of mobile phone dermatitis or mobile phone allergy, especially the mechanism between mobile phone use and contact dermatitis. As a result, research-based education, prevention, and intervention programs and regulations can be developed.

4.3 Risky Bacterial Infections within Hospitals

The review we will discuss next is entitled "Are healthcare workers' mobile phones a potential source of nosocomial infections? Review of the literature."[17] Nosocomial infections normally refer to infections that originate in a hospital rather than from the outside. This review synthesizes the literature on how bacterial contamination on mobile phones of medical staff members in hospitals might result in the spread of infection within a hospital. It was written by a group of Turkish medical scholars, Fatma Ulger, Ahmet Dilek, Saban Esen, Mustafa Sunbul, and Hakan Leblebicioglu. It was published in 2015 in *Journal of Infection in Developing Countries*, a new peer-reviewed journal established in 2007 with an impact factor of 1.3. Its Editor in Chief is Dr. Salvatore Rubino from the Università degli Studi di Sassari, Italy, a medical expert on Pathogens and publisher of over 130 articles. There is another widely cited review[18] on this topic published in 2009 in a journal with a higher impact factor. However, the 2015 article is preferable for our purposes, mainly because it reviews thirty-nine studies published between 2005 and 2013, whereas the 2009 review only includes ten articles published before 2009.

From this review, we can learn several important points. (1) The first publication was in 2005. As of 2003, thirty-nine studies have been published, which forms a good empirical base to understand bacterial contamination of mobile phones. (2) Many studies focused on health-care workers given the unique importance and popularity of this group of mobile phone users. (3) Mobile phone use in the medical setting leads to other potential risks, including noise, distraction, data safety, and patients' privacy, in addition to the possibility of transferring microorganisms for potential infections within the medical environment among clinicians, patients, devices, and general surfaces. (4) The review mainly used two methods to identify articles: database search and reference list checking. The thirty-nine studies included letters to the editor (i.e., brief reports), cohort studies, and cross-sectional studies. (5) The key finding is that the prevalence of infection ranged from 10 to 100 percent on all phones tested, with the most common isolated microorganisms being staphylococcus aureus (nearly 23 percent of all cases of

---

[17] Ulger, F., Dilek, A., Esen, S. *et al.* (2015). "Are healthcare workers' mobile phones a potential source of nosocomial infections? Review of the literature," *Journal of Infection in Developing Countries*, 9(10): 1046–1053.

[18] Brady, R. R. W., Verran, J., Damani, N. N., and Gibb, A. P. (2009). "Review of mobile communication devices as potential reservoirs of nosocomial pathogens," *Journal of Hospital Infection*, 71(4): 295–300.

infection). (6) Mobile phones are considered to be an ideal breeding site for bacteria because: (a) they provide ideal humidity and temperature for bacteria to thrive; (b) fingers and finger tips are used for touch screens and become good means to transfer pathogens, i.e., any disease-producing agent, especially a virus, bacterium, or other microorganism; and (c) health-care workers can bring them daily between home, work, and other public or private locations. (7) Potential technological solutions for the contamination and infection include hands-free earphones, antibacterial surface covers, washable phones, and disposable phone covers.

In the previous sections, we discussed Dr. Park's biology experiment of growing bacteria and the empirical study of identifying bacterial contamin-ation of patients' mobile phones. This review offers a synthesized scientific knowledge about bacterial infection within hospitals due to mobile phone use by medical workers. We now can have a current and broad picture of medical research in this area. Specifically, we can see two important points from the perspective of mobile phone behavior. First, as a special group of mobile phone users, medical workers in hospitals not only routinely use mobile phones in their professional work, but also often spread virus and bacteria through their contaminated mobile phones. In other words, they have a much higher risk of causing bacterial infection than Dr. Park's students or allergic patients treated in hospitals. Second, although the current prevalence of infection varies largely (10 to 100 percent), it is clear that mobile phones are an ideal breeding site for bacterial growth, and medical workers' mobile phones are a critical source of bacterial infection. Thus, from the perspective of mobile phone effects, mobile phones not only concern bacterial contamination in daily settings, but most importantly concern bacterial infection in hospital settings.

4.4   Debatable Phantom Vibration Syndrome

We now will discuss another short review, "Phantom vibration and phantom ringing among mobile phone users: A systematic review of literature."[19] It was written by Amrita Deb, an Indian scholar who is an Assistant Professor in Clinical Psychology at the Indian Institute of Tech-nology Hyderabad and has published articles on resilience. It was pub-lished in 2014 in Wiley's *Asia-Pacific Psychiatry*.

This is a clear, accessible, and thoughtful review. It offers several important insights into phantom vibration syndrome. (1) It lists several similar terms,

---

[19] Deb, A. (2015). "Phantom vibration and phantom ringing among mobile phone users: A systematic review of literature," *Asia-Pacific Psychiatry*, 7(3): 231–239.

ringxiety, phantom vibration, phantom ring, technopathology, and tinnitus. It reviews both phantom vibration and phantom ringing rather than just phantom vibration, a perception of feeling or hearing a mobile phone vibrating or ringing when it is not. (2) It identifies the earliest study by Laramie in his 2007 doctoral dissertation. (3) It used multiple methods to search the literature, including database searches, reference checking, grey literature search, and author consulting. From this, the author found twenty-nine articles, fifteen of which are newsletters, reports, or online magazine articles, four of which are review articles, and ten of which original research articles. Clearly, as the authors have indicated, this topic has been popular in the media; however, the research in this area is still at an early stage. (4) The majority of studies reviewed used university students as subjects and relied on self-reported questionnaires. (5) The prevalence rates of phantom vibration and phantom ringing range between 27 and 89 percent. (6) Factors related to phantom vibration and phantom ringing include hours spent calling or texting, ringtone or vibration type, device location, occupation, hours carried, frequency of using vibration mode, personality, stress, and depression. (7) Most people reported that it was not bothersome or only a little bothersome. (8) Causes include: (a) misinterpretation of incoming sensory signals by the brain; (b) high expectations during a special period of time in vigilance; (c) being on high alert, like a mother on alert for a crying baby; (d) desire for constant social contact, or anxiety in anticipation of an incoming message; and (e) phone dependence, addiction, or problematic use.

Although various cases like the one of Valerie Kusler have been observed in everyday lives and various studies like the one about phantom vibration syndrome among medical workers have been published, overall, in contrast to the broad media exposure, this review shows that it is still premature to identify phantom vibration syndrome as a widely accepted clinical condition with a strong scientific research support due to two major reasons. First, the empirical research on this topic is still limited as indicated by the review of only ten original research articles. Second, the quality of the research is also limited due to the currently wide use of non-experimental designs, self-report data collection, weak measurement development, and subjective speculations.

5. Comparative Analyses: From Device Allergy to Device Bacterial Contamination

After discussing the various mobile phone effects, we might ask a broader question: Are there any similarities and differences in the effects of different technologies such as television, computers, the Internet, and mobile phones on human beings? In other words, what kinds of effects are shared by various computation, information, and communication technologies? What kinds of effects are unique to mobile phones? This is a good but difficult question about media effects. Media effects can be considered to be the most discussed topic in technological behavior literature. There are television effects, computer effects, Internet effects, and now mobile phone effects. A general or philosophical discussion might only lead to an oversimplified answer. One of the workable ways is to discuss a specific example. Instead of comparing similar or different effects of different technologies, we will discuss two interesting articles that reveal shared or unique effects of different technologies.

5.1   Device Contact Dermatitis

The first comparative work is a literature review entitled "Modern electronic devices: An increasingly common cause of skin disorders in consumers."[20] It was written by a group of Italian medical doctors, Monica Corazza, Sara Minghetti, Alberto Maria Bertoldi, Emanuela Martina, Annarosa Virgili, and Alessandro Borghi. The article was published in 2016 in *Dermatitis*.

In this review, the authors used multiple strategies to search the existing medical literature on various skin disorders related to three modern technologies – game consoles, PCs, and mobile phones. The major findings specifically related to contact dermatitis or skin inflammation include the following: (1) There are only a few clinical reports on contact dermatitis of game devices; however, the literature on contact dermatitis of personal computers is very extensive. For contact dermatitis of mobile phones, clinical reports have been rapidly increasing over the last fifteen years. (2) Not only major devices per se (e.g., game controllers or handsets) but also various accessories are the source of contact dermatitis (e.g., chargers, batteries, mice, mouse pads, keyboard, keyboard wrist rests, phone covers, and headphones). Metallic elements (especially nickel) that are released from these devices are the most common cause of allergic contact dermatitis. (3) There are various kinds of symptoms related to allergic contact dermatitis. For game consoles, the allergic locations are only on fingers and palms. For personal computers, laptops, or tablets, the allergic areas are mainly on fingers, palms, wrists, and forearms. But for mobile phones, the

---

[20] Corazza, M., Minghetti, S., Bertoldi, A. M. *et al.* (2016). "Modern electronic devices: An increasingly common cause of skin disorders in consumers," *Dermatitis*, 27(3): 82–89.

allergic locations are widely spread, from hands, forearms, breasts, lower abdomen, faces, and ears.

For mobile phone allergy or dermatitis, we have already discussed an everyday observation of Jenny Fry, an empirical study of a new source of metallic allergy to mobile phones, and a review of consistent mobile phone dermatitis. From this comparative review, we can see the following: (1) Allergies to electronic devices is not very new or very rare. Contact dermatitis has been reported in various modern technologies, including video game devices, PCs, tablets, and now mobile phones. (2) Comparing with different devices, contact dermatitis to mobile phones is unique due to the rapid increase of the clinical reports and a wide variety of the allergic areas in a human body.

5.2   Device Bacterial Contamination

The second comparative study is entitled "Bacterial contamination of anaesthetists' hands by personal mobile phone and fixed phone use in the operating theatre."[21] It was cited 105 times according to Google Scholar. The authors are five Austrian scholars, Jeske, Tiefenthaler, Hohlrieder, Hinterberger, and Benzer. It was published in 2007 in *Anaesthesia*.

In this study, a within-subjects experimental design was used to examine whether mobile phones carry more bacteria than traditional fixed phones. The researchers recruited forty anesthetists to participate in the study. Note that while anesthetists and anesthesiologists are both involved in putting patients under anesthesia for various surgeries, an *anesthetist* is a specialized nurse and an *anesthesiologist* is a specialized medical doctor. First, these anesthetists were asked to use an alcohol-based hand rub to disinfect their hands. Cultures were then obtained from the fingers of both cleaned hands. Second, the anesthetists used their hands to make an approximately 1-minute-long phone call on their personal mobile phone. Cultures were taken again from their hands after making the phone call. Third, specimens were also collected from the keypad of the mobile phone. Fourth, after 48 hours, isolated microorganisms were identified using multiple laboratory procedures. Likewise, the same experiment was performed later using fixed wall phones in the anteroom of the operation room. The major results include the following: (1) Following the use of a

[21] Jeske, H. C., Tiefenthaler, W., Hohlrieder, M. *et al.* (2007). "Bacterial contamination of anaesthetists' hands by personal mobile phone and fixed phone use in the operating theatre," *Anaesthesia*, 62(9): 904–906.

mobile phone or a fixed wall phone, the rate of bacterial contamination of the anesthetists' hands increased, with thirty-eight out of forty anesthetists' hands contaminated by mobile phones and thirty-three out of forty anesthetists' hands contaminated by wall phones. (2) The keypad surface of the mobile phones (thirty-six out of forty) and of the fixed phones (thirty-eight out of forty) after these phones were used contained non-human pathogens (e.g. a bacterium or a virus) that can cause diseases, as well as some human pathogens.

For mobile phone bacterial contamination, we have already discussed the case of Dr. Simon Park's experiment, an empirical study of bacterial contamination in patients' mobile phones, and a review of bacterial infection by medical staff's phones. What can we learn from this comparative study?

First, although it was one of the earliest studies of this kind, the researchers thoughtfully chose both fixed phones and mobile phones to compare bacterial contamination. As we can imagine, television is almost incomparable with mobile phones, except for maybe the television remote controller; computers are almost incomparable with mobile phones, except for computer keyboards/mice and tablet computers with touch screens; whereas the Internet is special because it can be accessed from computers, mobile phones, and newer models of televisions (e.g., Samsung's smart television). It is quite creative to compare fixed telephones and mobile phones, while there are still many differences (e.g., the mobile phones are personal and the fixed wall phones are public). In addition, the same group of anesthetists followed the procedure twice. Thus, various individual differences are controlled for and the results of the comparison are more convincing.

Second, it was found that, after only 1 minute of use, mobile phones and fixed phones are contaminated at similar rates rather than at significantly different rates for both hands and keypads. However, a subtle but key difference between mobile phones and fixed phones is that mobile phones are always with the anesthetists in and out of the operation room, and are directly close to patients and close to doctors' hands, faces, and ears, whereas fixed phones are outside of the operation room and in the anteroom only. Thus, in the real clinical setting, the mobile phones are much more risky for bacterial contamination and infection than the wall phones.

Third, the study was conducted in 2007. As of 2016, it has been cited 105 times, even though the authors considered it to be a pilot study. It has been inspiring dozens of new comparative studies examining different groups, different settings, or different hygiene strategies. These comparative studies have made the accurate assessment of unique effects of mobile phones such as bacterial contamination possible. For instance, the bacterial contamination rate for different technologies after being used could be similar, but the high level of both mobility and personalization makes mobile phones much more hazardous in clinical settings.

6. Complex Thinking: A Complex Double-Edged Sword

At the beginning of this chapter, we discussed Frances' intuitive thinking about mobile phone effects. Recall that Frances covered various effects with various specific examples and stressed the core feature of mobile phones – using them anytime and anywhere. Meanwhile, Frances focused only on the positive effects and talked mainly about her everyday experience in China. After reading the entire chapter, we can easily see that mobile phone effects are much more complex than Frances thought intuitively. Now let us use a concept map again (see Figure 5.1) to summarize the major contents of the chapter and compare it with Frances' intuitive knowledge.

First, as shown in Figure 5.1, different from Frances' intuitive knowledge focusing only on positive effects, mobile phone effects concern different *directions*. Like various technologies invented by human beings,

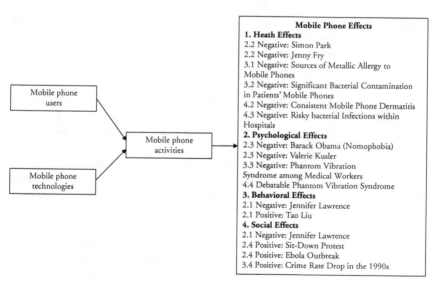

Figure 5.1   A Summary Diagram of Effect-Based Mobile Phone Behavior

a mobile phone itself as a technology does not have any positive or negative effects. However, mobile phone use or more broadly mobile phone behavior will lead to various mobile phone effects. These effects have both *negative* and *positive* sides in a wide spectrum. In other words, mobile phone behavior is a *double-edged* sword that could help us or hurt us, and thus lead to various positive and negative effects. This is the most critical point about mobile phone effects. The positive effects have been repeatedly demonstrated in the cases of Tao Liu getting her belongings back, the sit-down protest receiving live media coverage, and the use of mobile wallets to pay health-care workers in the battle against the Ebola breakout. Positive effects were also illustrated in the study of reporting the relationship between the large crime rate drop in the 1990s and the wide use of mobile phones in the United States. On the negative side, we have discussed the cases of Jennifer Lawrence's phone being hacked, Jenny Fry's suicide tragedy, Dr. Park's biological experiment, Valerie Kusler's phantom vibration syndrome experience, and the studies and reviews of contact dermatitis and bacterial contamination of mobile phone use.

Second, different from Frances' intuitive knowledge focusing only on her own everyday experience, mobile phone effects concern multiple *dimensions*, such as effects on people's physical and mental health, individuals' psychological processes, users' various behavior, and large-scale social practices. In other words, mobile phone behavior is not only a double-edged sword, but also a *complex* double-edged sword that could help us or hurt us in various ways directly and indirectly. In this chapter, we have discussed: (1) various health effects of mobile phone behaviors, including mobile phone dermatitis and allergy, and bacterial contamination and infection; (2) various psychological effects, including nomophobia and phantom vibration syndrome; (3) behavioral effects, such as the case of Jennifer Lawrence and Tao Liu; and (4) social effects, such as the case of the sit-down protest, the case of the Ebola outbreak, and the study of the large crime rate drop in the 1990s.

The future research of mobile phone effects should explore and examine multiple important topics. First, effects generally refer to causal effects based on well-controlled randomized experimental studies. However, many of the studies we have discussed in this chapter do not have a typical randomized experimental design, but rather follow a survey-based correlational study design. This type of design is useful to describe a behavior, but it is not sufficient to draw causality and determine effects. Therefore, future research needs better design as well as better measurement, data collection, and data analysis. Second, in addition to improving research quality, more research effects are needed to examine both the positive and negative effects so that our understanding of mobile phone effects will be balanced and complete. Third, future research should examine various dimensions of mobile phone effects, especially cognitive effects and moral effects rather than focusing on health effects. Fourth, research is urgently needed to study new issues, such as privacy, safety, and security of mobile phone use.

CHAPTER 6

Mobile Phone Behavior in Medicine

Outline

1. *Intuitive Thinking: From a Young Medical Doctor*
2. *Everyday Observations: From Dr. Christopher Spillers to Dr. John Tickell*
   2.1 *Users: Distracted Dr. Spillers*
   2.2 *Technologies: UNICEF Innovation Projects*
   2.3 *Activities: Monitoring Blood Sugar Levels*
   2.4 *Effects: Dr. John Tickell with Brain Tumors*
   2.5 *Effects: 176 Million Addicts*
3. *Empirical Studies: From HIV-Infected Pregnant Women to Links with Brain Cancers*
   3.1 *Users: HIV-Infected Pregnant Women*
   3.2 *Technologies: Mobile Phone Dispatch*
   3.3 *Activities: Smoking Cessation Intervention*
   3.4 *Medical Effects: Sleep Disturbance*
   3.5 *Medical Effects: Brain Cancers*
4. *Knowledge Syntheses: From Exponential Growth to Potential Brain Cancers*
   4.1 *Exponential Growth*
   4.2 *Dominant Themes*
   4.3 *Users: Older Adults' Health Care*
   4.4 *Effects: School Students' Sleep Disturbance*
   4.5 *Effects: Potential Brain Cancers*
5. *Comparative Analyses: From Television Addiction to Mobile Phone Addiction*
   5.1 *American Adults' Television Addiction*
   5.2 *British Adolescents' Computer Game Addiction*
   5.3 *British University Students' Internet Addiction*
   5.4 *American Undergraduates' Mobile Phone Addiction*
6. *Complex Thinking: The Best Diamond in the Crown*

1. Intuitive Thinking: From A Young Medical Doctor

Around Christmas of 2015, I heard from a good friend, who is a young medical doctor and highly proficient in using modern technologies, that he might visit Boston soon. We had an enjoyable and festive chat. Then I asked him: "What can people do with mobile phones in medicine or health care? Can you write down three to five words that quickly come to mind? I am writing a piece on mobile health and hope to hear a medical professional's initial responses."

He quickly emailed me back with the following five phrases: (1) real-time update; (2) remote control; (3) convenience; (4) database; (5) not high reliability. Upon my request, he further elaborated these five phrases as follows: (1) Mobile phones can update medical information such as people's heart rates and oxyhemoglobin saturation. (2) Doctors can control the data remotely from the mobile phone and monitor the health status of patients. (3) People can just stay at home and get help from doctors rather than go to a hospital. (4) Mobile phones can collect a patient's data over a long period for possible big data analytics. However, (5) the health data collected through the mobile phone is not so reliable compared to professional examination data from the hospital and can be used for references only.

These initial responses from a young medical doctor are informative for a few reasons. First, these responses are *specific*. He specified updating medical information, controlling the data remotely, monitoring the health status of patients, and performing possible big data analytics. As a medical professional rather than a technical professional, it is not easy to produce such technically specific responses. My friend is quite technically savvy. Second, these responses are *authentic*, a quite typical response from a doctor. From the perspective of a doctor, he considered using heart rates and oxyhemoglobin saturation, monitoring the health status of patients, patients being able to stay at home to get help from doctors, and he is concerned that the health data collected through mobile phones are not as reliable as professional examination data from the hospital. These responses represent what an active medical professional with good technical experiences would consider mobile phone use in medicine. Third, these responses are *incomplete* and *simple*. Based on the basic four-element model to analyze mobile phone behavior, he mentioned doctors and patients as the two types of mobile phone users and mainly focused on the process of collecting, updating, monitoring, and managing the medical data, but mentioned neither any specific technologies (he did mention databases as a phrase though) nor any specific effects of mobile phones.

In this chapter, using this intuitive knowledge as the starting point of learning, we will use the four-element framework to further discuss mobile phone behavior in medicine. We will briefly present multiple real-life observations, review multiple research examples in detail, offer an overview of the current knowledge in the area of mobile phone behavior in medicine, and compare different technologies in medicine. Our goals are to expand, extend, broaden, and deepen our intuitive knowledge about mobile phone behavior in medicine and develop a complex knowledge about mobile phone behavior in medicine and health care. Overall, we hope to develop a good picture of mobile phone behavior in medicine and health care and good analytic skills of studying mobile phone behavior in personal and professional settings.

2.   Everyday Observations: From Dr. Christopher Spillers to Dr. John Tickell

2.1   Users: Distracted Dr. Spillers

In April 2011, Dr. Christopher Spillers was an anesthesiologist during a routine heart surgery operation on Mary Roseann Milne, a 61-year-old woman in Dallas, Texas. Mary died after her surgery. Her family filed a medical malpractice suit, and one of the claims was *distracted doctoring* because Dr. Spillers was texting and reading an iPad during the operation and failed to notice Milne's dangerously low blood-oxygen levels for 15 or 20 minutes.[1] The case was set to go before a Dallas County jury in September. However, there is no information available about how the case ended. All we can find out on the Internet is that Dr. Christopher Spillers received his medical degree from the University of Texas Medical School, has been in practice as an anesthesiologist in Dallas for more than ten years, and currently is affiliated with multiple hospitals in the area, including Baylor Regional Medical Center and Baylor University Medical Center.

This case, as well as other similar cases, became headlines of multiple major newspapers and widely discussed in both the general public and the medical community. Of course, this type of case concerns various major issues, including medical ethics, medical malpractice, positive and negative

---

[1] See   www.dallasobserver.com/news/dallas-anesthesiologist-being-sued-over-deadly-surgery-admits-to-texting-reading-ipad-during-procedures-7134970.

effects of mobile phone use, and mobile phone use policy. Here, we can analyze this case from the perspective of mobile phone users in medicine.

First, by definition, this doctor is a mobile phone user in medicine, but clearly he is not a good mobile phone user. Doctors are a major group of mobile phone users in medicine, but their professional ethical levels of using mobile phones might vary widely. Many use mobile phones professionally, whereas some like Dr. Christopher Spillers use it unprofessionally.

Second, medical professionals carry their mobile phones all the time at work, as we can see in the hospitals and clinics, and they may be issued by their institutions or purchased by themselves. Their mobile phones may serve different professional and personal purposes.

Third, besides medical doctors, there are many other mobile phone users in medicine and health care, such as patients, families of patients, nurses, medical students, emergency bus drivers, and medical assistants. These diverse users will have different kinds of complex mobile phone behavior. In short, regardless of whether or how accurate this report was, this case deepens our knowledge in terms of mobile phone users in medicine. It is much more complex than we thought. This complexity was not mentioned in the intuitive response of my good friend.

On the basis of the four-element model, the mobile phone behavior related to Dr. Spillers can be illustrated in the following simple diagram, with the bold text highlighting the focus:

Dr. Christopher Spillers + iPhone/iPad → reading and texting during heart surgery operation on Mary Roseann Milne → Mary Roseann Milne passed away after surgery.

In the first major section of the book, we have discussed users, technologies, activities, and effects in four chapters. In the second major section of the book on mobile phone behavior in medicine, business, education, and daily life, we will apply the four-element model and use this simple diagram as often as possible to present and analyze mobile phone behavior.

2.2   *Technologies: UNICEF Innovation Projects*

Beginning in 2007,[2] UNICEF launched a program called UNICEF Innovation. With an interdisciplinary team of individuals around the world, the program has developed a series of innovative projects in integrating mobile technologies into health systems to improve the lives of children in

---

[2] See www.unicefstories.org/tech/mhealth/.

developing countries such as Senegal, Nepal, and Paraguay. In these developing countries, many remote villages in rural areas do not even have electricity, but people have started using mobile phones to solve problems of time, distance, and coordination in the delivery of health services.

For example, Patient Tracing and Results Delivery is one of such innovative projects in integrating mobile technologies into health systems to improve the lives of children in developing countries. It uses text messages rather than paper to deliver early infant HIV diagnosis results to rural and under-served communities in Zambia and Malawi and has improved the test result turn-around time by over 50 percent. Community health workers also use SMS to register births and trace patients to ensure that they receive key childhood interventions. Another example of such projects is Health Systems Management. It used a SMS-based disease surveillance and medicine tracking system called M-Trac. With this system, health-care workers can use mobile phones to monitor health service delivery performance and respond on a timely basis to health-care needs based on real-time data. The system also integrates an anonymous hotline and public dialog sessions to collect and show mobile-phone-based public opinions. UNICEF Uganda and the Ministry of Health are currently rolling this out nationwide.

From the perspective of mobile phone technologies, two merits of using mobile phones are worth noticing: (1) although these technologies, such as text messaging, are quite common, they are used *effectively* to address much needed real-life problems in developing countries; and (2) from the very beginning, the use of these technologies (e.g., M-Trac) started up with an aim to scale up results of various projects such as Patient Tracing and Results Delivery and Health Systems Management. This strategy makes the use of mobile phones more *efficient*. On the basis of the four-element model, the mobile phone behavior related to UNICEF Innovation can be illustrated in the following simple diagram, with the bold text highlighting the focus:

Health-care workers and patients in Zambia, Malawi, and Uganda + **text-based mobile technologies** → monitoring, managing, delivering community health-care systems → improved both effectiveness and efficiency of these health-care systems.

2.3   Activities: Monitoring Blood Sugar Levels

In November 2015, National Public Radio (NPR) reported that 16-year-old California teenager Blake Atkins was diagnosed with Type 1 diabetes.

His pediatric endocrinologist used Apple's app programming tool called *Healthkit* to monitor his blood sugar levels and share the information with his mother. He wears a continuous glucose monitor attached to his body and uses a tiny needle just under his skin to check his blood glucose levels every few minutes. The monitor has a Bluetooth connection and, with Blake's permission, the data travel to the *HealthKit* data repository on his mobile phone.

This is another interesting case. First, it concerns one mobile phone technology, *HealthKit* or *Health*. Technically, *HealthKit* is simply an app programming tool for software developers to develop apps that can interact with Apple's *Health*. Apple's *Health* is a general name of Apple's application within iOS 8 and iOS 9 that functions as a dashboard of all the fitness and health data of a specific iPhone user, such as the heart rate, calories burned, blood pressure, blood sugar, and cholesterol. Apple's *Health* has three major functions: (1) monitoring and analyzing health data for medical and general fitness purposes; (2) connecting various third-party wearable electronic hardware (e.g., Fitbit, Qardio, and iHealth) and software (e.g., Runmeter GPS, Sleep Cycle, and Nike+ Running); and (3) creating a Medical ID, an emergency card with important medical details and emergency details. From Apple's *Health* as an example, one may see that, after years of development, today's medical mobile technologies have become some of the most advanced and most exciting areas in mobile phone technologies.

Second, it deals with one disease, *Type 1 diabetes*. According to the American Diabetes Association,[3] Type 1 diabetes is a condition characterized by high blood glucose levels caused by a total lack of insulin. Our body needs energy. Energy comes from a process of breaking down the sugars and starches we eat into a simple sugar called glucose. This process needs insulin as a hormone to get glucose from the bloodstream into the cells of the body. Type 1 diabetes develops most often in children and young adults. With the help of insulin therapy and other treatments, even young children can learn to manage their condition and live long, healthy lives. In contrast, Type 2 diabetes is a condition characterized by high blood glucose levels caused by either a lack of insulin or the body's inability to use insulin efficiently. Type 2 diabetes develops most often in middle-aged and older adults. For both Type 1 and Type 2 diabetes, it is always vital for patients to monitor their blood glucose levels so they can

---

[3] See www.diabetes.org/diabetes-basics/type-1/.

manage their condition and live long, healthy lives. Mobile phones can be used as a good tool to monitor their levels.

Third, it is related to one specific medical procedure, *monitoring*, to keep track of blood sugar levels, as opposed to other medical procedures, like directly curing diabetes. There are various ways, such as monitoring, managing, counseling, therapizing, and treating, to tackle medical issues. Mobile phones are not prescription drugs or surgical procedures, but they have their own unique strengths and potential in medicine and health care.

Fourth, it involves *three parties* of the medical community – patients, doctors, and parents – rather than just doctors. Modern medical and health-care systems are complex. They involve a wide variety of members in the medical or health-care community, such as patients and their families, doctors, nurses, medical assistants, other medical team members, medical device producers, medical system managers, medical finance analysts, medical insurance companies, and medical attorneys. Many of them we know, and many others we might not know, but they might all use mobile phones.

On the basis of the four-element model, the mobile phone behavior related to Blake Atkins can be illustrated in the following simple diagram below, with the bold text highlighting the focus:

Blake Atkins, his pediatric endocrinologist, and his mother + Apple's *Health* → **monitoring and analyzing his blood sugar levels** → managed his Type 1 diabetes condition.

2.4   Effects: Dr. John Tickell with Brain Tumors

Dr. Tickell[4] is a well-known leading Australian doctor. He graduated from the University of Melbourne with a degree in Medicine and later became a general practitioner, obstetrician, and a specialist practitioner in sports medicine. He is a successful businessman and co-created the Heritage Golf and Residential Country Club in Victoria. He is an author and international public speaker. He has written several books, the most notable being *The Great Australian Diet* and *Laughter, Sex, Vegetables and Fish*. He has also appeared on television shows providing advice on how to turn stress into success and how to live a longer, healthier life.

In 2011, however, Dr. Tickell encountered an unexpected devastating challenge. He was on a flight from Sydney to Melbourne and suddenly had

---

[4] See www.dailymail.co.uk/news/article-3251669/Would-stick-head-microwave-Doctor-believes-mobile-gave-brain-cancer-says-use-patch-phone-reduce-radiation.html.

a seizure. A subsequent brain scan revealed five tumors in his head; one was the size of a golf ball. Dr. Tickell believes that radiation is a significant contributing factor to the increasing rate in brain tumors. He said: "There's a million more times radiation in the air today than there was fifty years ago – that is frightening." He is now becoming a leading advocate for the safer use of mobile phones, campaigning to make people aware of the risks of radiation, and promoting a new device that might reduce mobile phone radiation by up to 95 percent.

We can learn several good points about effect-based mobile phone behavior from this story. First, this case concerns Dr. Tickell. He is both a doctor, who should have more knowledge about cancers, and a cancer survivor, who has direct personal experiences. The then-65-year-old doctor said that he was certain his high mobile phone usage was a factor in his condition and he said he fears other people are unknowingly falling into the same trap. Although his personal testimony itself is not scientific research, it can carry more weight and draw more public attention than that from a non-medical person. Second, he specifies multiple reasons why mobile phone use leads to brain cancers. For example, he emphasized that on average we might spend 21 hours per week using mobile phones and we use mobile phones for an increasing number of different activities. Thus, we are exposed to lengthy and various electromagnetic radiations involved with mobile phones.

On the basis of the four-element model, the mobile phone behavior related to Dr. Tickell can be illustrated in the following simple diagram, with the bold text highlighting the focus:

Dr. John Tickell + radiation from mobile phones → being exposed to various lengthy radiation in his daily life → **experienced a seizure on a flight and had five tumors in his brain**.

2.5   *Effects: 176 Million Addicts*

On April 22, 2014,[5] Flurry, a mobile analytics company located in the San Francisco area of the United States, reported that, in 2014, the global mobile phone addiction population was 176 million. According to Flurry, addiction was defined as using apps at least sixty times per day, and its estimation of the global mobile phone addiction population was based on the usage data received from over 600,000 apps on 1.4 billion devices worldwide.

---

[5] See http://flurrymobile.tumblr.com/post/115191945655/the-rise-of-the-mobile-addict.

This is another interesting case for further analysis. First, it concerns medical effects. There are various effects due to mobile phone use, positive or negative. Mobile phone addiction is a widely discussed negative effect. Second, it concerns how to estimate mobile phone addiction. Why sixty times per day? How did Flurry access these data? Are these data valid and reliable? Will its estimation vary in different countries and different times (e.g., in Asia vs. in Africa? 2012 vs. 2016)? Third, this is one kind of effect caused by mobile phones, but also needs to be addressed by mobile phone behavior research to prevent, intervene, and reduce it. On the basis of the four-element model, the mobile phone behavior related to Flurry's estimation of mobile phone addiction can be illustrated in the following simple diagram, with the bold text highlighting the focus:

Mobile phones users in the world + 1.4 billion phones and 600,000 apps → using their apps sixty times per day → **176 million addicted to mobile phones in 2012**.

In summary, these real-life cases show diverse mobile phone behaviors in medicine from the perspective of mobile users, mobile technologies, mobile activities, and mobile effects. Compared with the intuitive thoughts by the doctor in the introduction to this chapter, these cases show a much broader scope of mobile phone behavior in medicine rather than mainly in clinic practice with mobile phones. However, these cases are not necessarily more complex in depth. This is partly because the intuitive responses and the everyday observations essentially are all anecdotal experiences rather than scientific evidence. We need to obtain scientific evidence through scientific research and can find scientific evidence in the journal article literature, a topic we will discuss in the next section.

3.   Empirical Studies: From HIV-Infected Pregnant Women to Links with Brain Cancers

3.1   Users: HIV-Infected Pregnant Women

The background. The first research example we will examine is an article entitled "An augmented SMS intervention to improve access to antenatal CD4 testing and ART initiation in HIV-infected pregnant women: A cluster randomized trial."[6] This article involved various medical terms.

---

[6] Dryden-Peterson, S., Bennett, K., Hughes, M. D. *et al.* (2015). "An augmented SMS intervention to improve access to antenatal CD4 testing and ART initiation in HIV-infected pregnant women: A cluster randomized trial," *PLOS ONE*, 10(2): e0117181.

For many of us who do not have a medical training background, the title itself is quite hard to understand. In order to understand the study, at least four key terms or acronyms should be briefly introduced, three relating to medicine and one relating to technologies.

First, HIV. HIV is a short term for human immunodeficiency virus, while AIDS is a short term for acquired immune deficiency syndrome. HIV infection causes AIDS. Following initial infection, a person may experience a brief period of influenza-like illness. This is typically followed by a prolonged period without symptoms. As the infection progresses, it increasingly interferes with the immune system, making the person much more susceptible to common infections, as well as opportunistic infections and tumors that do not usually affect people who have working immune systems. The late symptoms of the infection are referred to as AIDS. This stage is often complicated by an infection of the lungs, severe weight loss, skin lesions, or other AIDS-defining conditions. HIV is transmitted primarily via unprotected sexual intercourse, contaminated blood transfusions, hypodermic needles, and from mother to child during pregnancy, delivery, or breastfeeding. Common methods of HIV/AIDS prevention include encouraging and practicing safe sex, needle-exchange programs, and treating those who are infected. Antiretroviral treatment can slow the course of the disease and may lead to a near-normal life expectancy. Treatment is recommended as soon as the diagnosis is made. Without treatment, the average survival time after infection with HIV is estimated to be nine to eleven years. Pregnant women infected with HIV will transmit the virus to the child during pregnancy, delivery, or breastfeeding. Thus, early diagnosis and treatment is particularly important.

Second, CD4 count. In molecular biology,[7] CD4 is short for "cluster of differentiation 4." CD4 cells (often called T-cells or T-helper cells) are a type of white blood cells that play a major role in protecting our body from infection. They send signals to activate our body's immune response when they detect "intruders" (e.g., viruses or bacteria). Once a person is infected with HIV, the virus begins to attack and destroy the CD4 cells of the person's immune system. HIV uses the machinery of the CD4 cells to multiply and spread throughout the body. This process is called the HIV life cycle.

Based on AIDS.gov, a CD4 count is a lab test that measures the number of CD4 cells in a blood sample. In people with HIV, it is the most important laboratory indicator of how well our immune system is working

[7] See https://en.wikipedia.org/wiki/CD4.

and the strongest predictor of HIV progression. The higher our CD4 count, the better. For an uninfected healthy adult and adolescent, the CD4 count ranges from 500 to 1,200 cells/mm^3. Very low CD4 count indicates that a person living with HIV has progressed to Stage 3 infection, i.e., AIDS. Here, antenatal CD4 testing means that a CD4 test is performed when a human embryo or fetus gestates during pregnancy, from fertilization until birth.

Third, ART. It is a short form for antiretroviral therapy. Based on WHO, standard ART consists of the combination of antiretroviral drugs to maximally suppress the HIV virus and stop the progression of HIV disease. ART also prevents onward transmission of HIV. Huge reductions have been seen in rates of death and infections when use is made of a potent ART regimen, particularly in the early stages of the disease. WHO recommends ART for all people with HIV as soon as possible after diagnosis without any restrictions of CD4 counts.

Fourth, an augmented SMS intervention. The key word here is augmented, while the other two terms, SMS (short message service) and intervention, are common words that are easy to understand. Augmented reality is a live view of a real-world environment while some of its elements are augmented or supplemented by computer-generated sensory input such as sound, video, graphics, or GPS data. By contrast, virtual reality replaces the real-world environment by computer simulation.

In summary, this very long title, "An augmented SMS intervention to improve access to antenatal CD4 testing and ART initiation in HIV-infected pregnant women: A cluster randomized trial," simply means that the author reports a specially designed study (a cluster randomized trial) in which a mobile-phone-based method (an augmented SMS intervention) is used to encourage more HIV-infected pregnant women to partake in CD4 testing and ART initial treatment.

The authors and the journal. This article has eighteen authors from twelve medical research institutes. Scott Dryden-Peterson and Shahin Lockman, the first and last authors, are both experts in AIDS research and physicians of Immunology at Harvard and Infectious Diseases. They have published on AIDS research extensively, but this article is their first on mobile phone health care. The article was published in 2012 in *PLOS ONE*. Like *Frontier* and the *British Medical Journal*, *PLOS ONE* is an open access scientific journal published by the Public Library of Science (PLOS) since 2006. Open access journals have two basic features – publishing online and accessing for free. Since the 1990s, the open access movement has rapidly spread throughout the world. The PLOS organizers started to publish multiple open access journals, such as *PLOS Biology* in 2003 and *PLOS Currents* in 2009. In 2008, *PLOS ONE* became the most popular in the PLOS journal family, moved from a *weekly* publication schedule to a *daily* one through a typical peer review process, and is gaining a reputation of publishing high-quality articles as soon as they become ready. It is always useful for us to check authors and journals of an article and have an initial assessment of its credibility.

The study. The study took place in Botswana, Africa, a country among the poorest in the world and among the hardest hit by the HIV/AIDS epidemic (as high as one-quarter of adults aged 15 to 49 in 2009 had HIV/AIDS). The study focused on one research question: Can an augmented SMS intervention improve access to antenatal CD4 testing and ART initiation in HIV-infected pregnant women?

To answer this question, the researchers used a research design called cluster randomized trial, a special type of clinical study that randomizes participants based on certain groups or locations rather than typically randomizing individual participants. The authors first used 4,319 maternity recorders from twenty pregnancy clinics in Botswana and identified 396 HIV-infected women. They then randomly assigned these women in the twenty pregnancy clinics into the intervention group and the regular treatment group based on the locations of the clinics. The core device is an automated SMS-based system that directly collected and wirelessly distributed CD4 results to portable SMS-enabled printers located in each of the participating antenatal clinics. The system has an enhanced feature of alerting clinicians when testing frequency among pregnant women falls below expected ranges or laboratory validation results are delayed.

The results indicate that the augmented SMS-based programmatic intervention in the antenatal clinics improved neither timely CD4 testing nor ART initiation significantly among HIV-infected pregnant women. However, this SMS-based system did improve the speed and reduce the cost of laboratory reporting. The mobile method now takes six instead of sixteen days to deliver results from central laboratories to local clinics and costs $1.98 per result delivered instead of $2.73. For this scientific study, this is a useful and practical implication for HIV-infected pregnant women, particularly for those in resource-limited clinics in Botswana.

Comments. What we can learn about mobile phone behavior in medicine from this study? This article broadens and deepens our knowledge about mobile phone behavior in medicine in several ways. First, we can see a group of mobile phone *users* in medicine, all health-care workers involved in the study (designers, researchers, clinicians, and staff members). Besides them, there is another special group of hidden mobile phone users in this case, very vulnerable HIV-infected pregnant women in Botswana. Although they do not directly use the augmented SMS system, they might receive a mobile text message from that system or receive a mobile phone call from a clinician about their testing results. HIV is devastating in Botswana and these women can potentially benefit from mobile phone use. We can understand a little more about the complexity of the concept of mobile phone users in medicine. Second, we can see a special mobile phone *technique*, an augmented SMS system that is used in a clinic setting. The term sounds very high-tech, but the instrument used in the African setting is simple and straightforward. It demystifies the augmented reality to many of us. Third, we can see two special mobile phone *activities* – delivering CD4 testing information and managing ART intervention initiation. Fourth, although the results were not statistically significant, they are still scientifically and practically significant because they provide empirical evidence of how scientifically *effective* the mobile-phone-based treatment is in the study and how economically *useful* the augmented SMS system is in Botswana. Lastly, these four pieces of newly added knowledge are more specific, complete, and complex than the intuitive responses by the young doctor set out at the beginning of this chapter. They are also more scientific than the five cases observed in the everyday observations. They give us a specific, authentic, and scientific sense of how mobile phones are used in real clinical practice, including their strengths, weaknesses, and effectiveness. On the basis of the four-element model, the mobile phone behavior related to HIV-infected pregnant women in Botswana can be illustrated in the following simple diagram, with the bold text highlighting the focus:

Health-care workers in pregnancy clinics in Botswana + **the automated SMS-based system** → directly collecting and wirelessly distributing CD4 results → helped HIV-infected pregnant women in Botswana.

3.2   Technologies: Mobile Phone Dispatch

Background. Now let us discuss another journal article that focuses on medical technology-oriented mobile phone behavior. Its title is "Mobile-phone dispatch of laypersons for CPR in out-of-hospital cardiac arrest."[8]

---

[8] Ringh, M., Rosenqvist, M., Hollenberg, J. *et al.* (2015). "Mobile-phone dispatch of laypersons for CPR in out-of-hospital cardiac arrest," *New England Journal of Medicine*, 372(24): 2316–2325.

Three technical concepts used in the title should be introduced in order to understand the article.

First, mobile phone dispatch. Dispatch means to send messages to a destination or for a purpose. The mobile phone can be used to send an emergency dispatcher that instructs us in the proper procedures until help arrives.

Second, cardiopulmonary resuscitation (CPR). CPR is a lifesaving technique useful in many emergencies, including heart attack or near drowning. It normally begins with chest compressions. When the heart stops, a person may die within 8 to 10 minutes.[9] Its main purpose is to restore partial flow of oxygenated blood to the brain and heart in order to delay tissue death and to extend the brief window of opportunity for a successful resuscitation without permanent brain damage.[10] The rescuer may also provide breaths by either exhaling into the subject's mouth or nose or using a device that pushes air into the subject's lungs.

Third, cardiac arrest. This is a sudden stop in effective blood circulation due to the failure of the heart to contract. Medical personnel may refer to an unexpected cardiac arrest as a sudden cardiac arrest. Cardiac arrest is different from a heart attack, where blood flow to the muscle of the heart is impaired. It is also different from congestive heart failure, where circulation is insufficient but the heart is still pumping sufficient blood. Brain injury is likely to happen if cardiac arrest goes untreated for more than 5 minutes. For the best chance of survival and neurological recovery, immediate treatment is very important. However, since cardiac arrest will cause loss of consciousness, having someone get medical help is also very important.[11]

Here, the title "Mobile-phone dispatch of laypersons for CPR in out-of-hospital cardiac arrest" simply means that this study used mobile phones to call a layperson to perform CPR when one unexpectedly loses consciousness due to a cardiac arrest outside of a hospital.

The authors and the journal. The authors are Leif Svensson and other Karolinska Institutet researchers at several teaching hospitals and the Center for Resuscitation Science. Karolinska Institutet is one of the world's leading medical universities, with about 6,000 full-time medical students and 5,000 full-time employees.[12] Since 1901, the Nobel Assembly at Karolinska Institutet has selected the Nobel laureates in Physiology or

---

[9] See www.mayoclinic.org/first-aid/first-aid-cpr/basics/art-20056600.
[10] See https://en.wikipedia.org/wiki/Cardiopulmonary_resuscitation.
[11] See https://en.wikipedia.org/wiki/Cardiac_arrest.   [12] See http://ki.se/en/about/ki-in-brief.

Medicine. Leif Svensson published about 210 articles based on the database of PubMed, focusing on out-of-hospital cardiac arrest, emergency, and various diseases. The current article is the only article he has published related to mobile phones.

The *New England Journal of Medicine* (*NEJM*) is a medical journal published by the Massachusetts Medical Society. It is among the most prestigious peer-reviewed medical journals, as well as being the oldest medical journal, in publication since 1812. The journal usually has the highest impact factor of the journals of internal medicine. According to the Journal Citation Reports, *NEJM* had a 2014 impact factor of 56, the highest among 153 journals in general and internal medicine. By comparison, the second- and third-ranked journals in the category, *The Lancet* and the *Journal of American Medical Association*, had impact factors of 45 and 35 respectively, whereas *Nature*'s impact factor is 42 and *Science*'s impact factor is 31.[13]

In short, the initial check indicates that the authors are a team of experienced doctors and well-published researchers and the journal is one of the best. Thus, we should have initial trust in the methods used and results found in the article.

The study. The goal of the study is to examine whether a mobile phone positioning system can increase the number of CPR-initiated bystanders before the arrival of ambulance, fire, and police services. They used a study design of a blinded, randomized, controlled trial in Stockholm from April 2012 through December 2013. Participants were 9,828 people, and among them, 5,989 initial recruits were lay volunteers and trained in CPR. The authors developed a mobile phone positioning system that can locate individual mobile phones geographically for the present study. The study involved three types of persons: cardiac arrest patients, dispatchers, and trained lay volunteers. When suspecting that a patient had suffered a cardiac arrest, dispatchers activated the mobile phone positioning system. Then, the location of the patient with suspected cardiac arrest was compared with the current locations of trained lay volunteers. If a patient with suspected cardiac arrest was randomly assigned to the intervention group, then lay volunteers were located. If a volunteer was located within 500 meters of the patient, the volunteer was contacted automatically by means of text messaging and computer-generated telephone calls. If a patient was randomly assigned to the control group, then lay volunteers

---

[13] See https://tools.niehs.nih.gov/srp/publications/highimpactjournals.cfm.

who were trained in CPR were located, but no final contact was made by means of text messaging or telephone calls.

The main finding indicates that, among a total of 667 cases of out-of-hospital cardiac arrests occurring during the study, 61.6 percent of the patients in the intervention group (188 of 305 cases) received bystander-initiated CPR, as compared with 47.8 percent of the patients in the control group (172 of 360 cases). A significant difference was found in the percentage of the patients who received bystander-initiated CPR between these two groups.

Comments. This study can add to our understanding of mobile phone behavior in medicine in multiple ways. First, the mobile phone *users* in this case are both cardiac arrest sufferers and the CPR volunteers. These are two special groups of users: one will receive critical help and another can provide timely help. Second, the most salient point we can learn is about the technology. It is just a simple text message rather than a sophisticated app (like Apple's HealthKit) or most new *technologies* (e.g., augmented reality). However, one mobile phone message can help to save lives rather than regular trivial daily communication. Simple mobile phone dispatch is found to significantly save the life of cardiac arrest patients. This can only be possible when most people use and carry a mobile phone. Third, it is not a clinical treatment, but rather an emergency medical communication *activity* that is life-saving. Fourth, the strong scientific evidence indicates that *effects* of this mobile phone use are significant. This study provides better knowledge about mobile phone use in medicine than the young doctor's intuitive responses and the daily observations that we discussed earlier. The mobile phone behavior related to the mobile phone dispatch system used to better save lives of cardiac arrest patients can be illustrated in the following simple diagram, with the bold text highlighting the focus:

9,828 lay volunteers and cardiac arrest patients in Stockholm + a **text-based dispatch system** → searching and contacting lay volunteers with CPR training for cardiac arrest patients → significantly more cardiac arrest patients received timely bystander-initiated CPR.

3.3 Activities: Smoking Cessation Intervention

Background. The article we will discuss next is entitled "Smoking cessation support delivered via mobile phone text messaging (txt2stop): A single-blind, randomised trial."[14] The article has been cited 385 times

---

[14] Free, C., Knight, R., Robertson, S. *et al.* (2011). "Smoking cessation support delivered via mobile phone text messaging (txt2stop): A single-blind, randomised trial," *The Lancet*, 378(9785): 49–55.

based on Google Scholar. The authors are ten medical researchers from the United Kingdom, New Zealand, and Australia. The first author, Caroline Free, is a senior lecturer at the London School of Hygiene and Tropical Medicine, and has published several articles in the mobile health area. This article was published in 2011 in *The Lancet*, one of the world's oldest and best-known general medical journals by Elsevier since 1820, with a 2014 impact factor of 45, ranked second among general medical journals after the *New England Journal of Medicine*.

The study. From 2007 to 2009, 5,800 UK smokers (97 percent are adults) participated in the study. They were randomly assigned to the intervention group (2,915 smokers) and control group (2,885 smokers). The intervention group received smoking cessation support delivered via a mobile phone text messaging program called *text2stop*. This program can automatically generate text messages that consist of two types: 186 regular written messages to every participant in the intervention group and personalized messages to different participants selected from a database of 713 messages. These messages are either *motivational* ones (e.g., a text after the quit day is: "Quick result! Carbon monoxide has now left your body!"), or *behavioral-change* ones (e.g., a text message on the quit day is: "Quit day, throw away all your fags. Today is the start of being quit forever, you can do it!"). The intervention group received five text messages per day for the first five weeks and then three a week for the next twenty-six weeks. For the control group, the participants received text messages unrelated to quitting smoking (e.g., "Thanks for taking part! Without your input, the study could not have gone ahead!"). After the thirty-one-week intervention, participants self-reported their smoking abstinence and these self-reported data were further verified by standard biochemical lab test results. The major findings of the study include that: (1) the intervention group using *text2stop* doubled the quit rate at six months compared with the control group (10.7 vs. 4.9 percent); (2) no significant heterogeneity was found in any of the subgroups based on age or working status; and (3) no adverse side effects of the intervention were found in participants' thumb pain due to texting and traffic accidents due to texting on road.

Comments. From the perspective of mobile phone activities in medicine, the study provides multiple insights. First, typically, mobile phones are used in mental health clinics for monitoring patients, managing cases, or enhancing communication. *Clinic interventions* based on mobile phones are not common. The study we discussed above is one exception. It really used the text messaging programs of *text2stop* as the only intervention strategy to help people quit smoking. And the authors used rigorous data collection and data analysis methods to scientifically prove this intervention program works particularly well and thus recommended it to be used in the real clinical settings. Texts can heal people's souls and cure people's bodies! Second, the mobile phone activities involved in the study were mainly *text-based* interactions between smokers and clinicians for thirty-one weeks or nearly eight months. These text messages were sent to participants automatically based on computing algorithms and mainly either motivated or advised smokers how to best quit smoking and the intervention results were very significant. A total of 2,915 UK smokers used the program of *text2stop* and achieved the intervention results successfully. The activity-focused mobile phone behavior concerning this study can be summarized in a simple diagram, with the highlighted focus (in bold) on the mobile phone activity of the thirty-one-week intervention:

2,915 smokers in UK + *text2stop* → **receiving the thirty-one-week intervention** → the smoking quit rate of the intervention group was double that of the control group.

3.4   Medical Effects: Sleep Disturbance

Background. The next article to be discussed is entitled "The association between use of mobile phones after lights out and sleep disturbances among Japanese adolescents: A nationwide cross-sectional survey."[15] It was cited ninety-four times based on Google Scholar since being published in 2011. While it might not be well cited, it is one of the earliest articles examining the effect of mobile phone use on sleep. The authors are ten public health researchers from Japan. The first author, Takeshi Munezawa, is an expert of sleep and has published multiple articles on sleep problems in Japan. *Sleep* has been the official publication of the Sleep Research Society and American Academy of Sleep Medicine since 1978, with a 2015 impact factor of 4.793.

The study. In the study, 95,680 Japanese middle-school and high-school students participated in a survey. The questionnaire used in the survey mainly concerned these students' lifestyle, mental health, sleep problems, and mobile phone use. The major findings include: (1) over 84 percent of students reported using mobile phones daily; (2) nearly 30 percent of students reported making a call after lights were out and

---

[15] Munezawa, T., Kaneita, Y., Osaki, Y. *et al.* (2011). "The association between use of mobile phones after lights out and sleep disturbances among Japanese adolescents: A nationwide cross-sectional survey," *Sleep*, 34(8): 1013–1020.

about 52 percent of students reported sending text messages after lights were out; (3) 35 percent of students reported having a shorter sleep duration, 42 percent reported their sleep quality was poor, 46 percent reported experiencing excessive daytime sleepiness, and over 22 percent reported having insomnia symptoms; (4) their phone calls and text messages after lights were out significantly related to various forms of sleep disturbance such as shorter sleep duration or insomnia symptoms, independent of various covariates such as age and lifestyle and independent of calling vs. texting; and (5) girls and high-school seniors are the two special groups having a higher frequency of using mobile phones after lights were out, experiencing more sleep problems, and showing a higher relationship between their evening mobile phone use and their sleep disturbances.

Comments. What can we learn about mobile phone effects from this study? First, this study shows that nearly 30 percent of Japanese youth reported making a call after lights were out and about 52 percent of students reported sending text messages after lights were out. Thus, it is not uncommon for this student population to use mobile phones during sleeping time. Second, the study shows some evidence that these students' mobile phone use during sleeping time is associated with various sleep disturbances. In other words, for many young mobile phone users, mobile phone use, either calling, texting, or gaming, might have significant negative effects on one common but fundamental aspect of their lives, i.e., sleep. The mobile phone behavior related to this study can be summarized in a simple diagram, with a highlight (in bold) on the negative effect on sleep:

95,680 Japanese middle- and high-school students + mobile phones → calling and texting after lights were out → **experienced various forms of sleep disturbances**.

3.5 Medical Effects: Brain Cancers

Background. When we make or receive a call with our own small-sized, good-looking mobile phone, we may hardly think intuitively about whether there might be any serious direct negative effects on our health. Our worry-free impression perhaps would be similar to that with a telephone, a telegraph, a television, a CD player, a digital camera, a computer, and many other modern technologies. However, there could be multiple various health or even life-threatening concerns related to the use of mobile phones, including injuries after battery explosion, burns from overcharged or overheating phones, brain cancers, addiction, phantom vibration and ringing syndromes, germ accumulation, headaches, dizziness, memory loss, and sleep disturbances. Let us look at a recent article entitled "Pooled analysis of case-control studies on malignant brain tumours and the use of mobile and cordless phones including living and deceased subjects," by Lennart Hardell, Michael Carl Berg, and Kjell Hansson Mild.[16] The first author, Lennart Hardell, is a Professor of Oncology at the University Hospital in Orebro of Sweden. He is one of the leading researchers in mobile-phone-related brain cancers and has been publishing a series of studies examining the links between mobile phone radiation and brain cancers for a decade. This article is one of their latest empirical articles.

Extensive literature since the 1990s has indicated that daily use of mobile phones could be associated with brain cancers. The World Health Organization's International Agency for Research on Cancer (IARC) in 2011 classified mobile phone use and other radiofrequency electromagnetic fields as Group 2B, possibly carcinogenic to humans. The IARC classification is the most widely used system for classifying carcinogens. Over the past thirty years, the IARC has evaluated the cancer-causing potential of more than 900 materials, placing them into one of the following groups: Group 1: Carcinogenic to humans (e.g., coal gasification, indoor emissions from coal, engine exhaust from diesel, leather dust, outdoor air pollution, solar radiation, x- and gamma-radiation); Group 2A: Probably carcinogenic to humans (vinyl fluoride, vinyl bromide, manufacture of art glass, glass containers and pressed ware, occupational exposures in petroleum refining); Group 2B: Possibly carcinogenic to humans (e.g., carbon tetrachloride, lead, engine exhaust from gasoline, gasoline, magnetic fields with extremely low frequency, radiofrequency electromagnetic fields); Group 3: Unclassifiable as to carcinogenicity in humans; and Group 4: Probably not carcinogenic to humans. Among 900 candidates, only 116 are classified as "carcinogenic to humans" and most are listed as being of probable (73), possible (287), or unknown risk (503).

The study. In this article, Hardell and his collaborators aimed to find an association between the use of mobile and cordless phones and malignant brain tumors. Basically, there are two types of brain tumors: malignant tumors composed of cancerous cells rather than non-cancerous cells, and benign tumors composed of mainly non-cancerous cells. To achieve this

[16] Hardell, L., Carlberg, M., and Hansson Mild, K. (2011). "Pooled analysis of case-control studies on malignant brain tumours and the use of mobile and cordless phones including living and deceased subjects," *International Journal of Oncology*, 38(5): 1465.

goal, they used a design called case-control studies, an observational study used widely in epidemiology.[17] In such a design, the group of "case" (subjects who have a disease) and the group of "control" (subjects who do not have the disease, but are otherwise similar) are compared to examine the potential links of a possible risk factor and a disease. One of the most significant examples of the case-control study was the demonstration of the link between tobacco smoking and lung cancer (Doll & Hill, 1950).

Specifically, the case group consisted of patients with a histopathological diagnosis (using the microscopic examination of tissues to study the manifestations of diseases) of brain tumors during 1997 to 2003 (six-year duration, published in 2011, eight years later) aged 20 to 80 years in multiple regions in Sweden. The authors not only consider malignant tumors in general, but also glioma and even astrocytomas. There were three control groups: one living control group for healthy individuals drawn from the Swedish Population Registry, and two deceased control groups that either had died from other types of malignant diseases, but not brain tumors, or had died from other diseases, but not cancers. Relatives to both cases and controls were identified through the Swedish Population Registry at the Swedish Tax Agency. They were matched with the case group on age, sex, and residential area. A total of 1,251 cases and 2,438 controls participated in the study. These four groups, the case group and the three control groups, were the dependent variable in the study. The data collected about tumor localization was based on information in medical records and all tumor types were defined by using histopathology reports and through Swedish Population Registry and Death Registry.

The independent variables were different environmental and occupational exposures. The data were collected via a self-administered questionnaire that was sent to the living cases and controls or relatives of deceased patients. Use of mobile and cordless phones (together called wireless phones) was carefully assessed by the self-administered questionnaire. The information was, if necessary, supplemented over the phone by a trained interviewer using a structured protocol. In the study, 58.1 percent in the case group and 52.0 percent in the control groups used mobile phones.

Specifically, two indicators of wireless phone use were assessed: (1) latency period (between the year of first use of a wireless phone and the

[17] Schlesselman, J. J. and Stolley, P. D. (1982). *Case-Control Studies: Design, Conduct, Analysis.* Oxford University Press.

year of diagnosis), including three levels, >1–5 years, >5–10 years, and >10 years; and (2) cumulative hours (calculated based on number of years and average daily time), including three levels, 1–1,000, 1,001–2,000 and >2,000 h to further explore the dose-response relations. The unexposed category consisted of subjects that reported no use of mobile or cordless phones, or exposure ≤1 year before reference date. The exposed cases and controls were divided according to phone type – analog, digital, and cordless. The use of analog and digital phones were analyzed combined (i.e., mobile phone) in this presentation. Results for all phone types combined (wireless phone) are also presented. They used the unconditional logistic regression analysis with exposed status as the predictor variable and cancer status as the dependent outcome variable to calculate odds ratios and 95 percent confidence intervals. Adjustments were made for a few variables such as age, gender, year of diagnosis, and vital status.

The major findings regarding mobile phone use only rather than cordless phone use or a combination of both can be summarized as follows: (1) Overall, among all those who had malignant tumors, 574 used mobile phones for more than one year and 963 did not, and its odd ratio was 1.3, that is, the mobile phone users in general were 1.3 times more likely to have malignant tumors than those in the matched control groups. (2) Among different latency periods, the highest risk was in the largest latency period of >10 years; 134 mobile phone users had malignant tumors, while 106 non-mobile phone users had malignant tumors. Its odd ratio was 2.5, indicating that these mobile phone users were 2.5 times more likely to have malignant tumors than those in the matched control groups. (3) Among different cumulative lifetime use, the highest risk was in the longest cumulative lifetime use of >200 hours; sixty-one mobile phone users had malignant tumors, while thirty-three non-mobile phone users had malignant tumors. Its odd ratio was 3.0, indicating that these mobile phone users were three times more likely to have malignant tumors than those in the matched control groups. (4) Among different age groups, the highest risk was for the youngest group (<20 years old); nineteen mobile phone users had malignant tumors, while fourteen non-mobile phone users had malignant tumors. Its odd ratio was 2.9, indicating that these young mobile phone users were 2.9 times more likely to have malignant tumors than those in the matched control groups.

Comments. This study has several strengths. First, it included both living and deceased subjects due to cancers to expand the study's scope. Second, it carefully designed and executed the case-control study by matching on multiple aspects, given the ethical challenges for experimental studies of such a topic. Third, it covered several most common types of malignant cancers as dependent variables. Fourth, it used survey as well as interviews to collect the exposure data on latency periods, cumulative hours, and types of phones used, as well as other controlled variables such as age, sex, socio-economic status, and year of diagnosis. Fifth, the sample size is relatively large. Sixth, data analysis was appropriate, using unconditional logistical regression with statistical control. Seventh, it included different wireless phone types – analog, digital, and cordless.

This study has several limitations. First, the time period of 1997 to 2003 is a bit early, considering the exponential growth of mobile phone use since 2005. Second, the case-control study leads only to a finding about association between mobile phone use and brain cancers, but not about causation that mobile phone use causes brain cancers. Third, it should include more factors (e.g., personality, general health) and more paths (e.g., direct and indirect, moderation and mediation) that might exist. Fourth, it focused on Sweden, a country where people used mobile phones very early compared with other countries in the world. Fifth, more explanation is needed about why and how mobile phone use leads to brain tumors. Sixth, it did not cover contralateral (opposite sides of the head) and ipsilateral (the same side of the head) mobile phone use in relation to tumor localization. Seventh, it should compare the differences among the three control groups and different tumors more effectively.

Its major contributions are to provide initial empirical evidence, show the possibility of mobile phones being related to brain cancers due to exposure to the phones' electromagnetic field radiation, and show the complexity of mobile phone behavior. Its implication is to alert us to the potential risk and motivate further research.

From the perspective of effect-based mobile phone behavior, we can make two observations from the above example. First, it documents a specific type of effect-based mobile phone behavior in detail: of the 1,000 Swedish citizens who had brain cancers, over 700 used mobile phones on a daily basis for years, while among the nearly 2,500 who were healthy or did not have brain cancers, about half of them used mobile phones. Second, it demonstrates the complexity of effect-based mobile phone behavior. We can learn from this study that one should consider various important aspects of: (1) mobile users (e.g., years, frequencies, and ages of those using the mobile phones); (2) mobile phones (e.g., cordless vs. mobile, handheld vs. hands-free, analog vs. digital; (3) mobile activities (e.g. heavy use vs. non-heavy use); (4) mobile effects (e.g., brain cancers vs. other kinds of cancers, malignant brain tumors vs. benign tumors, contralateral vs. ipsilateral); and (5) mobile contexts (e.g., Sweden vs. other countries). In short, the mobile phone behavior related to this study can be summarized in a simple diagram, with a highlight (in bold) on the negative effect of brain cancers:

1,251 mobile phone users in Sweden + mobile phones → using mobile phones between 1997 and 2003 → **574 users had malignant tumors**.

4. Knowledge Syntheses: From Exponential Growth to Potential Brain Cancers

After studying five specific examples of empirical research, many of us might wonder what the current knowledge is in the area of mobile phone behavior in medicine. In this section, we will discuss the scope of the existing literature, relevant chapters of the *Encyclopedia of Mobile Phone Behavior*, and several review articles in order to have an overall picture of the current knowledge in this area.

4.1   Exponential Growth

Based on our review article,[18] medical research is the largest area in the entire field of mobile phone behavior research, making up about one-third of the published articles. In 2016, at least 2,400 articles can be found in PubMed, by using the keywords of public health and mobile phones or medicine and mobile phones. The general trend over the past twenty years has been an exponential growth, with the year of 2010 being the turning point (see Figure 6.1). Due to the delay of entering published articles into databases (typically around one year), the number of published journal articles should be much higher than that in 2014.

4.2   Dominant Themes

Empirical research published in journal article form is fundamental. However, it is useful to study review-based chapters of the *Encyclopedia of Mobile Phone Behavior* to develop a much broader picture of mobile phone behavior in medicine and public health. In the *Encyclopedia*, similar to the dominance in the m-health literature, at least 23 of a total of 108 chapters synthesize the literature of various topics in mobile phone behavior in

---

[18] Yan, Z., Chen, Q., and Yu, C. (2013). "The science of cell phone use: Its past, present, and future," *International Journal of Cyber Behavior, Psychology and Learning*, 3(1): 7–18.

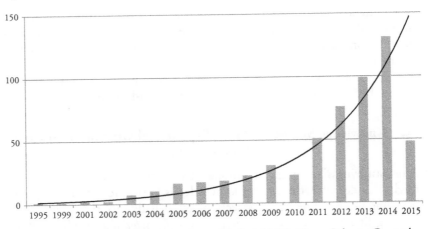

Figure 6.1 Trend of Published Articles on Medical Mobile Phone Behavior Research

medicine and public health. As shown in Table 6.1, these chapters can be grouped into four categories: medical users, medical technologies, medical interactions, and medical effects. Among them, at least twelve chapters focus on mobile phone effects as a dominant theme in the existing literature. For instance, mobile phone users reviewed in these chapters include medical doctors who use mobile phones in maternal, newborn, and child health programs, medical students who use smartphones for their medical education, and deaf or blind children who receive special therapy with mobile phones. Mobile phone technologies covered in these chapters include various smartphone apps used by professionals, students, and patients for health care and mobile sensors used in assessing, monitoring, tracking, and diagnosing. For mobile phone activities, these chapters review various medical activities in emergency care, plastic surgery, blood disease treatment, and mental health intervention. For medical phone effects, a well-studied area, various effects were reviewed, such as bullying, addiction, nomophobia, and brain tumors.

4.3 Users: Older Adults' Health Care

Another general way to develop an overview of the existing literature in a given area is to search and study published review articles, in addition to encyclopedias and handbooks. About 300 reviews have been published, as indicated in the database of Web in Science. Here, we will discuss three review articles, one on mobile users and two on mobile effects.

Table 6.1 *The* Encyclopedia *Chapters on Mobile Phone Behavior in Medicine*

Element	Chapter title
User	Divorced coparents' use of communication technology
User	mHealth in maternal, newborn, and child health programs around the world
User	Deaf adolescents' textisms
User	Use of mobile phones by individuals with visual impairments
Technology	Healthcare applications for smartphones
Technology	Smart phone health applications
Activity	Mobile health in emergency care
Activity	Mobile phones for plastic surgery and burns: Current practice
Activity	Mobile phones in haematology
Activity	Mobile tracking for mental health and wellbeing
Activity	Use of mobile phones to help prevent child maltreatment
Effect	Health effects of mobile phone usage
Effect	Mobile technostress
Effect	Mobile technology and cyberbullying
Effect	Sex, cyberbullying and the mobile phone
Effect	Students hurting students: Cyberbullying as a mobile phone behavior
Effect	Mobile phone addiction
Effect	Nomophobia
Effect	The conceptualization and assessment of problematic mobile phone use
Effect	Internet and mobile phone addiction
Effect	The digital drug: Understanding and treating mobile phone addiction
Effect	Mobile phones-like electromagnetic fields effects on human psychomotor performance
Effect	Long term mobile phone use leads to brain tumors

The first review we will discuss focuses on a special group of users in medicine – mobile phone users who are 60 years of age or older. Its title is "Older adults and mobile phones for health: A review."[19] The two authors are Jonathan Joe and George Demiris at the University of Washington. Jonathan Joe was then a PhD candidate studying how to help older adults with new technologies in the biomedical and health informatics program, while George Demiris is a Professor of Biomedical and Health Informatics and has published a series of articles on technology use among older adults. This review was published in 2013 in the *Journal of Biomedical Informatics*, an established Elsevier journal since 1967 (the original name was

[19] Joe, J. and Demiris, G. (2013). "Older adults and mobile phones for health: A review," *Journal of Biomedical Informatics*, 46(5): 947–954.

Computers and Biomedical Research, which changed to the current name in 2001), with an impact factor of 2.447.

In this review, the authors searched multiple databases (e.g., PubMed) and identified twenty-one journal articles that were published between 1965 and 2012 and met their specific inclusion/and exclusion criteria (e.g., utilizing a mobile phone as an intervention or emphasizing the mobile phone's use in health). They found that mobile phones were being used in ten areas of health interventions with older adults: (1) care for diabetes as a disease characterized by higher blood sugar levels, leading to increased urination, weight loss, fatigue, vomiting, skin infections, and other symptoms (e.g., sending text-based reminders to patients for their dietary management or blood sugar monitoring); (2) care for chronic obstructive pulmonary disease that is related to the lungs (e.g., providing a mobile-phone-based exercise training program with reminders to improve patients' fatigue, emotions, and breathlessness); (3) care for dementia and Alzheimer's disease that leads to a long-term decrease in the ability to think and remember (e.g., using GPS to track and locate wandering older patients); (4) care for osteoarthritis – a disease usually causing patients to experience joint pain and stiffness (e.g., using a mobile version of a testing instrument to assess the level of joint pain and stiffness); (5) care for non-melanoma skin cancers that are most common, less aggressive, hardly spreading to other tissues, and usually curable (e.g., using mobile phones for clinicians to take and transmit photos of skin lesions to dermatologists for further diagnosis); (6) care for accidental injury and death due to falls (e.g., using mobile phone sensors to detect older adults' falls and to minimize the amount of time between the fall and receiving medical attention); (7) care for congestive heart failure due to a chronic condition that affects the chambers of the heart (e.g., using mobile phones to detect and monitor early symptoms of heart failure at home to reduce the duration of hospital stays and mortality rate); (8) palliative care for relieving pain, symptoms, and stress among those who have serious and life-threating illnesses (e.g., using mobile phones for patients to report their symptoms regularly and for clinicians to review these symptoms remotely on a daily basis and offer self-care advice); (9) care for chemo-therapy symptoms as various side effects of chemotherapy treatment after using drugs to destroy cancer cells (e.g., using mobile phones for patients to report their adverse chemotherapy symptoms and receive help on a timely basis); and (10) elderly home care (e.g., using a mobile phone camera for older adults to record their activities of daily life in a rural home care setting).

As we can see from this review: (1) older adults are a special group of mobile users; they face a wide variety of special health-care challenges, from suffering from diabetes, chronic obstructive pulmonary disease, dementia, and Alzheimer's disease, to performing daily life activities; and (2) mobile phones have been widely used to help these older adults in various ways, including detecting early symptoms, managing interventions, relieving pains, and helping them to live better lives. Although this line of research overall is still at the early development stage, it shows that mobile phone use has a unique and promising potential for older adults' health care.

4.4 Effects: School Students' Sleep Disturbance

In the previous section, we discussed a survey study on associations between mobile phone use and sleep problems of Japanese middle- and high-school students. The review article we will discuss below provides a much broader picture of mobile phone use and sleep problems among school-aged children across the world. Its title is "Screen time and sleep among school-aged children and adolescents: A systematic literature review."[20] The two authors, Lauren Hale and Stanford Guan, are health science researchers at Stony Brook University. Lauren Hale is an Associate Professor of Family, Population and Preventive Medicine and has published extensively on sleep health. She is also the founding editor of *Sleep Health*, the journal of the National Sleep Foundation. Stanford Guan was then a pre-medical student. The review was published in 2015 in *Sleep Medicine Reviews*, a well-established Elsevier journal since 1990. It has a quite high impact factor of 7.341 in 2016 for a specialized journal.

The authors searched Web of Science as well as PubMed and Google Scholar and selected sixty-seven relevant journal articles for further review. The Munezawa article discussed above is one of them. Specifically, it includes twenty-seven studies in European countries, fourteen studies in the United States, seven studies in Japan, and five studies in Australia, as well as studies in eight more countries. For the independent variables, the authors focused on the use of four types of electronic media: televisions, computers, video games, and mobile phones. For dependent variables, six major types of sleeping outcomes, such as duration of sleep, delayed bedtime, sleep onset latency, and daytime sleepiness, were examined.

---

[20] Hale, L. and Guan, S. (2015). "Screen time and sleep among school-aged children and adolescents: A systematic literature review," *Sleep Medicine Reviews*, 21: 50–58.

The major findings include that: (1) overall, 90 percent of the reviewed articles show a significant negative association between time of media use and at least one of the sleep outcomes, indicating media use is consistently related to sleep disturbance among school students; (2) sleep disturbance varies with different media use: using computers (94 percent of studies showing significant sleep disturbance), playing games (86 percent of studies showing significant sleep disturbance), using mobile phones (85 percent of studies showing significant sleep disturbance), watching television (76 percent of studies showing significant sleep disturbance), suggesting interactive media use (e.g., playing games) leads to more sleep disturbance than passive media use (e.g., watching television); and (3) one major problem for the existing studies is that assessment of media use and sleep problems has largely relied on students' own reports or sometimes parental reports. For self-reported data, school students will normally overreport sleep time and underreport sleep problems. As a result, this might lead to an underestimate in the relationship between media use and sleep disturbance.

From this review, we can see clearly that sleep disturbance due to media use is clearly a pervasive problem among school students and mobile phone use is strongly and consistently associated with sleep disturbance. However, school students are using mobile phones like a computer, playing a game, surfing on the Internet, watching television, and doing various new things, in addition to calling or texting, thus, researchers should design better studies to accurately assess how much mobile phone use disturbs students' sleep.

4.5   Effects: Potential Brain Cancers

The literature on mobile phone use and brain cancers is particularly extensive. About 600 journal articles and fifty review articles can be found by searching the database of Web of Science. The three highest cited reviews are: (1) "Biological effects from electromagnetic field exposure and public exposure standards," by Hardell and Sage;[21] (2) "Mobile telephones and cancer – a review of epidemiological evidence," by Kundi, Hardell, and other co-authors;[22] and (3) "Mobile phones, mobile phone

---

[21] Hardell, L. and Sage, C. (2008). "Biological effects from electromagnetic field exposure and public exposure standards," *Biomedicine & Pharmacotherapy*, 62(2): 104–109.

[22] Kundi, M., Mild, K. H., Hardell, L., and Mattsson, M. O. (2004). "Mobile telephones and cancer – a review of epidemiological evidence," *Journal of Toxicology and Environmental Health, Part B*, 7(5): 351–384.

base stations and cancer: A review," by Moulder, Foster, Erdreich, and McNamee.[23] The last review we choose to discuss is "Systematic review of wireless phone use and brain cancer and other head tumors."[24] This is one of the most recent and most comprehensive reviews on mobile phone use and brain cancers and was written by thirteen scholars from nine countries across the world. The first and corresponding author, Michael Repacholi, was the team leader of the World Health Organization's Radiation and Environmental Health Program and has published extensively on health risks from radiofrequency fields and electromagnetic fields. The review was published in 2012 in *Bioelectromagnetics*, a well-established Wiley journal with a 2015 impact factor of 1.583. It is the official journal of the Bioelectromagnetics Society and publishes studies on all aspects of the science of biological effects of electromagnetic fields.

In this review, the authors reviewed two major types of existing literature – epidemiology studies (analyzing health risks and disease conditions in a population) and in vivo studies (studying whole living organisms, usually animals) – in order to examine the relationship between wireless/mobile phone use and brain cancers/other head tumors. The review has multiple highlights for us to read and learn: (1) Two basic technical features of mobile phones are that (a) the frequencies used by mobile phones are between 450 and 2,700 MHz, belonging to *radiofrequency* (RF) and (b) the energy power emitted by mobile phones is *low-powered*, typically with its maximum specific absorption rate (SAR) in the head between 0.2 and 1.5 watts per kilogram of weight (W/kg), compared with the international standard SAR of 2 W/kg. The higher the SAR of a mobile phone, the more radiation energy emitted from the phone to heads or brains. (2) For epidemiology studies, the authors identified ninety-six papers. Among them they specifically reviewed twenty-five case-control studies and cohort studies on four outcomes, the brain cancer (gliomas) and three head tumors (meningioma, acoustic neuroma, and parotid grand tumors) in detail. They did not find overall significant associations between short-term (<10 years) mobile phone use and gliomas, meningioma, acoustic neuroma, and parotid grand tumors, while there is no

[23] Moulder, J. E., Foster, K. R., Erdreich, L. S., and McNamee, J. P. (2005). "Mobile phones, mobile phone base stations and cancer: A review," *International Journal of Radiation Biology*, 81(3): 189–203.

[24] Repacholi, M. H., Lerchl, A., Röösli, M. *et al.* (2012). "Systematic review of wireless phone use and brain cancer and other head tumors," *Bioelectromagnetics*, 33(3): 187–206.

sufficient data on adults' long-term use ($\geq$ 10 years) or on children's use. (3) For in vivo studies, the authors identified forty-five studies and reviewed twenty-two original studies in detail, ten on genotoxicity studies (examining how chemical agents damage DNA that may lead to cancer) and twelve on tumor promotion studies (examining how existing tumors are stimulated to grow). They concluded that no strong evidence suggests that RF exposure either breaks down DNA in brain cells or promotes brain tumors. (4) While both the epidemiological studies and in vivo studies do not show a consistent causal relationship between mobile phone use and brain cancers and head tumors, the two major epidemiology studies, the Interphone Study and the Hardell studies, show substantial inconsistency, together with an insufficient number of studies on long-term use and children's use. Thus, further studies are still needed to fully understand potential brain cancers due to mobile phone use. At this moment, two cautious health policy recommendations for mobile phone use are taking adequate protective measures and limiting exposure to radiofrequency fields.

From the review, we can learn several important insights and develop further our understanding of the links between mobile phones and brain cancers. First, compared with the Hardell article discussed earlier, this review analyzes more than fifty studies, including the 2011 Hardell paper and Hardell's other papers, and paints a much more *complex* picture of whether mobile phone use leads to brain cancers. While no overall consistent evidence has been found to suggest that mobile phone use leads to brain cancers, large inconsistencies exist in two major studies as well as other studies, and sufficient data are not still available for long-term use and for children's use, two issues that will become increasingly critical as more adults and more children use mobile phones for longer periods of time. Thus, we still have a long way to go to find a full scientific answer. Second, the review consistently and rigorously assesses the quality of published studies and discusses various quality issues existing in these studies. One major issue identified by the review is that *self-report* is currently the dominant method of assessing exposure to radiation from mobile phones. Retrospective self-reported exposure has been found to be related to recall bias. With recall bias, for instance, people tend to substantially overestimate their number of calls or time of calling. Thus, objective data such as traffic records from mobile phone service companies or built-in records with special apps in the mobile phone should be used to significantly improve the quality of radiation exposure estimation, especially for long-term users and young users.

5. Comparative Analyses: From Television Addiction to Mobile Phone Addiction

It is useful to compare human behavior in medicine across different technologies, including television, computer, the Internet, and mobile phones. In the area of medicine and health care, similarities and differences have been observed in human behavior with different modern information and communication technologies. For instance, there exists considerable literature on the effects of overuse of different technologies on the muscle system (e.g., repetitive strain injury or RSI) or vision system (computer vision syndrome or CVS). However, it is only mobile phones that have the extensive literature on the effects on brain cancers. It is beyond the scope of this chapter to deal with the complicated and challenging task of performing a lengthy comprehensive study to compare behavior among television health, computer health, e-health, and m-health. Instead, let us focus on one behavior, addiction, across different technologies. Recall that we have discussed a report by Flurry estimating that 176 million users in 2012 across the world were addicted to mobile phones, or about a 2 percent prevalence rate for the 2012 world population of 7.043 billion. Now we can see a large picture of the existing literature on addiction to different technologies.

There exists very extensive literature on technology addiction. Table 6.2 provides an approximate estimation of the size of the literature on addiction to the four technologies, based on a preliminary search in PsycINFO by using the keywords of television, computers, Internet, and cellular phones, and addiction. Clearly, the smallest literature size is television addiction and the largest size is Internet addiction. Note that: (1) the literature size is different from but related to the prevalence rate of the addiction; (2) Internet addiction often includes computer addiction (e.g., online game addiction) and there is no clear line between these two; (3) nearly 90 percent of computer addiction concerns computer game addiction; and (4) the current literature size on mobile phone addiction is not the largest given that PsycINFO started to enter the data on cellular phones in 2008, but research has been growing rapidly.

Technology addiction is complex. Making comparisons among the technologies is even more complex. It is not feasible to review and compare all the existing literature or even review the published reviews. Thus, as the first step, let us review four empirical journal articles, one article from each of the four technologies (i.e., television, computer games, Internet, and mobile phones), in order to develop a basic knowledge about addiction to the four technologies.

Table 6.2 *Numbers of Journal Articles Published on Different Technology Addictions*

Technology Addiction	Number of Articles Published	Year of Entry
Television addiction	10	1962
Computer addiction	431	1967
Computer game addiction	386	1988
Internet addiction	652	2001
Mobile phone addiction	84	2008

5.1   American Adults' Television Addiction

The first article is about television addiction. Robert D. McIlwraith (1998) published an empirical article entitled "'I'm addicted to television': The personality, imagination, and TV watching patterns of self-identified TV addicts" in the *Journal of Broadcasting & Electronic Media*.[25] This article is well cited – 116 times by other scholars based on Google Scholar. Robert McIlwraith was an Associate Professor of Clinical Health Psychology at the University of Manitoba at that time and published several articles on television addiction. The *Journal of Broadcasting & Electronic Media* has been a well-established, peer-reviewed research journal for sixty years since 1957.

This article presents a survey study. Participants were 237 American adults who visited a science museum during one summer week and completed anonymous questionnaires in approximately 25 minutes. Two measures were used to assess television addiction, the *Television Addiction Scale*, which was developed by Smith,[26] and *Self-Identification as a TV Addict*, a single-item measure that asked participants to respond to the statement "I am addicted to television" on the five-point Likert scale (from "Strongly Disagree" to "Strongly Agree"). The major results of the study were as follows: (1) 10.1 percent of the participants labeled themselves as TV addicts; (2) self-identified TV addicts reported watching an average of 20.6 hours of TV per week, while the rest of the sample reported watching an average of 12.9 hours per week; (3) the participants reported reasons to

---

[25] McIlwraith, R. D. (1998). "'I'm addicted to television': The personality, imagination, and TV watching patterns of self-identified TV addicts," *Journal of Broadcasting & Electronic Media*, 42(3): 371–386.

[26] Smith, R. (1986). "Television addiction," in J. Bryant and D. Zillmann (eds.), *Perspectives on Media Effects*. Hillsdale, NJ: Erlbaum, pp. 109–128.

watch TV, such as being distracted from unpleasant moods, having nothing to do, having the TV on while doing other things, or playing computers or video games; and (4) total scores on Smith's TV Addiction Scale correlated with explicitly labeling oneself a TV addict.

This study has several strengths: (1) it is one of the few published empirical studies examining television addiction; (2) it provides an estimation of the prevalence rate of television addiction of 10 percent; and (3) it describes several motivations of television addiction. However, the study (1) did not describe specific symptoms of television addiction, except for reporting nearly 21 hours of television viewing among the addicts and (2) did not report the prevalence rate using the Smith's scale, but indicated a close relationship between the Smith's scale and the one-item self-assessment. In short, the study provides general empirical information about television addiction.

5.2 British Adolescents' Computer Game Addiction

The second article we will discuss is entitled "Dependence on Computer Games by Adolescents" published in *Psychological Reports* in 1998 by Mark Griffiths and Nigel Hunt from Nottingham Trent University in the United Kingdom.[27] This article is also well cited – 423 times by other authors according to Google Scholar. The first author, Mark Griffiths, is a Professor of Psychology and a highly productive researcher on game addiction, publishing over 400 referred articles mostly in the area of behavioral addiction. *Psychological Reports* is a peer-reviewed journal on experimental, theoretical, and speculative articles in the field of general psychology since 1955. This article is Griffiths' early study on computer game addiction, after which he focused on internet or online gaming.

This short six-print-page article reports a survey study where 387 adolescents at a comprehensive school in Exeter in the United Kingdom were administered a questionnaire examining factors in the acquisition, development, and maintenance of behaviors associated with playing computer games at home. The measure was an eight-question survey based on the DSM-111-R criteria for pathological gambling. Note that the *Diagnostic and Statistical Manual of Mental Disorders* (DSM), published by the American Psychiatric Association, offers standard criteria for clinical diagnosis of mental disorders in the United States and its latest edition, the

---

[27] Griffiths, M. D. and Hunt, N. (1998). "Dependence on computer games by adolescents," *Psychological Reports*, 82(2): 475–480.

fifth edition, was published in 2013. Eight questions to examine computer dependence included: (1) salience (Do you frequently play most days?); (2) tolerance (Do you frequently play for longer periods of time?); (3) euphoria (Do you play for excitement or a "buzz"?); (4) chasing (Do you play to beat your personal high score?); (5) relapse (Do you make repeated efforts to stop or decrease playing?); (6) withdrawal (Do you become restless if you cannot play?); (7) conflict (Do you play instead of attending to school-related activities?); and (8) conflict (Do you sacrifice social activities to play?). A cut-off score of four was assumed to indicate that a participant was dependent or addicted to computer games at the time of the study. The major findings were as follows: (1) Scores on the adapted DSM-III-R scale indicated that sixty-two players (19.9 percent) were currently dependent on computer games and that a further twenty-one players (6.8 percent) previously played at dependent levels. (2) The major reasons for these adolescents to first start playing computer games were to impress friends, to kill time, to have a challenge, and to meet friends. The major reasons for them to play computer games at the time of the study were to impress friends, an inability to stop playing, to have a challenge, and to meet friends.

This study is one of the early studies on computer game addiction. It is a simple survey study. Its major strength is its link with the DSM and its simple design of measurement. The weakness is that it is unclear about the quality of the measurement. From this study, we can learn that the estimated prevalence rate of computer addiction is about 20 percent, close to that of television addiction.

5.3   British University Students' Internet Addiction

For Internet addiction, we chose an article entitled "Prevalence of pathological internet use among university students and correlations with self-esteem, the general health questionnaire (GHQ), and disinhibition"[28] as an example for our discussion. The authors are Mark Griffiths and his two graduate students Katie Niemz and Phil Banyard.

In this study, the authors administered an online survey among 371 students at Nottingham Trent University in the United Kingdom. The instrument used in the study for determining Internet addiction is a

---

[28] Niemz, K., Griffiths, M., and Banyard, P. (2005). "Prevalence of pathological Internet use among university students and correlations with self-esteem, the General Health Questionnaire (GHQ), and disinhibition," *CyberPsychology & Behavior*, 8(6): 562–570.

thirteen-item questionnaire called *Pathological Internet Use Scale* that was originally developed by two established researchers, Morahan-Martin and Schumacher. Students respond to each of these items (e.g., "I have routinely cut short on sleep to spend more time online") in a four-point Likert scale. The relevant major results indicate that: (1) out of a total of 371 students, 68 (18.3 percent) were assessed to have strong symptoms of pathological Internet use, 190 students (51.2 percent) had limited symptoms, and 113 students (30.5 percent) had no symptoms; and (2) pathological Internet use was associated with various academic, social, and interpersonal problems among the university students.

From this study, we can learn that Internet addiction existed widely among this group of university students (about 70 percent of them had strong or limited symptoms of pathological internet use), with the prevalence rate of 18 percent.

5.4 American Undergraduates' Mobile Phone Addiction

The last article we will discuss is entitled "A preliminary investigation into the prevalence and prediction of problematic cell phone use" by Peter Smetaniuk, published in the *Journal of Behavioral Addictions*.[29] This article was published in 2014 and cited twenty times based on Google Scholar. Peter Smetaniuk is a graduate student of psychology and this is his first and only publication. The *Journal of Behavioral Addictions* is a new journal that was founded in 2012, but which has published multiple articles on mobile phone addiction.

This article consists of two studies. The first study aimed to use cell phone addiction inventories to assess problematic cell phone use. In the study, 301 undergraduate students comprised primarily of psychology majors attending San Francisco State University responded to a set of inventories via an online survey process. Using the measure of the *Adapted Mobile Phone Use Habits*, it was estimated that about 20 percent of the 301 respondents had symptoms of behavioral addiction, and about 12 percent have a moderate-to-severe degree of addictive mobile phone use. The second study aimed to test if age, depression, extraversion, emotional stability, impulse control, and self-esteem as independent variables predicted respondents' perceptions of problematic use. In the study, 362 participants with the average age of 32, comprised primarily of working

---

[29] Smetaniuk, P. (2014). "A preliminary investigation into the prevalence and prediction of problematic cell phone use," *Journal of Behavioral Addictions*, 3(1): 41–53.

adults, responded to a set of inventories via an online survey process. It was found that age, depression, extraversion, and low impulse control are the most suitable predictors for problematic use of mobile phones.

From this study, we can learn that researchers have started to develop instruments to assess mobile phone addiction and to collect empirical data to document mobile phone addiction. Based on this study, the prevalence rate of mobile phone addiction is about 20 percent among the undergraduate students.

In summary, comparing the four empirical articles on different types of technology addictions that we have discussed, we can see at least one similarity and one difference among various technology addictions. First, it is clear that addictive behavior has been consistently observed with each of the four technologies, from television, computer games, and the Internet, to mobile phones. Second, various prevalence rates are related to different technology addictions, 10 percent for television addiction, 20 percent for computer game addiction, 18.3 percent for Internet addiction, and 20 percent for mobile phone addiction. However, it is hard to say which technology has higher prevalence rates or which technology is easier for users to get addicted to due to different populations recruited in these studies (e.g., American adults or British adolescents) and different instruments to determine addiction (e.g., *Television Addiction Scale*, *Pathological Internet Use Scale*, and the *Adapted Mobile Phone Use Habits*). Third, although these technology addictions have been widely reported, only online games are formally recognized and included in the new edition of DSM-5. The literature on mobile phone addiction is rapidly growing; however, at present, mobile phone addiction is not considered a typical clinical phenomenon.

6. Complex Thinking: The Best Diamond in the Crown

To end this chapter, we can use two words to summarize the existing literature on mobile phone behavior in medicine: *largest* and *best*. First, about 2,400 journal articles have been published on mobile phone behavior in medicine since 1995. It consists of about one-third of the entire literature of mobile phone behavior. Thus, the research in this specific area has produced the largest amount of the literature on mobile phone behavior. Second, the research on this area is not only strong in quantity, but also outstanding in quality. Specifically, the research on mobile technologies (e.g., development of medical apps) and mobile phone effects (e.g., effects on brain cancers and sleep) has been published in the best journals in medical science, including the *New England Journal of Medicine, Lancet,* and *JAMA*. These studies have made significant contributions to the current scientific knowledge and generated major social impacts. In short, it is safe to say that the current knowledge about mobile phone behavior is the best diamond in the crown of the knowledge of mobile phone behavior.

As we might recall from the beginning of this chapter, the young doctor revealed his intuitive knowledge about mobile phone behavior in medicine. His focus is mainly on medical data collection and management from the perspective of a medical doctor. While it is understandable, however, this intuitive knowledge does not reveal the complexity of mobile phone behavior in medicine and health care. Let us now use Figure 6.2 to review the chapter and summarize mobile phone behavior in medicine.

First, as we can see in Figure 6.2, mobile phone behavior in medicine is much more rich and complex than we might initially think. Three perspectives concern complex understanding of mobile phone behavior in the domain of medicine. (1) Each behavior in medicine concerns all *four* basic elements of mobile phone behavior, users, technologies, activities, and effects, rather than one or two, as shown in the intuitive thoughts of the young doctor. (2) From the perspective of each element, each of the four elements is actually a *complex* system that involves diverse components and cases in medicine rather than a simple system. For instance, through daily observations, scientific studies, scientific reviews, and cross-domain comparisons, we can see that mobile phone effects, even potential brain cancers, are not simple and straightforward. (3) Most importantly, while there are similarities among the basic elements in general, each element of

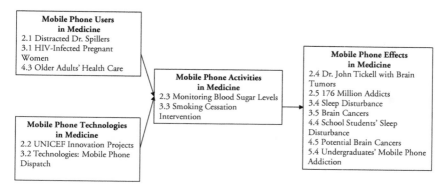

Figure 6.2   A Summary Diagram of Mobile Phone Behavior in Medicine

mobile behavior in medicine is *unique* in its complexity – users in medicine (e.g., doctors and patients), technologies in medicine (e.g., health apps and sensors), activities in medicine (e.g., management and treatment), and effects in medicine (e.g., sleep disturbance, brain cancer, and addiction). For instance, the mobile phone users are diverse and have complex components such as demographic characteristics (e.g., age and gender) and behavioral characteristics (bad, intelligence, disabled), and users in medicine include unprofessional doctors, diabetic patients with different diseases, families of patients, pregnant women, addicted teenagers, and medical staff, to name a few from an almost endless list.

Second, as we can see in Figure 6.2, future research should focus on at least the following areas to further broaden and deepen our current knowledge about the complexity of mobile phone behavior in medicine and health care: (1) for mobile phone users in medicine, further research is urgently needed to examine the effects on health of *young* children (an under-studied but crucial group); (2) for mobile phone technologies in medicine, further studies should be undertaken to investigate the latest developments and the effectiveness of *health apps* and *health sensors*; (3) for mobile phone activities in medicine, further studies should be undertaken to investigate the process of *therapy* and *treatment*; and (4) for mobile phone effects in medicine, further studies should be undertaken to assess the effects on *brain cancers* using behavior data and experimental designs.

CHAPTER 7

Mobile Phone Behavior in Business

Outline

1. *Intuitive Thinking: Henry's Quick Responses*
2. *Daily Observations: From Entrepreneurial Women in Africa to Andrew Hoog's Security Testing*
    2.1 *Business Users: Entrepreneurial Women in Africa*
    2.2 *Business Users: Sierra Leone's Girls in Transactional Sex*
    2.3 *Business Technologies: Full Mobile Phone Services in Airplanes*
    2.4 *Business Technologies: Airplanes Hacked with a Common Phone and a Special App*
    2.5 *Business Activities: Uber Operates an Innovative Taxi Business Service*
    2.6 *Business Activities: Jack Ma's Mother Cannot Get a Taxi*
    2.7 *Business Effects: From an Addicted Teen to a Millionaire CEO*
    2.8 *Business Effects: Andrew Hoog and Security Testing of Mobile Banking Apps*
3. *Empirical Studies: From Ugandan Women Entrepreneurs to Pro-Smoking Apps*
    3.1 *Business Users: Women Entrepreneurs in Uganda*
    3.2 *Business Technologies: Mobile Credit Cards*
    3.3 *Business Activities: Initial Acceptance of Mobile Banking*
    3.4 *Business Effects: Positive Effects of Travel Apps*
    3.5 *Business Effects: Negative Effects of Pro-Smoking Apps*
4. *Knowledge Syntheses: From Linear Growth to M-Payment*
    4.1 *Overview: Linear Gradual Growth*
    4.2 *Business Users: Mobile Commerce Adoption*
    4.3 *Business Activities: Mobile Payment*
5. *Comparative Analyses: From Advertisement Strategies to Economic Development Effects*
    5.1 *Advertisement*
    5.2 *Business Growth*
6. *Complex Thinking: From Henry's Quick Responses to Complex Knowledge*

1. Intuitive Thinking: Henry's Quick Responses

In the winter of 2015, I met with Henry, an old friend of mine who had been running a successful e-learning business and at the same time was a mobile phone lover. I asked him a quick question: What can people do with mobile phones in business? Can you quickly write down three to five words that come to mind? He quickly responded with four short phrases: communication; information that related to the business; business tools (planning, scheduling meetings, sales management or client management); and finance.

What can we see from his answers? First of all, he had some broad thoughts about mobile phone behavior in business. He sees mobile phones as communication and information technologies, meeting the various needs in operating and managing a business, and considers finance as one subarea of business. His short and quick responses suggest that his thoughts about mobile phones in business are *general* rather than specific (except for business management) and simple (implicitly focusing on *positive* aspects rather than both positive and negative ones). Using the four-element model, it seems that Henry mainly focused on four general activities of mobile business, but we do not see the specific complexity of users, technologies, activities, and effects involved in the mobile business behavior, even though Henry has a background of being in business for decades and has used mobile phones for years.

In this chapter, we will use this kind of general and simple thinking as our baseline knowledge. First, we will briefly introduce various cases that can be observed in daily life about mobile phone behavior in business. We will then present a few interesting empirical research examples of mobile phone behavior in business, followed by an overview of the current knowledge of mobile phone behavior in business. We will move on to compare mobile phone business behavior with different technologies, and finally, end with a summary of mobile phone behavior in business and a discussion of future research directions. After going through the intellectual journey of this chapter, we should have a better understanding of the richness and complexity of mobile phone behavior in business and develop a complex thinking about mobile phone behavior in this area.

2. Daily Observations: From Entrepreneurial Women in Africa to Andrew Hoog's Security Testing

There are many daily observations about mobile phone use in business. For instance, if you type "cases about mobile phone use in business" in

Google Search, you receive about 19,700,000 results in 0.40 seconds. Examples of topics include the serious business liability associated with employee cell phone use, increasing productivity and profitability with mobile technology, and the use of mobile phones by customers in retail stores. Let us now examine some cases that can often be observed in daily life, seen on TV, read in newspapers, or seen online. In this section, we will discuss a few interesting examples.

2.1 Business Users: Entrepreneurial Women in Africa

Lucia Njelekele is a mother of two children in Tanzania in Africa.[1] She is also a brave and smart female entrepreneur who runs a poultry farm with about 3,000 livestock. She heavily relies on her mobile phone for multiple daily business needs. These needs include: (1) to obtain real-time information about demand for her 3,000 livestock from one of Tanzania's biggest supermarkets; (2) to arrange transport; (3) to find feed; and (4) to consult her veterinarian. Recently, she planned to expand her business. She persuaded Fanikiwa Microfinance, a local finance company, to provide a loan by showing her consumption of mobile phone airtime, her mobile data purchases, and her social network interactions in her mobile phone records. First Access, a social enterprise that creates financial models for lenders such as Fanikiwa Microfinance, then used a credit scoring system designed for consumers without bank accounts and evaluated the creditworthiness of people like Lucia whose mobile data offer financial information. Going through these processes, finally, she got the loan.

In Africa, women are less likely than men to have home ownership papers, land titles, bank accounts, and other official documents. For a woman who cannot get a bank account in Tanzania, Lucia's mobile phone records become the best and actually only hard evidence of her strong financial credibility. Thus, mobile phones are not only invaluable to women as communication and transaction devices, but also offer a traceable record of activities that can then be used by companies like First Access and Fanikiwa Microfinance to further support and expand their businesses.

Similar to Lucia, Rebecca Kaduru is another entrepreneurial woman in Uganda. She started a passion fruit farm on a five-hectare plot several years ago. Passion fruit is the edible fruit of the passion flower. Early Spanish missionaries to South America felt the appearance of the passion flower

---

[1] See www.ft.com/cms/s/0/41dbff1a-8cfc-11e3-ad57-00144feab7de.html#axzz4FAW1BtmV.

symbolized many Christian beliefs and thus named the fruit in honor of the passion of Christ. Rebecca uses her mobile phone to communicate with a network of 600 young women between the ages of 14 and 20 who are part of a local passion fruit grower organization. By providing transport and relationship management with urban traders, she has helped hundreds of women obtain fair market value for their hard work. With her mobile phone, she also learned from an American development expert that her crop's earnings could increase by 200 percent if she drove 4 hours to Kampala. Her poor neighbors used to sell their crop for whatever price the local trader offered.

These two observations of mobile phone behavior in business illustrate how a unique group of users, female entrepreneurs in Africa, are benefitting from mobile phones. The mobile phone behavior involved in these two cases can be represented in the following simple diagram, with the bold text featuring the emphasized element (i.e., users in this case) from the four-element model of mobile phone behavior:

Lucia Njelekele in Tanzania + mobile phones → engaging in the poultry farm business → economic and social needs met.

Rebecca Kaduru in Uganda + mobile phones → engaging in the passion fruit farm business → economic and social needs met.

2.2   Business Users: Sierra Leone's Girls in Transactional Sex

Krystle Lai is a strategist of Africa Programs of KYNE, an international health communications consultant firm, with a graduate training in public health in developing countries from the London School of Hygiene and Tropical Medicine. Krystle speaks fluent Krio, a creole language spoken in Sierra Leone, and has worked in Sierra Leone for over five years. In January 2014,[2] she completed a case study for Save the Children and the National Secretariat for Reducing Teenage Pregnancy, two organizations in Sierra Leone. She learned several things from talking to teenage girls who served as informants for her study. The following are important highlights of the study with direct quotes from the teenage girls participating in it: (1) As one of the poorest nations across the world, mobile phones are important status symbols for Sierra Leone's teenage girls, as one girl said: "if you don't have a phone, you're not part of the civilised world." (2) In the nation's capital, Freetown, teenage girls from poor families are engaging in multiple

---

[2] See http://resourcecentre.savethechildren.se/sites/default/files/documents/mobile_phones_adolescent_
    girls_final.pdf.

forms of sexual relationships, concurrently, in order to access cash to purchase mobile phones, as a girl said: "Young girls are driven to seek older, richer men who can afford to buy them mobile phones." (3) When these girls do not have a mobile phone, they use a special way (e.g., flashlights) to communicate with different types of "papas" or "sugar daddies" to engage in transactional sex. One girl said: "For the sugar daddies, girls just flash them. They have wives so they don't like to be disturbed." (4) For some of these girls, having a mobile phone greatly increased opportunities for them to find men for prostitution, as one girl described: "the better your phone, the easier it is to find a man. Like if you have a phone, it is easier because you have Facebook. Then you can chat online. At one point, he will definitely say 'let's meet up'."

From the mobile phone behavior perspective, this study of Freetown girls is very unique for two reasons. First, when some girls in Freetown do not have a mobile phone, they use flashlights to communicate with sugar daddies. In other words, these girls are a special type of mobile phone users, i.e., non-mobile phone users. Although they cannot afford to buy a mobile phone yet, their purpose of engaging in transactional sex business is to buy a mobile phone, making this case a special type of mobile phone behavior. Generally speaking, non-mobile phone users (e.g., Russian President Putin refused to use mobile phones; some large IT company CEOs do not want their children to have mobile phones before high school) are a particularly interesting phenomenon for mobile phone behavior research. Second, when some girls in Freetown finally have a mobile phone, they move from the transactional sex business to the prostitution business and become sex workers. They are another special type of mobile phone users and mobile phones become their tools for their daily job. The above two observations are related to two special types of mobile phone behavior in business and can be illustrated in the following simple diagram, with the bold text highlighting the emphasized element:

Teenage girls in Freetown + flashlights → communicating with sugar daddies → engaged in transactional sex to earn money and buy mobile phones.

Teenage girls in Freetown + mobile phones → acquiring sex clients→ engaged in prostitution.

Comparing the two entrepreneurial women in Africa with the teenage girls engaging in transactional sex or prostitution in Freetown, we can see at least some of the complexity of mobile phone users in business. The entrepreneurial women and transactional-sex-motivated girls are all mobile phone users with the same gender and all already use or eventually use mobile phones as their business technologies. These two types of females, however, are engaging in very different business activities and resulting in very different business effects.

2.3   Business Technologies: Full Mobile Phone Services in Airplanes

On May 26, 2014,[3] Canada's Transport Minister, Lisa Raitt, announced that Canadian airlines are allowing passengers to use portable electronic gadgets such as mobile phones and tablets from the time they board an aircraft until they land, as long as they do not transmit data, thanks to new Transport Canada rules. The changes come, in part, to align with rules existing elsewhere, including the United States and Europe, which both relaxed their rules last year. This exemption applies to the use of mobile devices such as cameras, tablets, electronic games, and e-readers, from gate to gate, as long as they are in non-transmitting mode or flight mode, during takeoff and landing. Customers have been asking airlines to use their devices at all times on board an aircraft both for working and entertainment. Now using their mobile devices, airplane passengers who are businessmen can finish a memo, ordinary travelers can read a document while on the plane, and parents can have their child next to them playing Nintendo DS so the parents can have productivity time and the freedom to choose their own activities. This observation of mobile phone behavior in business can be illustrated in the following simple diagram, with the bold text representing the emphasized element:

Air Canada + **allow mobile phone devices** $\rightarrow$ providing new features and services $\rightarrow$ new good business incentives to compete with other airlines and meet passengers' demands.

2.4   Business Technologies: Airplanes Hacked with a Common Phone and a Special App

On April 12, 2013,[4] Hugo Teso, a German security analyst and licensed pilot, demonstrated in a conference that he could use just an Android phone and software he developed to remotely steal control of an airplane. Hugo spent three years developing *SIMON*, a framework of malicious code that could be used to attack and exploit airline security software, and

---

[3] See www.thestar.com/business/2014/05/26/air_travellers_can_use_electronic_devices_on_aircraft_in_canada.html.
[4] See www.cnn.com/2013/04/11/tech/mobile/phone-hijack-plane/.

PlaneSploit, an Android app for hacking. Using a flight simulator, Teso showed off the ability to change the speed, altitude and direction of a virtual airplane by sending radio signals to its flight-management system. People can use this system to modify almost everything related to the navigation of the plane. He told the crowd that the tools could also be used to do things like change what is on a pilot's display screen or turn off the lights in the cockpit. Teso told the crowd that he used flight-management hardware that he bought on eBay and publicly available flight-simulator software that contains at least some of the same computer coding as real flight software.

Teso is not the first so-called "white hat" hacker to expose what appear to be holes in air-traffic security. In 2012,[5] at the Black Hat security conference in Las Vegas, computer scientist Andrei Costin discussed weaknesses he said he found in a new US air-traffic security system set to roll out next year. The flaws he found were not instantly catastrophic, he said, but could be used to track private airplanes, intercept messages, and jam communications between planes and air-traffic control. In 2015,[6] Chris Roberts, a well-known computer security company CEO, used the last five years to improve aircraft security. The FBI accused him of overwriting code on the airplane's Thrust Management Computer while aboard a flight, successfully commanding the system to issue the "CLB" or climb command, and causing one of the airplane engines to climb, resulting in a lateral or sideways movement of the plane during flight. This mobile phone behavior can be illustrated in a simple diagram:

Hugo Teso + **an Android phone and an app** → hacking the airplane navigation system → the security vulnerability of the airplane navigation system is found.

2.5 *Business Activities: Uber Operates an Innovative Taxi Business Service*

On August 24, 2015,[7] Chris Ciaccia, a thoughtful and visionary technology journalist, predicted that Uber would have the chance of becoming one of the next big household names of the twenty-first century, just as Apple, Google, and Facebook have. The word *uber* literally means super or outstanding. *Uber* had its original company name called *UberCab* and its

---

[5] See www.cnn.com/2012/07/26/tech/web/air-traffic-control-security.

[6] See www.theregister.co.uk/2015/05/17/fbi_claims_infosec_bod_took_control_of_united_airlines_plane_midflight/.

[7] See www.nasdaq.com/article/5-next-big-tech-companies-to-go-public-cm512217#ixzz4FQR8zKw1.

current full company name is *Uber Technologies Inc.* In 2009, two San-Francisco-based entrepreneurs, Garrett Camp and Travis Kalanick, co-founded Uber. Its technical core idea is extremely simple: design, develop, and use a mobile phone application that connects passengers with drivers of vehicles for hire and ride-sharing services. Basically, a consumer with a smartphone can submit a trip request through the Uber mobile app and the request is then routed to Uber drivers who use their own cars. Uber's motto is "Everyone's private driver." Now, Uber is an American multi-national online transportation network company worth approximately $70 billion and ranked number 6 in Most Innovative Companies by Fast Company in 2013. As of May 2016, the service was available in over sixty-six countries and 449 cities worldwide. This mobile phone behavior can be illustrated in the following diagram:

Uber + Mobile phones and Uber app → **operating a new taxi business service** → helped more people to get a taxi.

2.6   Business Activities: Jack Ma's Mother Cannot Get a Taxi

On February 27, 2014,[8] Jack Ma or Yun Ma, a famous Chinese business magnate and the Founder and Chairman of Alibaba Group, texted a public message to many people. In this message, he said that his mother was having trouble getting a taxi because she did not know how to use the mobile taxi app, DiDi DaChe, China's mobile taxi app equivalent to Uber. Ironically, Jack's Alibaba invented and operates DiDi DaChe, but Jack had not taught his mother how to use it. DiDi DaChe requires the use of a specific mobile phone app, and that is why his mother was unable to get a taxi. While many elderly people own mobile phones, they do not know how to use this app. Jack's father said to him that he would have posted a big complaint already if it was not his own son's company operating the app and too many youngsters like the app. This message has very quickly spread in China. Many people share this concern and agree that if everyone uses the mobile taxi app, many old people, young kids, and even inter-national visitors would no longer be able to get a taxi easily because taxi drivers need to take those who use a taxi app to call them first. This mobile phone behavior can be illustrated in the following diagram:

Jack Ma's mom + a mobile phone and a taxi app without knowledge of using it → **trying to get a taxi she needed** → no taxi service was received.

---

[8] See http://tech.ifeng.com/bat3m/detail_2014_02/27/34263873_0.shtml.

2.7 Business Effects: From an Addicted Teen to a Millionaire CEO

In April of 2014,[9] Ruixu Wang, a Chinese undergraduate senior, developed a mobile phone app called *Student-Job Cat* for college students looking for part-time or summer jobs. After only two years, he now has become the CEO of an information technology company worth billions of dollars. Its business covers 200 cities in China, and 6 million students and 200,000 company clients use it, with 100,000 new jobs being updated every day.

Wang has come a long way to become a successful businessman. He grew up in a small business family and his parents do not have a higher education. When he was in middle school, his family's business went bankrupt and he became addicted to the Internet. Once, he and his brother stayed in a cyber bar for seven days, playing games for 12 hours per day. Soon, he became a problem teen, addicted to the Internet, smoking, drinking, and skipping classes. However, his family supported him and his late college experience provided him with scientific knowledge and business networks. Thus, he was able to turn his life around and became a Chinese version of Vincent Quigg or Grenneet Gree. This mobile phone behavior can be illustrated in the following diagram:

A cyber-addicted teen in China + the app Student-Job Cat → helping college students to find student jobs → **became a billion-dollar entrepreneur**.

2.8 Business Effects: Andrew Hoog and Security Testing of Mobile Banking Apps

Andrew Hoog is the CEO and co-founder of NowSecure, a Chicago-based mobile security company. In 2011,[10] he used viaForensics, a software program for automated testing for a variety of security flaws in apps, to test six of the most popular banking apps used by banks such as Wells Fargo, Bank of America, and the United Services Automobile Association for potential weaknesses. Only one banking app passed the test and the other five failed. There were multiple problems with the failed banking apps, including non-encrypted storage of critical information in plain text

---

[9] See http://baike.baidu.com/view/10863596.htm.
[10] See www.techrepublic.com/blog/it-security/mobile-banking-apps-may-be-vulnerable-testing-and-results/.

on the phone and easy cracking to get usernames, passwords, and all the customers' financial information in an account.

We can learn several important points from this story. First, mobile security is a real and serious problem, especially for business sectors such as banks, and especially as more technologies are developed (rapidly changing technology means developers put speed ahead of security) and more user growth is observed (this is a relatively new environment and crime follows growth). Second, problems in apps' mobile security are a small part of mobile security. Generally, mobile security concerns five major areas: (1) attacks on *communication* systems (e.g., attacks based on SMS and MMS or communication networks such as the GSM networks, Wi-Fi, and Bluetooth); (2) attacks on vulnerabilities in *software* applications, such as the web browser or operating system; (3) attacks on *hardware* vulnerabilities, such as electromagnetic waveforms and juice jacking (leaking data or installing malware through a USB charge port by utilizing malicious charging kiosks set up in public places or hidden in normal charge adapters); (4) attacks by cracking *passwords*; and (5) attacks using *malware*, such as viruses and Trojans, ransomware, and spyware. The third point we can learn from this story is that many technologies from NowSecure can be used to detect and fix the app security problems: NowSecure Forensics is a forensics tool that allows law *enforcement* users to perform a series of forensics tests on a mobile device; NowSecure Lab is a business tool that allows an *enterprise* to run attacks against their mobile apps to determine safety and privacy capabilities; NowSecure Mobile is a free mobile app for *individual* users to protect their phones using iOS or Android. The mobile phone behavior involved in this case can be illustrated in the following simple diagram:

Andrew Hoog + NowSecure → testing security of banking apps → **five of the six banking apps failed the test**.

In summary, from these cases, we can develop some new observations and knowledge about mobile phone behavior in business. First, these cases are real, specific, colorful, diverse, and complex, rather than general. They come from real life rather than from subjective ideas and pure imagination. Second, we can group these cases into four categories based on the four elements of mobile phone behavior framework: business users, business technologies, business activities, and business effects. These four basic elements are almost visible in each of the mobile phone business behaviors. Third, these cases are anecdotal observations rather than scientific evidence. Thus, some might be incomplete, some might be biased, and some might even be very much exaggerated. In short, these real-life observations can help us understand the complexity of mobile phone behavior, but cannot replace rigorous and systematic research works, which we will discuss in the following section.

3. Empirical Studies: From Ugandan Women Entrepreneurs to Pro-Smoking Apps

3.1 Business Users: Women Entrepreneurs in Uganda

Most often, the mobile phone users in business are clients, customers, or shoppers. In this section, we will start with a discussion of two types of users and their mobile phone business behavior. One type comprises 280 women entrepreneurs in Africa. The title of the article is "Usage of mobile technology among women entrepreneurs: A case study of Uganda."[11] The author is Mary Komunte, who received a Masters of Information Technology degree in 2007 from Makerere University in Kampala, Uganda. She is currently a lecturer in the Information Systems and Technology Department at the School of Computing and Engineering of Uganda Technology and Management University and a researcher undertaking PhD studies in Informatics Technology at Makerere University. Her publications and research have focused on comparative analysis or modeling and analysis of mobile phone usage among women entrepreneurs in Uganda and Kenya. She speaks English, Luganda, and Runyakitara.

The article was published in 2015 in the *African Journal of Information Systems*. Based on information available online,[12] the journal is indexed at the International Bibliography of the Social Sciences and Cabell's Directories. It aims at disseminating research on the transfer, diffusion, and adoption of information technology within the context of Africa. It is a peer-reviewed, online journal and the current editor is Peter Meso from Georgia Gwinnett College of the United States. The journal was founded with partial support from the National Science Foundation and is currently hosted at Kennesaw State University of the United States. It started in 2008 and has published quarterly for seven years. Clearly, it is a new and unique journal rather than a well-established general one. After the initial check of the author and the journal, let us now examine the article.

---

[11] Komunte, M. (2015). "Usage of mobile technology in women entrepreneurs: A case study of Uganda," *African Journal of Information Systems*, 7(3): 3.
[12] See http://digitalcommons.kennesaw.edu/ajis/about.html.

The research purpose of this mixed-methods design study was to study mobile phone usage among women entrepreneurs in Uganda. The field work was carried out between April and July 2011. The questionnaires were administered and data were collected from 280 women entrepreneurs and forty focus group participants. The major findings include the following: (1) The majority of women entrepreneurs (82.9 percent) owned micro enterprises (less than ten employees), small-scale enterprises (between ten and fifty employees) were represented by 11.8 percent of the women, while a few (5.4 percent) owned medium enterprises (between 50 and 100 employees). (2) There were seven types of businesses run by women entrepreneurs: textiles (61 percent), agricultural products (38.3 percent), beauticians (25.5 percent), hotels and restaurants (19.3 percent), schools (19.3 percent), clinics (28.3 percent), and mobile money (8.5 percent), which ranked lowest because of the high capital needed to start such a business venture. (3) A total of 47 percent of the women used both texting and calling to carry out their business transactions. The majority of the women entrepreneurs (46.1 percent) purchased their mobile phones for convenience, the next most frequently cited motivation was communication purposes (41 percent), followed by mobility (4.5 percent), and affordability (3.6 percent). (4) These women entrepreneurs reported that mobile phone services increased efficiency, productivity, and effectiveness, provided better customer service, reduced transaction costs, and encouraged price comparison and negotiations. (5) A total of 54.6 percent of these women entrepreneurs agreed that there was a tremendous increase in profits as a result of using mobile phones. The reasons cited for the increase in profits were: quick service delivery (10.4 percent), reduced transport costs (25 percent), cheaper communication (13.6 percent), easy business networking (32.1 percent), and immediacy (6.8 percent).

Although the study involves preliminary survey research, it makes contributions to the field by providing empirical descriptive evidence for what kinds of unique groups of users in Africa use mobile phones for their business, why they use them, and what kinds of effects they have had on their business. What can we learn from this article about mobile phone users in business? First, these women are unique mobile phone users, a group of women entrepreneurs in Africa. Second, they mainly needed basic mobile phone technologies to call or text rather than mobile Internet or various specific apps. They did not demand many sophisticated technologies. Third, they engaged in various business activities using mobile phones, from textiles and agricultural products, to beauticians and restaurants. Fourth, mobile phones have substantial positive effects in helping their business, including speeding up service delivery, reducing transport costs, having cheaper communication, and engaging in easy business networking. The mobile phone behavior involved in this study can be represented in the following simple diagram, with the bold text featuring the emphasized element:

280 women entrepreneurs in Uganda + mobile phones → engaging in various small business → received substantial positive effects on their business.

3.2 Business Technologies: Mobile Credit Cards

The next article is "NFC mobile credit card: The next frontier of mobile payment?"[13] NFC stands for near field communication, a short-range wireless communication technology. The authors are technology management researchers from Malaysia: Garry Wei-Han Tan, Keng-Boon Ooi, Siong-Choy Chong, and Teck-Soon Hew. The first author, Garry Wei-Han Tan, has published multiple articles on acceptance of m-payment, m-TV, and m-music. The study was published in 2014 in *Telematics and Informatics*, an interdisciplinary journal by Elsevier established in 1984 with an impact factor of 2.261, and which examines the social, economic, political, and cultural impacts and challenges of information and communication technologies. Since 2014, it has been cited sixty-one times based on Google Scholar.

In the study, the authors conducted a survey in a major bank of Malaysia. They used a very simple sampling method: every second customer who entered the bank was recruited to complete a survey. A total of 187 customers aged around 20 to 30 years old who own both a credit card and a mobile phone completed the survey. The dependent variable was intention to use mobile credit cards. The six independent variables were divided into three groups: (1) technology-related variables: perceived usefulness of mobile credit cards (e.g., believing mobile credit cards have a faster transaction time and do not need a signature) and perceived ease of using mobile credit cards (e.g., believing that using mobile credit cards does not require a lot of mental effort); (2) psychology-related variables: social influence (e.g., other people's views) and innovation technology attitude (e.g., willingness to adopt a new technology); and (3) finance-related variables: perceived financial cost (e.g., concerning mobile phone

---

[13] Tan, G. W.-H., Ooi, K.-B., Chong, S.-C., and Hew, T.-S. (2014). "NFC mobile credit card: The next frontier of mobile payment?" *Telematics and Informatics*, 31(2): 292–307.

bills, known and hidden transaction fees, or annual service fees) and perceived risk (e.g., concerning potential financial loss).

It was found that customers reported that their perceived usefulness of mobile credit cards, perceived ease of using mobile credit cards, social influence, and innovation technology attitude were significantly related to their intention to use mobile credit cards, but perceived risk and perceived financial cost were not. In other words, in Malaysia, young bank customers cared about whether mobile credit cards have more technical advantages (e.g., more useful or easier to use) than using cash or regular credit cards. These young customers were more likely to be influenced by their families, friends, and colleagues and willing and more likely to accept new technologies. However, these customers in Malaysia were not concerned about various risks and potential financial cost.

This study helps us learn more about mobile phone behavior in business. First, the mobile phone users in the study are unique: 187 young customers walking into a bank in 2013 in Malaysia, a country that has an emerging rather than established mobile payment market. Second, mobile phone technology covered in the study is unique: Mobile credit cards are a contactless credit card payment method using mobile phones and the near field communication technology. For instance, if customers need to pay a bill in a bank, they can wave their mobile phones over a special reader within 10 to 20 centimeters of distance. The reader will collect and send the mobile phone information to the bank system through the near field communication network. A wireless transaction will be completed. Mobile credit cards differ from traditional credit cards because they use mobile phones. Thus, they are wireless and digital. Mobile credit cards differ from existing mobile payment methods such as Wireless Application protocol or General Pocket Radio Service because they are based on a short-range wireless technology to transfer data between two nearby devices. Thus, they are touchless and easy to use. However, this method of choice for mobile payment has not been widely adopted, while mobile credit cards have been on the market since 2010. This puzzling situation makes mobile credit cards a good technology to study further. Third, the mobile phone activity involved in the study is very common: adopting or accepting a mobile credit card. Technology adoption or acceptance in general and mobile phone adoption and acceptance is one of the most frequently studied topics in the literature. Fourth, the mobile phone effects involved in the study are also very common: various factors contributing to early adoption were identified. The mobile phone behavior involved in the study can be summarized in a simple diagram:

187 young bank customers in Malaysia + **mobile credit cards** → deciding whether they want to use mobile credit cards → identified technology-related and psychology-related factors contributed to early adoption.

3.3 Business Activities: Initial Acceptance of Mobile Banking

Another article on mobile business activity is entitled "Examining multi-dimensional trust and multi-faceted risk in initial acceptance of emerging technologies: An empirical study of mobile banking services."[14] The authors are four researchers on management information systems from four American universities, Xin Luo, Han Li, Jie Zhang, and J. P. Shim. The article was published in 2010 in *Decision Support Systems*. Since its publication, it has been cited 100 times based on Web of Science as a highly cited paper and 372 times based on Google Scholar.

The study aimed to understand how various perceived risks and perceived trusts among young people influence their mobile banking acceptance. A total of 180 American undergraduate students participated in a survey study. The dependent variable used in the study is intention of accepting mobile banking services. The eight risk-related independent variables are: performance risk (e.g., the risk that a banking app performs very poorly), financial risk (e.g., the risk that a banking service has financial fraud), time risk (e.g., the risk of taking too long to learn a new banking app), psychological risk (e.g., the risk of experiencing extra anxiety), physical risk (e.g., the risk of getting brain cancers due to cell phone use for a longer time), social risk (e.g., the risk of getting embarrassed in front of friends), privacy risk (e.g., the risk of losing privacy after using mobile banking apps), and overall risk. The three trust-related independent variables were: (1) overall trust in humankind; (2) general trust in mobile banking (e.g., whether mobile banking has high-quality legal and technical systems in place); and (3) specific trust in the vendor (e.g., whether a bank respects and cares about its customers).

The major findings include the following: (1) Among all the eight risk-related variables, all but physical and social risk were not significant indicators of perceived risk. Perceived risk significantly and negatively influenced participants' intention of accepting mobile banking services.

---

[14] Luo, X., Li, H., Zhang, J., and Shim, J. P. (2010). "Examining multi-dimensional trust and multi-faceted risk in initial acceptance of emerging technologies: An empirical study of mobile banking services," *Decision Support Systems*, 49(2): 222–234.

In other words, when customers decide if they use mobile banking, they are concerned about mobile banking in terms of its potential performance risk, financial risk, time risk, psychological risk, privacy risk, and overall risk, but not about physical and social risks. (2) Among the three trust-related variables, except for specific trust in a vendor, general trust in mobile banking and overall trust in humans indirectly influence participants' intention of accepting mobile banking services only through perceived risk. In other words, between perceived risk and perceived trust, perceived risk is the primary factor negatively related to the initial acceptance, and perceived trust is the secondary factor negatively related to the initial acceptance.

From the mobile phone behavior perspective, the most useful insight from this study is that the early acceptance of mobile banking is a specific mobile activity and potential customers will worry about various kinds of risk involved in mobile banking. Thus, it is critical to address these perceived risks (i.e., potential performance risk, financial risk, time risk, psychological risk, privacy risk, and overall risk) to attract more mobile phone users to use mobile banking. The mobile phone behavior involved in this study can be represented in the following simple diagram, with the bold text featuring the emphasized element:

180 undergraduate students in the United States + mobile banking → **engaging in early acceptance of mobile banking** → six perceived risks were directly related to mobile banking acceptance.

3.4   Business Effects: Positive Effects of Travel Apps

The empirical article we examine now reveals a positive effect of mobile phone behavior in business. Its title is "The role of smartphones in mediating the touristic experience."[15] The three authors are: Dan Wang and Daniel Fesenmaier from Temple University in the United States and Sangwon Park from the University of Surrey in the United Kingdom. It was published in 2012 in *Journal of Travel Research*, the premier research journal focusing on travel and tourism behavior, management, and development, published by Sage. It has been the official research publication of the Travel and Tourism Research Association since 1968, with an impact factor of 2.905. Since its publication, this article has been cited 192 times according to Google Scholar.

---

[15] Wang, D., Park, S., and Fesenmaier, D. R. (2012). "The role of smartphones in mediating the touristic experience," *Journal of Travel Research*, 51(4): 371–387.

In this study, the authors creatively used custom reviews posted in the 100 most popular travel apps as the data to analyze the effects of smartphones on the experience of tourists. Among a total of 37,133 records of custom reviews related to travel, through a three-step screening procedure, the author identified 202 viable storytelling reviews as the narrative data for further content analysis. The major findings are as follows: (1) The 100 most popular travel apps serve various specific needs. These needs belong to eleven categories, such as flight information manager, destination guides, online travel agency, entertainment, food finder, and language assistant. (2) The travel apps have fourteen types of positive effects on traveling experiences, such as (a) getting good value out of trips (e.g., the app *Line* guides a family visiting Disney World to attractions with the shortest waiting lines), (b) improving efficiency (e.g., the app *Flight Update Pro* informs tourists about flight delays and terminal changes on a timely basis), (c) making life easy (e.g., the app *TripIt* quickly generates a detailed itinerary for a businessman's complicated eleven-day trip), (d) making trips more fun (e.g., the app *Air Traffic Control* enables travelers to hear interesting conversations between flight pilots and the ground control team), (e) visiting more places (e.g., the app *Roadside America* leads vacationers to great places they have never heard about), and (f) sharing happiness (e.g., the app *MouseWait* developed an online community for Disney World visitors to meet amazing new friends).

We can learn quite a lot from this study about various types of interesting mobile phone behavior in the tourism business. First, there are many mobile phone users involved in tourism: tourist providers, government officers, involved communities, indigenous groups, and, of course, tourists with diverse needs. Second, there are many great mobile apps for tourists on the market. The study introduced a few from the 100 most popular apps such as *Roadside America* or *TripIt*. Third, there are many mobile activities related to travel, including planning reservations, navigation, finding resting rooms, estimating waiting time, sending travel photos to family members, and generating online word of mouth to share experiences. Fourth, there are many positive effects of these apps on tourists physically (e.g., saving waiting time), cognitively (e.g., inspiring vacationers with new places), socially (e.g., meeting new friends), and emotionally (e.g., sharing happiness). The mobile phone behavior involved in this study can be represented in the following simple diagram, with the bold text featuring the emphasized element:

202 tourists who used travel apps and posted storytelling reviews + 100 most popular traveling apps → engaging in various travel activities → **had fourteen kinds of positive experiences with travel apps.**

3.5   Business Effects: Negative Effects of Pro-Smoking Apps

The empirical article we will now examine is entitled "Pro-smoking apps for smartphones: The latest vehicle for the tobacco industry?"[16] In contrary to the previous study which focused on a positive effect, this study reveals a negative effect of mobile apps. The authors are Nasser BinDhim, Becky Freeman, and Lyndal Trevena, three public health researchers from the University of Sydney in Australia. The article was published in 2012 in *Tobacco Control*, a well-established journal publishing the nature and consequences of tobacco use worldwide since 1992, with an impact factor of 6.321. It has a mobile site at http://m.tobaccocontrol.bmj.com/ and even an iPad app. The publisher is the BMJ (originally called the British Medical Journal or BMJ Group), a well-known international health-care publication company owned by the British Medical Association. Over the past fifty years, it has pioneered digital publication and open access.

The study was conducted in 2012. The authors searched the Apple App Store and Android Market to find apps that provided explicit pro-smoking contents (e.g., various brands of tobacco and specific locations to buy cigarettes) and encouraged smoking behavior (e.g., smoking games). No human subjects were involved. The major findings include the following: (1) From the initial search result of 1,400 apps, the authors identified 107 pro-smoking apps. (2) There are six major types of pro-smoking apps, tobacco shop apps (e.g., listing famous cigarette brands with images), smoking simulation apps (e.g., a cartoon game where users can have game characters smoke or pass the cigarettes to other characters), wallpaper apps (e.g., showing the famous brand Marlboro in 3D images), cigarette battery (e.g., using an image of burning cigarettes to indicate the battery life percentage), smoking advocacy (e.g., promoting the freedoms of cigar enthusiasts), and cigarette rolling demonstration (e.g., showing how to roll a cigarette in various shapes). (3) In the Android Market, in one month of 2012, about 11 million unique users downloaded the pro-smoking apps. Among all the six categories of pro-smoking apps, the most popular app categories were smoking simulation apps and tobacco shop apps.

From the perspective of mobile phone behavior in business, the findings of this study teach us a few things. First, mobile phones can be used to bring a *negative* rather than a positive effect to users. This study shows that 107 apps were created to promote smoking, a harmful health behavior, in

---

[16] BinDhim, N. F., Freeman, B., and Trevena, L. (2014). "Pro-smoking apps for smartphones: The latest vehicle for the tobacco industry?" *Tobacco Control*, 23(1): e4–e4.

six major categories. Second, the 107 pro-smoking apps have a *large* rather than small market. For instance, 11 million users from around the world downloaded these pro-smoking apps from the Android Market alone within one month. The mobile phone behavior involved in this unique empirical study can be represented in the following simple diagram, with the bold text featuring the emphasized element:

11 million mobile users in the world + 107 pro-smoking apps → downloading these apps from Apple App Store and Android Market → **exposed to six types of pro-smoking experiences.**

4. Knowledge Syntheses: From Linear Growth to M-Payment

4.1 Overview: Linear Gradual Growth

To estimate the scope of the existing literature on mobile phone behavior, let us search three major databases: Web of Science, PsycINFO, and Business Source Complete. An initial search on Web of Science (one of the largest databases on social and natural sciences) with two keywords, business and mobile phone, in combination, yields 334 journal articles and seven reviews. An initial search on Business Source Complete (one of the best databases on business) using the combination of keywords mobile phone and business yields 165 journal articles. An initial search of the existing literature on PsycINFO (one of the widely used databases on behavioral science) using the combination of keywords cellular phones/ mobile device and business/commerce leads to 124 journal articles. From these articles, we can see the following features: (1) These articles cover a wide variety of topics, such as consumer behavior, product quality, self-efficacy, privacy, travel, health, advertisement, retail, adoption, diffusion, and client switch. (2) These articles are scattered around various outlets for dissemination, including *Computers in Human Behavior* and *Decision System.* Many of these journals are familiar to neither regular readers nor those from the major business science journals such as *Harvard Business Review, Business Science Quarterly,* or *Business Science Quarterly Review.* (3) Three to four dissertations are included, an important sign of emerging paradigms based on Thomas Kuhn's theory.[17] This is because younger generations of researchers are in training, supported by established scholars on their dissertation committee. (4) Rather surprisingly, the trend of journal article publications over time is a gradual linear growth rather than

[17] Kuhn, T. S. (2012). *The Structure of Scientific Revolutions.* University of Chicago Press.

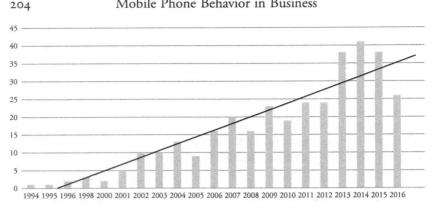

Figure 7.1   The Linear Growth Trend of Journal Article Publications on Mobile Phone
Behavior in Business

an exponential growth, different from the general trend of the mobile phone
behavior literature (compare Figure 7.1 with Figure 1.3 in Chapter 1). This
trend is interesting, indicating that researchers have been consistently contributing to the literature of mobile phone behavior in business for the past
two decades rather than over the past few years.

After seeing some general features for the business mobile phone
behavior literature, let us take a look at the coverage of mobile phone
behavior in business in the *Encyclopedia of Mobile Phone Behavior*. One of
the benefits of checking the *Encyclopedia* is to *easily* see how some of the
established researchers in the field of business science have reviewed *major*
research achievements in mobile phone behavior. Although, like all the
publications, the *Encyclopedia* is not perfect, it does provide some baseline
information in this area to help us learn about the existing knowledge a bit
more effectively and efficiently, compared to searching for the literature by
ourselves.

As shown in Table 7.1, the *Encyclopedia* has a major section on mobile
phone behavior in business that consists of twelve chapters. These chapters
synthesize the literature on the four basic elements of mobile phone
behavior in business, i.e., business users, business technologies, business
activities, and business effects. From these chapter titles, we can see at least
a few things. First, for business users, *consumers* are the users that have
been reviewed the most (e.g., the chapter on "Consumer adoption of
mobile e-WOM messages"), although business users are much more
diverse (e.g., human resource managers in the chapter on "Human
resource recruiting and selection using cellphone apps"). Second, for

Table 7.1 *The* Encyclopedia *Chapters on Mobile Phone Behavior in Business*

Element	Chapter Title
Users	Generation Y and mobile marketing in India
Users	Consumer adoption of mobile e-WOM messages
Technologies	Human resource recruiting and selection using cellphone apps
Technologies	Mobile coupons: Adoption and use
Technologies	Branded mobile apps: Possibilities for advertising in an emergent mobile channel
Activities	Consumer acceptance of the mobile Internet
Activities	Empirical research methods for evaluating affective satisfaction of consumer products
Activities	Understanding mobile phone usage through a value-based approach: Marketing implications
Activities	Generation, collection and recycling of used and end-of-life mobile phones
Activities	Communication privacy management and mobile phone use
Activities	Sustainability of the use of mobile phones
Effects	Mobile technostress

business technologies, *business apps* are often examined (e.g., "Human resource recruiting and selection using cellphone apps"). Third, for business activities, *adaptation* is the most examined topic, reflecting on the initial stage of adoption, use, and diffusion of mobile phones based on the technology diffusion theory.[18] This is consistent with the empirical articles discussed in the previous section. Fourth, for business effects, it seems that we do not have a good coverage in the *Encyclopedia* on this topic as the major focus, although every chapter has to deal with business effects directly or indirectly as an inherent element of any mobile phone behavior.

4.2 Business Users: Mobile Commerce Adoption

The second review article we will discuss focuses on another specific and popular topic – how people will adopt mobile commerce. It is entitled "A meta-analysis of mobile commerce adoption and the moderating effect of culture."[19] As of 2016, it was cited ninety-five times in Google Scholar. The authors are three Chinese scholars in information technology and management, Liyi Zhang, Jing Zhu, and Qihua Liu. It was published in

[18] Rogers, E. M. (2010). *Diffusion of Innovations*. New York: Simon & Schuster.
[19] Zhang, L., Zhu, J., and Liu, Q. (2012). "A meta-analysis of mobile commerce adoption and the moderating effect of culture," *Computers in Human Behavior*, 28(5): 1902–1911.

2007 in *Computers and Human Behavior*, a well-established scholarly Elsevier journal dedicated to examining the use of computers from a psychological perspective since 1985, with an impact factor of 2.880.

This review mainly focuses on what factors will significantly impact m-commerce adoption. It consists of the following sections: introduction, theoretical models, methods, results, and discussion. The highlights of the review include the following: (1) Mobile commerce is a new form of electronic commerce and refers to various business activities conducted via wireless telecommunication technologies, such as mobile ticketing, mobile banking, mobile marketing, and mobile transaction. (2) Three major theories have been used in various studies to examine how different factors influence mobile commerce adoption, that is, the Technology Acceptance Theory (focusing on individual perceptions such as attitudes), the Theory of Planned Behavior (focusing on social perceptions such as the perceived social norm held by other people), and the Innovation Diffusion Theory (focusing on innovation features such as technical advantages). Based on these theories, the authors developed an analytic framework to review the literature. (3) A total of fifty-three articles were carefully selected for meta-analysis, including thirty-nine journal articles, eleven conference proceeding papers, two theses, and one program report. The total sample size from all of these articles is nearly 20,000. (4) Based on these fifty-three articles, the strongest relationship is found between individuals' *attitudes* toward m-commerce and their intention to adopt m-commerce and between individuals' *perceived usefulness* and their attitudes. (4) Cultural differences exist. In Eastern culture, the perceived *ease* of use plays the most important role in m-commerce adoption, whereas in Western culture, the perceived *usefulness* is the most vital factor.

This is a well-written and high-quality meta-analysis. It provides a big picture of how to improve m-commerce adoption. From the perspective of mobile phone behavior in business, we can learn two important lessons from this meta-analysis. First, mobile phone users' attitudes and perceptions matter. To attract more people to use m-commerce and achieve higher levels of m-commerce adoption, we should pay more attention to how users will think about m-commerce rather than what technologies should be developed. Specifically, the two most user-related factors are individuals' attitudes toward m-commerce and its perceived usefulness, besides various other user-related factors such as social norms and perceived cost. Second, mobile phone users' cultural backgrounds matter. To persuade more users to adopt m-commerce, we should consider certain cultural differences; for uses with the Eastern culture background, the perceived *ease* of use should be emphasized, whereas for users with the Western culture background, the perceived *usefulness* should be emphasized.

4.3   Business Activities: Mobile Payment

After briefly discussing the *Encyclopedia* chapter, let us now discuss a review article entitled "Past, present and future of mobile payments research: A literature review."[20] This paper is well cited, 467 times based on Google Scholar. The four authors – Tomi Dahlberg, Niina Mallat, Jan Ondrus, and Agnieszka Zmijewska – are from three European countries. The first author, Professor Tomi Dahlberg, has published multiple studies on mobile payment. The article was published in 2008 in *Electronic Commerce Research and Applications*, a relatively established Elsevier journal publishing e-commerce research since 2002, with an impact factor of 2.139.

This review consists of four major sections: framework, method, results and discussion. In other words, the authors followed the general structure of empirical studies to present their review work. The major points from this review include the following: (1) Mobile payments are payments for goods, services, and bills with a mobile device (such as a mobile phone, smartphone, or personal digital assistant) by taking advantage of wireless and other communication technologies. (2) Mobile devices can be used in a variety of payment scenarios, such as payment for digital content (e.g., ringtones, logos, news, music, or games), tickets, parking fees, transport fares, or to access electronic payment services to pay bills and invoices. Payments for physical goods are also possible, both at vending and ticketing machines, and at manned point-of-sale terminals. (3) A mobile payment is carried out with a mobile payment instrument such as a mobile credit card or mobile wallet. (4) Mobile payments, as all other payments, fall broadly into two categories: payments for daily purchases and payments of bills (i.e., credited payments). For purchases, mobile payments complement or compete with cash, checks, credit cards, and debit cards. For bills, mobile payments typically provide access to account-based payment instruments such as money transfers, Internet banking payments, direct debit assignments, or electronic invoice acceptance. (5) In the early 2000s, mobile payment services became a hot topic. Hundreds of mobile

---

[20] Dahlberg, T., Mallat, N., Ondrus, J., and Zmijewska, A. (2008). "Past, present and future of mobile payments research: A literature review," *Electronic Commerce Research and Applications*, 7(2): 165–181.

payment services, including access to electronic payments and Internet banking, were introduced all over the world. Strikingly, many of these efforts failed. For example, most, if not all, of the dozens of mobile payment services available in countries of the European Union and listed in the database of electronic point-of-sale terminals in 2002 have been discontinued. (6) In total, the authors identified seventy-three peer-reviewed journal articles and conference papers that were published between 1999 and 2006, after searching nine databases and fifteen conferences. Among the seventy-three publications, twenty-nine are about m-payment techniques and twenty are about m-payment consumers; among the thirty empirical studies, fifteen are qualitative and ten are quantitative. (7) The authors developed and used a conceptual framework to analyze the existing literature and predict future directions. This framework has four environmental factors (technological, cultural, commercial, and legal factors) and five business factors (competition among m-payment service providers, consumer power, merchant power, traditional payment services, and new e-payment services). (8) Most studies focus on technical factors (e.g., system design, tools and protocols) and consumer factors (e.g., adaptation and perception), specifically in three areas (attractiveness, risk, and anxiety).

Although this review focuses more on mobile payment services from the business management perspective, it shows that a substantial number of studies have examined mobile payment behavior. As a result, we can see an overall complex picture of mobile payment and a specific synthesis of diverse mobile payment behavior.

5.   Comparative Analyses: From Advertisement Strategies to Economic Development Effects

5.1   Advertisement

One of the common marketing strategies is to use advertisements. Will mobile advertisement differ from newspaper advertisement, television advertisement, and Internet advertisement? The first comparative study we will discuss next addresses this question. Its title is "Effective advertising on mobile phones: A literature review and presentation of results from 53 case studies."[21] As one of the most comprehensive studies on m-

---

[21] Park, T., Shenoy, R., and Salvendy, G. (2008). "Effective advertising on mobile phones: A literature review and presentation of results from 53 case studies," *Behaviour & Information Technology*, 27(5): 355–373.

advertisement, it was cited ninety-six times based on Google Scholar. The authors are Taezoon Park, Rashmi Shenoy, and Gavriel Salvendy from Purdue University. The corresponding author Gavriel Salvendy is an eminent scholar in human factors and ergonomics. The article was published in *Behaviour & Information Technology*, a well-established Taylor & Francis journal specializing in human factors since 1982, with an impact factor of 1.211.

The review consists of four main sections on mobile advertisement: concepts, models, factors, and cases. The major points include the following: (1) Advertisement is a common marketing strategy to develop an image of products, services, and business to stimulate direct purchase. The three generations of advertisement are (a) billboards, newspapers, and magazines, (b) radio and TV, and (c) Internet and mobile networks. Each of them has different features such as mode, presentation type, and advertisement type. (2) Mobile advertising includes messages (short message service, enhanced messaging service, and multimedia messaging service), mobile banners, ringtones, screen savers, wallpapers, and mobile games. It can be used for promotions, event marketing, branded content marketing, and branded customer relationship marketing. (3) There are four basic models of advertisement processing (i.e., market response model, intermediate effect model, hierarchy effect model, and hierarchy-free model), explaining how consumer behavior is related to experience, cognition, and emotion. (4) Three types of factors influence the effects of mobile advertisement: advertisement factors (e.g., design and content), environmental factors (e.g., exposure time and repetition), and audience factors (e.g., experience and attitude). (5) Fifty-three cases were examined, indicating that most mobile advertisement is for entertaining companies, targeting young populations, and involves multimedia. (6) Mobile advertisement features limited space, multimedia support, and personal involvement.

Overall, the article functions as a hybrid of theory integration, literature review, and case studies. It does not specify the literature scope and search strategies. However, it provides a clear picture of differences in advertisement between the three generations of media. It helps us better understand the mobile advertisement in a broad context.

5.2   Business Growth

The second comparative study is entitled "The economic impact of information and communication technologies (ICTs) on microenterprises in the context of development."[22] It was written by two Michigan State University scholars, Han Ei Chew and Mark Levy, and one scholar from India, P. Vigneswara Ilavarasan. Mark Levy is an eminent scholar in communication and technologies. Han Ei Chew was one of his mentees and is now an established scholar. The three authors have published multiple articles on the impacts of mobile phones on economic and social development. The article we will be discussing was published in 2010 in the *Electronic Journal on Information Systems in Developing Countries*, a widely recognized journal specializing in technologies for social and economic development. The journal has seventy-five volumes and has been edited by David Robinson, a Professor in Cross-Cultural studies of Information Systems at the City University of Hong Kong, since 2000. As a unique and strong peer-reviewed open-access e-journal (www.ejisdc.org), the journal is becoming the foremost international forum for practitioners, teachers, researchers, and policy makers to share their knowledge and experience in the design, development, implementation, management, and evaluation of information systems and technologies in developing countries.

This empirical study examined how four information and communication technologies (landline phones, mobile phones, computers, and the Internet), influence economic development for microenterprises (with one to twenty employees) owned by women microentrepreneurs in Mumbai, the commercial capital of India. A random cluster probability sampling was used to obtain research participants. A total of 231 women microentrepreneurs participated in a 30-minute interview conducted in 2009. The interview covered multiple issues about these women microentrepreneurs, including: (1) *business growth* (e.g., their annual incomes); (2) *technology access* (e.g., whether they had mobile phones for business); (3) *business formality* (how formally they ran their business, e.g., whether they registered their business with the government or had business bank accounts); (4) *motivations* to use technologies for their business (e.g., having mobile phones to know price information on a timely basis); and (5) *perceived social status* (e.g., receiving more respect from friends and neighbors). The major findings include the following: (1) Among 231 women microentrepreneurs, 87 percent were married, had on average two children, were aged 35 years old on average, and 52 percent had high-school or middle-school

---

[22] Chew, H. E., Ilavarasan, P. V., and Levy, M. R. (2010). "The economic impact of information and communication technologies (ICTs) on microenterprises in the context of development," *Electronic Journal of Information Systems in Developing Countries*, 44(4): 1–19.

educations. They typically hired six workers, most of them had been in business for ten years, 56 percent of them were in the sales business, including restaurants, clothing sales, groceries, and small electronics, 43 percent of them were in the service business, including medical care, taxicabs, tours, tutoring, or beauty salons, and only over 1 percent of them were in the manufacturing business, typically making dresses or leather goods. (2) Mobile phones were the most used technologies by the women microentrepreneurs (88 percent of them), whereas computers and Internet were used only by about 15 percent of them. (3) About 50 percent of women microentrepreneurs had a positive attitude toward mobile phones, and felt that mobile phones could help their business survive and grow, and could enable them to always receive important business calls. (4) Technology access and business formality were two significant predictors of their business growth (technology access was positively related and business formality was negatively related), but business motivations and perceived social status were not significant predictors.

In the section on everyday observations, we discussed how two African women entrepreneurs used the mobile phones for their poultry farm business or passion fruit farm business. In the section on empirical studies, we also discussed how mobile phones benefited 280 African women entrepreneurs. This empirical study generates interesting comparative data from 231 Indian women microentrepreneurs. It provides scientific evidence that mobile phones were the most used technologies by the women microentrepreneurs, compared with landline phones, computers, and the Internet, and technology access is both significantly and positively associated with their business growth, compared with business formality, business motivations, and perceived social status. These kinds of comparative findings make it easier to see important impacts of mobile phone use on women microentrepreneurs.

6. Complex Thinking: From Henry's Quick Responses to Complex Knowledge

Recall that Henry's responses to mobile phone behavior in business were quite simple (primarily focusing on the positive effects) and quite general (mainly mentioning four broad aspects of business activities). Starting from that baseline knowledge, we discussed nearly ten daily observations, five empirical studies, two reviews, and two comparative studies and have gone through quite an interesting intellectual journey.

Let us now use Figure 7.2 and briefly review the complexity of mobile phone behavior in business. First, for business users, we discussed two

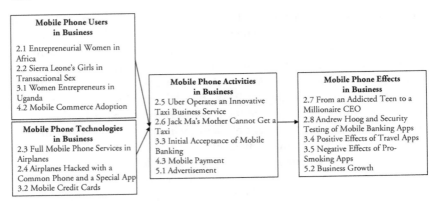

Figure 7.2   A Summary Diagram of Mobile Phone Behavior in Business

amazing entrepreneurial women in Africa who ran their farm business successfully. We also discussed a special group of teenage girls in Freetown in Sierra Leone engaging in transactional sex and prostitution. They are all female mobile phone users in Africa, but are involved in two very different businesses – one flourishing, but another devastating. We then further discussed one empirical study about how mobile phones helped 280 entrepreneurial women in Uganda. In the end, we discussed an excellent meta-analysis of fifty-three empirical studies about what factors influence mobile phones users' adoption of mobile commerce. We have learned that users' attitudes and cultural backgrounds play an important role. Compared with Henry's responses in which he hardly considered mobile users, we now have much more sophisticated knowledge about business users – the first basic element in mobile phone behavior.

Second, for business technologies, we discussed two somehow contrasting cases, one about airplane companies adding full mobile phone services to compete for more clients, and another about Hugo Teso using an Android phone and an app to hack the airplane navigation system, showing its security vulnerability. As a modern technology, mobile phones could either lead to increased airline business or decreased flight security. We then discussed an empirical study on how 187 young bank customers in Malaysia decided whether they will consider using a relatively new technology – mobile credit cards. Compared with Henry's responses in which he did not mention any mobile phone technologies, we can have more insights into the complexity of technologies in business: technologies can lead to both positive and negative effects and good technologies might not be adopted automatically.

Third, for business activities, we discussed two somehow contrasting cases again. One was about Uber enjoying tremendous business success primarily based on its mobile phone apps, and another was about the mother of the CEO of a mobile taxi company in China not being able to get a taxi simply because she did not know how to use the taxi app. For the same mobile taxi business, it can either help people get the taxi service or prevent people from getting a taxi. Through an empirical study on initial acceptance of mobile banking among 180 American undergraduate students, we learned that early acceptance of mobile banking itself is an important mobile activity since it is a gateway to various other mobile phone activities. Furthermore, this activity is influenced by potential performance risk, financial risk, time risk, psychological risk, privacy risk, and overall risk in the minds of these students. We also discussed a review article on mobile payment. The authors reviewed seventy-three peer-reviewed journal articles and conference papers and synthesized a comprehensive knowledge of mobile payment as an important mobile phone activity. Finally, from the comparative study on advertisement using different technologies, we can see the uniqueness and complexity of mobile advertisement processes. From mobile taxi operations, mobile banking, mobile payment, to mobile advertisement, we can see many more diverse activities than Henry's four general business management activities (planning, scheduling, sales management, and client management).

Fourth, for business effects, again, we started with two somehow contrasting cases. One was about how a young Chinese man grew up from an addicted teen to become a billionaire CEO, and another was about how various security problems were found in mobile banking apps (from a negative effect). The first case shows a surprising turnaround from a negative effect (being addicted to online games) to a positive effect (developing a great company); and the second case shows another surprising turnaround from a positive effect (developing mobile banking apps) to a negative effect (finding various security holes). After that, we learned about two empirical studies on the positive effects of traveling apps and negative effects of pro-smoking apps. We ended with a comparative study of effects of different technologies on business growth, while mobile phones stand out as the best used and best valued means for women entrepreneurs in India. Again, we should have a much richer and more comprehensive understanding of the complexity of effects of mobile phone behavior in business.

In short, Figure 7.2 displays an overall picture of mobile phone behavior in business and summarizes the essential contents discussed in this chapter.

We might be a bit surprised to see that: (1) ordinary people's intuitive responses could be so simple and general; (2) scientific knowledge in this area could be so complex and specific; (3) although the current literature is extensive, it is not as extensive as it is in mobile phone behavior in medicine; and (4) many new or remaining questions (e.g., diversity of business users, emerging business technologies, business activities in various sections, and complexity of business effects) need to be addressed to better understand mobile phones in business.

CHAPTER 8

Mobile Phone Behavior in Education

Outline

1. *Intuitive Thinking: Tom's Quick Responses*
2. *Daily Observations: From Generation Text to Sexting*
   - 2.1 *Educational Users: Generation Text and a Retired Teacher*
   - 2.2 *Educational Technologies: A Campus App and Pokémon Go*
   - 2.3 *Educational Activities: Texting Champion and Sexting Ring*
   - 2.4 *Educational Effects: A Learning Aid and a Student Lawsuit*
3. *Empirical Studies: From Generation Text to Learning Distraction*
   - 3.1 *Educational Users: Norwegian Youths*
   - 3.2 *Educational Technologies: Bar Code*
   - 3.3 *Educational Activities: Learning in a Biology Class*
   - 3.4 *Educational Effects: Learning Distraction*
4. *Knowledge Syntheses: From Disabled Learners to Distractive Effects*
   - 4.1 *Overview: A Relatively Small Research Area*
   - 4.2 *Educational Users: Learners with Special Needs*
   - 4.3 *Educational Technologies: Tablets*
   - 4.4 *Educational Activities: Mobile Learning Trends*
   - 4.5 *Educational effects: Mobile Phone Multitasking*
5. *Comparative Study: Media Multitasking for Youth*
6. *Complex Thinking: From Tom's Responses to Complex Behavior*

1. Intuitive Thinking: Tom's Quick Responses

Tom is a well-known Chinese language professor and a good friend of mine. I asked him during the Christmas holiday season of 2015: What can people do with mobile phones in education, teaching, or learning? Can you quickly write down the first three to five words that come to mind? With a festive mood, he quickly replied with the following responses:

1. Study/learn foreign languages.
2. Send homework assignments to students.

3. Send links to YouTube videos for foreign language study.
4. Look up Chinese characters or words I do not know or have forgotten.

Tom's responses offer a good profile of him as a mobile phone user: a university professor who loves teaching and whose expertise is studying Chinese. From the perspective of mobile phone behavior in education, we can learn a few interesting things. First, from the mobile user perspective, his responses represent a typical educational user – a professor teaching and studying Chinese at university. Second, from the mobile technology perspective, the educational technologies involved are general and limited, mainly concerning mobile texting, mobile video, and mobile Internet. Third, from the mobile activity perspective, his mobile activities focus on learning, studying, and teaching Chinese as a foreign language. Fourth, from the mobile effect perspective, he focused on positive cognitive effects on learning, studying, and teaching. In short, his responses are quite normal and understandable based on his own professional experience. Thus, these responses are personalized based on his own unique experience and limited to a specific area of his profession.

However, are these responses typical of other people's perspectives or everyday observations? Are they consistent with current research? How much do we know about mobile phone behavior in education? Do we know more about mobile phone behavior in education than we know in other domains such as medicine or business? What needs to be studied to promote learning, teaching, instruction, schooling, and education? This chapter is intended to address these questions. Overall, after reading this chapter you will be able to appreciate much more the complexity of mobile phone behavior in education.

2.   Daily Observations: From Generation Text to Sexting

2.1   Educational Users: Generation Text and a Retired Teacher

Generation Text.[1] Dr. Larry Rosen is a Professor of Psychology at California State University, Dominguez Hills. He is an expert on the psychology of digital technologies and meanwhile is a happy dad of four children. One of his research areas is generational differences, that is, generational characteristics, values, and beliefs that differ among and between the Baby Boomers (born around the 1940s to 1960s), Generation

---

[1] See www.cnn.com/2010/OPINION/02/08/rosen.texting.communication.teens/.

X (born around the 1960s to 1980s), the Net Generation (born around the 1980s to 1990s), and the iGeneration (born around the 2000s to 2010s, relating to the use of iPhone, iPod, or iTunes). He himself is a Baby Boomer and has raised four children: two Generation Xers, one Net Generation young adult, and one iGeneration teenager. He has learned firsthand that the generations are different in their lifestyles, attitudes, and use of technology. On February 11, 2010, he told a story on CNN about trying to contact his youngest daughter, Kaylee, who was 19 years old at that time. One day, he called her and left a voicemail and sent an e-mail, but did not get a response. He finally texted her and told her to check his voice message on the phone and his e-mail to her. Seconds later, he received a text from his daughter with one single letter: "K" (i.e., OK). He said that his daughter has been sending and receiving over 3,000 texts per month, i.e., 300 per day, but this is normal and she is not unusual at all. According to Nielsen Mobile, a leading market information company, in 2009, the average US teen sent and received 3,146 messages per month. Thus, Larry Rosen called the iGeneration of his daughter Generation Text.

His daughter is a *typical* mobile user in education because she is a student and uses a mobile phone. Students in elementary school, middle school, high school, and college are the largest group of mobile phone users in today's education. However, on the other hand, she belongs to Generation Text rather than the Net Generation. Thus, she is a *special* mobile phone user in education because she shares several unique characteristics of her Generation Text. The mobile phone behavior observed in this case can be illustrated in a simple diagram:

Dr. Larry Rosen's youngest daughter Kaylee + mobile phones → texting rather than calling very frequently in her daily life → exemplified characteristics of Generation Text.

A retired teacher.[2] On June 16, 2015, Miriam Morgenstern, a history and English-as-second-language teacher in Lowell High School, decided to retire after twenty years of teaching. One of the major reasons was that she no longer wanted to compete with mobile phone distraction at school. She told *Boston Global*, a Boston-based daily newspaper, that texting, tweeting, and Snapchatting during class time are an incredible distraction, and make it much more difficult to teach. Many in the pro-technology camp say that students are not distracted if their teachers are engaging, a statement that irritates Miriam Morgenstern. One day, she brought a Holocaust survivor

---

[2] See www.bostonglobe.com/lifestyle/style/2015/06/15/cellphones-school-teaching-tool-distraction/OzHjXyL7VVIXV1AEkeYTiJ/story.html.

into class to talk about World War II, and noticed that one of her students was tweeting during the talk. She asked herself if she should have told the Holocaust survivor in advance to be a little more engaging.

Morgenstern is an *atypical* mobile phone user in education. We do not know if she owns or uses a mobile phone for personal use. By a typical definition, if she does not have a mobile phone, she might not be called a mobile phone user. However, she certainly got extremely frustrated by the significant distraction from mobile phones used by her students in the classroom, which became one of reasons why she decided to retire. Thus, she is indirectly and closely related to her students who are heavy mobile phone users or Generation Mobile Phones. Thus, her negative experience with students' mobile phone use in classrooms made her an atypical mobile phone user, a teacher being perhaps without a mobile phone of her own and strongly against distractive use of mobile phones by her own students. The unique mobile phone behavior involved in this case can be illustrated in a simple diagram:

Miriam Morgenstern in Lowell High School + mobile phones used by her students → experiencing significant distraction and extreme frustration by her students' mobile phone use in class → ended her twenty-year teaching career in 2015.

2.2   Educational Technologies: A Campus App and Pokémon Go

A campus app.[3] In May 2014, Shivam Parikh and Matthew Gilliland, two undergraduates majoring in computer science, received bachelor of science degrees from University at Albany. They spent their final undergraduate semester developing and creating the university's first official mobile app, giving their alma mater a unique gift fit for the digital age. Many universities have special campus apps to be used for various campus services such as textbook purchase and sports ticket sales. Most of these apps are developed by professional for-profit vendors. The University at Albany had long needed such an app, but budget constraints did not allow for developing it. Mr. Parikh proposed the project to the web-services department, where he was an intern, to develop their computer skills and at the same time serve the campus needs because students know more about what other students might be looking for in an app. Starting in January of 2014, Mr. Parikh and Mr. Gilliland, two long-time schoolmates, each

---

[3] See www.chronicle.com/blogs/wiredcampus/for-125-2-students-build-official-app-for-suny-albany/ 52687.

spent about 15 hours a week on the development of the app as their senior project. The work was based on an open-source mobile app development framework called PhoneGap. They also studied as many as twenty-five apps in use at other institutions. The app cost the university only about $125. Since August of 2014, the app is available to download for free and it functions on both Android and Apple iOS devices. After their graduation, Mr. Parikh and Mr. Gilliland will spend an additional year at Albany studying computer science as graduate students. In the near future, we might see a great mobile app company co-founded by these two bright students!

This story has at least two interesting points. (1) Campus apps have become a specific type of popular mobile app. These apps are serving various university campuses and benefiting university students' lives. (2) Two undergraduate students with a very limited budget can design and develop a successful app within one semester. This was hardly imaginable before. Traditionally, software companies like Microsoft normally might need multiple years to develop a commercial software program such as Microsoft Word by using a large team of hundreds of professional computer programmers. The unique mobile phone behavior involved in this case could be illustrated in two related diagrams:

Shivam Parikh and Matthew Gilliland at University at Albany + **the open-source app development tool PhoneGap** → each spending about 15 hours a week developing an app as their senior project → developed the university's first official mobile app called UAlbany App.

Members of the university community + **UAlbany App** → using the app → benefited their campus lives.

Pokémon Go.[4] On July 13, 2016, a 16-year-old boy was catching Pokémon with a middle-aged man on a county courthouse lawn. Two probation officers identified the man as Randy Zuick, a 42-year-old convicted child molester and registered sex offender in Indiana. One officer ran inside and asked a security officer to take Zuick into custody. The courthouse is a landmark in the game called a *pokéstop*, a checkpoint in the game that usually has cultural or historical significance. It has been attracting enthusiastic players like the 16-year-old boy since the app's release. Zuick was accused of fondling a child his girlfriend was babysitting in 2015. He later pleaded guilty to a felony charge of child molestation. Since then, he's been on probation and banned from interacting with

---

[4] See www.nydailynews.com/news/crime/indiana-sex-offender-arrested-playing-pokemon-teen-article-1.2710477.

children. Now, for his new legal violation, Zuick is being held in the county jail until a judge determines whether to revoke his probation.

This story has at least two important messages. First, Pokémon Go is one of the best examples of what augmented reality is. As a new technology, augmented reality has been talked about by an increasing number of people. However, it is not very clear to us what exactly it is and how it can really benefit us. With Pokémon Go and the Pokémon phenomenon, we can see now that augmented reality can be an extremely useful and interesting technology for ordinary users in general and for school students in particular. Students can learn about landmarks in their community and walk around more by playing Pokémon Go and visiting various pokéstops. Thus, Pokémon Go has a huge potential to become a very useful mobile technology in education. Second, mobile games like Pokémon Go can have various unique positive effects on school-aged children (e.g., walking outside to get more exercise, playing it in after-school programs, using it on museum field trips). However, it can certainly also have various negative effects for young children. As shown in the case we discussed just now, children might play with a registered sex offender or visit unsafe places with drug dealers, people suffering from mental illness, or sex offenders, making them easy targets for sex offenders and criminals. Thus, the Pokémon phenomenon also generates various new concerns such as child safety or game addiction. From the perspective of analyzing technology-based mobile phone behavior, the users in the study are the 16-year-old boy and the 42-year-old sex offender, the technology involved is Pokémon Go, the activity involved is playing Pokémon Go together on a county courthouse lawn, and the effect is that the boy became a potential victim of the registered sex offender. This mobile phone behavior can be illustrated in a simple diagram:

The 16-year-old boy and the 42-year-old sex offender + **Pokémon Go** → playing Pokémon Go together → the boy became a potential victim of the sex offender.

2.3   *Educational Activities: Texting Champion and Sexting Ring*

Texting championship.[5] On August 8, 2012, Austin Wierschkem, a 17-year-old, handsome high-school senior from Wisconsin, won the sixth annual US LG National Texting Competition, with a $50,000 prize, for the second year in a row. Even after winning the championship last year,

[5] See http://usatoday30.usatoday.com/tech/news/story/2012-08-08/texting-championship/56867966/1.

Austin worked hard to prepare for this year's competition and sent almost 500 texts a day to his friends. It was observed that, as the fastest texter in the United States, he has abnormally fast thumbs, and while he was texting, his thumbs were flying. The preliminaries started several months ago when the competition had about 100,000 contestants. Of these, eleven contestants from all over the United States qualified for the final competition and went through three rounds of texting to test their speed (spelling out text abbreviations while blind-folded), accuracy (copying phrases shown on the screen as fast as possible), and dexterity (texting backwards based on jumbled words that had to be figured out by the texters). Since LG is the sponsor of the contest, contestants all use the same type of cell phone – an LG Optimus Zip phone with a QWERTY keyboard. Anan Arias, 17, came out to see the competition final. As an avid texter, she sends more than 100 texts a day and told a reporter: "Texting is part of the new generation." In collaboration with this year's event, LG teamed up with Cartoon Network's "Stop Bullying: Speak Up" campaign to help raise money for anti-bullying toolkits that will be sent out to middle and high schools across the United States. LG has been sponsoring the LG Mobile World Cup, the worldwide texting competition since 2010. Ha Mok-Min, aged 16, and Bae Yeong-Ho, aged 17, won the first competition with prizes of $100,000. Over 6 million people registered to compete in the tournament.

Sexting ring.[6] Newtown, a small, scenic town in southwestern Connecticut about 60 miles from New York City, was known in 2012 as the site of a mass shooting. Adam Lanza, aged 20, killed himself after killing his mother and twenty-six people at Sandy Hook Elementary School. After four years, the town drew national attention again. On January 25, 2016, three students from Newtown High School were arrested and accused of involvement in a "sexting" ring that circulated sexually explicit images and videos of other students. Since May 2015, these students began transmitting sexually explicit images and videos via cell phone text messaging apps such as Snapchat, Facetime, iMessage, and KiK. These sexually explicit materials quickly spread throughout a school of roughly 1,800 students. The charges were brought after a six-month investigation that included dozens of interviews with students and parents, as well as executions of search and seizure warrants. Nationally, there are twenty states including Connecticut with modern sexting laws, whereas thirty states are without modern sexting laws. However, even with all the new laws, most of the

[6] See www.cnn.com/2016/01/27/us/connecticut-high-school-sexting-ring/.

country remains far behind the fast-moving pace of teens and technology, including sexting.

These two stories observed in daily life show two opposite sides of a mobile phone activity, i.e., texting among high-school students. The first story indicates that texting is popular among youths as Generation Text, and some of them have an extremely high level of texting skill in speed and accuracy, and that skill can lead to winning a national or international competition. For educators, more educational programs should be designed to take advantage of the popularity of texting and texting competitions to develop students' cognitive development (e.g., promoting spelling and linguistic skills) and social development (e.g., linking with anti-bullying campaigns). The second story illustrates that sexting, an activity of texting sexually explicit images and videos, occurs more commonly among youths now and leads to serious negative consequences for school-aged victims and offenders in educational settings. Thus, further efforts are needed to develop effective strategies of prevention and intervention to deal with sexting rings in schools.

From the perspective of analyzing activity-based mobile phone behavior, the mobile phone behavior involved in these two cases can be illustrated in a simple diagram:

Austin Wierschkem from a Wisconsin high school + LG Optimus Zip phone with a QWERTY keyboard → **practicing texting by sending about 500 texts a day to prepare for the texting competition** → won the sixth annual US LG National Texting Competition with $50,000 in prize money for the second year in a row as the fastest American texter.

Three students from Newtown High School + cell phone text messaging apps such as Snapchat, Facetime, iMessage, and KiK → **transmitting sexually explicit images and videos of other students in school** → arrested for their involvement in a sexting ring.

2.4   *Educational Effects: A Learning Aid and a Student Lawsuit*

A learning aid.[7] On March 25, 2013, Giselle Barkley, a contributing author of *Statesmen*, a student newspaper at Stony Brook University that has informed the university for more than fifty years, wrote a story summarizing how students are using new methods of taking notes in the classroom. Students can be seen taking a snapshot with their phones' cameras in large lecture halls. Such digital note-taking predominantly

---

[7] See www.sbstatesman.com/2013/03/25/students-use-new-methods-of-taking-notes-in-the-classroom/.

occurs in science-related courses such as biology and chemistry in addition to social science classes. For example, students sometimes take pictures of structure diagrams on the slides or clicker questions with iPhones to refer back to. Others take pictures of lecture slides because the lecture slides used in class and those posted on Blackboard may differ. Some students may take pictures especially when a lecture is fast-paced. Taking pictures of the lecture allows students to devote more time to writing down what is being said, while pictures account for what is actually on the slide. For other students, digital note-taking not only allows for a better quality shot, but also the ability to take close-up images, even from the back row of a lecture hall. In short, though traditional note-taking practices may not die out completely, students are increasingly using a variety of technological devices for academic purposes.

A student lawsuit.[8] On May 22, 2007, Marsha Pechman, a US District Judge, denied a case requesting to end the 40-day suspension of a high-school student, rejecting the student's argument that this punishment violated his First Amendment rights. The judge upheld the suspension of the student due to his involvement in the production and YouTube posting of a video insulting a teacher.

This case involves two key parties: one is Gregory Requa, the high-school senior in Kentridge High School of Seattle; and another is Joyce Mong, Requa's English teacher. In early 2007, a video surfaced online, dubbed "Mongzilla," which criticized Joyce Mong's personal hygiene and classroom mess. The video was recorded using a hidden video camera secured in Mong's English classroom. Requa denied any involvement in creating the video, but he did acknowledge posting a link to it on his MySpace page, and he removed it after a local television station reported this video. School officials punished Requa by suspending him after other students alleged that he helped to edit and post the video. However, Requa and his attorney argued that his involvement in the video was irrelevant, saying that the suspension of a student for criticizing a teacher is a violation of the First Amendment. The school district then responded that the punishment was for the classroom disruption that occurred in the production of the video, not for his criticism. After the court debate, Judge Marsha Pechman ruled as follows. (1) One student filming another student standing behind a teacher or a student filming the buttocks of a teacher as she bends over in the classroom constitutes a substantial

---

[8] See www.firstamendmentcenter.org/federal-judge-upholds-student%E2%80%99s-suspension-for-video.

disruption to the work and discipline of the school. (2) While it is a legitimate and important right for students to critique the performance and competence of their teachers, it is in the public interest to have a classroom without inappropriate behavior. (3) The First Amendment does not extend its coverage to disruptive in-class activity of this nature. (4) Students' disruptive behavior in a classroom is not allowed, but overtly taped videos even without the teachers' knowledge or permission could be allowed as evidence in the legal process.

These two stories, again taking place in real-life educational settings, show the complexity of mobile phone behavior in education in general and the complex impacts of mobile phone technologies on education in particular. First, these two stories involved the same mobile phone technology – the mobile phone camera. However, the first story tells us the positive side of the mobile camera – a new trend for a traditional learning method of taking notes. This use is actually very common if one attends a conference talk or professional workshop. The second story shows the complexity of using cameras by students, involving various serious legal issues, including teachers' privacy, students' First Amendment right, rights for schools to use these tapes for discipline or promotion processes, and public monitoring of teachers' behavior in the classroom. Many educators, parents, and students might not be aware of these issues.

From the perspective of analyzing effect-based mobile phone behavior, the mobile phone behavior observed in these two cases can be illustrated in two simple diagrams:

Students at Stony Brook University + mobile camera → taking digital notes during the class → **helped students' learning in various ways.**

Gregory Requa from Kentridge High School of Seattle + mobile Camera → filming, editing, and distributing a clip named *Mongzilla* about his English teacher Joyce Mong's teaching → **Requa was suspended for substantial classroom disruption.**

To end the discussion of the eight cases presented above, we should see now that the mobile phone behavior in education is very complex, especially compared to Tom's intuitive responses. Users range from a professor of Chinese to a teenager of Generation Text to a retired teacher; technologies range from smartphones to special apps to hot games featuring augmented reality; activities range from teaching and studying to winning text championships and sexting at school; effects encompass positive effects on teaching and studying, including a positive effect on memorization, and a negative effect on privacy concerning mobile camera use in the classroom. However, these cases are just the tip of a gigantic iceberg in real life: there is even more complexity regarding mobile phone behavior in education. We will encounter endless issues, such as addiction, bullying, policy, disabled students, gifted education, campus gunfire, distraction, and First Amendment rights. However, now it is time for us to examine the current scientific research in mobile phone behavior in education.

3. Empirical Studies: From Generation Text to Learning Distraction

3.1 Educational Users: Norwegian Youths

The next article we will discuss is "The socio-demographics of texting: An analysis of traffic data,"[9] a string computational study of mass mobile phone data in Norway. It has been cited fifty-nine times in Google Scholar. The authors are Rich Ling, a pioneering scholar in mobile communication, Troels Fibæk Bertel, and Pål Roe Sundsøy. It was published in 2011 in *New Media & Society*.

In the study, the authors accessed and analyzed 394 million anonymous text exchanges provided by Telenor, a Norwegian major telecommunications company, during the fourth quarter of 2007 in Norway. Only two demographical variables were available in the fourth quarter of 2007 from Telenor's anonymized billing records: age and gender of the mobile phone users. The dependent variable was these users' mobile phone data traffic volume (e.g., 900 MB per month). The following are the major findings: (1) Among the age groups between 10 and 90 years old, most of the texting traffic occurs between similarly aged texting partners, particularly between same-aged teens who send and receive almost sixty times more texts than the average texts sent by the entire society. (2) For text messages from female to male, from male to female, between females only, and between males only, most of the texting traffic occurs between females only. (3) 50 percent of all texts involved only about five different texting partners. In other words, users send the majority of their texts to a few individuals with strong ties.

This big data study is particularly interesting for us to understand Generation Text, a special group of mobile phone users in education. First, different from various survey studies relying on self-reported

---

[9] Ling, R., Bertel, T. F., and Sundsøy, P. R. (2012). "The socio-demographics of texting: An analysis of traffic data," *New Media & Society*, 14(2): 281–298.

subjective data, this study used mass mobile phone data and analyzed the objective patterns of mobile phone use. It confirmed that *school-aged teenagers* are the dominant users of texting or we can call this age group Generation Text. Second, different from various studies focusing on only one age group, this study examined almost all the age groups in Norway from ages 10 to 90 in 2007 in a cross-sectional comparison. Thus, the finding that *texting use peaks during adolescence* in relation to all other age groups is particularly convincing. From the perspective of analyzing user-based mobile phone behavior, the users in the study are Norwegian youths, the technology involved is texting technology, the activity involved is texting to the same age and gender, and the effect is that evidence for Generation Text is generated. It can be illustrated in a simple diagram:

Norwegian youths in 2007 + mobile texting technologies → various texting activities among youths with the same age and gender → the phenomenon of Generation Text observed.

3.2   Educational Technologies: Bar Code

Now let us examine and discuss another article entitled "Integrating mobile multimedia into textbooks: 2D barcodes."[10] A barcode is a method of coding and representing data that are read by an optical machine with almost perfect accuracy compared to the key entry method. A one-dimensional barcode or a linear barcode was invented and used around the 1970s and was read by special optical scanners. A two-dimensional or matrix barcode became widely available after the year 2000 and represents more data per unit area and is read by smartphone cameras. In this study, using the 2D barcode in a textbook, students will scan the 2D barcode tag by using a mobile camera and then automatically view relevant multimedia materials on the mobile phone screen through a textbook website. This article was well written and published in 2012 in *Computers & Education*. The authors are Celebi Uluyol and R. Kagan Agca, from the Department of Computer Education and Instructional Technologies at Gazi University in Turkey. The first author has a PhD in educational technology and has published nearly ten articles on educational technologies, but this article is the first one on mobile phones. He is a junior researcher, but has published some good work.

[10] Uluyol, C. and Agca, R. K. (2012). "Integrating mobile multimedia into textbooks: 2D barcodes," *Computers & Education*, 59(4): 1192–1198.

In the experimental study, the participants were 188 Turkish undergraduate students majoring in instructional technologies. The two dependent variables were how well students can retain and transfer their
understanding of a computer science concept – the seven-layer network
model. The one independent variable concerns four experimental conditions: text only (students learn by reading text only); text plus picture
(students learn by using both text and illustrative pictures); online animation plus narration (students learn through online animation along with
narration); and text plus mobile phone (students learn by reading text and
using mobile phones that were activated by the 2D barcode in the
textbook). The procedure included a pre-test of previous knowledge using
five Likert-scale questions, the experiment with four conditions (studying
the instructional materials for 20 minutes), and a post-test on both
knowledge retention by using five open-ended questions and knowledge
transfer by using three open-ended questions. The major findings included
that: (1) retention scores were, from the lowest to the highest, Text-only,
Text-plus-picture, Computer-based, and Text-plus-mobile phone; and (2)
similarly, transfer scores were, from the lowest to the highest, Text-only,
Text-plus-picture, Computer-based, and Text-plus-mobile phone. It was
concluded that a printed textbook with camera-equipped mobile devices
and 2D barcodes linked to supplemental information may increase the
effectiveness of learning.

What can we learn about this experimental study from the mobile
phone behavior perspective? We can now use the four-element model to
analyze this mobile phone behavior in education. First, the mobile users in
the study are 188 normal undergraduate technology-major students in
Turkey, with relatively strong knowledge about technology. However,
other kinds of normal students (e.g., undergraduates with different majors,
students in middle or high schools, students in different cultures), gifted
students, and students with disabilities should be studied in the future.
Second, the mobile technologies involved are textbook 2D barcodes used
widely for mobile phones and mobile cameras (the technical features of the
mobile phones and cameras used in the study are not reported). These
technologies are common, but we can see how these common technical
features can be creatively used in learning complex concepts of computer
science. Third, the mobile activities are reading and studying the online
instructional materials on a computer network model. However, various
other mobile learning activities in real-life classrooms such as field trips,
team collaborations, or afternoon programs should be further explored.
Fourth, the mobile effects are positive retention and transfer based on the

strong experiment evidence. However, besides the cognitive effect, other possible physical (e.g., the small mobile screen and touch screen experience), emotional (e.g., motivation and interest), and social effects (e.g., knowledge sharing and peer support) could be included. The following simple diagram can represent the mobile phone behavior in education reported in the study:

188 Turkish undergraduates + **2D barcodes and mobile camera** → learning a computer science concept → cognitive learning effectiveness increased.

3.3   Educational Activities: Learning in a Biology Class

The next article is "An interactive concept map approach to supporting mobile learning activities for natural science courses,"[11] and examines how a mobile learning experiment can help elementary students learn biology. A concept map is a graphic representation of the relationship among various concepts. The authors are three scholars – Gwo-Jen Hwang, Po-Han Wu, and Hui-Ru Ke – from three universities in Taiwan. The article was published in 2012 in *Computers & Education.*

In the study, the researchers designed a true experiment to compare both learning achievements and learning attitudes during a mobile learning activity using computerized concept map tools in a butterfly ecology garden. Thirty elementary-school students from Taiwan were randomly assigned to an experimental group and a control group before the experiment. The entire study took place in a butterfly garden that had a local wireless communication network. In this location-aware mobile learning environment, an RFID tag was placed in each target ecology area and students used a PDA equipped with an RFID reader to guide their efforts to find the target ecology areas. Note that: (1) radio-frequency identification (RFID) is a tracking system that uses intelligent barcodes (tags) to track items in a location by using RFID readers; (2) personal digital assistant (PDA), also known as a handheld PC, is a mobile device that functions as a personal information manager; and (3) the local wireless communication network in this garden functions as a WiFi network.

The procedure consisted of the following steps: Students (1) learned the basic knowledge about butterfly ecology; (2) took a pre-test of their

---

[11] Hwang, G.-J., Wu, P.-H., and Ke, H.-R. (2011). "An interactive concept map approach to supporting mobile learning activities for natural science courses," *Computers & Education,* 57(4): 2272–2280.

knowledge of butterfly ecology and completed a questionnaire about their attitude toward butterfly ecology; (3) observed the four growing stages of a butterfly called *Idea leuconoe clara* (eggs, larvas, pupas, and imago) in the garden and developed concept maps. The experimental group received immediate assistance via the mobile learning system, but the control group did not have mobile learning assistance; and (4) took a post-test of their knowledge of butterfly ecology and completed the same questionnaire about their attitude toward butterfly ecology. It was found that: (1) the experimental group received significantly higher scores on their concept maps than the control group; (2) the experimental group significantly improved their attitude scores in comparison to the control group; and (3) the experimental group highly valued the mobile learning system.

We can use the basic element model to analyze this study. First, the mobile users are thirty elementary-school students for both of the groups. Second, the mobile technologies used in the study were as follows: first, the wireless network in the garden, PDA, and RFID tags and readers for both groups to observe butterflies and second, the mobile learning system used by the experimental group to develop concept maps. Third, the mobile activities in which students participated were guided natural observation by the two groups and assisted mobile learning with a mobile learning system. Fourth, the mobile effects were that students in the experimental group had a positive impact on their concept map work and their attitude toward learning natural sciences. In short, the mobile behavior in education can be presented in the following diagram:

Thirty elementary students + local network/PDA/RFID/mobile learning system → **observing butterflies and developing concept maps** → positive learning outcomes in both knowledge and attitude achieved.

3.4 Educational Effects: Learning Distraction

The next article we will discuss is entitled "No A 4 U: The relationship between multitasking and academic performance."[12] This is one of the earliest and well-cited studies (232 times based on Google Scholar). The authors are Reynol Junco and Shelia Cotten, two American scholars from Lock Haven University and University of Alabama respectively. The article was published in 2012 in *Computers & Education*, a well-established Elsevier journal that has published a series of strong studies on mobile learning.

---

[12] Junco, R. and Cotten, S. R. (2012). "No A 4 U: The relationship between multitasking and academic performance," *Computers & Education*, 59(2): 505–514.

In this study, 1,774 American undergraduate students from one university completed an online survey. The measure was a multitasking questionnaire with a Likert scale designed by the authors. Major independent variables included information and communication technology usage, frequency of multitasking, Internet skills, high-school GPA, and parental education. The dependent variable was students' overall grade point averages. Hierarchical regression analysis was used for data analysis. The major findings were as follows: (1) Students reported that the frequency of texting multitasking, Facebook multitasking, and e-mail multitasking were the highest, whereas Instant messaging was the least often used when multitasking. (2) Controlling for high-school GPA, time preparing for class, Internet skills, and demographic variables, students' overall college GPAs were significantly and negatively related to reported frequency of Facebook multitasking and texting multitasking, but not e-mail multitasking, searching multitasking, and talking multitasking. It was concluded that the type and purpose of ICT use matters in terms of the educational impacts of multitasking.

We can use the four-element model to analyze the mobile phone behavior demonstrated in this study. First, the mobile users are 1,774 American undergraduate students at one university who frequently use technologies (e.g., they reported sending an average of ninety-seven text messages per day). Second, the mobile technologies featured in the study are Facebook, texting, e-mailing, or searching technologies. Third, the mobile activities are typically Facebook multitasking, texting multitasking, e-mail multitasking, online searching multitasking, and phone-calling multitasking. Fourth, the mobile effects are that GPA is negatively related to Facebook multitasking and texting multitasking, but not e-mail multitasking, information searching multitasking, and talking multitasking. Again, the following diagram summarizes this mobile phone behavior:

1,774 American undergraduate students + mobile phones → multitasking using Facebook, texting, e-mail, searching information, and calling → **GPA decreased with Facebook multitasking and texting multitasking**.

4.   Knowledge Syntheses: From Disabled Learners to Distractive Effects

4.1   Overview: A Relatively Small Research Area

After discussing multiple specific cases and empirical studies, we will examine mobile phone behavior in education from a much broader perspective, by first overviewing the scope of the existing literature, core journals, and major topics, and then discussing four review articles in detail.

To know the current scope of the existing literature on mobile phone behavior in education, again, let us do an initial literature search. PsycINFO and ERIC were chosen as two primary databases related to education. Second, the keywords *cellular phones* and *mobile devices* were entered, then the keywords *education, teaching, learning,* and *instruction* to search the literature. Third, over 400 journal articles were identified by combining the search results of *cellular phones/mobile devices* and *education/learning/teaching/instruction*. Finally, a search among the literature review articles found six published reviews. Compared with the existing literature on mobile phone behavior in medicine or business, we can see that the scope of the literature on mobile phone behavior in education is much smaller.

Major journals in this area include: (1) *Education & Computers* (publishing the majority of and best studies in this area); (2) *Computers in Human Behavior* (publishing a wide variety of topics in this area); (3) the *International Journal of Mobile and Blended Learning* (publishing studies on e-learning and m-learning); (4) the *Journal of Computing Education Research* (starting to publish relevant articles in recent years); (5) the *Journal of Assistive Education* (publishing articles on learners with disabilities); (6) the *British Journal of Educational Technology* (publishing technology-oriented articles); (7) the *Australasian Journal of Educational Technology* (publishing a few but strong articles in the area); and (8) *IEEE Transactions* (sometimes publishing emerging mobile phone technologies related to education).

Topics in mobile phone behavior in education are quite broad. The *Encyclopedia of Mobile Phone Behavior* has a special section with over forty chapters examining mobile phone behavior in education. As shown in Table 8.1, various topics concern mobile users in education, mobile technologies in education, mobile phone activities in education, and mobile effects in education. Among them, nearly twenty chapters mainly focus on mobile phone activities in education, such as learning, gaming, texting, assessing, and bullying.

4.2 Educational Users: Learners with Special Needs

The first review we will discuss is "The case for mobile devices as assistive learning technologies: A literature review on assistive technologies."[13] The

---

[13] McKnight, L. (2014). "The case for mobile devices as assistive learning technologies: A literature review," *International Journal of Mobile Human Computer Interaction,* 6(3): 1–15.

Table 8.1 *The* Encyclopedia *Chapters on Mobile Phone Behavior in Education*

Elements	Chapter Title
Users	Children, risks and the mobile internet
Users	Exploring the use of mobile devices to support teacher education
Users	Deaf adolescents' textisms
Users	Generation Y and mobile marketing in India
Users	Keitai and Japanese adolescents
Users	Mobile phone use by middle school students
Users	Mobile phone: Repurposed assistive technology for individuals with disabilities
Users	The use of mobile phone technology to support people with Autism Spectrum Disorders (ASD)
Users	Use of mobile phones by individuals with visual impairments
Technology	Educational potentials of SMS technology
Technology	Mobile games
Technology	Mobile phones and libraries/information centres
Technology	Texting: Its uses, misuses and effects
Technology	Digital mobile games in education
Activity	Adolescent text messaging
Activity	Teenage sexting: Sexual expression meets mobile technology
Activity	Using smartphones in the college classroom
Activity	Harnessing mobile technology for student assessment
Activity	Microlearning and mobile learning
Activity	Mobile games and learning
Activity	Mobile learning
Activity	Mobile literacies: Learning in the mobile age
Activity	Mobile phone multitasking and learning
Activity	Mobile phone use and children's literacy learning
Activity	Mobile seamless learning from the perspective of self-regulated learning
Activity	Mobile technology-enhanced learning
Activity	Science learning games for mobile platforms
Activity	The use of mobile phones in K-12 education
Activity	Using mobile phones for educational assessment
Activity	Sex, cyberbullying and the mobile phone
Activity	Textism use and language ability in children
Effect	Mobile phone etiquette
Effect	Use of mobile phones to help prevent child maltreatment
Effect	The impact of mobile phones on teenagers' socialization and emancipation
Effect	Connecting 'round the clock: Mobile phones and adolescents' experiences of intimacy
Effect	mHealth in maternal, newborn, and child health programs around the world
Effect	Mobile phone addiction
Effect	Mobile phone behavior in the college classroom: Effects on student learning and implications for students and teachers
Effect	Mobile technology and cyberbullying
Effect	Mobile technology and social identity
Effect	Nomophobia
Effect	Students hurting students: Cyberbullying as a mobile phone behavior

author is Lorna McKnight, from the University of Bolton in the United Kingdom. She has published multiple articles on mobile phone design for children and assistive learning technologies. The article was published in 2014 in the *International Journal of Mobile Human Computer Interaction*, a relatively new journal by IGI Global in publication since 2009.

This review consists of three major sections: background overview, use of mobile device as assistive learning technologies, and limitations of mobile technologies. The major results of the review include the following: (1) The author identified over 100 journal articles and conference papers based on database searches, reference follow-up, journal and conference proceeding search, and expert consultation. The goal was to examine if mobile technologies can be suitable assistive technologies to support students with learning difficulties at different stages of education. (2) The review discusses three important concepts: assistive technologies (the broadest, any technology that supports people with disabilities in all aspects of life), assistive learning technologies (focusing on technologies that can support learners with diverse needs), and mobile-phone-based assistive learning technologies (the narrowest, focusing on mobile or portable technologies that can support learners with special needs). (3) Learners with special needs can benefit from six aspects of mobile phone technologies, namely: various mobile apps (e.g., speech-to-text, text-to-speech, mind maps, audio notetaking), portable features (e.g., autistic teenagers can carry a mobile phone and press a "panic button" to call for social support wherever they feel most anxious), mobile sensors (e.g., sensors of face recognition can help autistic students to sense other people's emotions), touch screens (e.g., encouraging multiple autistic students to work together by touching the screen), classroom learning tools (e.g., showing activities both on mobile phones and on the large classroom screen to help students organize their activities), and regular mobile phones (e.g., using mainstream phones that are more affordable and more socially attractive to students with visual impairments). (4) Several limitations exist. For instance, assistive tools on mobile phones (e.g., voice recognition apps such as Dragon Dictate, Google Voice typing, and Apple's Siri) demand more battery power; students with dyslexia need more customized text format functions; students with cerebral palsy cannot control one finger to touch a small menu item; and students with visual impairments need screen readers instead of touch screens.

From the mobile phone user perspective, this review shows that students with various disabilities are a special group of mobile users in educational settings; mobile phones can provide various physical, cognitive, and social assistance; and using mobile phones to best serve the diverse needs of these students is still a large challenge.

4.3   Educational Technologies: Tablets

The review article we will discuss next is entitled "Tablet use in schools: A critical review of the evidence for learning outcomes,"[14] a systematic review of school learning effects and contributing factors of tablets. In this review, tablets (e.g., iPads) are considered to be a type of mobile technology. The three authors are all affiliated with the Faculty of Education at the University of Cambridge. Bjoern Haßler is currently a research fellow in the Centre for Commonwealth Education and has published several articles specifically focusing on tablet use in education. Louis Major is a research associate studying the use of digital technology for education. Sara Hennessy is a reader (equivalent to full professor in the United States) in Teacher Development and Pedagogical Innovation and has published extensively on educational uses of digital technology. The review article was published in 2016 in the *Journal of Computer Assisted Learning*, a well-established specialty journal by Wiley in publication since 1985, with an impact factor of 1.679 in 2015.

In this review, the authors used manual and automated searches and identified twenty-three studies with good methodological quality and content relevance. The major findings include: (1) sixteen studies reported positive learning outcomes, that tablet use supports learning in science, social studies, and mathematics; five reported no difference in learning outcomes for literacy, reading, math, and science; and two reported negative outcomes in reading comprehension and collaboration in creativity and writing; and (2) factors contributing to learning outcomes included hardware affordance (high usability and good integration, easy customization and good personalization, good touch screen use, portability), effective teaching implementation, good content and instruction design, and learning interaction.

This review has been cited only five times according to Google Scholar as of August 2016, not yet a highly cited review. A good review will normally be widely cited, but it is too early to tell since it was just recently published online in 2015 and in hard copy a few months ago in the second issue of the journal in 2016. However, from the perspective of technology-based mobile

---

[14] Haßler, B., Major, L., and Hennessy, S. (2016). "Tablet use in schools: A critical review of the evidence for learning outcomes," *Journal of Computer Assisted Learning*, 32(2): 139–156.

phone behavior in education, it is particularly unique and insightful for us to examine for a few reasons. First, the mobile users were all elementary- or middle-school students rather than college students, the population discussed most frequently in the literature. Second, the review focused on tablets, one mobile technology typically welcomed in schools, compared with personal mobile phones, the use of which in classrooms has been debated for years. It discussed extensively hardware affordance issues, including usability integration, customization and personalization, touch screen use, and portability. Third, it analyzed pedagogical factors within the mobile learning activities, including teaching implementation, content and instruction design, and learning interaction. Fourth, it presents a trustable synthesis on learning effects: (a) It first explicitly excluded motivation studies, which is a thoughtful decision to focus more on cognitive achievements. Note that motivational outcomes (or emotional outcomes) and social outcomes (e.g., collaborative learning) are an inherently important part of learning outcomes based on modern learning sciences and should be included in a comprehensive assessment of learning outcomes. (b) It assessed the quality of studies and rated them in terms of methodological rigor and content relevance before the review. This rigorous and auditable approach has improved the review quality because low quality studies will bring biases into the knowledge synthesis process and should not be included in the review. (c) It presents a general conclusion that tablets have mixed impacts on cognitive and social achievement.

4.4 Educational Activities: Mobile Learning Trends

Generally speaking, published qualitative literature reviews are a good indicator of productive research in a given area. Published meta-analyses and quantitative literature reviews are a particularly important indicator of highly productive empirical research in a given area. Fortunately, in the area of mobile phone behavior in education, several meta-analyses have been published.[15] Among them is "Review of trends from mobile learning studies: A meta-analysis."[16] It was cited 268 times according to Google Scholar. The authors are a group of researchers in information management from five universities in Taiwan: Wen-Hsiung Wu, Yen-Chun Jim

---

[15] Alrasheedi, M. and Capretz, L. F. (2013, August). "A meta-analysis of critical success factors affecting mobile learning," in *IEEE International Conference on Teaching, Assessment and Learning for Engineering: TALE 2013*, pp. 262–267.
[16] Wu, W.-H., Wu, Y.-C. J., Chen, C.-Y. *et al.* (2012). "Review of trends from mobile learning studies: A meta-analysis," *Computers & Education*, 59(2): 817–827.

Wu, Chun-Yu Chen, Hao-Yun Kao, Che-Hung Lin, and Sih-Han Huang. It was published in 2012 in *Computers & Education*.

In this review, built on two published reviews (one on 154 articles published between 2003 and 2008; another on 154 articles published between 2001 and 2010), the author searched over ten education-based databases and seven core journals and identified 164 articles on mobile learning published between 2000 and 2010. Major findings included the following: (1) The articles focused on four goals: assessing effectiveness of mobile learning programs (58 percent), presenting new mobile learning system designs (32 percent), examining affective aspects (5 percent), and evaluating learners' characteristics (5 percent). (2) Five types of methods were most often used: surveys, experiments, descriptive, observation, and case studies. (3) 142 articles (87 percent) reported positive learning outcomes, sixteen (9 percent) did not report outcomes, six (4 percent) reported neutral outcomes, and only one (0.6 percent) reported negative outcomes. (4) Mobile devices studied in the existing literature included mobile phones (sixty-nine articles), PDAs (sixty-four articles), and iPods (seven articles).

The title of the review indicates that it is a meta-analysis. Clearly this is an error because no effect size estimation has been used in the review. Despite this error, we can still learn several important trends of activity-based mobile phone behavior in education from this detailed review. First, the majority of mobile users in the reviewed studies were college students (52 percent), and other groups were elementary students (12 percent), middle- and high-school students (8 percent), and students with disabilities (only 0.56 percent). The content of mobile learning activities mainly involved languages (thirty articles), computer sciences (twenty-three articles), environmental studies (eighteen articles), and health sciences (eighteen articles). Second, mobile phones and PDAs were the most often studied technologies. Third, the main mobile activities involved were effectiveness assessment and new mobile learning system implementation for learning. Fourth, the majority of the studies presented positive learning outcomes.

4.5   Educational Effects: Mobile Phone Multitasking

The last review article we will discuss is "Does multitasking with mobile phones affect learning? A review."[17] The first author, Quan Chen, is one of

---

[17] Chen, Q. and Yan, Z. (2016). "Does multitasking with mobile phones affect learning? A review," *Computers in Human Behavior*, 54: 34–42.

my doctoral students at University at Albany. She has published multiple articles on mobile phone multitasking. The article was published in 2016 in *Computers in Human Behavior*.

In the review, Quan and I identified 104 empirical articles explicitly examining the effects of mobile phone use while learning. Extending the existing two reviews,[18] this review focused on three specific issues in synthesizing distractive effects of mobile phone multitasking: sources of distraction (where do distractions come from?), targets of distraction (what activities does distraction impact?), and subjects of distraction (who is more easily distracted?). The review indicated that: (1) distraction sources include rings of mobile phones, texting, and various information and communication technologies (e.g., Facebook use); (2) distraction targets mainly include various dimensions of reading and attention (e.g., reading speed or reading comprehension); and (3) distraction subjects include diverse individuals with main characteristics such as personality, gender, culture, and motives. The review also discussed four theories that have been used to explain why mobile phone multitasking impairs learning: multimedia learning theory, continuous partial attention theory, multitasking continuum theory, and attention blink theory.

This review can help us better understand the multitasking effect of mobile learning. First, the multitasking effect is related to different kinds of mobile phone users (e.g., personality plays an important role). Second, the multitasking effect is related to different kinds of mobile phone technology (e.g., texting vs. calling). Third, the multitasking effect is related to different kinds of mobile phone activities (e.g., reading or focusing). Lastly, the multitasking effect is related to different kinds of mobile phone effects (e.g., negative vs. positive ones).

5. Comparative Study: Media Multitasking for Youth

In the previous sections, we discussed an empirical study and a review article on distracting effects of mobile phone use on learning. We can see not only the empirical evidence (decreasing GPA among nearly 2,000 undergraduates) and synthesized evidence (104 empirical articles) of distracting effects of mobile phone use, but also the complexity of this

---

[18] Levine, L. E., Waite, B. M., and Bowman, L. L. (2012). "Mobile media use, multitasking and distractibility," *International Journal of Cyber Behavior, Psychology and Learning,* 2(3): 15–29; and Carrillo, R. and Subrahmanyam, K. (2015). "Mobile phone multitasking and learning," in Z. Yan (ed.), *Encyclopedia of Mobile Phone Behavior.* Hershey, PA: IGI Global, pp. 82–92.

issue (e.g., this effect depends on different sources, targets, and users). Are distracting effects unique to mobile phones? Do other technologies also cause distractive effects on learning? Let us now discuss a comparative study on distraction, entitled "The consequences of media multitasking for youth: A review."[19] It is a review article comparing multitasking effects of different media on young users. As of July 2016, it has been cited only five times in Google Scholar and two times in Web of Science. However, this is largely because of its publication date (December 2016) rather than its quality. It is a very well-written review and will become well-cited in due course. The authors are a research group from the University of Amsterdam: Winneke van der Schuur, Susanne Baumgartner, Sindy Sumter, and Patti Valkenburg. The last author, Patti Valkenburg, is an internationally renowned expert in communication and has published multiple high-quality reviews. The review was published in *Computers in Human Behavior*.

The review consists of three major sections, reviewing the existing literature on effects of media multitasking among youth on three aspects: cognitive control, academic performance, and socioemotional functioning. The major results include the following: (1) Media multitasking generally consists of simultaneous media multitasking or academic media multitasking. The multiple media reviewed by the authors include televisions, cell phones, social network sites, Facebook, text messaging, laptops, and instant messaging. (2) Since 2014, a total of fifty-six highly relevant empirical studies on media multitasking have been published. To synthesize this existing literature, this review focused on examining various mixed findings of media multitasking effects on young populations. (3) About 30 percent of youth use multiple media simultaneously or use media while studying. (4) For cognitive control, only nine studies partially support the negative effects of media multitasking on cognitive control (an ability to select and maintain concentration). More studies support the idea that multitasking leads to attention splitting, where some studies support the idea that multitasking leads to attention improvement. (5) For academic performance, nearly forty-five studies indicate that multitasking while studying is negatively related to academic performance, but the effect size is small or moderate. (6) Several studies found that the effect of media multitasking on academic performance was dependent on the specific type

---

[19] van der Schuur, W. A., Baumgartner, S. E., Sumter, S. R., and Valkenburg, P. M. (2015). "The consequences of media multitasking for youth: A review," *Computers in Human Behavior*, 53: 204–215.

of media used during academic activities. In particular, using Facebook during academic activities was related to lower GPA and test scores. (7) For socioemotional functioning, four studies indicate that media multitasking is negatively related to emotion functioning and sleeping, but not to social functioning.

This comparative review shows the complexity of the effects of media multitasking. First, different conceptualizations, designs, and measurements lead to mixed findings. Second, while mobile phones are one of the modern media or modern technologies, mobile phone multitasking is not the dominant focus of the reviewed existing studies before 2015. However, one complex issue is that modern mobile phones are a technology integrating multiple media (e.g., mobile television, mobile Internet) that has been used for multiple functions, including social networking, Facebook checking, text messaging, and instant messaging. This is a special challenge for empirical, theoretical, and methodological studies comparing different media or technologies.

6. Complex Thinking: From Tom's Responses to Complex Behavior

Recall that at the beginning of this chapter we discussed Tom's quick responses about mobile phone behavior in education. For mobile phone users, he focused on himself as a university professor; for mobile technologies, he considered mobile texting, mobile video, and mobile Internet; for mobile activities, he talked about learning, studying, and teaching Chinese; and for mobile effects, he focused on positive cognitive effects on learning, studying, and teaching. After reading this chapter, we can now see that mobile phone behavior in education is much deeper, much broader, and much more complex than Tom's intuitive thinking. We can use Figure 8.1 to summarize the complexity of mobile phone behavior in education.

First, for educational users, we discussed: (1) a girl of Generation Text as a typical user, and she sends 3,000 texts per month – Generation Text are the new generation of students and the new generation of mobile phone users; (2) a case of a teacher as an atypical mobile user, who decided to retire as she no longer wanted to deal with mobile phone distraction; (3) a study of Norwegian youths, who texted very often, most often to their close circle with the same age and same gender; and (4) a review on learners with special needs as a special group of users, who benefit from mobile phones and at the same time challenge the design of mobile phones.

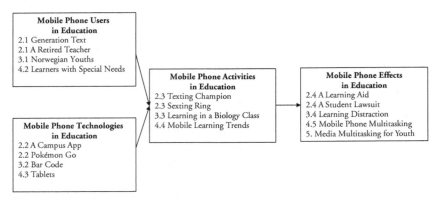

Figure 8.1   A Summary Diagram of Mobile Phone Behavior in Education

Mobile phone users in education are diverse and complex rather than just concerning regular teachers.

Second, for educational technologies, we discussed: (1) a case of a campus app that was developed by two undergraduate students, showing that a mobile app can benefit the entire university campus; (2) a case of a sex offender who played Pokémon Go with a boy, indicating that Pokémon Go as a mobile game can be used to hurt innocent teenagers; (3) a study of using bar codes to help students understand a concept of computer science; and (4) a review on how students used tablets with mixed effects on their cognitive achievement. Mobile phone technologies in education are diverse and complex rather than just concerning texting or going online.

Third, for educational activities, we discussed: (1) a high-school student who won the national texting championship in two consecutive years, engaging in an extraordinary texting activity; (2) three high-school students involved in a sexting ring, engaging in an illegal texting activity; (3) a study of a biology class that used a local mobile network to develop an effective learning process; and (4) a review on diverse users, contents, technologies, and outcomes of mobile learning. Mobile phone activities in education are diverse and complex rather than just being about language learning and teaching.

Lastly, for educational effects, we discussed: (1) a case of how university students benefited from mobile phone use in taking digital notes during class; (2) a case of how a student disturbed his English class by videotaping his teacher and posting it online, ending up in a highly visible lawsuit; (3) a study of nearly 2,000 college students who reported using mobile phones during their study and negatively impacted their grades; (4) a review on the distracting effects of mobile phone multitasking; and (5) a comparison of media multitasking, indicating media multitasking actually impacts students' cognitive control, academic achievement, and socioemotional functions quite differently. Mobile phone effects in education are diverse and complex rather than just being either positive or negative.

CHAPTER 9

Mobile Phone Behavior in Daily Life

Outline

1. *Intuitive Thinking: Cindy's Quick Responses*
2. *Daily Observations: From a Refugee Bringing a Mobile Phone to a Husband Witnessing the Stabbing of His Wife*
   - 2.1 *Everyday Users: Iqbal as an Afghanistan Refugee*
   - 2.2 *Everyday Users: A Coloradan Girl*
   - 2.3 *Everyday Technologies: GPS Helped Police to Find Murderers*
   - 2.4 *Everyday Technologies: WomanLog*
   - 2.5 *Everyday Activities: Amanda Kloehr Drove to See Her Friend in Virginia*
   - 2.6 *Everyday Activities: Walking in the Cell Phone Lane in DC*
   - 2.7 *Everyday Effects: Mobile Phone Saved Garett Kolsun*
   - 2.8 *Everyday Effects: Witnessing the Stabbing of His Wife*
3. *Empirical Studies: From Australian Twins to Reduced Loneliness*
   - 3.1 *Everyday Users: 518 Australian Twins*
   - 3.2 *Everyday Users: 371 Low-Income Mothers*
   - 3.3 *Everyday Technologies: Brain–Computer Interface*
   - 3.4 *Everyday Activities: Calling While Driving Before Car Crashes*
   - 3.5 *Everyday Activities: Planning Everyday Family Activities*
   - 3.6 *Everyday Activities: Dining in Restaurants*
   - 3.7 *Everyday Effects: The Negative Spillover Effect*
   - 3.8 *Everyday Effects: Reduced Loneliness in Public Spaces*
4. *Knowledge Syntheses: From Older Users to Calling While Driving*
   - 4.1 *Overview: A Boundless Research Area*
   - 4.2 *Everyday Users: Older Users*
   - 4.3 *Everyday Activities: Calling While Driving*
5. *Comparative Analyses: Family Functioning*
6. *Complex Thinking: A Common Topic but a Complex Behavior*

1. Intuitive Thinking: Cindy's Quick Responses

One day, I asked Cindy, a proud mother of four children, what mobile phones can be used for in daily life for individuals and families. I told her to be quick and simple, and to say whatever came to mind. Her quick responses are as follows: "As a mother of four, mobile phones (1) provide me with the security that my kids can always reach me if they need me, (2) provide me with the security that if my son's car breaks down that he will have a phone to call for help, (3) make me feel that I am closer to my kids even when I am at work because I know that they can easily call if they need something, and (4) keep us connected in our crazy lives of sports, activities, work and school. Overall, I think mobile phones provide me with a sense of connection and security in that my kids can always contact me no matter where I am or where they are. Nothing else really matters to me in regards to the mobile phone. Although I would probably miss it if I couldn't use it for other things!"

What a great mom caring so much about her children! What can we learn about mobile phone behavior in daily life from Cindy's quick responses? It is not difficult to see at least four features. First, her knowledge about mobile phone uses in daily life was directly based on her personal knowledge of her personal experience. It is very concrete and very specific. Second, her responses focused on her family, especially her children. Clearly, she considers and uses her mobile phone as a basic tool for family communication. Third, her responses focused on security for her children anywhere and anytime. Fourth, they focused on connections to and coordination with her children. Furthermore, using the four-element model, we can see more specifically that in her case, mobile phone users were mainly her four kids and her as a mother, her mobile phone technologies involved merely the basic calling feature, her mobile phone activities focused on family communication, and her mobile phone effects were about security and connections among her family. Her experiences of mobile phone behavior in daily life can be illustrated in the following simple diagram:

Cindy and her children + calling feature → making calls between themselves → security and connections were achieved in her family.

Using Cindy's responses as the baseline, this chapter will further discuss and analyze a few daily observations, a few research studies, a few literature reviews, and a few comparative studies with the hope of developing a good knowledge of mobile phone behavior in daily life and appreciating the dynamics and complexity of mobile phone behavior in daily life. Our goal is to expand and deepen our understanding of the complexity of the mobile phone behaviors in daily life and to motivate further effective analyses and research efforts.

Sometimes it is not easy to distinguish mobile phone behavior in daily life from that of other contexts such as medicine, business, or education. For instance, K-12 mobile phone learning can be considered either in the daily context because school is a regular daily event or in the education context because K-12 is part of the education system. Another example relates to mobile phone payment, which is a business topic, but also a daily topic, because many people use mobile phones for payment on a regular basis. Mental health is a medicine topic because it is a branch of medicine in general and a daily topic because our modern daily life is often stressful. To clarify this potential ambiguity and for the sake of simplicity and convenience, we will look at the four aspects of mobile phone behavior: user, technology, activity, and effect. If a behavior concerns a regular rather than a professional user, a regular rather than a professional technology, a regular activity rather than a professional activity, or a regular effect rather than a professional effect, then we will consider the behavior in a *daily context* rather than in a *professional context*.

2. Daily Observations: From a Refugee Bringing a Mobile Phone to a Husband Witnessing the Stabbing of His Wife

2.1 Everyday Users: Iqbal as an Afghanistan Refugee

In September of 2015, thousands of refugees were heading to Europe. Among them, Iqbal was a 17-year-old refugee teenage boy from Afghanistan.[1] Iqbal had travelled hundreds of miles to escape his home, the warring province of Kunduz in northern Afghanistan. He fled east to Iran, and then travelled on foot through Turkey and by boat to Lesbos. He was unsure of where to go next. In his small brown backpack, he packed a few items to take with him. Among them were one pair of pants, one tissue, one pair of shoes, a pair of socks, a roll of bandages, 100 US dollars, 130 Turkish lira, one smartphone, one extra old phone, and SIM cards used in Afghanistan, Iran, and Turkey. Carrying a mobile phone with them as a vital tool for survival or even the only lifeline is extremely common among refugees from Afghanistan and Syria. They use their

---

[1] See http://metro.co.uk/2015/09/15/these-are-the-things-refugees-pack-when-fleeing-for-their-lives-5392880/.

mobile phones for various purposes, such as contacting or reconnecting with relatives and friends, taking selfies and using Instagram to document their travels, sharing life-or-death information, using GPS to find their way safely through Europe, alerting Greek coastguards to the sinking of their boat, searching online to reduce dangers of trafficking, and getting help from non-profit organizations such as Welcome to Europe to get practical and legal advice to find temporary shelter or a new home. This mobile phone behavior can be illustrated in a simple diagram, with the bold text highlighting the focus:

Afghanistan refugee Iqbal + smartphone/old phone/sim cards → using the phones during his escape → Iqbal escaped from his warring hometown and arrived in Turkey as a refugee.

2.2 *Everyday Users: A Coloradan Girl*

On March 20, 2015, a 12-year-old Coloradan girl was arrested by the police in Boulder County for attempting to poison her mother.[2] The girl, whose name was not released for reasons of protection, had an iPhone, but it was taken away by her mother because she was using it too much. The girl was extremely upset and decided to put bleach into her mom's drink twice in a week. Her mom eventually found out about the girl's plan to kill her. The girl was taken to a juvenile detention facility where she is being held pending the filing of charges:

A 12-year-old Coloradan girl + iPhone → overuse of her phone results in her mom taking it away → she tried to poison her mom twice and was arrested and taken to a juvenile detention facility.

These two cases based on daily observations involved two very different teenage mobile phone users. They both had similar smartphones. However, due to completely different life situations, their mobile activities and mobile effects were completely different. Iqbal used his phone to survive as a refugee and the Coloradan girl overused her phone, resulting in it being confiscated by her mom. Consequently, Iqbal fortunately escaped from his home country, but the Coloradan girl ended up in a juvenile detention facility after attempting to poison her mother. We can see that mobile phone users in daily life can be very different – a refugee trying to escape a war-torn province or a pre-teen girl poisoning her mom – leading to complex mobile phone behavior.

---

[2] See www.reuters.com/article/us-usa-colorado-poison-idUSKBN0MG2KQ20150320.

2.3   Everyday Technologies: GPS Helped Police to Find Murderers

In the morning of April 11, 2012, two electrical engineering graduate students at the University of Southern California, Ming Qu and Ying Wu, both 23 years old, were shot dead in their parked car near the campus.[3] Afterward, the Los Angeles Police Department found that someone used Wu's missing iPhone to make calls. Using the GPS in Wu's iPhone, the police were able to track down its whereabouts and found one suspect named Bryan Barnes. The police found further evidence that Barnes allegedly talked to another suspect named Javier Bolden about this killing. On February 5, 2014, Barnes and Bolden, both 21 years old, pleaded guilty to the murder of the two students after their botched robbery attempt. The mobile phone behavior diagram is as follows:

LAPD + GPS in a stolen iPhone → finding suspects and collecting criminal evidence → two murderers were arrested and pleaded guilty to the murder.

2.4   Everyday Technologies: WomanLog

On July 30, 2013, a local court in Taiwan found a married man guilty of having an affair with a young woman, ruling that the man should be jailed for 8 months and pay the young woman's family 30,000 New Taiwan Yuan.[4] The key evidence that the court collected and used against the man came from the young woman's mobile phone. On this phone, the woman had a special mobile application called WomanLog, a tool to keep track of her menstrual and fertility calendar, but she also recorded each time they slept together. The mobile phone behavior diagram is as follows:

A young Taiwanese woman + **WomanLog on her mobile phone** → recording the details of her affair with a married man → the court found the man guilty.

These two cases discussed above show the complexity of technology-based mobile phone behavior in daily life. For the first case, Bryan Barnes and Javier Bolden were two special mobile phone users because they stole an iPhone from two students. However, it was the GPS signals from the stolen iPhone that the LAPD used to identify the suspects and gather the criminal evidence, and the two murderers were eventually found guilty.

---

[3] See http://articles.latimes.com/2014/feb/05/local/la-me-usc-killings-conviction-20140206.
[4] See http://fashion.taiwan.cn/styleshow/201307/t20130731_4524528.htm.

On a technical note, in general, GPS (Global Positioning System) is run by the US military, but is commonly used by civilians in their everyday lives. In particular, in order to make GPS on our cell phones work, our phones need to have a regular GPS receiver and an active cell phone service. We typically turn on the GPS receiver in our cell phones, then our GPS receiver starts communicating with our cell phone service, and finally the GPS satellite sends back our location information. Because it uses up some cellular bandwidth, by default, most cell phone companies turn off the GPS in the phone except for emergency calls unless we manually turn it on, but a company can always automatically record our locations without giving us notice and this is one of reasons why some people are seriously concerned about privacy and security.

For the second case, the young woman as the regular mobile phone user used the app WomanLog to record her affair with a married man. It is these records on WomanLog that became the legal evidence for the court to make a ruling. Note that, as one of millions of apps used in daily life, WomanLog has multiple user interface languages and dozens of specific features such as keeping track of the menstrual cycle, ovulation and fertility forecast, basal body temperature chart, weight tracking, mood, pregnancy mode, and cervical mucus monitoring. All the main functions are accessible via the calendar. Tapping a finger on the calendar date, you can add and edit the settings for each day. Menstruation, ovulation, and fertility day forecast have to be understood as theoretical predictions which may not coincide with the actual menstruation, ovulation and fertility days.

2.5   Everyday Activities: Amanda Kloehr Drove to See Her Friend in Virginia

On June 20, 2008, Amanda Kloehr, then a college student of 20 years old, drove from McGuire Air Force Base in New Jersey to Newport News in Virginia to visit a friend.[5] She was on Route 13, enjoying the summer breeze from the North Atlantic Ocean, and approaching her trip destination. She was not speeding, she had not been drinking or taking drugs, and she was wearing her seatbelt. She was doing nothing terribly wrong. All she was doing, then, was driving while just briefly checking her text messages or her GPS on her cell phone, but in the few seconds she was distracted, she did not see a tractor-trailer in the left lane waiting to make a left turn. Immediately, her car slammed into the back of the tractor-trailer,

---

[5] See www.pennlive.com/midstate/index.ssf/2012/07/distracted_driving_cost_her_an.html.

slid underneath the truck, and was nearly crushed flat. Her leg was broken. Her face hit a forklift in the back of the truck-trailer and the right side of her face was basically gone. Blood was everywhere.

Fortunately, she survived this horrific car accident. It took her more than a year to learn to walk again. She lost her right eye and had more than twenty surgeries to rebuild her smashed face. To share this real experience and take her serious message to other young drivers, she has been giving talks about the dangers of distracted driving in many schools and colleges and developed a special website called AmandaReconstructed.com. She said: "I want to tell as any people as I can so I can save as many lives as possible."

2.6 Everyday Activities: Walking in the Cell Phone Lane in DC

On July 17, 2014, near the National Geographic Museum of Washington DC, a sidewalk on the 18th Street Northwest was divided into two lanes.[6] One was labeled *No Cellphones*, and another was labeled *Cellphones: Walk in This Lane at Your Own Risk*, designating this lane for those who walk while using cell phones. National Geographic Channel – the National Geographic Society's American television channel – was making a TV series. With the city's permission, the TV series team marked the cell phone lane to see how people would react. Interestingly enough, many pedestrians stopped and smiled when seeing the cell phone lane sign. They then brought out their mobile phones and took a picture of the lane as a fun photo-souvenir.

This kind of social experiment of pedestrian management has also been seen in New York City and Philadelphia in the United States and a few cities in the world (e.g., Chongqing in China and Antwerp in Belgium). Given that minor and major cell phone walking accidents have rapidly increased, people are concerned about pedestrian safety. The designated cell phone lane is one of the current strategies to deal with the pedestrian safety issue.

The two cases we have just discussed concern activity-based mobile phone behavior that has been very often observed in our everyday lives. More specifically, these two cases show a unique and complex issue in studying activity-based mobile phone behavior: *mobile phone multitasking activities* – That is, people use mobile phones while simultaneously engaging in various other activities (e.g., reading while texting, juggling

---

[6] See www.yahoo.com/tech/cellphone-talkers-get-their-own-sidewalk-lane-in-d-c-92080566744.html.

while listening to music from the mobile phone, studying while searching information online, and calling or texting while driving). However, among all the mobile phone multitasking activities, calling or texting while driving is both the most dangerous activity to be concerned about and the most challenging to stop. The Amanda story represents one of hundreds of real terrible accidents as a result of calling or texting while driving. The DC cell phone lane case suggests that, besides distracted driving, there are still more issues leading to various accidents due to using mobile phones while walking or biking. For these reasons, distracted driving has been one of the second most studied topics in mobile phone behavior research, next to research on the possible links between brain cancer and mobile phone use. The two diagrams illustrating the two cases of activity-based mobile phone behavior are as follows:

Amanda Kloehr + mobile phone $\rightarrow$ **using her mobile phone while driving** $\rightarrow$ resulted in a terrible car accident, causing her to lose the right-hand side of her face, including her right eye.

Pedestrians in cities + mobile phones $\rightarrow$ **using their mobile phones while walking** $\rightarrow$ a special mobile phone lane was designated for pedestrian safety.

2.7 *Everyday Effects: Mobile Phone Saved Garett Kolsun*

On the Saturday morning of September 7, 2013, Garett Kolsun, a 40-year-old Canadian Border Services officer, walked alone on the street in the small port town of Churchill, Canada.[7] Suddenly, he saw a polar bear running toward him. He screamed loudly for help, waved his hands, and ran in a circle, trying to stop the bear. He finally saw a bakery and tried to open the door. At this time, the bear was on top of Garett and put her paw on him. He could not do anything but pull his cell phone out of his pocket. He turned it on and the screen lit up. He thrust the cell phone into the face of the bear, and the light distracted and scared the bear enough that she stepped back and Kolsun had a second to run away and enter another house. He only suffered scratches and superficial puncture wounds to his hip. The bears are more active at that time of year, before the ice freezes. The local government captured the 3-year-old bear and, instead of euthanizing it, decided to move it from the wild to the International Polar Bear Conservation Centre of a local zoo. This case is illustrated in the simple diagram below:

---

[7] See www.cbc.ca/news/canada/manitoba/winnipeg-man-wards-off-polar-bear-with-cellphone-1.1705973.

Garett Kolsun + mobile phone light → used it to startle and distract an attacking polar bear → **survived the bear attack.**

2.8   *Everyday Effects: Witnessing the Stabbing of His Wife*

On October 30, 2013, Justin Pele Poole, an American soldier stationed for about nine months in Southwest Asia, used FaceTime, an iPhone app, to videochat with Rachel Poole, his wife, who was in her ninth month of pregnancy in her home in Texas.[8] Suddenly, he saw a young man allegedly attack Rachel from behind with a knife. Rachel recognized this man and shouted his name several times to her husband over the iPhone. Justin helplessly watched via the iPhone while the young man stabbed the face and stomach of Rachel multiple times. Ultimately, Rachel Poole was transported to University Medical Center, and was still in a critical condition when her baby, Isabella, was born after doctors performed a successful emergency cesarean section. Her baby was born healthy. The attacker was charged with criminal attempted capital murder.

Justin Pele Poole + FaceTime on iPhone → chatting with his pregnant wife → **he witnessed his wife being stabbed multiple times by a young man who was later arrested.**

These two cases presented above show the complexity of effect-based mobile phone behavior. For the first case, the mobile user was Garett Kolsun. He used the mobile phone light to scare the polar bear and survived the bear attack. The phone literally saved his life, demonstrating an unexpected, amazing life-saving effect. For the second case, the mobile phone users were Justin Pele Poole and his 9-month-pregnant wife Rachel Poole. The couple used the iPhone to videochat thousands of miles away from each other. The mobile phone allowed him to witness the process of his wife being stabbed, demonstrating an unexpected, devastating life-threatening effect.

3.   Empirical Studies: From Australian Twins to Reduced Loneliness

As we discussed in the previous section, mobile phones are very common in daily life; however, mobile phone behavior in daily life is more complex than many of us might expect. Now we will move from the everyday

---

[8] See www.cnn.com/2013/11/02/justice/texas-stabbing-videochat/?hpt=zite_zite9_featured.

observations to the scientific studies and further examine the complexity of mobile phone behavior in daily life.

3.1 Everyday Users: 518 Australian Twins

The next study we will discuss is entitled "The heritability and genetic correlates of mobile phone use: A twin study of consumer behavior."[9] Heritability is normally defined as the proportion of phenotypic variation that is due to variation in genetic values. The authors are Geoffrey Miller from the Psychology Department at the University of New Mexico in the United States, and Gu Zhu, Margaret Wright, Narelle Hansell, and Nicholas G. Martin from the Department of Genetic Epidemiology at the Queensland Institute of Medical Research, Australia. Geoffrey Miller has published two articles on smartphone psychology, while his primary research area is on sexual selection in human evolution. The article was published in 2012 in *Twin Research and Human Genetics*, the official journal of the International Society for Twin Studies and the Human Genetics Society of Australasia by Cambridge University Press since 1998.

This study aimed to examine the heritability and genetic correlates of mobile phone use. In the study, two samples of teenage twins in Australia were recruited, with a total sample size of 1,036 teens or 518 twin pairs. Whether the twins were identical (a single fertilized egg with the same DNA) or fraternal (two fertilized eggs with different DNA) was determined by using a commercial kit and cross-checking with blood group and other phenotypic data. Mobile phone use between 2005 and 2010 was measured by a five-item questionnaire. The major findings include the following: (1) About 25 percent of the twins reported making voice calls two to four times per week and about 15 percent of the twins sent text messages four to ten times per day. (2) Using mobile phones, either making more voice calls or sending text messages, among these twins had more to do with heritabilities, ranging from 34 to 60 percent in explained variance, than shared family environment, ranging from 5 to 24 percent in explained variance. (3) Identical or monozygotic twins consistently showed more similarities in using mobile phones, making more voice calls, and sending text messages than fraternal or dizygotic twins. The authors believe that their results have implications for: (1) assessing the risks of mobile phone use such as radiofrequency field

---

[9] Miller, G., Zhu, G., Wright, M. J. *et al.* (2012). "The heritability and genetic correlates of mobile phone use: A twin study of consumer behavior," *Twin Research and Human Genetics*, 15(1): 97–106.

exposure and driving accidents; (2) studying the adoption and use of other emerging technologies; (3) understanding the genetic architecture of the cognitive and personality traits that predict consumer behavior; and (4) challenging the common assumption that consumer behavior is shaped entirely by culture, media, and the family environment.

This is the first and perhaps only study examining mobile phone behavior from the perspective of behavior genetics. We can learn a few key points about mobile phone behavior in daily life from this study. First, heritabilities of twins, whether they are identical or fraternal twins, might influence their mobile phone behavior, in addition to common demo-graphical and psychological characteristics of mobile phone users. Second, for mobile technologies and mobile activities (using mobile phones to call or text), no different behavioral patterns were observed in making voice calls vs. sending text messages among these twins. Heritabilities of twins do not lead them to make more calls or text more messages. Third, the study did not examine mobile effects on these twins. The mobile phone behavior diagram is as follows:

518 pairs of Australian teenage twins + mobile phones → calling or texting in daily life → the impact of heritability on calling and texting was observed, but no mobile effects on behavioral patterns were reported.

3.2   Everyday Users: 371 Low-Income Mothers

Judith Carta is a Professor of Special Education at Kansas University and has published multiple articles on using mobile phones to enhance parenting interventions. She and her collaborators published an article entitled "Randomized trial of a cellular phone-enhanced home visitation parenting intervention" and provided a good case for mobile phone users.[10] The article was published in 2013 in *Pediatrics*.

This study focused on one core research question: Does a parenting intervention supported by family coaches or a similar intervention enhanced by cell phones increase low-income mothers' use of good parenting strategies? To examine this question, the researchers designed a randomized control trial study. They recruited 371 low-income mothers (being 18 years old at first child's birth, having less than a high-school diploma, receiving financial assistance, or meeting the income eligibility requirement for a program such as Head Start), who – together with their

---

[10]   Carta, J. J., Lefever, J. B., Bigelow, K. *et al.* (2013). "Randomized trial of a cellular phone-enhanced home visitation parenting intervention," *Pediatrics*, 132(Supplement 2): S167–S173.

young children – were randomly assigned to three conditions: a regular parenting intervention called Planned Activities Training (PAT); a cellular phone-enhanced version of Planned Activities Training (CPAT); or a wait-list control (WLC) group. The six dependent variables assessing the intervention effects included: (1) mothers' correct use of the PAT strategies (e.g., explaining activities, establishing rules and consequences, giving choices, using positive interaction skills, ignoring minor misbehavior); (2) the quality of mother–children interactions in twelve dimensions (e.g., sensitivity, reasonable expectations); (3) mothers' depression levels; (4) mothers' stress levels; (5) children's adaptive and externalizing and internalizing problem behaviors; and (6) children's positive engagement and responsiveness. They assessed both the short- and long-term intervention effects, at post-intervention and six months after post-intervention. Analysis of covariance was used to assess the six intervention effects, controlling for pre-intervention measures. The study had two major findings: there were significant intervention effects (1) on both mothers' parenting strategies and quality of mother–children interactions at the two time points, with a relatively better effect by the cell-phone-enhanced intervention, and (2) on both children's positive engagement and internalizing/externalizing behaviors, with a relatively better effect by the cell-phone-enhanced intervention.

This case shows three aspects of the complexity of mobile phone behavior. First, it documents a specific mobile phone behavior, with an emphasis on intervention effects. Specifically, one-third of 371 low-income mothers were provided with the PAT training delivered through home visits, but also received a cellular phone and cellular phone service. The cellular phone enhancement mainly consisted of text messages that occurred between mothers and family coaches. Text messages were sent twice per day, with one message prompting mothers to use a specific PAT strategy or to engage in positive interactions with their child, and a second text inquiring about the mothers' use of PAT, their implementation of a planned activity or interactions with their child, or their child's behavior. Text message content was individualized for each mother and related to the focus of recent intervention visits. This cell-phone-enhanced intervention with two text messages per day substantially improved these mothers' parenting strategies and their children's behavior. Second, instead of a simple view, it reveals the complexity of the mobile effects and thus shows the complexity of mobile phone behavior. Intuitively and typically, one tends to think that mobile phone effects are one single effect that stands alone (e.g., adolescents text each other daily leading to one effect – sustaining their friendship). This case shows more complex effects: text messages were added to the existing human-based intervention and generated significant effects on parenting behaviors and children's behaviors for low-income families, both short and long term. The mobile phone behavior related to this study can be illustrated in the following simple diagram:

371 low-income mothers + mobile phones → receiving phone-enhanced training → mothers' parenting strategies, quality of mother–children interactions, children's positive engagement, and children's internalizing/externalizing behaviors improved.

3.3   Everyday Technologies: Brain–Computer Interface

The next study we will discuss is "A cell-phone-based brain–computer interface for communication in daily life."[11] This study is uniquely interesting in terms of our everyday lives because someone might encounter a challenge in moving their hands, arms, feet, legs, or entire bodies (e.g., injured, disabled, or elderly) and may be unable to carry out even very simple daily tasks (e.g., making a phone call or moving a wheelchair). It would be very convenient for us to just use our brains to do things. The authors Yu-Te Wang, Yijun Wang, and Tzyy-Ping Jung are a research group from the Swartz Center for Computational Neuroscience, Institute for Neural Computational, at the University of California, San Diego (UCSD). Yu-Te Wang graduated with a PhD from the Department of Computer Science and Engineering at UCSD, and is currently a research staff associate at UCSD. He has published multiple articles on cell-phone-based wireless and mobile brain–machine interfaces. This article was published in 2011 in the *Journal of Neural Engineering*, a relatively new journal published by IOP Publishing since 2004, with an impact factor of 3.493 in 2015. IOP Publishing is part of the Institute of Physics Publishing (IOP), a leading scientific society promoting physics and bringing physicists together for the benefit of all with a worldwide membership of around 50,000 physicists from all sectors.

The goal of the study was to test the practicality of a new device that can use a brain–computer interface to send brain signals wirelessly to a cell phone in daily life so that the phone can perform tasks (e.g., remotely turning off a kitchen oven or turning on a home heating system without physically moving our bodies). In the study, ten individuals participated in

---

[11] Wang, Y.-T., Wang, Y., and Jung, T.-P. (2011). "A cell-phone-based brain–computer interface for communication in daily life," *Journal of Neural Engineering*, 8(2): 025018.

the experiment. The device consisted of three parts: (1) a computer screen shows digital numbers from 0 to 10, as well as two keys for *Backspace* and *Enter*; (2) a headband functioning as an EEG brain signal acquisition unit to detect, amplify, process, and send out brain signals; and (3) a mobile phone to receive, process, and execute brain signals wirelessly through Bluetooth. The experimental task was to ask each participant to gaze at a ten-digit phone number and a key of *Enter* or *Backspace* on the computer screen and assess the accuracy and efficiency of using human brains rather than human fingers to dial a mobile phone. The results indicated that: (1) all of the ten participants passed the phone-dialing task with their brains, with an average accuracy of nearly 96 percent and with an average completion time of nearly 89 seconds; and (2) the information transfer rate of the device was close to 30 bits per minute, which is comparable to similar devices using high-end PCs rather than mobile phones.

This is the first study of this kind that links human brain signals with mobile phones. We can learn from this study that: (1) mobile phones can be operated via the human brain rather than via actual human fingers; (2) mobile phones as a regular technology can be linked with a regular brain–computer interface to make a wireless, mobile, portable, convenient, and low-cost device; (3) individuals with no or extremely limited motor abilities (e.g., those with a disability or those with motor restraints) can use this device to carry out various daily tasks (e.g., make a phone call or move a wheelchair). The mobile phone behavior diagram is as follows:

Human brains + **brain–computer interface via mobile phones** → detecting, processing, delivering brain signals to a mobile phone → successfully carried out daily-life tasks by using mobile phones.

3.4 *Everyday Activities: Calling While Driving Before Car Crashes*

In the previous section, we discussed the Amanda Kloehr case and the DC cell phone lane case. Now let us see some scientific evidence about the serious dangers involved in the activity of using mobile phones while driving. The article is called "Association between cellular-telephone calls and motor vehicle collisions."[12] It is one of the classic studies on distracted driving and has been cited 1,122 times according to Google Scholar. The article was published in 1997 in the *New England Journal of Medicine*, widely considered the oldest and best medical journal in the world with a

---

[12] Redelmeier, D. A. and Tibshirani, R. J. (1997). "Association between cellular-telephone calls and motor vehicle collisions," *New England Journal of Medicine*, 336(7): 453–458.

2015 impact factor of 59.558 – the highest among academic journals. The authors are two eminent Canadian scholars, Donald Redelmeier and Robert Tibshirani. Donald Redelmeier is a Professor of Medicine at the University of Toronto and has published extensively on major studies related to driving accidents. Robert Tibshirani is a Professor of Health Research and Policy and Statistics at Stanford University and has published extensively on statistics.

The study was conducted from 1994 to 1995 in Toronto. The participants were 699 drivers who had car accidents with major property damage and came to the North York Collison Reporting Center during Monday to Friday, 10 am to 6 pm. Drivers who had personal injuries or were involved in criminal activities did not come to the center and thus were not included in the study. The independent variable, *use of cell phones*, was based on phone records from the cell phone companies. The dependent variable, time of motor vehicle collision, was based on the combined examination of participants' statement, police reports, and emergency service records. Case-cross-over analysis was used to compare each driver's cell phone use immediately before the accident (i.e., case) to the cell phone use at the same time on various comparable days before the accident (i.e., cross-over) in order to find an association between car accidents and cell phone use. The major findings were as follows: (1) Cell phone use right before a car accident was associated with 4.3 times higher risk of a car accident than that of the same drivers when they were not using cell phones. (2) The relative risk was higher for younger drivers, less experienced drivers, less educated drivers, and drivers who were on high-speed roads. (3) Using handheld cell phones was not safer than using hands-free cell phones. (4) 70 percent of these drivers used cell phones (e.g., calling emergency services) immediately after the accident.

From the perspective of mobile phone behavior in daily life, this classic study can offer a few insights. First, a large group of daily mobile phone users are drivers who use mobile phones while driving every day. Various characteristics (e.g., age, experience, and education) are associated with their distracted driving risks. However, distracted driving is their daily habit, which could be very costly, even costing their lives. Second, different specific mobile phone technologies are involved, for instance, using features of calling or texting and hands-free or handheld phones. Third, there are various distractive mobile phone activities during driving, for instance, dialing, reaching for phones, calling, texting, and checking GPS. These are all risky activities while driving. Fourth, there are both negative and positive effects of using cell phones. Cell phone use right before a car accident was associated with four times higher risk of a car accident, similar to or even higher than the risk of drunk driving. On the other hand, many drivers used their phones to call emergency services after their accidents. The mobile phone behavior involved in the study can be illustrated in the following simple diagram:

699 drivers in Toronto + mobile phones → **calling while driving right before a car accident** → had four times higher accidental risk before their accidents and phones used to call emergency services after their accidents.

3.5 *Everyday Activities: Planning Everyday Family Activities*

We will next discuss an article entitled "The mobile phone as a tool in family life: Impact on planning of everyday activities and car use."[13] It has been cited twenty-eight times according to Google Scholar. The author is Randi Hjorthol, Chief Research Sociologist at the Institute of Transport Economics of Norway, who has published multiple articles on travel behavior and mobility. This article was published in 2008 in *Transport Reviews*, a well-established Taylor & Francis journal publishing authoritative and current research-based reviews since 1981, with an impact factor of 2.452 in 2015.

The research goal of this study was to examine the relationships among time norms, planning of everyday activities, use of the mobile phone, and use of the car in families with children. The study was a survey study conducted in 2005 with a random sample of 2,030 parents of Norwegian families with children 18 years of age or younger living at home with their parents. The major findings include the following: (1) 98 percent of parents had mobile phones and 93 percent had connections to the Internet. A total of 51 percent of the parents reported having one car in the household and 39 percent reported having two. These two pieces of background information – percentage of parents having mobile phones (the communication tool) and percentage of parents having cars (the transportation tool) – help us to understand how these parents organize their children's everyday activities. (2) Three everyday activities were related to communication of planning and the frequency of daily car use: shopping for groceries, transporting children to and from day-care or school, and transporting children to or from friends' houses and other unorganized leisure activities. (3) In families with children, the most

---

[13] Hjorthol, R. J. (2008). "The mobile phone as a tool in family life: Impact on planning of everyday activities and car use," *Transport Reviews*, 28(3): 303–320.

common shopping frequency was three to four times a week. A total of 73 percent of the parents indicated that their most common way to make family car arrangements for grocery shopping was face to face; 40 percent of them indicated that they called with mobile phones to make shopping arrangements, 23 percent used mobile texting, and only 16 percent used landline telephones. (4) Over 60 percent of the parents used cars to accompany children to day-care or school. For the parents who used cars multiple times a day for their children, 63 percent called with mobile phones (the highest percentage), 58 percent used mobile phone SMS, 50 percent used face-to-face communication, and 48 percent used landline telephones. In contrast, for the parents who used the car for children once a day, 38 percent used landline telephones (the highest percentage), 34 percent communicated face to face, 27 percent used mobile phones to call, and 25 percent used mobile phone SMS.

We can learn from this study that: (1) these 2,030 parents were mobile phone users; (2) they mainly used their mobile phones to call or text; (3) many of them used mobile phones to call or text their spouses for their everyday family car usage; and (4) mobile phones helped them coordinate family cars for shopping and sending kids to school. The mobile phone behavior diagram is as follows:

2,030 Norwegian parents + mobile phones → **planning car use** → helped them use their cars for their children's daily activities more efficiently with less planning time.

3.6   Everyday Activities: Dining in Restaurants

The next article we will discuss is entitled "Patterns of mobile device use by caregivers and children during meals in fast food restaurants."[14] The authors are a group of medical researchers from Boston University Medical Center. The first author is Jenny Radesky. She is a developmental and behavioral pediatrician at Boston Medical Center and has done multiple studies examining how mobile devices, such as smartphones and tablets, impact the interaction between children and caregivers and mobile phone use by young children and caregivers. The article was published in 2014 in *Pediatrics*, the official journal of the American Academy of Pediatrics since 1948, with an impact factor of 5.473 in 2014.

---

[14] Radesky, J. S., Kistin, C. J., Zuckerman, B. *et al.* (2014). "Patterns of mobile device use by caregivers and children during meals in fast food restaurants," *Pediatrics*, 133(4): e843–e849.

The research goal of this study was to examine how mobile phone use affects caregiver–child interactions. In this study, the researchers conducted fifty-five naturalistic, anonymous observations during lunch or dinner times in fast food restaurants in Boston. Three researchers mainly used detailed field notes to independently observe parenting behavior and child behavior without direct participation for 10 to 40 minutes. They then used the grounded theory approach (a qualitative data analysis method to systematically review qualitative data and detect emerging themes) as the data analysis method to develop themes and subthemes. The major findings were as follows: (1) Among fifty-five caregiver–child observations, forty involved mobile phone use. (2) The observed dominant theme was that caregivers' attention was absorbed with mobile phone use rather than interactions with their children during the meal time. (3) Five patterns of caregiver–child interactions were observed: (a) sixteen of fifty-five observations involved high degree of absorption, meaning caregivers continuously typed text or swiped screens throughout the meal; (b) eight observations involved a relatively high absorption, where caregivers made mobile phone calls while maintaining some eye contact with their children; (c) nine observations involved less absorption, where caregivers quickly checked their phones, typed briefly, or made quick calls; (d) three observations involved caregivers' partial attention to their phones while holding their phones in their hand and doing other things; and (e) eighteen observations had no mobile phone use, neither bringing out the phone or just placing the phone on the table. (4) Three impacts of mobile phone use were specified: while using the mobile phone during the meal: (a) caregivers reduced their responsiveness to children; (b) caregivers reduced conversation with children and children showed passiveness in conversation; and (c) children intensified their actions to draw caregivers' attentions and caregivers responded with discouragement.

This medical anthropological study provided rich and unique evidence of activity-based mobile phone behavior from a very special angle, i.e., family mealtimes. (1) The mobile users are the caregivers who used or did not use their phones during the mealtime. Their children should also be considered mobile phone users because they directly used (e.g., co-viewing a phone screen) and indirectly used (e.g., seeing and getting annoyed by their parents' mobile phone use) mobile phones. (2) The specific types of mobile technologies, whether texting, swiping, calling, or even holding, generated different interactions. (3) Specific negative impacts on caregiver–child interactions have been observed. The mobile phone behavior diagram is as follows:

Fifty-five caregiver–child pairs + mobile phones → **absorption with the phone during the meal** → negative reactions from both children and caregiver were observed.

3.7   Everyday Effects: The Negative Spillover Effect

The next study we will discuss is entitled "Blurring boundaries? Linking technology use, spillover, individual distress, and family satisfaction."[15] The author is Noelle Chesley, an Associate Professor of Sociology at the University of Wisconsin-Milwaukee, who has published multiple articles on technology use and work–family relationships. The article was partially based on her dissertation in 2004. It was published in 2005 in the *Journal of Marriage and Family*, a well-established Wiley journal of the National Council on Family Relations published since 1938, with an impact factor of 1.873 in 2015.

In this study, the researcher defined two types of technology use – computation-based use (using computers) and communication-based use (using mobile phones) – and aimed to examine whether technology use was associated with work–family overlap and eventually with personal distress and family satisfaction. This is essentially a secondary data analysis based on existing interview data collected twice from seven organizations in the state of New York from 1998 to 1999 and 2000 to 2001. Major measures included: technology use (computer use and mobile phone use); spillover on a two-item scale for assessing negative or positive spillover from work to family (e.g., job problems distract you when you are at home) or from family to work (e.g., personal problems distract you when you are at work); psychological distress on a five-item scale; and family satisfaction on a five-item scale. The findings included: (1) Regarding the spillover from work to family, for the entire sample with both men and women, mobile phone use over two years but not computer use over two years was significantly associated with negative but not positive spillover. This effect was further significantly linked with personal distress and family dissatisfaction. (2) Regarding the spillover from family to work, only for women but not for men, mobile phone use over two years was significantly associated with negative but not positive spillover. This effect was significantly linked with personal distress and family dissatisfaction.

---

[15] Chesley, N. (2005). "Blurring boundaries? Linking technology use, spillover, individual distress, and family satisfaction," *Journal of Marriage and Family*, 67(5): 1237–1248.

From a daily-life perspective of mobile phone behavior, this study examined a very interesting phenomenon – the *spillover phenomenon*. First, for mobile phone users, the study shows gender differences in the spillover effect: women's family demands will spill over into their workplace and their work demands will also spill over into their family life; whereas men's work demands will spill over into their family life, but not the other way around. Second, for mobile phone technologies and activities, different technologies have different spillover effects. In general, mobile phone use but not computer use leads to negative work-to-family spillover. Second, for mobile effects, the study does not support the boundary theory arguing that technology use provides a flexible boundary between work and family and thus better meets the needs for work and family. Instead, it partially supports the spillover theory that technology use produces a permeable work–family boundary and leads to negative but not positive spillover outcomes from work to family for both men and women and from family to work for women only. Technology use may be blurring work–family boundaries with negative consequences for working people's daily lives. The mobile phone behavior diagram is as follows:

1,367 New York couples + mobile phones → using mobile phones for work and home → **produced the negative work–family spillover effect, leading to increased personal distress and decreased family satisfaction.**

3.8   Everyday Effects: Reduced Loneliness in Public Spaces

The next article we will talk about is entitled "Change in the social life of urban public spaces: The rise of mobile phones and women, and the decline of aloneness over 30 years."[16] The author is Keith N. Hampton from Rutgers University in the United States. Hampton is an Associate Professor in the Department of Communication at Rutgers University and has published multiple articles on mobile phones and social changes. This article was published in 2014 in *Urban Studies*, a journal published by Sage since 1964, with an impact factor of 1.934 in 2015.

In the study, the authors compared two sets of films, one set made thirty years ago in 1979 to 1980 and another made recently in 2008 to 2010, to compare behavior and characteristics of nearly 150,000 people in the same four public spaces (e.g., Steps of the Metropolitan Museum of Art in New

---

[16] Hampton, K. N., Goulet, L. S., and Albanesius, G. (2015). "Change in the social life of urban public spaces: The rise of mobile phones and women, and the decline of aloneness over 30 years," *Urban Studies*, 52(8): 1489–1504.

York City). The goal was to examine whether Americans have become more or less socially isolated when using public spaces. In total, there were 38 hours of footage. The authors sampled the films at 15-second intervals, leading to 9,173 observation periods, and coded them based on gender, activity (alone or in groups), mobile phone use (alone or in groups), and other characteristics. The major findings include the following: (1) From the period of 1979 to 1980 to the period of 2008 to 2010, people staying alone decreased and people interacting in groups increased in three of the four public spaces where leisure and shopping were the main functions. In other words, there is an observed general trend that now people interact more in groups rather than staying alone. (2) From the period of 1979 to 1980 to the period of 2008 to 2010, in one public space which people mainly used to transit from a subway station to an office tower and a hospital, people staying alone increased and people interacting in groups decreased. (3) During the years 2008 to 2010, the majority of these observed people did not use their mobile phones and only 3 to 10 percent of them used them in all four public spaces. Among these mobile phone users, they tended to use phones alone rather than in a group. No such data were collected in the years 1979 to 1980.

This study shows two surprising findings. First, it does not support the popular perception that people are more alone in public spaces than they were in the past. Instead, it was found that people spending time in groups was more prevalent in 2010 than it was thirty years ago. Second, it does not support another popular perception that mobile phone use is popular in public, making people alone but together. It was observed that the percentage of people using mobile phones when walking in public spaces was quite low and people rarely used their phones in groups. One simple diagram of the mobile phone behavior involved in the study is as follows:

Over 50,000 American people in four public areas in 2008 to 2010 + mobile phones → did not use their mobile phones in four public areas unless they were not in a group → **limited mobile phone use in public is associated with reduced public isolation over thirty years.**

4. Knowledge Syntheses: From Older Users to Calling While Driving

4.1 Overview: A Boundless Research Area

In medicine, business, or education, as we discussed in the previous three chapters, it is relatively easy to set a boundary to search the relevant literature in a given domain. However, it is quite difficult to set a boundary for the literature on mobile phone behavior in daily life. This is because, by design, mobile phones are generally for everyday use by ordinary people. Thus, mobile phone behavior in daily life is essentially boundless. For the convenience of analysis in this book, we could loosely define the literature in this area as not being close to the areas of medicine, business, or education. In the *Encyclopedia of Mobile Phone Behavior*, there are at least forty-two chapters that examine mobile phone behavior in daily life rather than specifically related to medicine, business, or education (see Table 9.1). Among these chapters, some focus on mobile users in daily life (e.g., church goers, divorced coparents, romantic partners, or Mexican users), others focus on mobile technologies in daily life (e.g., mobile diary methods, antisocial texting, or environmental geo-sensors), others focus on mobile activities in daily life (e.g., social interactions, mobile phone beeping, hyper-coordination, or of course calling while driving), and others also focus on mobile effects in daily life (e.g., emotional effects, ethical effects, social effects, and cultural effects).

4.2   Everyday Users: Older Users

In addition to the *Encyclopedia* chapters, we will discuss two review articles to further illustrate the breadth and depth of the literature in this area. The first review we will examine is "Mobile applications in an aging society: Status and trends."[17] The authors are four engineering researchers from Spain, Inmaculada Plazaa, Lourdes Martína, Sergio Martin, and Carlos Medrano. It was published in 2011 in the *Journal of Systems and Software*, a well-established specialist journal published by Elsevier since 1980, with an impact factor of 1.424 in 2015.

This review is not easy to read mainly due to its uncommon organization. However, it provides unique and much-needed knowledge about elderly mobile phone users in daily life. (1) It is well known that people live and work longer and healthier than ever, e.g., in Europe, the population of age 65 and over was about 23 percent in 2005 and is predicted to be about 30 percent in 2050. (2) *Gerontechnology* as a new research field has emerged to meet the needs of an aging society with information technologies. (3) *Quality of life* has been an important contemporary concept in the past five decades stressing physical, mental, social, spiritual, and economic needs for

---

[17] Plaza, I., Martína, L., Martin, S., and Medrano, C. (2011). "Mobile applications in an aging society: Status and trends," *Journal of Systems and Software*, 84(11): 1977–1988.

Table 9.1 *The* Encyclopedia *Chapters on Mobile Phone Behavior in Daily Life*

Elements	Chapter Title
Users	Mobile phones and libraries/information centres
Users	Religious use of mobile phones
Users	Divorced coparents' use of communication technology
Users	The role of mobile phones in romantic relationships
Users	Texting and Christian practice
Users	Mobile communications in Mexico in the Latin American context
Users	Focus on text messages: A review of studies in French
Users	Mobile user behaviors in China
Users	Portable social groups
Technologies	Mobile diary methods in studying daily family life
Technologies	Text messaging as a forum for negative and antisocial communication
Technologies	The usage and applications of mobile apps
Technologies	Mobile games
Technologies	Cognitive phone for sensing human behavior
Technologies	Mobile phones as ubiquitous social and environmental geo-sensors
Activities	Using mobile phones to control social interactions
Activities	Mundane mobile maintenance, entrapment, and hyper-coordination
Activities	Mobile communication tools as morality-building devices
Activities	The impact of mobile phones on teenagers' socialization and emancipation
Activities	Mobile phone beeping
Activities	Sustainability of the use of mobile phones
Activities	Generation, collection and recycling of used and end-of-life mobile phones
Activities	Mobile phones: News consumption, news creation, and news organization accommodations
Activities	Cell phone conversation while driving
Activities	Teenage sexting: Sexual expression meets mobile technology
Activities	Adolescent text messaging
Effects	Emoticon use in mobile communications :-)
Effects	The new frontier of mobile communication ethics
Effects	Dimensions of mobile phone behaviors in environmental communication
Effects	Attachment to mobile phones across social contexts
Effects	Mobile phone addiction
Effects	Mobile technostress
Effects	Mobile phone use enhances social connectedness
Effects	Mobile technology and social identity
Effects	Mobile phone culture: The impacts of mobile phone use
Effects	Use of mobile phones to help prevent child maltreatment
Effects	Connecting 'round the clock: Mobile phones and adolescents' experiences of intimacy
Effects	Sex, cyberbullying and the mobile phone
Effects	An exploration of intrusive mobile phone behavior
Effects	Communication privacy management and mobile phone use
Effects	Mobile phone etiquette

older people. (4) In contrast to the popular stereotype that older people reject new technology or are unable to learn new technology, about 60 percent of 60 to 74 year olds and 27 percent of 75 year olds and older use a mobile phone, a higher adaptation rate than that of PCs and the Internet. They accept and adopt mobile phones very well. (5) There are five major types of mobile phone needs for older people: feeling safe and secure (e.g., need for getting help when they move around and fall down); memory aids (e.g., need for an appointment or medication reminder); communication (e.g., need for contacting families and friends); mobility (e.g., need for movement freedom); and a healthier life (e.g., need for physical and mental wellbeing). (6) The current mobile phones challenge older people in multiple aspects, including buttons being too small to press, too many menus to understand and remember, text size being too small to read, and handsets being too small to hold. (7) The current research work concerns multiple specific areas: health and home care (e.g., DGhome, a home-care service that uses mobile phones to remind the older users to take medicine); safety and security (e.g., using mobile phones with GPS and compass to assist older people and their families when the older people get lost in the outdoor environment; using SMS to remotely monitor mobility levels of older people in their daily lives); learning (e.g., Hermers, a product for cognitive care and cognitive training with mobile phones); religion (e.g., religious calendars, daily audio podcasts, news updates, religious ringtones); social interaction (e.g., mobile phone communications between grandparents and grandchildren); hobbies (e.g., games for older people like PopCap Games); and working life (e.g., working at home as teleworkers). (8) Several mobile phones have been designed specifically for older people (Auto-Mobile, Emporia) with special features such as a much larger keypad, an SOS button for automatic emergency calls, a flashlight to help users with visual difficulties, a louder volume if needed to aid hearing, and a motion sensor to detect fallen or motionless users.

Older people might have various special needs in their daily lives. This review shows various mobile phone behaviors in daily life among older mobile phone users. We can learn a few important points from this review. (1) Older people are not only a special user group with various special needs, but also a heterogeneous group with diverse needs. (2) Mobile phone technologies need to have various special designs to meet these special and diverse needs. (3) Older people like to use mobile phones for various activities. (4) Mobile phones can help older people live better, healthier, and happier lives.

4.3   Everyday Activities: Calling While Driving

We will now discuss a meta-analysis study entitled "A meta-analysis of the effects of cell phones on driver performance."[18] The four authors are all from the University of Calgary in Canada, Jeff Caird, Chelsea Willness, Piers Steel, and Chip Scialfa. The first author, Jeff Caird, is the Director of the Cognitive Ergonomics Research Laboratory and has published multiple articles on transportation human factors. This study was published in 2008 in *Accident Analysis & Prevention*.

In this review, the authors carefully identified and selected thirty-three relevant empirical articles published between 1969 and 2007 that explicitly examined the effects of cell phones on driver performance. The major findings were as follows: (1) calling with either hands-free or handheld mobile phones while driving significantly slows users' reaction times, especially for older users; (2) calling with either hands-free or handheld mobile phones while driving does not significantly influence lane position; (3) calling with either hands-free or handheld mobile phones while driving increases the distance between two cars; (4) calling with either hands-free or handheld mobile phones while driving makes the users drive cars significantly slower; and (5) the publication bias, a tendency that journals tend to publish studies with significant rather than insignificant results, does not have a significant impact on the above results.

Calling while driving perhaps is the most studied topic in mobile phone behavior in daily life. This meta-analysis review provides a quantitative synthesis of the existing literature, strongly suggesting that, in general, calling with either hands-free or handheld mobile phones while driving will reduce reaction time, increase the distance between cars, and reduce the speed of driving cars.

5.   Comparative Analyses: Family Functioning

Recall that at the beginning of this chapter, we discussed Cindy's intuitive understanding of mobile phone use in daily life. As a mother, understandably, she focused on using mobile phones for her family. The review article we will discuss next will tell us the research findings about how technologies, including mobile phones, are related to family functioning. Its title is "Family functioning and information and communication

---

[18] Caird, J. K., Willness, C. R., Steel, P., and Scialfa, C. (2008). "A meta-analysis of the effects of cell phones on driver performance," *Accident Analysis & Prevention*, 40(4): 1282–1293.

technologies: How do they relate? A literature review."[19] The authors are Joana Carvalho, Rita Francisco, and Ana Relvas from two universities in Portugal. It was published in 2014 in *Computers in Human Behavior*.

In this comprehensive review, the authors identified forty-five relevant journal articles published between 1998 and 2013 and reviewed them in two major sections: how various information and communication technologies (ICTs) are used in families and how various ICTs impact family functions. Some of the major results were as follows: (1) The literature of ICTs initially focused on professional work and later focused on personal and family life. (2) Three major theories exist: the network theory, suggesting that ICTs change today's family and social networks; the uses and gratification theory, suggesting that personal and contextual needs determine the use of ICTs; and, finally, the domestication theory, suggesting that new technologies change the environment, structure, and process of interactions within families through a process of domestication. (3) Face-to-face used to be a family's main method of communication and their Christmas card list used to be the best representation of a family's social network. Now, medial multitasking, media multiplexity, multi-communication, and perpetual connectivity are common patterns. (4) The use of ICTs in families can be classified into three levels: *low* technology density (e.g., using TV); *medium* technology density (e.g., multimedia and PC); and *high* technology density (e.g., Internet and mobile phones). (5) The user of ICTs was influenced by multiple factors. For example, in terms of different stages of family life cycle, in the stage of families with young children, children are key reasons for families to use televisions, PCs, and the Internet; in the stage of families with adolescents, "room culture" has emerged and adolescents are more often isolated in their own rooms playing and communicating with friends via e-mails, games, and mobile phones; in adulthood, adults tends to use e-mails and chat to communicate and interact with extended families; in parenthood, mothers tends to use Facebook more than fathers. Consider another example concerning geographic distance among family members: people will use e-mails and mobile phones more if the distance between them is larger, whereas people will use face-to-face communication and telephones more if they live close to each other. (6) Mobile phones are a major way for modern families to keep in touch instantly, such as making plans in real

[19] Carvalho, J., Francisco, R., and Relvas, A. P. (2015). "Family functioning and information and communication technologies: How do they relate? A literature review," *Computers in Human Behavior*, 45: 99–108.

time and monitoring children's safety and calling for emergencies. Parents normally prefer to call rather than text children, whereas children prefer to text rather than call. (7) ICTs impact various aspects of family functioning, including family communication (e.g., maintaining family bonds vs. reducing actual interactions), family cohesion (e.g., sharing online activities together vs. isolating teens from their parents), family relationships (e.g., playing games leading to couple conflicts or teenagers as a technology guru of a family making parents uncomfortable), and family boundaries (e.g., having unrestricted access to outside information vs. blending the external world with families). (8) ICTs qualitatively change modern family life. However, there is no consensus about whether these changes are all positive or negative.

We can learn more about mobile phone behavior in daily life from this comparative review. First, mobile phones are one of the ICTs and their functions should be considered with other ICTs rather than by themselves. Second, mobile phones play unique roles in family functions (e.g., making family decisions in real time). Third, it is complex to view how ICTs including mobile phones impact family functioning in daily life, due to multiple users, technologies, activities, and the effects being involved in multiple contexts.

6. Complex Thinking: A Common Topic but a Complex Behavior

At the beginning of this chapter, we discussed Cindy's intuitive responses regarding mobile phone behavior in daily life. Her responses showed four features: her mobile phone users were mainly her four children and herself as a mother; her mobile phone technologies involved merely the basic calling feature; her mobile phone activities focused on family communication; and her mobile phone effects were about security and connections among her family. After reading this chapter, we can see more clearly and easily that Cindy's intuitive response in general is quite simple and mobile phone behavior in our daily lives actually is very diverse and very complex.

The content of this chapter can be summarized in Figure 9.1. Comparing Cindy's intuitive responses with the rest of the chapter, we can observe several major differences. First, from the mobile user perspective, in daily life, mobile users are much more complex, from refugees bringing their mobile phones with them to the Coloradan girl who poisoned her mother, from twins to low-income mothers, and from young children to older users. Parents and children are important and common users in our daily lives as mentioned by Cindy, but clearly are not the only users. Second,

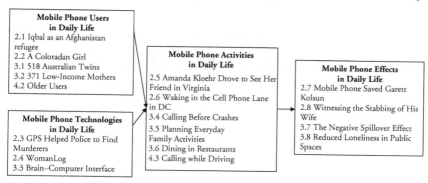

Figure 9.1   A Summary Diagram of Mobile Phone Behavior in Daily Life

from the mobile technology perspective, mobile technologies are much more complex, from GPS to WomanLog, from brain–computer interfaces to text-based interventions. Calling and texting are two common technologies as indicated by Cindy, but clearly there are more and newer technologies involved. Third, for mobile activities, the most studied topic is about using mobile phones while driving, walking, or biking. Besides that, there are various activities involved, e.g., their use during meal times or for planning family activities. Lastly, for mobile effects in daily life, mobile phones can have various complex effects, such as positive (e.g., escaping from a polar bear attack and reducing loneliness in public spaces), negative (e.g., witnessing a wife being stabbed and experiencing negative spillover consequences), and both negative and positive at the same time (e.g., distractive effects of using mobile phones before car accidents and making emergency calls after car accidents).

CHAPTER 10

The Complexity of Mobile Phone Behavior

Outline

1. The Three Systems
2. System 1: Intuitive Thinking
3. System 2: Complex Thinking
    3.1 The basic knowledge of the complexity of mobile phone behavior
    3.2 The basic skill of understanding the complexity of mobile phone behavior
    3.3 The extended knowledge of the complexity of mobile phone behavior
4. System 3: Intuitive Complex Thinking

1. The Three Systems

In this final chapter, we will use three concepts, System 1, System 2, and System 3, to explore the process of understanding the complexity of mobile phone behavior and to conclude the intellectual journey we have travelled together.

As we briefly introduced in Chapter 1, Nobel Laureate Daniel Kahneman uses *System 1* to symbolize people's *intuitive thinking*. Based on his theory, System 1 operates quickly, automatically, and effortlessly. People often use their intuitive thinking, but it is associated with various cognitive biases such as the saliency bias, confirmation bias, availability bias, anchoring bias, or halo bias. In contrast, *System 2* is another specific term used by Daniel Kahneman to symbolize *rational thinking*. System 2 operates slowly, deliberately, and requires effort. People rely on their rational thinking to construct complex thoughts, but it is associated with training, education, learning, and practice rather than developing naturally. In this book, we consider complex thinking to be a specific rational thinking and use it throughout the book. In addition to System 1 and System 2, Daniel Kahneman and other researchers often discussed *expert intuition* in their work.[1] It refers to the skill of certain experts to make quick and complex judgements. For example, outstanding doctors make timely diagnosis in the emergency room, experienced firefighters respond quickly in a burning building, or a chess master recognizes complex chess patterns and makes winning moves in a short period of time. We can call expert intuition *System 3* since it is built on Systems 1 and 2 as a more advanced thinking approach. According to Kahneman and Klein,[2] development of expert intuition needs adequate learning opportunities, prolonged learning practice with timely feedback, and a highly supported learning environment.

Together, Systems 1, 2, and 3 are helpful for us to discuss our intuitive thinking about mobile phone behavior, to summarize the complex thinking about mobile phone behavior that we hope to achieve through the book, and to highlight a final message to end the book.

2. System 1: Intuitive Thinking

At the very beginning of this book, we summarized and discussed quick responses from a group of graduate students about mobile phones, mobile phone behavior, and mobile phone behavior research. Many students thought that a mobile phone has two key features, calling and texting, mobile phone behavior is mainly about sending texts, checking e-mails, and using Facebook, and mobile phone behavior research has about 200 published journal articles. These responses represent these students' intuitive thinking about mobile phones, mobile phone behavior, and mobile phone behavior research and can be considered the outcomes of System 1.

In addition, in the beginning of eight chapters, we presented various quick responses about a specific topic of mobile phone behavior from ordinary individuals. For example, Chapter 2 starts with the quick responses about mobile phone users from three graduate students. Each of them focused on one aspect of mobile phone users such as their ages or their time spent on mobile phones, showing that their intuitive knowledge is not deep, broad, or sophisticated. These responses can also be considered the outcomes of System 1.

In short, these quick responses discussed in the book are examples of outcomes of System 1. They are simple but authentic, general but

---

[1] Kahneman, D. and Klein, G. (2009). "Conditions for intuitive expertise: A failure to disagree," *American Psychologist*, 64(6): 515–526; and Kahneman, D. (2011). *Thinking, Fast and Slow*. New York: Macmillan.

[2] Kahneman and Klein, above n. 1.

informative. We used these responses as the baseline knowledge to develop our thinking about mobile phone behavior from System 1 to System 2.

3.　System 2: Complex Thinking

As presented in Chapter 1, we would like to achieve two goals in this book: to *understand* the complexity of mobile phone behavior and to *analyze* the complexity of mobile phone behavior. To achieve these two goals, we have used a six-step learning sequence in each chapter to develop System 2 complex thinking about mobile phone behavior:

Intuitive Thinking ▶ Daily Observations ▶ Empirical Studies ▶ Knowledge Syntheses ▶ Comparative Analyses ▶ Complex Thinking.

Now let us summarize what we have learned about mobile phones, mobile phone behavior, and mobile phone behavior research.

3.1　The basic knowledge of the complexity of mobile phone behavior

Mobile phones. As discussed in Chapter 1, classic mobile phones do function mainly as typical telephones for oral and written communications. However, modern mobile phones have transformed into multi-function personal technologies, functioning as a powerful command center of information, communication, and computation technologies. As for a future mobile phone, it might even become a powerful artificial organ of human beings.

Why, then, was the intuitive thinking about mobile phones of these graduate students so simple when they gave their intuitive responses? According to Kahneman's theory, one cognitive bias, *the saliency bias*, can be used to explain why mobile phones are mainly viewed as a traditional phone rather than a multiple-functioning personal device. The saliency bias refers to a tendency that people will judge one uncertain object based on an analogy of a salient object in their memory.[3] For instance, a manager will judge a new business plan largely based on his most successful business project. It is likely that the saliency bias makes ordinary people consider mobile phones as traditional phones. This is because traditional phones are the closest technology to mobile phones. The most basic function of traditional phones is to make a phone call and the original function of mobile phones is to make a phone call wirelessly. Plus, linguistically, mobile phones and traditional phones share one

---

[3] Kahneman, D., Lovallo, D., and Sibony, O. (2011). "Before you make that big decision," *Harvard Business Review*, 89(6): 50–60.

keyword, *phones.* Thus, it is not surprising that ordinary people misjudge mobile phones based on an analogy of salient features of traditional phones. However, using the term by renowned innovation expert Clayton Christensen,[4] mobile phones are a *disruptive* technology that unexpectedly and significantly revolutionized traditional phones, just like e-mail after postal mail or digital photography after chemical photography. From the perspective of System 2, mobile phones are no longer a subtype of traditional phones, but rather multi-functional personal technologies. However, the saliency bias might significantly mislead ordinary people.

Mobile phone behavior. From the perspective of System 2, mobile phone behavior is particularly complex. It involves complex mobile phone users, complex mobile phone technologies, complex mobile phone activities, complex mobile phone effects, and complex contexts of mobile phone use. Just consider mobile phone users, only one basic element of mobile phone behavior. Who are mobile phone users? This question is not as simple as many ordinary people would expect. First, it is not easy to define mobile phone users based on whether a person owns a mobile phone, subscribes to a mobile service, or uses a mobile phone. Second, there are a wide variety of mobile phone users, including bad and good users (e.g., criminal users or addicted users), users with diverse demographic characteristics (e.g., age and gender), diverse behavioral characteristics (e.g., personalities or disabilities), and special characteristics (e.g., political leaders). Third, mobile phone users can be seen in diverse contexts, such as users in medical, business, educational, or everyday settings. The complexity of mobile phone users contributes to the complexity of mobile phone behavior. The complexity of mobile phone behavior that has been discussed throughout the book can be summarized in Figure 10.1.

Why was the graduate students' intuitive thinking about mobile phone behavior merely about sending messages, checking e-mails, and using Facebook? According to Kahneman's theory, a cognitive bias, the *availability bias,* can offer one explanation. The availability bias refers to the tendency to overestimate the likelihood of events with greater availability in memory. People tend to think or judge based on readily available information or immediate examples that come to mind. For example, right after an earthquake in California, survivors were more motivated to buy property insurance. For these graduate students we discussed earlier, what was immediately available to them was their own daily experience of

[4] Christensen, C. (2013). *The Innovator's Dilemma: When New Technologies Cause Great Firms to Fail.* Boston, MA: Harvard Business School Press.

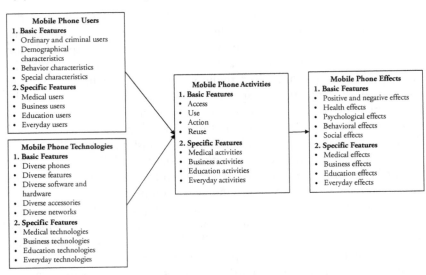

Figure 10.1   A Summary of the Complexity of Mobile Phone Behavior

using their own mobile phones. Because of the availability bias, when they think about mobile phone behavior, they heavily use their personal daily experience of using mobile phones (e.g., being a nice user, having a regular phone, texting often, seeing good effects). Thus, their intuitive thinking is very personal and very simple, directly reflecting their own daily experience. However, from the perspective of System 2, mobile phone behavior is extremely complex due to complex users, technologies, activities, effects, and contexts. Here, the availability bias substantially prevents ordinary people from thinking complexly.

Mobile phone behavior research. In Chapter 1, we discussed the big picture of mobile phone behavior research, indicating that the science of mobile phone behavior has a twenty-five-year history and has accumulated more than 3,000 published journal articles. In the eight chapters that followed, we discussed nearly fifty empirical studies, nearly twenty review articles, nearly ten comparative studies, and introduced nearly 100 *Encyclopedia* chapters, showing various specific examples of mobile phone behavior research.

Why is there such a large discrepancy between the students' intuitive guess of the number of published journal articles on mobile phone behavior (on average 173 articles) and the actual number of the published journal articles (more than 3,000 articles)? We can use Kahneman's well-known concept, the *anchoring bias*, to give an explanation. Kahneman used the anchoring effect to name a very reliable and robust experimental finding that people often use a particular value as a cognitive anchor to guess an unknown quantity, which thus leads to the anchoring bias. One example he used is that a house's list price for sale influences how much we are willing to pay. The higher the list price, the more valuable the house would appear to us, even if we try deliberately to resist the anchoring effect of the list price.

Mobile phone behavior research has at least three important features that might lead to three anchoring biases. First, mobile phone behavior research in essence is an *interdisciplinary* field. Researchers from a wide variety of disciplines, such as medicine, business, education, politics, sociology, human factors, psychology, and communication, have made contributions to the field. As a result, published articles are scattered around more than fifty different types of journals in different disciplines, from the *New England Journal of Medicine* and *Nature*, to *Mobile Communication* and *Computers in Human Behavior*. Thus, ordinary people, including general graduate and undergraduate students, might only rely on their observations of a very small number of published articles in their own field (e.g., education, psychology, business) to make a narrow-minded guess rather than a comprehensive one. Second, although mobile phone behavior literature emerged in the early 1990s, over twenty-five years ago, it has experienced an *exponential growth* since 2010. Thus, ordinary people, including general graduate and undergraduate students, might only rely on their observations of the early history of a very small number of published articles (e.g., publications in the 1990s rather than publications in the 2010s) to make an out-of-date guess rather than a more recent one. Third, there is not a wide availability of good courses, good books, and good TV programs offering good education and training about the entire field of mobile phone behavior. Thus, ordinary people, including general graduate and undergraduate students, might only rely on their own limited daily experiences and observations, making *naive guesses* rather than educated ones. However, from the perspective of System 2, mobile phone behavior research is an emerged interdisciplinary field with a twenty-five-year history and over 3,000 published journal articles rather than a small, new area with 173 published journal articles. Here, the anchoring bias makes ordinary people underestimate the broad scope of mobile phone behavior research to a considerable extent.

3.2   *The basic skill of understanding the complexity of mobile phone behavior*

In addition to developing a usable knowledge of mobile phone behavior, the second goal we want to accomplish through this book is to develop a workable skill to analyze the complexity of mobile phone behavior. The usable knowledge, as we briefly reviewed in the previous section, provides a conceptual framework, and the workable skill we will briefly review in this section will provide specific tools. Both help develop our System 2 complex thinking about mobile phone behavior. Here, we will focus on two basic tools that are useful for us to either analyze or synthesize the complexity of various types of mobile phone behavior.

The simple diagram as an analyzing tool. After introducing and discussing the four basic elements of mobile phone behavior from Chapters 2 to 5, we have used a simple diagram to analyze and present various types of mobile phone behavior from Chapters 6 to 9. For instance, on the basis of the four-element model, we used the following diagram to analyze and present the mobile phone behavior relating to Dr. Spillers:

Dr. Christopher Spillers + iPhone/iPad → reading and texting during heart surgery operation on Mary Roseann Milne → Mary Roseann Milne passed away after surgery.

To analyze and present the mobile phone behavior relating to Dr. Tickell, we used the following simple diagram:

Dr. John Tickell + radiation from mobile phones → being exposed to various forms of lengthy radiation in his daily life → **experienced a seizure on a flight and had five tumors in his brain**.

This kind of simple diagram is a useful analyzing and presentation tool for us to understand the complexity of a given mobile phone behavior for three reasons. First, this diagram helps us to explicitly break down a specific mobile phone behavior into four basic elements – user, technology, activities, and effects – to show different aspects of mobile phone behavior. Second, it helps us easily highlight a specific element with the bold text (e.g., in the first diagram shown above, the focus of the mobile phone behavior is placed on "**Dr. Christopher Spillers**"). Third, it helps put the four basic elements of the specific mobile phone behavior back together into a simple flowchart to show the dynamic relationship among the basic elements.

The summary diagram as a synthesizing tool. In the end of Chapters 2 to 9, we have used a summary diagram as a useful synthesizing and presentational tool to understand the complexity of mobile phone behavior in a given area. For example, at the end of Chapter 3, a diagram was used to synthesize and present the element of technologies of mobile phone behavior. At the end of Chapter 6, a diagram was used to synthesize and present the mobile phone behavior in medicine and health care.

This kind of summary diagram, as shown in Figure 10.2, is useful for us to understand the complexity of mobile phone behavior in a given area for three

(a)

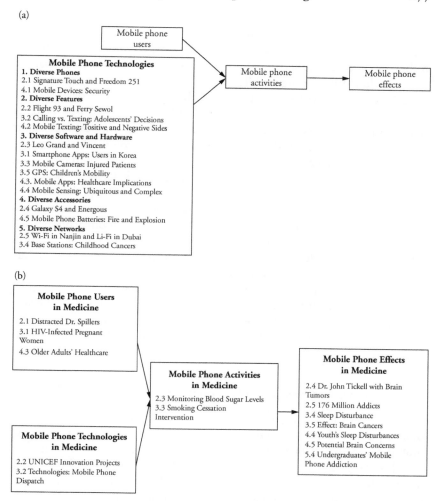

(b)

Figure 10.2 Two Examples of the Summary Diagrams: (a) the Summary Diagram of Technology-Based Mobile Phone Behavior and (b) the Summary Diagram of Mobile Phone Behavior in Medicine

reasons. First, this diagram helps us use keywords (i.e., both the subheading of a specific section and the focus or emphasis of a given mobile phone behavior) to efficiently organize and symbolize various examples of mobile phone behavior from daily observations or empirical studies. For example, in the first summary diagram, *Signature Touch* and *Freedom 251* are two of the keywords used. These two keywords are both the subheading of a small section discussing two very different mobile phones and the two examples of technology-focused mobile phone behavior. These two keywords and all the others included in the big mobile phone technology box are organized to systematically represent each aspect of mobile phone technology: phones, features, software and hardware, accessories, and networks. Second, it helps us to place these examples of various mobile phone behavior into the four major element boxes to visually show a big picture of the complexity of mobile phone behavior in a given area. For instance, the second diagram contains a total of fourteen examples of various mobile phone behavior which were placed into the four boxes to showcase the diversity of the medical users (e.g., distracted doctors and HIV-infected pregnant women), technologies (e.g., UNICEF's large-scale innovation projects and simple mobile phone dispatch), activities (e.g., monitoring blood sugar levels and smoking cessation intervention), and effects (e.g., brain cancers, sleep disturbance, and mobile addiction). This kind of diagram shows the complexity of mobile phone behavior in medicine and motivates us to think complexly rather than intuitively. If we continue using this summary diagram well, we will be able to relatively easily see a landscape of mobile phone behavior research so that we can see both the most productive areas and much-needed future research directions.

3.3   The extended knowledge of the complexity of mobile phone behavior

The book, by design, is to serve as an introductory-level presentation of mobile phone behavior. As a result, we use the four-element basic model of mobile phone behavior to promote a basic understanding of its complexity. However, various types of mobile phone behavior in the real world and in the scientific literature are more complex than the four-element basic model can adequately embrace. In fact, in this book, we have already encountered some complex cases.

For instance, in Chapter 5, we discussed the case of the American actress Jennifer Lawrence, whose private pictures were saved in her iCloud account, which was then hacked, and the case of the Chinese actress Tao Liu, whose property was stolen and then returned, suggesting that an initial positive effect might turn into a negative one (in the case of Lawrence) and an initial negative effect of mobile phone use might turn into a positive one (in the case of Liu). In each of the two cases, different mobile phone behaviors (e.g., having positive and negative effects) were involved. Thus, we need to use two simple diagrams instead of one to fully describe these mobile phone behaviors. For the case of Jennifer Lawrence, the two diagrams are as follows:

(1) Jennifer Lawrence + iPhone camera → taking her own pictures → the pictures automatically stored in iCloud.

(2) Hackers + iBrute → hacking into iCloud → the pictures were stolen and posted online.

For the case of Tao Liu, the two diagrams are as follows:

(1) Tao Liu + iPhone texting→ texting friends for help after property stolen → news spreads rapidly.

(2) Friends + Weixin → finding cues and solutions → all the property found within 12 hours.

Another good example suggesting we should develop more advanced knowledge of the complexity of mobile phone behavior is the discussion of various comparative studies in the book. For various topics, such as writing, sleep disturbance, bacterial contamination, addiction, advertisement, multitasking, and family functions, we can easily see that mobile phones almost always function with other technologies together rather than separately. This makes mobile phone behavior more complex because we need to see the *forest* (various technology behaviors) in order to better understand the *tree* (mobile phone behavior).

For instance, it was reported that, for Japanese middle-school and high-school students, their phone calls and text messages after lights were out were significantly related to various forms of sleep disturbance; 35 percent of them reported having a shorter sleep duration, 42 percent reported that their sleep quality was poor, 46 percent reported experiencing excessive daytime sleepiness, and over 22 percent reported having insomnia symptoms.[5] However, we can develop a much better overall picture through the review article by Lauren Hale and Stanford Guan, comparing screen time of different media.[6] On the basis of twenty-seven studies in European countries, fourteen studies in the United States, seven studies in Japan, and five studies in Australia, as well as studies in eight more countries, it was found that, while media use is consistently related to sleep disturbance among school students, it is interactive media use (e.g., playing games) that leads to more sleep disturbance than passive media use (e.g., watching television).

---

[5] Munezawa, T., Kaneita, Y., Osaki, Y. *et al.* (2011). "The association between use of mobile phones after lights out and sleep disturbances among Japanese adolescents: A nationwide cross-sectional survey," *Sleep*, 34(8): 1013–1020.

[6] Hale, L. and Guan, S. (2015). "Screen time and sleep among school-aged children and adolescents: a systematic literature review," *Sleep Medicine Reviews*, 21: 50–58.

The existing literature indicates that mobile phones do disturb students' sleep, but are not the technology that has the highest disturbing effect.

To further develop a more advanced understanding of the complexity of mobile phone behavior, we will briefly introduce two advanced strategies, structural equation modeling and dynamic system modeling, and add them to our repertoire of analytical tools for examining the complexity of mobile phone behavior.

Structural equation modeling. Structural equation modeling[7] is a well-established research method. It aims at building powerful and flexible models to examine complex empirical research questions, such as multi-level questions (e.g., how five *observed variables* at the measurement level are related to one *general factor* at the structure level via different sequences), multi-path questions (e.g., how six independent variables are related to three dependent variables *directly* and *indirectly*), multi-group questions (e.g., how six independent variables are related to three dependent variables *differently* between female students and male students), and multi-wave questions (e.g., how six independent variables are related to three dependent variables *differently* over multiple months).

In this book, all of the simple diagrams and the summary diagrams have been deliberately developed to have a strong association with structural equation modeling so that we can easily use them in empirical studies. In fact, these diagrams are actually the theoretical or hypothesized models in structural equation modeling that are ready to fit empirical data and obtain the best or estimated models.

For instance, as shown in Figure 10.3(a), the four-element basic model can be considered a general theoretical model for structural equation modeling. If we attempt to address a research question of how high-school students become addicted to taking selfies, as shown in Figure 10.3(b), we can first consider various issues related to mobile phone users (e.g., possible sample sizes, ages, locations, school types, and personalities), mobile phone technologies (e.g., different cameras or different service plans), mobile phone activities (e.g., taking selfies and posting selfies), and mobile phone effects (e.g., addiction to selfies). And then, based on the literature review, we can decide to focus on personality styles, mobile phone data plans, frequency of taking and posting selfies, and degree of selfie addiction as four variables (see the bold text in the figure) and estimate a hypothesized model of how personality styles and mobile phone data plans influence high-school students' frequency of taking and posting selfies, leading to their degrees of

---

7 Bollen, K. A. (1989). *Structural Equations with Latent Variables*. New York: Wiley.

(a)

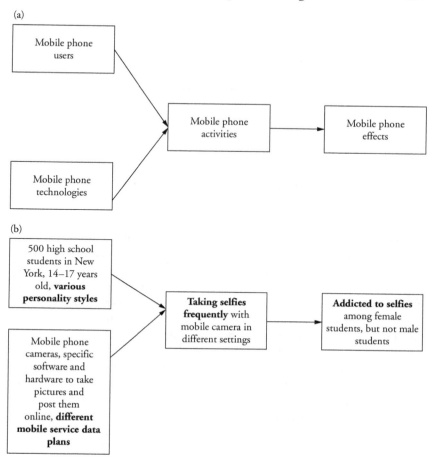

(b)

Figure 10.3   (a) The Four-Element Basic Model as a General Model for Structural Equation Modeling and (b) the Specific Hypothesized Model for Structural Equation Modeling

addiction. There are at least two major advantages of using structural equation modeling: (1) it helps us to turn a conceptual model into an empirical model relatively easily; and (2) it expands a model from a relatively simple one (four variables are involved in our example on selfie addiction here) to a very complex one (e.g., include three variables of mobile phone users, age, gender, and service plan). In short, structural equation modeling will be a strong tool to use for designing complex empirical studies and to understand the complexity of mobile phone behavior.

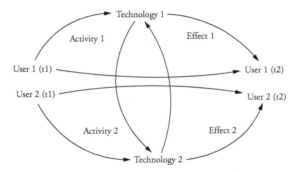

Figure 10.4   A Simple System Dynamics Model of Two Friends Sending or Receiving
Text Messages Reciprocally and Developing Together over Time through Co-Construction

Dynamic system modeling. Similar to structural equation modeling, dynamic system modeling is also a well-established research method that is powerful and flexible. However, different from structural equation modeling, whose theoretical foundation is statistical theories, the theoretical foundation of dynamic system modeling is non-linear dynamic system theories. There exist various approaches and techniques to running dynamic system modeling, and here we introduce one good example – Jay Forrester's system dynamics modeling.[8]

Forrester is known as the founder of *system dynamics*. He has used various concepts of system dynamics (e.g., feedback loops and time delays) and a computer program called *DYNAMO* to successfully simulate complex interactions between objects over time in various dynamic systems, such as industrial dynamics, urban dynamics, and even world dynamics. We can use this modeling method to gain insights into the complexity of mobile phone behavior. For instance, the real-life situations of using mobile phones very often involve co-constructions of different pairs of mobile users: callers vs. listeners, senders vs. receivers, offenders and victims, parents and children, game leaders vs. game followers, and close friends vs. new friends. Figure 10.4 illustrates one common scenario that two mobile users (e.g., two friends as User 1 and User 2) use two mobile phones to send or receive text messages reciprocally so that they both develop together over time through co-construction with each other.

Specifically, this complex model specifies three functions. First, the upper part of the model represents how a user's (User 1) development

[8] Forrester, J. W. (1969). *Urban Dynamics*, vol. 114. Cambridge, MA: MIT Press.

occurs from Time 1 (t1) to Time 2 (t2) when the user interacts with a mobile phone (Technology 1) to form a mobile phone activity (Activity 1) and generates a mobile phone effect (Effect 1). Second, the lower part of the model represents how another user's (User 2) development occurs from Time 1 (t1) to Time 2 (t2) when the user interacts with a mobile phone (Technology 2) to form a mobile phone activity (Activity 2) and generates a mobile phone effect (Effect 2). Third, User 1 and User 2 interact with each other through two mobile phones (Technology 1 and Technology 2) through co-construction. Although this model is extremely simple from the perspective of system dynamics, it can be used for a complex longitudinal study of complex interactions among multiple elements through multiple links at multiple time points, which is already much more complex than some statistical models we have often seen.

There are several major advantages of using system dynamics modeling: (1) it can be used to simulate a wide variety of dynamic systems that are *extremely complex* with more than hundreds of variables and connections (e.g., the worldwide environmental change or the entire system of mobile phone behavior); (2) it is particularly strong in examining *complex relationships* among multiple elements (e.g., the positive and negative effect relationship, the circular relationship, the reciprocal causal relationship, or the time-delayed relationship) rather than just on multiple elements; and (3) it uses only a few core concepts and chooses one of many user-friendly system dynamics programs (e.g., *Vensim* and *JDynSim*)[9] and the initial *learning curve* of learning to run system dynamics models is rather small. In short, system dynamics modeling will be a very useful tool for us to develop our System 2 complex thinking and to understand the complexity of mobile phone behavior.

4. System 3: Intuitive Complex Thinking

It is our primary goal to be able to think about and analyze the complexity of mobile phone behavior. However, with adequate learning opportunities, prolonged learning practice with timely feedback, and a highly supported learning environment, we can even further develop our ability of System 3 (expert intuition or intuitive complex thinking), that is quick and sophisticated, effortless and insightful. With expert intuition, we can understand the complexity of various kinds of existing or emerging mobile phone behavior even faster and better. It is obviously not an easy job, but

---

[9] See https://en.wikipedia.org/wiki/Comparison_of_system_dynamics_software.

one thing we should and can do immediately is to think of mobile phone behavior as a double-edged sword consistently and intuitively so that it eventually becomes second nature.

As we have seen in the intuitive responses from various people in various chapters of the book, one of the most striking similarities is that people often think of mobile phone behavior only from the positive perspective or sometimes only from the negative perspective, but hardly ever from both the positive and negative perspectives at the same time. For instance, mobile phone users are often considered to be good or normal individuals (e.g., always nice users, but never Boston Marathon bombers), mobile phone technologies are often thought to be of good quality (e.g., flawless password protection features or harmless batteries), mobile phone activities are mainly viewed as good ones (e.g., thinking often of useful m-learning, but hardly thinking about distractive learning), and mobile phone effects are often considered to be beneficial only (e.g., helping to coordinate family activities), but sometimes to be harmful only (e.g., causing brain cancers). Throughout this book, we deliberately collected and discussed various examples that can help us develop a balanced thinking habit that considers mobile phone behavior from both the positive and negative perspectives rather than from one single perspective. If we can develop this thinking habit into an expert intuition, then we can consistently and intuitively consider good and bad users, poorly and well-designed technologies, constructive and destructive activities, and beneficial and harmful effects.

In conclusion, looking back at our discussion from the first chapter to the last, it has been an interesting intellectual journey for all of us. We now see that it is critical to transform our System 1 intuitive thinking into our System 2 complex thinking; it is also useful to transform our System 2 complex thinking into our System 3 intuitive complex thinking. This way, we move from simplicity to complexity, and then to complex simplicity. The book has now come to an end, but for us, it should not be a final ending point, but rather the new starting point of our intellectual journey. Our efforts of further exploration of the complexity of mobile phone behavior will benefit millions of mobile phone users across the world, including ourselves. Please bear in mind whenever we pick up a mobile phone: a little device, a complex world!

Index

accessibility, 88–89, 106, 112
action, 90, 97
activities,
    complexity of, 106, 111–113
    family, 253, 257–258, 268
    general, 10, 86–88, 102–103, 153–154, 183
    hacking, 91
    in business, 186–187, 190–192, 194, 196,
        199, 204, 206, 211, 213–214
    in daily life, 90, 180, 243, 245, 247–248,
        252, 263
    in education, 216, 227, 229–230, 236,
        239–240
    in medicine, 150, 158, 161–162, 170, 184
    older people, 172–173, 265
    recycling, 92
    technology and, 261
    travel, 201
    usage, 168
    using a mobile phone while driving, 255–256,
        266
activity-based mobile phone behavior, 11
addiction, 153, 177–182
allergy, 133
apps, 66, 74, 151, 153, 190–194, 199–202, 205,
    212–213, 218–219

bad users, 29, 54
behavioral characteristics, 54–55, 184
behavioral effects, 124, 144
brain cancers, 154, 169
business, 17–20, 62, 74, 185–213

calling, 67, 252, 266, 269
complex thinking, 21–22, 270, 272, 283
complexity, 270

Daniel Kahneman, 3
demographic characteristics, 27, 37, 48, 54–55,
    184
device bacterial contamination, 141

device contact dermatitis, 115, 140
disabled learners, 230
distraction, 217, 239
driving, 249, 255, 257, 262, 266
dynamic system modeling, 280, 282
dyslexia, 40

education, 10–11, 17–21, 67, 72, 74, 78, 84,
    216–218, 220, 222, 224–231, 233–236,
    239–241
educational activities, 228, 235, 240
educational effects, 240
educational technologies, 216, 226, 240
educational users, 239
effect-based mobile phone behavior, 11
effects,
    addiction, 178
    complexity, 133, 143
    contamination, 138
    general observations, 10, 117, 125
    in business, 193–194, 196–198, 204, 209,
        211–214
    in daily life, 243, 245, 250, 256, 260–261,
        263
    in education, 227, 229–231, 239
    life-saving, 161, 249
    medical, 170, 183–184
    of intervention, 162, 253
    on behavioral patterns, 252
    on drivers, 256, 266
    on health, 122, 152–154, 168, 174, 177, 182
    on sleep, 163–164, 173
    on travel, 200–202
    positive and negative, 116, 120, 144, 164
    psychological, 124
    reporting of, 172

gaming, 90–94, 97, 99–100, 102–103, 106–108,
    113
GPS, 58, 62, 70–71, 76, 83, 245–247, 256, 265,
    269

health effects, 144–145
health care, 69, 74, 76, 78, 121, 146–150, 152, 156–157, 170, 173, 177, 183–184
human side, 9

intuitive thinking, 3, 19, 21, 58, 143, 270–272

learners with special needs, 231
learning, 87, 113, 216, 222, 224–225, 227–229, 231, 233–237, 239–240

medicine, 10–11, 17–18, 20, 70, 72, 74, 84, 147, 149–150, 152, 154–155, 157, 160–163, 169, 171, 173, 177, 182–184
mobile banking, 193, 199–200, 206, 213
mobile commerce, 185, 205, 212
mobile credit cards, 197–198, 212
mobile devices, 73
mobile Internet, 216, 239
mobile payment, 197–198, 207–208, 213
mobile phones, 3, 5–6, 8, 60, 62–64, 72, 74–75, 78, 87, 242–246, 248, 250–253, 255–260, 262–263, 265–266, 268–269
mobile phone school policy, 23
mobile sensing, 75–76
mobile video, 216, 239
multi-function technology, 7
multiple user, 30
multitasking, 230, 237, 239

negative and positive effects, 118, 256

penetration rates, 23, 30
personal technology, 7, 9
personalities, 38
phantom vibration syndrome, 123, 125, 130, 138
problematic users, 23, 47, 54
psychological effects, 115, 122, 144
psychological processes, 144

radiation exposure, 23, 47, 49, 52
rational thinking, 3, 21
reuse, 91, 100

science of mobile phone behavior, 11
screen time, 110
security, 72–73, 78, 83, 190–191, 193, 212–213
sexting, 23, 33, 45, 54, 97, 216, 220–221
social effects, 124–125, 144
special characteristics, 29, 45, 54, 56

structural equation modeling, 280
system, 3, 270–275, 283–284

tablets, 234
technologies,
    addiction, 177, 182
    and families, 243, 266, 268
    and economic development, 209–211
    and older people, 265
    in general, 10, 19
    in business, 190, 196, 204, 206, 212–213
    in daily life, 246, 252, 254, 256, 259, 261, 263, 269
    in education, 227, 229–231, 233, 239–240
    in medicine, 149–151, 154, 155, 158, 161, 164, 170–171, 186
    mobile credit cards, 197–199
    mobile payments, 207
    security, 194
technology-based mobile phone behavior, 11
text-based interventions, 269
texting, 61, 65, 67–68, 72, 74, 78, 81–83, 216–217, 220–222, 225–226, 230–231, 237, 239–240, 248, 252, 256, 258–259, 263, 269
tweeting, 110–111, 113

use, 85, 87, 89, 93, 95–97, 102, 106–107, 112, 124, 126, 132–133, 135–136, 138, 144–145, 218, 226, 237, 240
user-based mobile phone behavior, 11
users,
    addicted, 177, 182
    attitudes towards m-commerce, 206
    drivers, 266
    in Africa, 196
    in business, 194, 196, 198, 200, 204–206, 211–212, 214
    in education, 217–218, 225, 239
    in everyday life, 246, 250–252, 256, 258–259, 261–263, 265, 268
    in general, 5, 7, 10, 22, 49
    in medicine, 149, 154, 157, 161, 170, 176, 183–184
    multitasking, 237
    non-users, 189
    older, 173
    of smoking apps, 201–202
    with brain tumors, 167–168
    young, 164

visual impairment, 23, 46, 49